CW00548053

Sylvia Pankhurst designing a part of the decorations of
the Prince's Skating Rink

THE
SUFFRAGETTE

THE HISTORY OF THE WOMEN'S
MILITANT SUFFRAGE MOVEMENT

SYLVIA PANKHURST

PREFACE BY
EMMELINE PANKHURST

DOVER PUBLICATIONS, INC.
MINEOLA, NEW YORK

Bibliographical Note

This Dover edition, first published in 2015, is an unabridged republication of the work originally published in 1911 by the Sturgis & Walton Company, New York. In the original edition, several chapters were numbered incorrectly; these errors have been retained to keep the present volume as close to the original as possible.

ILibrary of Congress Cataloging-in-Publication Data

Pankhurst, E. Sylvia (Estelle Sylvia), 1882-1960
    The suffragette : the history of the women's militant suffrage movement / Sylvia Pankhurst ; preface by Emmeline Pankhurst. — Dover edition.
        pages cm
    Originally published: Sturgis & Walton Company, New York, 1911.
    Includes index.
    ISBN-13: 978-0-486-80484-2
    ISBN-10: 0-486-80484-4
    1. Women—Suffrage—Great Britain. I. Title.
JN979.P3 2015
324.6'230941—dc23

                                                                2015014171

Manufactured in the United States by RR Donnelley
80484401   2015
www.doverpublications.com

PREFACE BY MRS. PANKHURST

THIS history of the Women's Suffrage agitation is written at a time when the question is in the very forefront of British politics. What the immediate future holds for those women who are most actively engaged in fighting for their political freedom no one can foretell, but one thing is certain: complete victory for their cause is not far distant.

When the long struggle for the enfranchisement of women is over, those who read the history of the movement will wonder at the blindness that led the Government of the day to obstinately resist so simple and obvious a measure of justice.

The men and women of the coming time will, I am persuaded, be filled with admiration for the patient work of the early pioneers and the heroic determination and persistence in spite of coercion, repression, misrepresentation, and insult of those who fought the later militant fight.

Perhaps the women born in the happier days that are to come, while rejoicing in the inheritance that we of to-day are preparing for them, may sometimes wish that they could have lived in the heroic days of stress and struggle and have shared with us the joy of battle, the exaltation that comes of sacrifice of self for great objects and the prophetic vision that assures us of the certain triumph of this twentieth-century fight for human emancipation.

E. PANKHURST.

4, Clement's Inn, W. C., *London.*
JANUARY, 1911.

PREFACE

In writing this history of the Militant Women's Suffrage Movement I have endeavoured to give a just and accurate account of its progress and happenings, dealing fully with as many of its incidents as space will permit. I have tried to let my readers look behind the scenes in order that they may understand both the steps by which the movement has grown and the motives and ideas that have animated its promoters.

I believe that women striving for enfranchisement in other lands and reformers of future days may learn with renewed hope and confidence how the " family party," who in 1905 set out determined to make votes for women the dominant issue of the politics of their time, in but six years drew to their standard the great woman's army of to-day. It is certain that the militant struggle in which this woman's army has engaged and which has come as the climax to the long, patient effort of the earlier pioneers, will rank amongst the great reform movements of the world. Set as it has been in modern humdrum days it can yet compare with any movement for variety and vivacity of incident. The adventurous and resourceful daring of the young Suffragettes who, by climbing up on roofs, by sliding down through skylights, by hiding under platforms, constantly succeeded in asking their endless questions, has never been excelled. What could be more piquant than the fact that two of the Cabinet Ministers who were carrying out a policy of coercion towards the women should have been forced into the witness box to be questioned and cross-questioned by Miss Christabel Pankhurst, the prisoner in the dock? What, too, could throw a keener searchlight upon the methods of our statesmen than the evidence put forward in the course of that trial?

To many of our contemporaries perhaps the most remarkable feature of the militant movement has been the flinging-aside by thousands of women of the conventional standards that hedge us so closely round in these days for a right that large numbers of men who possess it scarcely value. Of course it was more difficult for the earlier militants to break through the conventionalities than for those who followed, but, as one of those associated with the movement from its inception, I believe that the effort was greater for those who first came forward to stand by the originators than for the little group by whom the first blows were struck. I believe this because I know that the original militants were already in close association with the truth that not only were the deeds of the old time pioneers and martyrs glorious, but that their work still lacks completion, and that it behoves those of us who have grasped an idea for human betterment to endure, if need be, social ostracism, violence, and hardship of all kinds, in order to establish it. Moreover, whilst the originators of the militant tactics let fly their bolt, as it were, from the clear sky, their early associates rallied to their aid in the teeth of all the fierce and bitter opposition that had been raised.

The hearts of students of the movement in after

PREFACE

years will be stirred by the faith and endurance shown by the women who faced violence at the hands of the police and others in Parliament Square and at the Cabinet Minister meetings, and above all by the heroism of the noble women who went through the hunger strike and the mental and physical torture of forcible feeding.

A passionate love of freedom, a strong desire to do social service and an intense sympathy for the unfortunate, together made the movement possible in its present form.   Those who have worked as a part of it know that it is notable not merely for its enthusiasm and courage, but also for its cheery spirit of loyalty and comradeship, its patient thoroughness in organisation which has made possible its many great demonstrations and processions, its freedom from bitterness and recrimination, and its firm faith in the right.

E. Sylvia Pankhurst.

London, May, 1911.

ILLUSTRATIONS

ILLUSTRATIONS

THE
SUFFRAGETTE

THE SUFFRAGETTE

CHAPTER I

EARLY DAYS

<small>From the Formation of the Women's Social and Political Union to the Summer of 1905.</small>

From her girlhood my mother, the founder of the Women's Social and Political Union, had been inspired by stories of the early reform movements, and even before this, at an age when most children have scarcely learnt their alphabet, her father, Robert Goulden, of Manchester, set her to read his newspaper to him at breakfast and thus awakened her lasting interest in politics.

The Franco-German War was still a much-discussed event when Robert Goulden took his thirteen-year-old daughter to school in Paris, placing her at the Ecole Normale, where she became the room-companion of Henri Rochfort's daughter, Noémie. Noèmie Rochfort told her little English schoolfellow much of her own father's adventurous career, and Emmeline Goulden soon became an ardent and enthusiastic republican. She was now delighted to discover that she had been born on the anniversary of the destruction of the Bastille and was proud to tell her friend that her own grandmother had been an earnest politician, and one of the earliest

3

members of the Anti-Corn Law League, and that her grandfather had narrowly escaped death upon the field of Peterloo. Even before her school days in Paris she had been taken by her mother to a Women's Suffrage meeting addressed by Miss Lydia Becker.

On returning home to England, Emmeline Goulden settled down at seventeen years of age to help her mother in the care of her eight younger brothers and sisters, and when she was twenty-one she married Dr. Richard Marsden Pankhurst, who was many years older than herself, and had long been well known as a public man.

Dr. Pankhurst had been one of the founders of the pioneer Manchester Women's Suffrage Committee and one of its most active workers in the early days. He had drafted the original Women's Enfranchisement Bill, then called the Women's Disabilities Removal Bill, to give votes to women on the same terms as men, which had first been introduced by Mr. Jacob Bright in 1870 and had then passed its Second Reading in the House of Commons by a majority of thirty-three. With Lord Coleridge, Dr. Pankhurst had acted as counsel for the women who had claimed to be put upon the Parliamentary Register in the case of Chorlton v. Lings in 1868. He was also at the time one of the most prominent members of the Married Women's Property Committee and had drafted the Bill to give married women the absolute right to their own property and to sue and be sued in the Courts of Law, which was so soon to be placed as an Act upon the Statute Book. Two years before this great Act became law, Mrs. Pankhurst was elected to the Married

Women's Property Committee, and at the same time she became a member of the Manchester Women's Suffrage Committee.

In 1889 my parents helped to form the Women's Franchise League. My sister Christabel and I, then nine and seven years old, already took a lively interest in all the proceedings, and tried as hard as we could to make ourselves useful, writing out notices in big, uncertain letters and distributing leaflets to the guests at a three days' Conference held in our own home. About this time we two children had begun to attend Women's Suffrage and other public meetings, and these we reported in a little manuscript magazine, which we both wrote and illustrated. When some few years afterwards, owing chiefly to lack of funds and the ill health of its most prominent workers, the Women's Franchise League was discontinued, Dr. and Mrs. Pankhurst returned to Manchester and worked mainly for general questions of social reform. Years before, my mother had joined the Women's Liberal Federation in the hope that it would work to remove both the political and economic grievances of women and to raise the status of women generally, but finding that the Federation was being used merely to forward the interests of the Liberal Party, of which women could not be members and in the formation of whose programme they were allowed no voice, she had resigned her membership. In 1894 she and Dr. Pankhurst joined the Independent Labour Party, one of the decisive reasons for this step being that, unlike the Liberal and Conservative parties, the Independent Labour Party admitted men and women to membership on equal terms. In the same year Mrs. Pankhurst was elected to the Chorlton Board of Guardians, and remained a member of that body for four years. This experience taught her much of the pressing needs of the poor, and of the bitter hardships, especially, of the women's lives.

After Dr. Pankhurst's death, in 1898, Mrs. Pankhurst retired from the Board of Guardians and became a Registrar of Births and Deaths.

For the next few years, my mother took no active part in politics, except as a member of the Manchester School Board,[1] but in 1901 my sister Christabel became greatly interested in the Suffrage propaganda organised by Miss Esther Roper, Miss Eva Gore-Booth, and Mrs. Sarah Dickinson amongst the women textile workers. She was also elected to the Manchester Women's Suffrage Committee, of which Miss Roper was Secretary. Christabel soon struck out a new line for herself. Impressed by the growing strength of the Labour Movement she began to see the necessity of converting to the question of Women's Suffrage the various Trade Union organisations, which were upon the eve of becoming a concrete force in politics. She therefore made it her business to address as many of the Trade Unions as were willing to receive her.

We were all much interested in Christabel's work and my mother's enthusiasm was quickly re-awakened. The experiences of her later years had brought her a keener insight into the results of the political disabilities of women, against which she had rebelled as a high-spirited girl, and she now realised

[1] When the School Boards were abolished, Mrs. Pankhurst became the Trades Council Representative on the Education Committee.

more strongly than ever before, the urgent and immediate need for the enfranchisement of her sex. She
became filled with the consciousness that her duty lay
in forcing this one question into the forefront of
practical politics, even if in so doing she should
find it necessary to give up all her other work. The
Women's Suffrage cause, and the various ways in
which to further its interests were now constantly
present in all our minds. A glance at the early
history of the movement, to say nothing of personal
experience, was enough to show that the Liberal and
Conservative parties had no intention of taking the
question up, and, after mature consideration, my
mother at last decided that a separate women's
organisation must be formed. Therefore, on October 10, 1903, she invited a number of women to
meet at our home, 62 Nelson Street, Manchester,
and the Women's Social and Political Union was
formed. Almost all the women who were present
on that original occasion were working-women,
Members of the Labour Movement, but it was decided from the first that the Union should be entirely
independent of Class and Party.

The phrase " Votes for Women " was now for the
first time in the history of the movement adopted
as a watchword by the new Union. The propaganda
work was at first mainly carried on amongst the
women workers of Lancashire and Yorkshire and,
in the Spring of 1904, as a result of the Women's
Social and Political Union's activities, the Annual
Conference of the Independent Labour Party instructed its Administrative Council to prepare a Bill
for the Enfranchisement of Women to be laid before
Parliament in the forthcoming session. This Reso-

lution, though carried by an overwhelming majority, had been bitterly opposed by a minority of the Conference, who asserted that the Labour Party should not concern itself with a partial measure of enfranchisement, but should work directly to secure universal adult suffrage for both men and women.

Therefore, before preparing any special measure, the National Administrative Council of the Independent Labour Party went very carefully into the whole question. They were advised by Mr. Keir Hardie and others who understood Parliamentary procedure that a measure for universal adult suffrage, which would not only bring about most sweeping changes, but would open countless avenues for discussion and consequent obstruction, could never hope to be carried through Parliament except by the responsible Government of the day. It was, therefore, useless for the Labour representatives to attempt to introduce such a measure. In addition to this, it was pointed out that, whilst a large majority of the Members of the House of Commons had already pledged themselves to support an equal Bill to give votes to women on the same terms as men, no substantial measure of Parliamentary support had as yet been obtained for adult suffrage, even if confined to men. Taking into consideration also the present state of both public and Parliamentary feeling and with a million more women than men in the British Isles, there was absolutely no chance of carrying into law any proposal to give a vote to every grown man and woman in the country. Having thus arrived at the conclusion that an adult suffrage measure was out of the question, the Council now carefully inquired into the various classes of women who were possessed of the qualifications which would have entitled them to vote had they been men.   On its being ascertained that the majority would be householders, whose names were already upon the register of Municipal voters, the following circular was addressed to all the Independent Labour Party branches.

We address to your branch a very urgent request to ascertain from your local voting register the following particulars : —

(1) The total number of electors in the Ward.
(2) The total number of women voters.
(3) The number of women voters of the working classes.
(4) The number of voters not of the working classes.

It is impossible to lay down a strict definition of the term " working classes," but for this purpose it will be sufficient to regard as working-class women, those who work for wages, who are domestically employed, or who are supported by the earnings of wage-earning children.

It was not unnatural, that the majority of the branches failed to comply with a request which obviously entailed a very extensive work.   Nevertheless returns were sent in from between forty and fifty different towns and districts in various parts of the country and these showed the following results : [1]

Total of electors on the Municipal register...... 423,321
Total of Women Voters.................... 59,920
Total of Working Women Voters as defined above 49,410
Total of Non-working Women Voters.......... 10,510
Percentage of Working Women Voters.......... 82.45

[1] In Booth's classic book, *Life and Labour in London,* the result of a canvass of the then 186,982 women occupiers, shows

On receiving these figures, the National Council of the Independent Labour Party decided to adopt the original Women's Enfranchisement Bill, which passed its Second Reading in 1870. The text of the Bill was as follows:

In all Acts relating to the qualifications and registration of voters or persons entitled or claiming to be registered and to vote in the election of members of Parliament, wherever words occur which import the masculine gender the same shall be held to include women for all purposes connected with and having reference to the right to be registered as voters and to vote in such election, any law or usage to the contrary notwithstanding.

Meanwhile we of the Women's Social and Political Union were eagerly looking forward to the new session of Parliament. It is indeed wonderful, in

that of that number 94,940 were wage earners who were divided into the following categories: —

Charwomen, office-keepers, laundresses 30,334
Dressmakers and milliners 14,361
Shirt and blouse-makers, seamstresses 6,525
Waitresses, matrons, etc. 5,595
Tailoresses 4,443
Lodging and coffee-house keepers 4,226
Medical women, nurses, midwives 3,971
Teachers 2,198

On the basis of Booth's figures, Miss Clara Collett, the Government's Senior Inspector for Women's Industries, writing in the *Journal of the Royal Statistical Society* for September, 1908, estimated that the women occupiers of London might be divided as follows: —

Occupied women (who work out) .... 51 per cent.
Housewives (without servants) 38   "
Housewives (with one servant) 5   "
Housewives (with two or more servants) 6   "

the midst of the great Women's Movement that is present with us to-day, to look back upon its small beginnings in that dreary and dismal time not yet six years ago. It seemed then well-nigh impossible to rouse the London women from their apathy upon this question, for the old Suffrage workers had lost heart and energy in the long struggle and those who had joined them in recent days saw no prospect that votes for women would ever come to pass.

I myself was then a student at the Royal College of Art, South Kensington, but I decided to absent myself in order to help my mother, who had come down from Manchester to "lobby," as it is called, on those few important days. The House met on Tuesday, February 13, and during the eight days which intervened before the result of the Private Members' ballot was made known we spent the whole of our time in the Strangers' Lobby striving to induce every Member who had pledged himself to support Women's Suffrage to agree that his chance in the ballot should be given to a Women's Suffrage Bill. It was my first experience of Lobbying. I knew we had an uphill task before us, but I had no conception of how hard and discouraging it was to be. Members of Parliament all told us that they had pledged themselves to do "something for their constituents" or had some other measure in which they were interested, or had not been in Parliament long and preferred to wait until they had more experience before they would care to ballot for a Bill at all. Oh, yes, they were "in favour" of Women's Suffrage; they believed that "the ladies ought to have votes," but they really could not give their places in the ballot for the question; it was always " anything but that," and during the whole of the week we spent in the Lobby we did not succeed in adding one single promise to that which we had originally received from Mr. Keir Hardie.

On the fateful Wednesday on which the result was declared, my mother and I were the only women in the Lobby. We sat there on the shiny black leather seats in the circular hall waiting for the result, and at last we saw with relief Mr. Keir Hardie's pictur-esque figure coming hurrying towards us from the Inner Lobby. He was so kind and helpful, the only kind and helpful person in the whole of Parliament, it seemed. At once he told us that his name had not been drawn in the ballot and explained that only the first twelve, or, at most, fourteen, places that had been drawn could be of any use to the Members who had secured them, and that, owing to the limited number of days upon which private Members' Bills could be discussed, only the first three or four had even a moderately good chance of becoming law.[1] Our next move must therefore be to get in touch with the successful fourteen Members and to en-deavour to persuade one of them to devote his place in the ballot to a Women's Suffrage Bill. After considerable trouble we finally got into communication with all of them, and they all said " No," with the exception of Mr. Bamford Slack, who held the four-teenth place, and who at last agreed to introduce our Bill, largely because his wife was a Suffragist and helped us to urge our cause. Of course the four-teenth place was not by any means a good one, and

[1] Even a first place is useless if the Government and the Speaker are hostile.

the Bill was set down as the Second Order of the
Day for Friday, May 12.

In the meantime we drafted a petition in support
of it and set ourselves to procure signatures. One
Sunday evening I went with a bundle of petition
forms to a meeting addressed by Mr. G. K. Chesterton at Morriss Hall, Clapham. The lecturer's
remarks were devoted to a eulogy of the French
Revolution, from which he asserted all ideas of popular representation had sprung. An opening, which
I seized, was given for a question on the subject of
votes for women in relation to the Government of
our Colonies. Whilst the audience were asking
questions and offering criticisms, Mr. Chesterton was
busily making sketches of us all, but, though I saw
myself being added to the picture gallery, in replying to the questions raised in the debate afterwards,
he did not answer my point. Afterwards, however,
he came up and told me that he had forgotten to
deal with it and then gave me an explanation. I
had not asked, " Are you in favour of Votes for
Women ? " I had assumed that he was and he
replied on the same assumption, and afterwards voluntarily signed his name to my petition. It was with
surprise, not untempered with amusement, therefore,
that I afterwards found Mr. Chesterton coming forward as an active anti-suffragist, but his attitude
seemed to me to be an augury of our speedy success,
for he delights to champion unpopular causes and to
oppose himself to the overwhelming and inevitable
march of coming events.

Many other women's societies, suffrage, organised
petitions at this time, for the fact of having a Bill
before the House of Commons for the first time for

eight years, had sent a thrill of new life through
them all. The result of our united efforts was that,
when the twelfth of May came round, the Strangers'
Lobby was densely crowded, and many of the women
had to be drafted on to the Terrace, or to stand
in the various passages leading from the Lobby.
As well as the members of the various suffrage societies, women of all classes, from the richest to the
poorest, were represented in the gathering, and
amongst the rest was a large contingent of women
Co-operators, accompanied by Mrs. Nellie Alma
Martel, of Australia, who had helped to win votes
for women there, and had afterwards been run as a
candidate for the Commonwealth Parliament, having polled more than 20,000 votes.

Many of the women were quite pathetically con-
fident that we were going to get Women's Suffrage
then and there, but those of us who knew rather more,
both of the stubborn character of our opponents and
the antiquated Parliamentary procedure which renders it possible for a handful of obstructionists to
block any private Member's measure unless the Government will come to its aid, knew that the Women's
Enfranchisement Bill stood in a very precarious position. The question which occupied the first place on
the day for which our own measure had been set
down, was a simple, practically non-contentious little
Bill, the object of which was to provide that carts
travelling along the public roads by night should
carry a light behind as well as before. We had spent
weeks in bringing all possible pressure to bear, both
upon the promoters of the Roadway Lighting Bill,
that they might withdraw their measure, and upon
the Conservative Government, in the hope that they

would give special facilities for the further discussion of the Bill. In both directions we met with a refusal, but we would not give up hope. Finally on the very day of the Second Reading, when the anti-suffragists (as we had already foreseen would be the case) were amusing themselves by spinning out the debate on the Roadway Lighting Bill by pointless jokes and contemptible absurdities, Mrs. Pankhurst sent a message to Mr. Balfour telling him that if facilities for the passing into law of the Women's Enfranchisement Bill were not granted, the Women's Social and Political Union would work actively against the Government at the next General Election. This message produced no apparent effect; and from the meeting of the House, at twelve o'clock until half-past four in the afternoon, the discussion upon the Roadway Lighting Bill continued. Then only half an hour remained for our Bill, and this, amid irresponsible laughter, was "talked out."

The news of what was being done had gradually filtered into the Lobby, and the attitude of the assembled women had changed from one of pleased expectancy to anger and dismay. A feeling of tense excitement seemed to run through the gathering. Some of the faces were flushed and others white, whilst many had tears in their eyes. Especially amongst the working women Co-operators feeling was running high. These women were eagerly looking forward to the time when they would be able to take their part side by side with men in settling the terrible social problems with which they were met on every hand. They bitterly resented the way in which they were being insulted by Members of the House of Commons; they wanted to do

something to express their feelings of disapproval
and when the order for strangers to leave the House
was given, many of them seemed disinclined to go.
Then some of the women who had been listening
to the debate from behind the Grille in the Ladies'
gallery, came down into the Lobby and told us that
a strange man in the adjoining gallery had suddenly
sprung up to protest against the way in which our
question was being " talked out," he had been thrown
out of the House by the police, and was now at
the entrance to the Lobby. This piece of news
created a diversion. The women flocked out to
thank him. It was not until afterwards that we
or they learned that the man was one of the unemployed bootmakers who had marched up from
Leicester, and that he had not made his protest in
our favour, but because he saw that the House was
wasting hour after hour in laughing and joking,
though the Government had assured him that it had
no time to attend to the grievances of starving men.

My mother now suggested that a meeting of
protest should be held outside, and Mrs. Wolstenholme Elmy, the oldest worker in the Suffrage movement present, began to speak. The women crowded
round to listen, but almost at once the police ordered
us away and began striding in and out amongst us
and pushing us apart. We thereupon moved to the
foot of the Richard I statue, which stands just
outside the door of the House of Lords, but again
the police intervened, till, at last, after much argument, the Inspector of Police offered to take us
to a place where a meeting might be held. Mrs.
Pankhurst then called upon Mrs. Martel, as an
Australian woman voter, to lead us and, joined by a

single Member of Parliament, Mr. Keir Hardie, we
marched with the police to Broad Sanctuary, close
to the gates of Westminster Abbey. Here we
adopted a Resolution condemning the procedure of
the House of Commons, which had made it possible
for a small minority of opponents to prevent a vote
being taken upon the Women's Enfranchisement
Bill, and calling upon the Government to rescue it
now and carry it into law. The meeting then dispersed, vowing political vengeance upon the Government if this should not be done.

It will be remembered that during the summer of
1905 it was evident to the most casual observer
that the resignation of the Conservative Government
could not be long delayed. Mr. Chamberlain's
Tariff Reform proposals were causing dissent in the
Cabinet, and the resignation of several Ministers had
already taken place. The South African War had
brought a measure of overwhelmingly enthusiastic
support to the Conservative Government but, as
almost always happens in such cases, a reaction had
set in, now that the war taxes had to be met. At the
same time there was grave depression in the cotton
trade, and consequent distress in the industrial districts. In order to cope with the trouble, Mr.
Walter Long, on behalf of the Government, had
introduced a Bill to provide relief work for the
unemployed. This had met with serious opposition
from his own party, and it had been subsequently
announced that no further time could be found for
the discussion of the measure. At this point the
dispute which had arisen between the Scottish Free
Church and the United Free Church of Scotland had
become acute, and on June 7, Mr. Balfour had intro-

duced the Scottish Churches Bill, which was hurried
through its various stages and finally passed on
July 26. It was urged that the Government ought
not to have brought forward this new measure
whilst the unemployed workmen Bill, to which they
were already committed, had been set aside for lack
of time. But Mr. Balfour excused himself by protesting that he had been obliged to carry the Scottish
Churches Bill because a " crisis " had arisen.

The unemployed and their leaders now stated that
if Mr. Balfour needed a crisis to make him act,
they would certainly provide him with a crisis. An
uprising on a small scale accordingly took place in
Manchester, in the course of which the unemployed,
in spite of police prohibition, persisted in holding a
meeting in Albert Square. Afterwards they marched
in an irregular mass along Market Street, spreading
all over the roadway and obstructing the traffic. A
struggle with the police ensued, during which four
men were arrested. The question of the Manchester
" riot," as it was called, was at once raised by Mr.
Keir Hardie as a matter of urgency in the House
of Commons and, as a result, it was hastily carried
through its remaining stages, though in a modified
form.

We of the Women's Social and Political Union
had been much interested by the situation that had
arisen, both in regard to the Unemployed and the
Scottish Churches, and we determined to profit by
the example of those who, by determined and decisive
action, had secured a certain measure of consideration for their claims. It was only a question now
of how much longer militant tactics were to be delayed, and as to how they were to be inaugurated.

A favourable opportunity for their dramatic commencement had not yet presented itself, but there was plenty of necessary propaganda work for the Women's Social and Political Union to do.

One Sunday evening in June, Mrs. Pankhurst had been invited to speak on Women's Suffrage to a meeting held under the auspices of the Oldham Independent Labour Party. During the proceedings glees were sung by a choir of men and women cotton operatives, and one of the members of the choir was Annie Kenney, who was afterwards to take so prominent a part in the Votes for Women Movement. Annie Kenney was deeply impressed by all that Mrs. Pankhurst had to say, and shortly afterwards, when my sister Christabel also lectured in Oldham, she asked to be introduced to her. Christabel then asked her to pay a visit to our home in Manchester, and the friendship which was to have such far-reaching results began.

Annie Kenney was born at Lees, near Oldham. She was the child of working-class parents, and, to supplement her father's earnings, her mother, in addition to all her household cares, had been obliged to go out to work in a cotton mill most of her married life. Annie Kenney herself had early become a wage-earner, for at ten years of age she secured an engagement as a half-timer in one of the Oldham cotton factories. Then, wearing her heavy steel-tipped clogs, her fair hair hanging down her back in a long plait covered by a shawl, she had gone into the hot, crowded spinning mill, and working amid the noisy jarring of the machinery as a " little tenter " at the disposal of three older women, she had learnt to fit into place the big bobbins covered with fleecy strands of soft, raw cotton; and to piece these same fleecy strands when they broke, as they did so often, whilst they were being spun out thinner and stronger. Once, as she seized the broken thread in her tiny fingers, one of them was caught somehow and torn off by the whirling bobbins. Whilst she was still a half-timer she worked alternately, one week from six o'clock in the morning till midday in the mill, and during the afternoon at the elementary school; and the next week she spent the morning at school and four hours of the afternoon in the mill. At thirteen, her school days had ceased, and she had become a " full-timer," working in the mill from six o'clock in the morning till six at night.

This premature launching forth into the world of wage-earners had left its mark upon Annie Kenney. Her features had been sharpened by it, and her eager face that flushed so easily was far more deeply lined than are the faces of girls whose childhood has been prolonged. Those wide, wide eyes of hers, so wonderfully blue, though at rare moments they could dance and sparkle like a fountain in the sunshine, were more often filled with pain, anxiety and foreboding, or with a longing restless, searching, unsatisfied and far away. A member of a very large family, Annie had four sisters — Nellie, Kitty, Jennie, and Jessie — who came nearest her in age and had been her companions in the cotton mill. In spite of the fact that they were constantly obliged to rise at four or five in the morning, in order to reach the factory gates at six o'clock, and on returning home were obliged first to help to do the housework and prepare the evening meal for the rest of the family, these girls were all determined to continue their education, and they regularly attended the Oldham night schools. At the time when we first met Annie, Nellie and Kitty, the two eldest of the sisters, had both worked their way out of the cotton mill. Nellie had become a shop assistant, and had soon proved herself so able that she had been put in charge of two of her employer's shops, whilst Kitty had passed the necessary examinations and had obtained a post as an elementary school teacher, and Jennie, though still in the mill, was studying with the same object. Jessie, who was but sixteen, was learning typewriting and shorthand.

Annie, who was then twenty-five, was unlike her sisters in many ways. She frequently said that she was not so " clever " as her sisters, but when any decisive step was to be taken or any question of principle to be decided, it was always Annie who took the lead. There is not much that is beautiful in a small Lancashire manufacturing town, but what little there was, Annie Kenney contrived to make the most of. She was a regular attendant at the Church, and delighted in the beauty of the music; the Whitsuntide processions, in which she walked with the other Sunday-school children all in their white dresses, being vivid memories with her still. She early commenced to carry on a literary campaign amongst her work-mates and, having come across a copy of the penny weekly paper " The Clarion," in which Robert Blatchford was publishing a series of articles on his " favourite books," contrived to procure some of the works which were there mentioned, and introduced them to her companions.

On the few holidays which fall to the lot of the cotton worker, or when the mills were stopped owing to bad trade, Annie Kenney and her sisters and some of their favourite work-mates would put together a simple luncheon and set off roaming for miles across the moors.   The grass and the trees might be blackened with the smoke of the factories, the sight of whose tall chimneys the girls could never leave behind, but, blighted as it was, this was the only country that Annie had ever known, and it was all beautiful to her.   When they had walked till they were tired, the girls would lie down on the grass, and then they would read to each other in turn, and Annie would talk to them about the flowers and the sky.

Just as she was intensely alive to all that was beautiful, so too Annie Kenney realised keenly the ugly and sordid side of life.   When speaking of her early days to a conference of women in Germany, in 1908, she said:

I grew up in the midst of women and girls in the works, and I saw the hard lives of the women and children about me.   I noticed the great difference made in the treatment of men and women in the factory, differences in conditions, differences in wages and differences in status.   I realised this difference not in the factory alone but in the home. I saw men, women, boys and girls, all working hard during the day in the same hot, stifling factories.   Then when work was over I noticed that it was the mothers who hurried home, who fetched the children that had been put out to nurse, prepared the tea for the husband, did the cleaning, baking, washing, sewing and nursing.   I noticed that when the husband came home, his day's work was over; he took his tea and then went to join his friends in the club or in the public house, or on the cricket or foot-ball field, and I used to ask myself why this was so.   Why was the mother the drudge of the family, and not the father's companion and equal?

From the first we found Annie ready with excellent ideas for spreading our propaganda. In Lancashire every little town and village has its "Wakes Week." The "Wakes" being a sort of Fair, at which there are "merry-go-rounds," "cocoanut shies," and numberless booths and stalls where human and animal monstrosities are shown and all kinds of things are sold. In every separate town or village the "Wakes" is held at a different date, so that within a radius of a few miles one or other of these fairs is going on all through the summer and autumn. Annie told us that on the Sunday before the "Wakes" almost all the inhabitants of the place go down to the "Wakes-ground" and walk amongst the booths, and that Salvation Army and other preachers, temperance orators, the vendors of quack medicines and others seize this opportunity of addressing the crowds. She suggested that we should follow their example. We readily agreed, and all through that summer and autumn we held these meetings, going from Stalybridge to Royton, Mosely, Oldham, Lees where Annie lived, and to a dozen other towns.

CHAPTER II

THE BEGINNING OF THE MILITANT TACTICS

ARREST AND IMPRISONMENT OF CHRISTABEL PANKHURST AND ANNIE KENNEY. OCTOBER, 1905.

WHILST the educational propaganda work of the Women's Social and Political Union was being quietly carried on, stirring events were in preparation. The resignation of the Conservative Government was daily expected. The Liberal leaders were preparing themselves to take office, and every newspaper in the country was discussing who the new Ministers were to be. A stir of excitement was spreading all over the country and now the organisers of the Liberal Party decided to hold a great revival meeting in that historic Manchester Free Trade Hall, which stands upon the site of the old franchise battle of Peterloo. The meeting was fixed for October 13, and here it was determined that the old fighting spirit of the Radicals should be revived, the principles and policy of Liberalism should be proclaimed anew and, upon the strength of those principles and of that policy, the people should be called upon to support the incoming Government with voice and vote.

When the evening of the thirteenth came, the great hall was filled to overflowing with an audience

mainly composed of enthusiastic Liberals, for the
meeting was almost entirely a ticket one, and the
tickets had been circulated amongst the Liberal Associations throughout the length and breadth of Lancashire. The organ played victorious music, and then
the Liberal men, whose party had been out of office
for so long and who now saw it coming into power,
rose to their feet and cheered excitedly as their leaders came into the hall. After a few brief words from
the chairman, words in which he struck a note of
triumphant confidence in the approaching Liberal
victory, Sir Edward Grey was called upon to speak.
The future Cabinet Minister, in a speech full of fine
sentiments and glowing promises, named all the
various great reforms that the Liberal Government
would introduce, and appealed to the people to give
the Liberal Party its confidence, and to return a
Liberal ministry to power. Whilst he was speaking,
Sir Edward Grey was interrupted by a man who
asked him what the Government proposed to do for
the unemployed. Sir Edward paused with ready
courtesy to listen. " Somebody said the unemployed," he explained to the audience; " well, I will
come to that," and he did so, saying that this important question would certainly be dealt with. Then
he came to his peroration; he spoke of the difficulties
of administration, difficulties which were especially
great at the present time. " We ask for the Liberal
Party," he said, " the same chance as the Conservative Party has had for nearly twenty years. . . .
There is no hope in the present men, but there is hope
in new men. . . . It is to new men with fresh
minds, untrammelled by prejudice and quickened by
sympathy, and who are vigorous and true, that I

believe that the country will turn with hope. What
I ask for them is generous support and a fair
chance." The thunder of applause that greeted his
final words had scarcely died away when, as if in
answer to Sir Edward Grey's appeal and promise, a
little white cotton banner, inscribed with the words,
" VOTES FOR WOMEN," was put up in the centre
of the hall, and a woman was heard asking what
the Government would do to make the women politically free. Almost simultaneously two or three men
were upon their feet demanding information upon
other questions. The men were at once replied to,
but the woman's question was ignored. She therefore stood up again and pressed for an answer to
her question, but the men sitting near her forced her
down into her seat, and one of the stewards of the
meeting held his hat over her face. Meanwhile,
the hall was filled with a babel of conflicting sound.
Shouts of "Sit down!" "Be quiet!" "What's the
matter?" and "Let the lady speak!" were heard
on every hand. As the noise subsided a little, a second woman sitting beside the first got up and asked
again, "Will the Liberal Government give women
the vote?" but Sir Edward Grey made no answer,
and again arose the tumult of cries and counter cries.
Then the Chief Constable of Manchester, Mr.
William Peacock, came down from the platform to
where the women were sitting, and asked them to
write out the question that they had put to Sir
Edward Grey, saying that he would himself take it
to the Chairman and make sure that it received a
reply. The women agreed to this suggestion, and
the one who had first spoken now wrote:

Will the Liberal Government give votes to working women?

Signed on behalf of the Women's Social and Political Union,

ANNIE KENNEY,

Member of the Oldham Committee of the
Card and Blowing Room Operatives.

To this she added that as one of the 96,000 organ-ised women cotton workers, and for their sake, she earnestly desired an answer. Mr. Peacock took the paper on which the question had been written back to the platform, and was seen to hand it to Sir Edward Grey, who, having read it, smiled and passed it to the Chairman, from whom it went the round of every speaker in turn. Then it was laid aside, and no answer was returned to it. A lady, sitting on the platform, who had noticed and understood all that was going on, now tried to intervene.[1] " May I, as a woman, be allowed to speak — ?" she began, but the Chairman called on Lord Durham to move a vote of thanks to Sir Edward Grey. When this vote had been seconded by Mr. Winston Churchill, and when it had afterwards been carried, Sir Edward Grey rose to reply. But he made no reference, either to the enfranchisement of women, or to the question which had been put. Then followed the carrying of a vote of thanks to the Chair, and by this time the meeting showed signs of breaking up. Some of the audience had left the hall, and some of the people on the platform were preparing to go. The women's question still remained unanswered and

[1] She had no connection with the two women, and no previous knowledge that the question was to be put.

seemed in danger of being forgotten by everyone concerned. But the two women were anxiously awaiting a reply, and the one who had first spoken now rose again, and this time she stood up upon her seat and called out as loudly as she could, "Will the Liberal Government give working women the vote?" At once the audience became a seething, infuriated mob. Thousands of angry men were upon their feet shouting, gesticulating, and crying out upon the woman who had again dared to disturb their meeting.

She stood there above them all, a little, slender, fragile figure. She had taken off her hat, and her soft, loosely flowing hair gave her a childish look; her cheeks were flushed and her blue eyes blazing with earnestness. It was Annie Kenney, the mill girl, who had gone to work in an Oldham cotton factory as a little half-timer at ten years of age. A working woman, the child of a working woman, whose life had been passed among the workers, she stood there now, feeling herself to be the representative of thousands of struggling women, and in their name she asked for justice. But the Liberal leaders, who had spoken so glibly of sympathy for the poor and needy, were silent now, when one stood there asking for justice; and their followers, who had listened so eagerly and applauded with so much enthusiasm, speeches filled with the praise of liberty and equality, were thinking now of nothing but Liberal victories. They howled at her fiercely, and numbers of Liberal stewards came hurrying to drag her down. Then Christabel Pankhurst, her companion, started up and put one arm around Annie Kenney's waist, and with the other warded off their blows, and as she did so, they scratched and tore her hands until the blood ran down on Annie's hat that lay upon the seat, and stained it red, whilst she still called, " The question, the question, answer the question ! " So, holding together, these two women fought for votes as their forefathers had done, upon the site of Peterloo.

At last six men, Liberal stewards and policemen in plain clothes, seized Christabel Pankhurst and dragged her away down the central aisle and past the platform, then others followed bringing Annie Kenney after her. As they were forced along the women still looked up and called for an answer to their question, and still the Liberal leaders on the platform looked on apparently unmoved and never said a word. As they saw the women dragged away, the men in the front seats — the ticket holders from the Liberal clubs — shouted " Throw them out ! " but from the free seats at the back, the people answered " Shame ! "

Having been flung out into the street, the two women decided to hold an indignation meeting there, and so, at the corner of Peter Street and South Street, close to the hall, they began to speak, but within a few minutes, they were arrested, and followed by hundreds of men and women, were dragged to the Town Hall. Here they were both charged with obstruction, and Christabel Pankhurst was also accused of assaulting the police. They were summoned to attend the Police Court in Minshull Street next morning.

Meanwhile, as soon as the women had been thrown out of the hall, there came a revulsion of feeling in their favour and the greater part of the meeting broke up in disorder. Believing that some explanation was expected of him, Sir Edward Grey now said that he regretted the disturbance which had taken place. " I am not sure " he continued " that unwittingly and in innocence I have not been a contributing cause. As far as I can understand, the trouble arose from a desire to know my opinion on the subject of Women's Suffrage. That is a question which I would not deal with here to-night because it is not, and I do not think it is likely to be, a party question." He added that he had already given his opinion upon votes for women and that, as he did not think it a " fitting subject for this evening," he would not repeat it.

Thus, within a few days of the fortieth anniversary of the formation of the first Women's Suffrage Society (perhaps even upon that very anniversary), and after forty years of persevering labour for this cause, Sir Edward Grey announced that Women's Suffrage was as yet far outside the realm of practical politics, and the two women who had dared to question him upon this subject were flung with violence and insult from the hall.

The next morning the police court was crowded with people eager to hear the trial. The two girls refused to dispute the police evidence as to the charges of assault and obstruction, and based their defence solely upon the principle that their conduct was justified by the importance of the question upon which they had endeavoured to secure a pronouncement and by the outrageous treatment which they had received. But though ignoring the violence to which they had been subjected and exaggerating the disturbance which they had made, the Counsel for the prosecution had dwelt at length upon the scene

in the Free Trade Hall; the women were not allowed
to refer to it and, though it was evident that but
for what had taken place in the meeting they would
not have been arrested for speaking in the street,
they were ordered to confine their remarks to what
had taken place after they had been ejected. Both
defendants were found guilty, Christabel Pankhurst
being ordered to pay a fine of ten shillings or to go
to prison for seven days and Annie Kenney being
fined five shillings with the alternative of three days'
imprisonment. They both refused to pay the fines
and were immediately hurried away to the cells.

Now the whole country rang with the story. In
Manchester especially, the news created tremendous
excitement. The father of one of the prisoners,
was, as we have seen, a Manchester man. Dr.
Pankhurst's [1] remarkable ability and learning, his
wonderful eloquence, his wide range of interests, and
the number of causes in which he had taken a foremost part, had secured for him an unusually large
amount of public recognition. There was scarcely
a man or woman in the city to whom he was not
a familiar figure. Moreover, his fascinating personality, and his well-known tenderness of heart, illustrated as it was by thousands of kindly acts, as well
as by his long life of service and sacrifice for the
public good, had endeared him to many of his strongest political opponents. Whatever bitterness may
have been aroused against him by his strenuous ad-
vocacy of advanced and frequently unpopular causes,
had disappeared when the news of his sudden death,
which took place in the midst of a legal case that
he was conducting on behalf of the Manchester Cor-

---

[1] See biographical note at the end of this chapter.

poration, had become known, and public sympathy
had gone generously forth to Mrs. Pankhurst in her
tragic home-coming when she had read of her great
loss in the evening papers in the train.   Mrs.
Pankhurst by her work on public bodies was also
known of course, and Christabel Pankhurst herself
had recently attracted notice because, having wished
to follow her father's profession, she had applied
to the Benchers of Lincoln's Inn for admission to
the Bar.   Her application had been refused on the
ground of her sex, as had also a request to be heard
by the Benchers in support of her claim, but she
had not abandoned her endeavours to secure the
opening of this avenue of employment to women and
she was now a Law student at the Victoria University of Manchester.

Votes for Women in those days was regarded by
the majority of sober, level-headed men as a ladies'
fad which would never come to anything and the
idea that it could ever be a question upon which
governments would stand or fall, or be associated
with persecution, rioting and imprisonment had been
alike unthinkable to them.   Therefore, for many
reasons, this trial and imprisonment came as a tremendous shock to the general public of Manchester.
Questions addressed to political speakers by men in
the audience both during and at the close of the
speeches were, as everyone knew, the invariable ac-
companiment of every public political meeting in this
country.   These questions were almost always replied to.   When dissatisfied with the answer the
interrogators frequently began a running commentary of disapproval, which sometimes terminated in
their ejection, but not until they had become a source

of general disturbance to the meeting.   These facts
were of course a matter of common knowledge, but
the newspapers now ignored them and treated the
questioning of Sir Edward Grey in the manner
adopted by the two women in the Free Trade Hall
as an absolutely new and entirely reprehensible departure.   They were all agreed that such behaviour
would inevitably injure the Women's Suffrage Cause
of which, though they had hitherto boycotted it,
most of them now implied that they were supporters.
Extracts from two newspapers are enough to convey the attitude which in varying degrees of severity
was adopted by them all.   The *Evening Standard:*

> The Magistrates were lenient in inflicting a small fine.
> . . . If Miss Pankhurst desires to go to gaol rather
> than pay the money, let her go. Our only regret is that
> the discipline will be identical with that experienced by
> mature and sensible women, and not that which falls to
> the lot of children in the nursery.

The Birmingham *Daily Mail:*—

> If any argument were required against giving to ladies
> political status and power, it has been furnished in Man-
> chester, and by two of the people who are most strenuously
> clamouring for the franchise.

The reason why the Press as a whole was against
the women was of course because every great newspaper in this country is a special pleader, for one or
other of the two great political Parties — the Liberals
and the Conservatives — and both these Parties
looked upon the question which the women were
striving to urge forward, as something of a nuisance.
Unfortunately, vast numbers of people, instead of

examining into and thinking out a thing for themselves, begin, at any rate, by allowing their opinions to be formed for them by the particular newspapers which they happen to read. Therefore some people at once made up their minds that the women were entirely in the wrong, because the papers said so. Others, with strange obliquity of vision, because they did not like the idea of women mixing themselves up in scenes of violence, found it easier to disapprove of the women who had been ill-used than of those who had ill-used them. Besides the unthinking ones, there were also many who had become so much inflamed by Party spirit that their sole idea was to whitewash and bolster up the Liberal leaders and to cast a slur upon the character of any who had dared to turn too fierce a light upon their faults and weaknesses.

But with all this the imprisoned women were not friendless and though for the time being, stone walls and iron bars might prevent their speaking, there were those outside who were determined to defend and uphold them and to turn what they had done to good. The Women's Social and Political Union at once published a statement explaining that in view of the approaching general election the intentions of the Liberal leaders with regard to Women's Suffrage had been recognised to be of immense importance, and Sir Edward Grey had therefore been asked to receive a deputation of members of the Union, in which the questions it was desired that he should answer were clearly stated. No reply or acknowledgment of this request had been received, and it had thereupon been decided that two delegates from the Union should

Christabel Pankurst and Annie Kenney

attend the Free Trade Hall meeting to question Sir Edward Grey.

Many who witnessed the scene in the Free Trade Hall wrote to the newspapers expressing their sympathy with the women.

A " sympathiser " apologised for having helped to shout the women down saying that he would never have done so had he realised what was really taking place. On first reading the accounts, Mr. Keir Hardie, the only Member of Parliament to come forward in support of the prisoners, telegraphed, " The thing is a dastardly outrage, but do not worry, it will do immense good to the Cause. Can I do anything ? " Sir Edward Grey's wife, Lady Grey, made no public statement but she told her friends that she considered the women justified in the means they had adopted of forcing their question forward. " What else could they do ? " she asked. Whilst Mr. Winston Churchill, fearing probably that his approaching candidature in Manchester might be damaged by the imprisonment of the women, visited Strangeways Gaol and offered to pay their fines, but the Governor refused to accept the money from him.

On Friday, October 20, a crowded demonstration was held to welcome the Ex-prisoners in the Free Trade Hall from which they had been flung out with ignominy but a week before, and now, as they entered, the audience rose with raised hats and waving handkerchiefs and greeted them with cheers. Christabel Pankhurst and Annie Kenney did not speak of their imprisonment. We knew that they had been treated as belonging to the third and lowest class of criminals, and that they had been dressed in the prison clothes, fed on " skilly " and brown bread, and kept in solitary confinement in a narrow cell both day and night; that they had attended services with the other prisoners in the Chapel and with them had gone out to exercise in the prison yard, that they had performed the daily routine of prison tasks and, losing their own names, had answered only to the number of their cell. These things we know, but *they* refused to speak of them then, wishing that all attention should be concentrated upon the cause of the enfranchisement of women for which they had been willing to endure all.

But in spite of their own silence we have one picture of Christabel during that first imprisonment. It was brought out to us by one of the Visiting Justices, a friend of her father, who, in the hope of inducing her to allow her fine to be paid, had gone in to see her in the prison cell. He found her clad in strangely made, coarse serge garments, with large heavy shoes upon her feet and with a white cap framing her rosy face, and partly covering her soft brown hair. Seated on a wooden stool she was working away at her allotted task — the making of a shirt for one of the men prisoners. Her dinner, consisting of two or three small sodden-looking unpeeled potatoes and a chunk of coarse brown bread, was lying beside her and she was taking a bite of the bread every now and then. "Don't you think you're a very silly girl to sit here eating brown bread and potatoes and sewing that shirt when you might be freely doing what you please outside?" the Justice asked her. But she smiled up at him brightly "Oh, no," she said, "I always liked brown bread."

Fresh and bright and full of cheer as she had been in her cell, though more serious, she was now, as she stood on the Free Trade Hall platform to make her speech. When she began to tell the meeting of the disturbance that had taken place upon the previous Friday there were some cries of protest from Liberals who disagreed with her, but she stopped them saying " I am sure you want to hear my side of the story," and when she had finished, Resolutions calling for the immediate extension of the franchise to women, commending the bravery of the released prisoners' action and condemning the behaviour of those who had refused to answer their question were carried with tremendous enthusiasm.

DR. PANKHURST — BIOGRAPHICAL NOTE

In addition to his activities for Women's Suffrage, and indeed, for all questions affecting the welfare of women, which have been already referred to, Dr. Pankhurst had taken an important part in many other reform movements. He had been one of the most distinguished of the students of Owen's College which paved the way for, and became incorporated with, the newer Victoria University of Manchester. Having studied at Owen's, he had taken his B.A. degree at the London University in 1858, his LL.B., with honours in Principles of Legislation in 1859, and LL.D. with the gold medal in 1863. Called to the Bar in Lincoln's Inn in 1867 he had joined the Northern Circuit and become a member of the Bar of the County Palatine and Lancaster Chancery Court. He had been Honorary Secretary to the Union of Lancashire and Cheshire Institutes from 1863 to 1876 in which years he had laboured zealously in the promotion of education, devoting much time to visiting the various Mechanics Institutes, which largely owing to his work were beginning to spring up as the forerunners of the Technical Schools and Municipal Evening Classes of to-day, teaching and addressing the students on educational questions, and enlisting public sympathy in this important work. Later, when in 1893, the subject of citizenship had, owing primarily to his influence, been made a part of the teaching of the evening continuation schools in Manchester, Dr. Pankhurst had issued a scheme of political studies in the form of an outline of political and social theory, and in 1894 he had delivered a series of addresses on the " Life and Duties of Citizenship," which were afterwards published. In 1882 he had become a member of the Manchester Chamber of Commerce and was recognised to be an authority upon many commercial questions. He was one of the earliest and most active workers of the Social Science Association which did so much to educate public opinion upon many questions affecting the welfare of women and the community in general. Dr. Pankhurst had also been the author of many important papers on the Patent Laws, Local Courts and Tribunals, International Law, the study of Jurisprudence, and other subjects. He had interested himself greatly in public health and the general field of sanitation, and had been concerned in many public inquiries in regard to this matter. He had been a life member of the Association for the Reform and Codification of the Law of Nations, and had laid before that body a scheme of international arbitration as a substitute for war, a principle for which he had for many years strenuously contended. He had three times been a candidate for Parliament, having contested Manchester in 1883, Rotherhithe in 1885, and Gorton in 1895, but because, admittedly, he was too fearlessly honest and outspoken he had on each occasion failed to secure election. Even by his bitterest political opponents he was respected, for it was a matter of common knowledge that, for the sake of his principles, he had over and over again sacrificed his own material advancement. He had begun life as an advanced Radical, having been a friend of John Stuart Mill, also of Ernest Jones, and other well-known Chartists. So long ago as 1873 he had been a pronounced Home Ruler. He had been a member of

the executive of the National Reform Union, and the declaration of principles which he had issued in his candidature
of 1883 has been ascribed as "a third Charter in itself."
By his fearless championship of their interests, and his sympathy for them in time of trouble, he had especially endeared himself to the working people.   So early as the days
of George Odger and other leaders of the Labour cause,
he had taken part in a movement which resulted in the re-
casting of the labour laws.   He had acted as arbitrator for
the men in many cases of trade dispute.   Whilst taking an
active part in the effort to secure both the later extensions
of the franchise which took place in 1867 and 1884, Dr.
Pankhurst had, as we have seen, done all he could to get
women included under them.

CHAPTER III

THE GENERAL ELECTION OF 1906

AFTER the inauguration of the militant tactics on October 13th, we determined not to let the matter rest until we had obtained a definite pledge that the incoming Liberal Government would give votes to women. On December 4th came the long-expected resignation of Mr. Balfour, and the King then called upon Sir Henry Campbell-Bannerman, the Liberal leader, to form an Administration. It was now announced that a great demonstration should be held on December 21st in the Royal Albert Hall, at which, surrounded by every member of his Cabinet, Sir Henry should make his first public utterance as Prime Minister.

The importance of raising our question at this meeting was of course apparent, and we at once endeavoured to procure tickets of admission. But, even so early in the fight as this, the Liberals did not scruple to refuse tickets to women who might be going to ask awkward questions. On one occasion just as two tickets were about to be delivered over to me, I was accused of having questioned Mr. Asquith at a meeting in the Queen's Hall, and, though I had really not been present at that meeting, I was obliged to go away empty-handed. I had been mistaken for Annie Kenney who had come to London to attend both the Queen's Hall and the

Albert Hall meetings. We both of us thought the
incident most absurd, for we do not in any way
resemble each other. But it put us on our guard,
and when on the very morning of the Albert Hall
meeting, a friend sent me three tickets, we made up
our minds that they should not be rendered useless
by those who presented them being turned away at
the doors. I had been twice interviewed in two
different sets of clothes by the Liberal officials who
had eventually refused me the tickets and Annie herself had been paraded before a row of stewards; it
was therefore clear that if either of us went to the
meeting we must go disguised. We decided at last
that the three tickets should be used by Theresa
Billington, who had recently joined the Union and
was coming from Manchester for the meeting, by
Annie herself, and by a working woman from the
East End, a recent convert. Nevertheless, we intended first to give the Prime Minister a chance to
answer fairly, so that no disturbance need be made.
Shortly before the meeting, therefore, Annie Kenney
dispatched by express messenger a letter to Sir Henry
Campbell-Bannerman on behalf of our Union, asking him whether the new Government would give
Women the vote, and stating that she should be
in the hall that night in the hope that this important
question would be answered without delay. If this
were not done, she added that she should feel
bound to rise in her place and make a protest.

The next thing to do was to disguise Annie. We
understood that most of the ladies would wear
evening gowns, but it was essential to show as little
of her face, neck, and hair as possible, so, after
dressing her up in a light cream-coloured frock,

we added a fur coat and a thick dark veil. She told us afterwards that she felt very hot in these clothes which she was afraid to remove, but, with the little East End convert walking closely behind her as her maid, she was allowed by the scrutineers to pass into a private box which we afterwards found had been specially set apart for the use of Mr. John Burns' family and friends.

The immense brilliantly lighted hall was filled from floor to ceiling. The platform was gaily decorated with flowers. As the Prime Minister began to speak Annie Kenney sat anxiously awaiting his answer, and at last, as he did not give it, she rose suddenly up and hanging over the edge of the box a little white calico banner with the words " Votes for Women " painted upon it in black letters, she called out in a loud clear voice, " Will the Liberal Government give women the vote? " Immediately afterwards came an answering cry from the opposite end of the hall, and Theresa Billington let down from the orchestra above the platform a great banner, nine feet in length inscribed in black with the words " Will the Liberal Government give justice to working-women? " For a moment there was a hush, whilst the people waited for the Prime Minister's answer, but he and his Cabinet remained silent. Then the whole vast audience broke into a tumultuous, conflicting uproar, in the midst of which the Chairman vainly called for order. The organ played to drown the women's questions, and the women were flung out of the hall.

The next day we returned to Manchester for Christmas to find that Christabel was already planning a General Election campaign, and all through

the holidays, whilst Cabinet Ministers were resting
from their labours, we were busy making white
calico banners, and inscribing them in black letters
with the fateful words, "Votes for Women" and
"Will the Liberal Government give women the
vote?" We had no longer a doubt either that the
new Liberal Government was hostile to our cause
or that it was our duty to fight them until they were
ready to capitulate or to retire from office. Had it
been possible we should have opposed the election
of every candidate running under their auspices, but
as we had neither the funds nor the membership for
so extensive a work, we decided to carry out a definite Election campaign against one member of
the Government,— Mr. Winston Churchill. Mr.
Churchill was selected not for any personal feeling
against him, but because he was the most important
of the Liberal candidates who were standing for
constituencies within easy reach of our home.

On the opening night of the campaign Mr.
Churchill had arranged to hold several meetings in
halls in different parts of his constituency and, as the
intentions of the Women's Social and Political Union
were now well-known, considerable excitement and
expectancy prevailed. The first meeting was held
in a school at Cheetham Hill. There were a number of doors to the meeting room, one opening in
the middle of a side wall and communicating with
a passage leading from the main entrance to the
building; another, a big emergency exit at the back
of the room farthest from the platform, and several
others on each side of the platform opening into
class-rooms and ante-rooms. The first of these
doors was the one by which the audience came in.

No tickets were needed and the solitary Suffragette who presented herself was able to walk quietly in unnoticed and to take a seat in the middle of the room. If her heart beat so loud that it seemed that all must hear it, if she felt sick and faint with suspense, no one knew.

The whole audience was eagerly looking for " The lady Suffragists." A party of women in a little gallery above the door, attracted considerable attention. " Those are the Suffragists, look up there," was whispered from all quarters. A man who sat next to the unrecognised Suffragette fixed his gaze upon these ladies, and turning to his companion said: " That is Miss Pankhurst; she has aged very much since I saw her last. The ladies have got their eyes on us; they will begin putting their question soon." The hall filled up rapidly and at last became so densely crowded that, owing to the press of people, the emergency doors at the back of the hall were burst open and a large crowd collected outside. Mr. Churchill was late, and during the Chairman's remarks and the speeches that followed little attention was paid to what was being said for everyone was waiting for what was to happen next.

At last Mr. Winston Churchill came in. He spoke of the unsatisfactory behaviour of the late Government. The will of the people, he declared, had been ignored, " But now," he said, " you have got your chance! " " Yes, we have got our chance, and we mean to use it. Will the Liberal Government give women the vote? " The reply came prompt and sharp as a pistol shot. It was a woman's voice, and there was a woman standing up with a little white banner in her hand. There was a moment's breathless waiting for Mr. Churchill's answer which did not come, and then the usual uproar burst forth. The man who " knew " Miss Pankhurst was the first to snatch the banner from the Suffragette, but it was evident that sitting around her were many unknown friends.

For some time it was impossible to proceed with the meeting. Whilst the noise was at its height the interrupter sat down and waited; then, as soon as quiet was restored and Mr. Churchill attempted to continue his speech without replying, she again got up and pressed for an answer to her question. The Chairman endeavoured to induce Mr. Churchill to give an answer, but without success. The stewards threatened to throw the woman out but were afraid to do so because many of the men showed that they were prepared to fight for her, and in any case, the meeting was so crowded that it would have been difficult to get her through the press of people. The woman asking for votes seemed likely to have the best of it for once. Someone suggested that if Mr. Churchill would only answer, or if the men in the audience would not get so very much excited, things might go better, but the advice was unheeded.

At last the Chairman announced that, if the lady would promise to be quiet afterwards, she should speak from the platform for five minutes. To this she was not disposed to agree, but went up to the foot of the platform to explain that all she wanted was an answer to her question. Speaking directly to Mr. Churchill she said, " Don't you understand what it is I want? " But hiding his face with a quick impatient movement of his arm he answered crossly, " Get away, I won't have anything to do with you." Then the Chairman appealed to her: " You had better come up to the platform," he said, " we can hear you then; as it is, half the people in the meeting do not know what all the fuss is about." She consented, and for the next five minutes tried to make her explanation, but the enthusiastic Liberals of the three front rows set up the wildest tumult of shouts and yells in order to drown her words.

When the five minutes were over the woman turned to go, but Mr. Churchill seized her roughly by the arm and forced her to sit down in a chair at the back of the platform saying, " No, you must wait here, till you have heard what I have to say," then turning to the audience he began complaining of the way in which the women were treating him and concluded, " nothing would induce me to vote for giving women the franchise," and, " I am not going to be henpecked into a question of such grave importance." As he finished this declaration of hostility the men on the platform rose, as if by prearranged agreement, and the woman questioner stood up also, wishing to leave. Instantly two men hurried her to the side of the platform where, screened from the audience by a group of others, they swung her roughly over the edge and dragged her into an ante-room.

Thinking that she was merely to be put outside she had made no resistance, but now one of the men went to find the key to lock her in whilst the other remained in the room, standing with his back to the door. As soon as they were alone he began to use the most violent language and, calling her a cat, gesticulated as though he would scratch her face with his hands. Knowing that the room was on the ground floor, she ran to the window, and threw it open, only to find that it was barred. She called to some people who were passing in the side street saying: " I want you to be witnesses of any-thing that takes place in this room," and they came running up and shouted to the man to behave himself. He at once became quieter, and presently on a key being brought to him, he locked the door and went away. Now, some of those in the street discovered that one of the windows had no bars, and they called to the prisoner to go and open it in order that they might help her to escape. This was easily done and an indignation meeting was immediately held on a piece of waste ground near by. Meanwhile Mr. Churchill was going on to his other meetings, but he found a woman readily to question him at every one.

Next day there were long columns in the Man-chester papers dealing with these incidents whilst Mr. Churchill's angry assertion that he would not be " henpecked " drew forth innumerable jokes from the humorous writers. A verse from one of these, entitled " The Heckler, and the Hen-pecker, with apologies to Lewis Carroll " ran as follows: —

" ' The price of bread ' the Heckler said, ' is what we have to note.
Answer at once, who caused the war, and who made Joseph's coat? '
But here the Hen-pecker, shrieked out, ' Will women have the vote? '
' I weep for you ' the Heckler said, ' I deeply sympathise,
We have asked a hundred questions and yet had no replies.'
But here the Hen-pecker spread out a flag of largest size."

Day by day the warfare with Mr. Churchill continued, a large proportion of the inhabitants of the district gradually becoming more and more completely converted to the women's point of view. In some cases after violent scenes of disorder, the entire audience got up and left the meeting to show their sympathy with them.

In our Manchester election campaign we did not confine ourselves, however, merely to questioning and Heckling Mr. Churchill. We also held numberless meetings of our own and distributed thousands of leaflets.

One day my brother Harry, who was then fifteen years of age, suggested to us a scheme which, though it involved some risk of prosecution, we found irresistible. Accordingly, in the small hours of the last two mornings before polling, he and two of his school fellows set off with brush and paste can and some long narrow slips called " fly, posters," with " Votes for Women " printed in black letters upon them. Whilst the other two boys kept a lookout for passing policemen, Harry pasted these slips cornerwise across Mr. Churchill's great red and white posters which appeared on every hoarding in the constituency, just as the ordinary advertiser does when he wishes to bring out special points of attraction to heighten the public interest.

Though Mr. Churchill won the Election, his majority was smaller than that of any of the other Manchester Liberal candidates.

One of the most active workers in the new militant campaign was Mrs. Flora Drummond, a cheery, rosy-faced little woman, a native of the Island of

Arran. As a girl Flora Gibson had been daring
and high-spirited, a good swimmer, a splendid
walker, and the leader in all kinds of out-door sports
and games. On leaving school she successfully
passed all examinations for the position of post mistress, but immediately afterwards the Post Master
General raised the height standard for all post
masters and mistresses to five feet, two inches, the
same standard being exacted both for men and
women although the average height of men is of
course greater than that of women. Flora Gibson
was only five feet one inch in height, and as it had
been only at considerable sacrifice that her widowed
mother had been able to pay for her education,
poor Flora was in despair; but her father's relations agreed to pay the necessary fees for her to
learn shorthand and typewriting. She soon became
exceedingly skilled and took a Society of Arts cer-
tificate. Shortly after this she married Mr. Drummond, a journeyman upholsterer, and removed to
Manchester, his native place. Soon after her marriage she was obliged to resume her typewriting because bad trade threw Mr. Drummond out of regular employment. Eventually she became manager
of the Oliver Typewriter Company's office in Manchester. She had joined the W. S. P. U. on hearing of the imprisonment of Annie Kenney and
Christabel Pankhurst.

Mrs. Drummond was invaluable for the work of
questioning Cabinet Ministers which was carried on
continuously in spite of our Manchester election campaign. When, early in January, 1906, we heard
that the Prime Minister was to speak at the Sun
Hall, Liverpool, she and several other members of

the Union agreed to go over and question him. Mr. Balfour, who was then fighting a losing battle in the effort to retain his old seat in East Manchester, had agreed to receive a deputation from our Union. Nothing very important came of the interview, though Mr. Balfour's reply was kindly and sympathetic, but long before Mr. Balfour's hotel had been reached the deputation had discovered that they were being shadowed by detectives. As it had been arranged that some of the women should go straight on to Liverpool, they made every attempt to shake off their pursuers. Proceeding first in one direction and then in another, they were tracked all over Manchester and Liverpool until finally Christabel said good-bye to her companions and returned to Manchester. Then, instead of breaking up into two parties the detectives all followed her, whilst the other women, in company with a number of Liverpool members of our Union, quietly made their way to the Sun Hall, where nine of them subsequently questioned the Prime Minister and were all thrown out of the hall without receiving a reply. After the first woman had been rejected Sir Campbell-Bannerman said: " If I might have done so, I could have calmed that lady's nerves by telling her that I am in favour of Women's Suffrage," but this, of course, was no answer to the question as to whether the Government was prepared to enfranchise the women of the country.

On January 15th Mrs. Drummond and a number of her friends in Glasgow attended a meeting of the Prime Minister's in the St. Andrew's Hall there. Heckling is a regular institution in Scotland, and the Glasgow women declared that they would certainly receive courteous replies. On asking the usual question Mrs. Drummond was at once flung out by the stewards and immediately afterwards one of her companions who had hitherto been a staunch Liberal approached her with hat awry and dishevelled clothing saying in bewilderment, " Oh my, they pet me oot ! "

During these weeks questions were also put at several other meetings including that of Mr. Asquith in the Sheffield Drill Hall. Everywhere the women were ejected. On January 25th one of the last big Liberal meetings of the General Election was held at Altrincham in Cheshire, Mr. Lloyd George being the principal speaker. The members of the W. S. P. U. who were present did not interrupt him during his speech but waited until he had finished before asking him the usual question. Mr. Lloyd George then said: " I was going to congratulate myself that I had escaped this; however, at the last meeting of the campaign the spectre has appeared." That was all, and the women were quickly hauled out to prevent their again raising their voices.

So the General Election ended, and we were still left without that pledge from the Liberal leaders which we had set ourselves to gain. Those of us who went through the campaign will be ever at a loss to understand the motives which led the Liberal leaders to treat our first orderly and considerate questioning and even the later, more persistent heckling, as they did. They obviously had neither the wish nor the intention of giving votes to women during their term of office, and it was probably the fear of offending the ladies who canvassed for them that prevented their plainly saying so. Yet after all, they were accustomed to parrying the questioning of men and it was surely unwise, even from their own standpoint, to deal so violently with women.

All that had been done by the new militant suffragists up to now had been merely the brilliant skirmishing of an intrepid and resourceful little band of enthusiasts driven to employ somewhat unconventional methods, both by the old established custom of boycotting their cause and by the ruthless brutality of the forces that were arrayed against them. Our opponents called us " a stage army " and " a family party," and the designations were not inapt, but the little stage army was always cleverly marshalled, and its soldiers were as cheerfully and affectionately loyal to the mother of the movement and to the young general who had initiated the new tactics as though in reality they had all been members of a single family.

During the General Election various attempts to press forward the question of Women's Suffrage had also been made by the non-militant Suffragists. Miss Llewellyn Davies and others had organised a joint Manifesto on this question from a large number of societies. These included, amongst others, the Women's Co-operative Guild with 20,700 members, the Women's Liberal Federation with 76,000 members and the Scottish Women's Liberal Federation with 15,000 members. The North of England Weavers' Association, with 100,000. The British Women's Temperance Association with 109,890 members, the Independent Labour Party with 20,000 members, and the Lancashire and Cheshire Textile and others Workers' Representation Committee,

whose Secretaries were Miss Eva Core-Booth and
Mrs. Sarah Dickinson. The Women Textile Workers' Committee had also run Mr. Thorley Smith
as a Women's Suffrage candidate for Wigan.
Though Mr. Smith had not been elected, a good fight
had been made and a very creditable vote secured;
the figures had been : —

      Powel (Conservative) 3,573
      Smith (Women's Suff.) 2,205
      Woods (Liberal) 1,900

CHAPTER IV

JANUARY TO MAY, 1906

ANNIE KENNEY SETS OFF TO ROUSE LONDON — THE
SCENE IN THE LADIES GALLERY AND THE DEPUTATION
TO SIR HENRY CAMPBELL-BANNERMAN.

As soon as the General Election was over, we
began to make preparations for the opening of Parliament. It was decided that the work of our Union
must be carried to London, and that we must have
an Organiser there who would be able to devote
the whole of her time to it. Annie Kenney, who,
after her imprisonment, had never gone back to the
Mill, was chosen for this post. The Election campaign had put a severe strain upon the resources of
the Union, and from the first the raising of funds
had been our greatest difficulty. Therefore, it was
with only £2 in her pocket and the uncertainty as to
whether more would be forthcoming that Annie
Kenney set off " to rouse London." Perhaps no one
realised what a heavy task, and how many bitter
rebuffs were before this sensitive, fragile girl. I
took a room for her in the house where I was staying at 45, Park Walk, Chelsea, in order that we
might consult, and as far as possible, work together.

The Committee in Manchester had not formulated
any definite plans of campaign, but we came to the

conclusion that we must organise a procession of women and a demonstration in Trafalgar Square for the day of the opening of Parliament. When Annie went to Scotland Yard to inform the police of our intentions, however, she was told that no meeting in Trafalgar Square could be allowed whilst Parliament was sitting. This forced us to the conclusion that we must hire a Hall somewhere near Westminster for our meeting place, but we knew not where to find the money to pay for it. This and other difficulties, however, were one by one smoothed away. Mr. Keir Hardie and Mr. Frank Smith (afterwards elected to the London County Council as member for Lambeth) were the first to help us, and they advised us to take the Caxton Hall, Westminster, and put us in touch with a sympathiser who agreed to pay the rent of it.

As soon as we had taken the Hall, we drafted a little handbill to announce the Meeting, and then, armed with her bills and her wonderful faith in the goodness of her fellow men and women, Annie Kenney proceeded with her mission, calling day by day upon people of whom she knew practically nothing, and to whom she herself was entirely unknown. One of those who kindly helped us was Mr. W. T. Stead, who published in the *Review of Reviews* a character sketch of Annie Kenney, in which he likened her to Josephine Butler. It was soon plain to us that it would be easier to ask for help if we formed a London Branch of the W. S. P. U., and with my aunt, Mrs. Clarke, and Mrs. Lucy Roe, our landlady, we therefore formed a Preliminary Committee.

In about a fortnight's time my mother joined us. She was surprised to learn that so many arrangements had been made and at first was almost inclined to be appalled at the boldness of our plans. She was afraid that we should never induce more than a handful of women to walk in procession through the public streets, and that the Caxton Hall could not be filled. But the die was cast, and she threw herself into the work determined to do her very best to prevent failure.

A few days after this we heard that Mrs. Drummond was coming from Manchester to help us. Her husband was earning little at the time, and the Union had no money to provide her railway fare, but she had walked miles through the snow in order to collect the necessary funds from her friends. When she arrived, we were all of us growing very weary and overwrought. It seemed almost impossible to stir this great city, filled with its busy millions who appeared to have no time to think of anything but their own affairs. The thoughtless apathy of those whom we met with money and leisure at their disposal, the dull, hopeless inertia of those who agreed that we were right, but would not stir themselves to help, were to us in our anxiety, almost maddening. But Mrs. Drummond, with her practical ways and her inexhaustible fund of good humour, brought with her a spirit of renewed hope and energy. Her first act was to go to the office of the Oliver Company and borrow a typewriter from them. The secretarial duties were thus enormously lightened, and after rattling off the correspondence she was always ready to join us in delivering handbills, canvassing from house to house, or writing announcements of the forthcoming meetings with white chalk upon the city pavement.

At last the day of the opening of Parliament, February 19th, 1906, arrived, and a crowd of some three or four hundred women, a large proportion of whom were poor workers from the East End, met us at St. James' Park District Railway Station. We formed in procession and put up a few simple banners, some of which were red with white letters, and had been made by working people in Canning Town, whilst the rest I had made of white linen and lettered with India ink in the little sitting-room at Park Walk. Our procession had gone but a few yards when the police came up and insisted upon the furling of the banners, but they did not prevent our marching to the Caxton Hall near by. Here we found that a large audience had already assembled, and soon the hall was crowded with women, most of whom were strangers to us. We were told afterwards that amongst the rest were many ladies of wealth and position, who, inspired with curiosity by the newspaper accounts of the disturbances which we were said to have created, had disguised themselves in their maids' clothes in order that they might attend the meeting unrecognised.

Mrs. Pankhurst, Annie Kenney and others who spoke, were listened to with much earnestness and presently the news came that the King's speech, the Government's legislative programme for the session, had been read, and that it had contained no reference to the question of Women's Suffrage. My mother at once moved that the meeting should form itself into a " Lobbying " Committee and should at once proceed to the House of Commons in order to induce its members to ballot for a Women's Suffrage Bill. This resolution was carried with acclamation, and the whole meeting streamed out into the street and made its way to the House. It was bitterly cold and pouring with rain, but when we arrived at the Strangers' Entrance, we found that for the first time that anyone could remember, the door of the House of Commons was closed to women. Cards were sent in to several Private Members, some of whom came out and urged that we should be allowed to enter, but the Government had given its orders, and the police remained obdurate. All the women refused to go away, and permission was finally given for twenty women at a time to be admitted. Then hour after hour the women stood outside in the rain waiting for their turn to enter. Some of them never got into the House at all, and those who did so went away gloomy and disappointed for there was not one of them who had received any assurance that Parliament intended to give women the vote.

Now, after a chance meeting with Mrs. Pankhurst and a second long talk with her and with Annie Kenney, a new recruit had entered our movement. This was Mrs. Pethick Lawrence, the daughter of Mr. Henry Pethick, of Wesern Super-Mare, and a member of a Cornish family. As a child at school she had read the story of Hetty Sorrell in George Eliot's "Adam Bede," had seen "Faust," and Marguerite in her prison cell. Later she had learnt from Sir Walter Besant's *Children of Gideon* of the cheerless struggle to eke out an existence upon starvation wages, which falls to the lot of working-girls. Then and there she had resolved to spend her life in striving to alter these conditions. She determined that as soon as she left school she would go to " the East End," and begin. When the time came she at once acted upon this decision. Without seeking help or advice from anyone, she wrote to Mrs. Hugh Price Hughes, of the West London Mission and asked that she might be received into her sisterhood. When her request had been granted she told her parents of what she had done, and they readily gave their full approval and sympathy.

After four years of useful training and varied experiences in the West London Mission, during which she had had at some times the charge of a Working-Girls' Club and at others had been sent out at night on to the London Streets in order to save and succour the homeless and outcast women there, she and her friend, Miss Mary Neal, took rooms in a block of artisans' dwellings and gathered round them a small colony of social workers. Together they founded the Esperance Working-Girls' Club, to which was attached a co-operative dress-making establishment, and a holiday hotel at Littlehampton called " The Green Lady." Later on, after her marriage Mrs. Pethick Lawrence built a small cottage near her house at Holmwood called " The Sundial," where the junior members of the Esperance Club were invited during the summer.

Writing of these early years, and of her own decision to take part in the Votes for Women Movement she says:

Out of that part of my life there stand out many memories. . . . I remember a little girl belonging to the Children's Happy Evening Club, who went mad with grief because her widowed mother lost her work, and was in despair. The dread of being separated in the workhouse was upon the whole family, and the child was taken to the asylum, crying, " Poor, poor mother." I remember a girl about twenty, alone in the world, earning a pittance as a waitress in a tea-shop. She was a quiet, gentle creature, who made no complaint. All the greater was the shock when the girl put an end to her life, leaving a little note, with the words, " I am tired out." These two cries still ring out at times in my memory with their terrible indictment against life as men have made it. . . . We recognised the fact that we were only making in a great wilderness a tiny garden, enclosed by the wall of human fellowship. As we saw more and more of the evil plight of women, we realised ever more clearly that nothing could really lift them out of it until the power had been put into their hands to help themselves. . . . Suddenly a light flashed out. News came of the arrest and imprisonment of Christabel Pankhurst and Annie Kenney. Here at last was action.

So it was that Mrs. Pethick Lawrence had prepared herself to take part in the great Votes for Women Movement.

We had now decided to organise our London Committee on a more formal basis. Mrs. Lawrence was asked to become one of its members and I well remember her coming to my little room in Park Walk to take part in the formation of the new Central Committee. It was the first time I had seen her, and I can never forget how much I was attracted by her dark expressive eyes, and the quiet business-like way in which she listened to what was being said, only interposing in the debate when she had something really valuable to suggest. It was later that I noticed the untrammelled carriage and the fine free lift of the head.

That first meeting was towards the end of February and it was arranged that Mrs. Lawrence, her friend, Miss Mary Neal, myself, Annie Kenney, my aunt, Mrs. Clarke, Mrs. Roe, Miss Irene Fenwick Miller, daughter of a well-known early suffragist, and Mrs. Martel, of Australia, should form the London Committee with my mother and Mrs. Drummond, who were returning to Manchester. It was decided that I was to become the Honorary Secretary, and Mrs. Lawrence was asked to be Honorary Treasurer.

We now felt that our next move must be to secure an interview with the Prime Minister, and we therefore wrote to Sir Henry Campbell-Bannerman asking him to receive a deputation from our Union. He replied that he could not spare the time to see us. Our answer was that, owing to the urgency of the question, we could take no refusal, and that a number of our members would call upon him at the Official Residence, No. 10 Downing Street, on the morning of March 2nd, 1906.

Downing Street is a short road opening out of Parliament Street and ending in a flight of steps leading into St. James' Park. There are now only three houses left in the Street, the others having been pulled down to make way for Government Buildings. The Official Residence itself was not built for its present purpose and consists of two comfortable-looking Georgian houses knocked into one, each of which is three stories high with attics above, and has three windows along the front of the first and second floors and two windows and a door below. The door is dark green, almost black, and has a black iron knocker, a lion's head with a ring in its mouth.   Above this knocker is a small, circular, brass knob about half an inch in diameter and very highly polished and under the knocker is a brass plate, equally well polished, inscribed " First Lord of the Treasury."   There is one shallow, well whitened doorstep and on each side of it are black iron railings that protect the house from the street. The next house, No. 11, is a slightly more ornate building in the same style, which was then occupied by Mr. Herbert Gladstone.

On presenting themselves at the door of the Official Residence, the deputation from the Women's Social and Political Union were told that Sir Henry Campbell-Bannerman could receive no one, as he had been ill and was still confined to his room.   A request to see the Prime Minister's secretary was also refused, and the door was shut.   Then, deciding to wait there until they were attended to, the deputation sat down to rest on the doorstep and displayed a little white " Votes for Women " banner.

We had notified the various newspapers [1] that we intended to call on Sir Henry Campbell-Bannerman and by this time a number of Press photographers had collected.   This greatly embarrassed the inhabitants of No. 10, and presently the hall porter opened the door again, and looking very uncomfortable, begged the women to go away.   Annie

[1] From the first, the London papers and especially the newly inaugurated *Daily Mirror,* had been somewhat interested in our unusual methods of propaganda. It was just at this time that the *Daily Mail* began to call us " Suffragettes " in order to distinguish between us and the members of the older Suffrage Society who had always been called " Suffragists," and who strongly objected to our tactics.

Kenney assured him that she and her companions would remain all day if need be, and after arguing for some time, scratching his head and looking very much puzzled, he finally asked two members of the deputation to go inside, where they were received by Mr. Ponsonby, the secretary, who promised to give their message to his chief.

The same evening we held another Committee meeting and drafted a further letter to the Prime Minister asking for an early opportunity of laying our case before him. In response to this letter, he returned an evasive reply in which he stated that any representations that the Union wished to make to him must be put in writing.

We therefore decided that another attempt must be made to interview him and after waiting until he had made a complete recovery and was again able to take his part in the House of Commons debates, a larger deputation, consisting of several members of our Committee and some thirty other women, made their way to Downing Street about 10 o'clock on the morning of March 9th. They again asked to see the Prime Minister and the door-keeper promised to give their message to the secretary. After they had been waiting for three-quarters of an hour two men came out and said to them, " You had better be off; you must not stand on this doorstep any longer." The women explained that they were waiting for a reply but were abruptly told that there was no answer and the door was rudely shut in their faces.

Angered by this Miss Irene Miller immediately seized the knocker and rapped sharply at the door. Then the two men appeared again and one of them

called to a policeman on the other side of the road,
" Take this woman in charge." The order was at
once obeyed, and Miss Miller was marched away to
Canon Row Police Station. Spurred on by this
event Mrs. Drummond, exclaiming that nothing
should prevent her from seeing the Prime Minister,
darted forward and pulled at the little brass knob
in the middle of the door. As she did so, she discovered that the little knob, instead of being a bell,
as she had imagined, was something very different indeed, for suddenly the door opened wide.
Without more ado she rushed in and headed
straight for the Cabinet Council Chamber, but before
she could get there she was caught, thrown out of the
house and then taken in custody to the police station.
Meanwhile Annie Kenney began to address the gathering crowd, but the man who had first called the
policeman again looked out and said, " Why don't
you arrest that woman? She is one of the ringleaders. Take her in charge." Then she was
dragged away to join her companions.

The three women were detained at Canon Row for
about an hour. Then a police inspector told them
that a message to set them at liberty had been sent
by the Prime Minister, who wished them to be informed that he would receive a deputation from the
Women's Social and Political Union, either individually or in conjunction with other women's societies.
Of course we published Sir Henry Campbell-Bannerman's promise broadcast. Shortly afterwards, two
hundred Members of Parliament, drawn from every
party, petitioned Sir Henry to fix an early date for
receiving some of their number in order that they
might urge upon him the necessity for an immediate

extension of the franchise to women.   He then formally announced that on May 19th he would receive a
joint deputation both from Members of Parliament
representing the signatories to this petition and all
the organised bodies of women in the country who
were desirous of obtaining the Suffrage.

All the women's societies now began to make preparations for an effective Demonstration on May 19th.
The National Union of Women's Suffrage Societies
decided to hold a meeting in the Exeter Hall, but
we of the Women's Social and Political Union wished
to do something very much more ambitious than that,
and we resolved to organise a procession and a demonstration in Trafalgar Square.   In view of the immense work that this would entail, we felt the necessity of engaging another organiser, and my mother
now recommended that Miss Billington should be
asked to undertake the work.

Born in Blackburn in 1877, Theresa Billington,
the daughter of a shipping clerk, had been educated at
a Roman Catholic convent school.   Owing to financial difficulties at home, she had been set to learn
millinery at thirteen years of age.   At seventeen she
had made up her mind to be a teacher, and having obtained one of the Queen's Scholarships, she eventually
became a teacher under the Manchester Education
Committee.   When she was first introduced to us she
had come into conflict with the authorities because of
her refusal to give the prescribed religious instruc-
tion to her pupils.   My mother, who was then a
member of the Education Committee, intervened to
secure that she should be transferred to a Jewish
school, where she would not be expected to teach
religion, and thus prevented her dismissal.   In 1904,

at my mother's request, she had been appointed as an organiser for the Independent Labour Party.

About the middle of April, a few weeks after the Prime Minister had given his promise to receive the deputation, a Parliamentary vacancy occurred in the Eye division of Suffolk, and Christabel wrote to our London Committee, saying that she thought it advisable that we should go down to the constituency and intimate to the Liberal candidate that, unless he could obtain a pledge from his Government to give Votes to women, we should oppose his return, and that we should take a similar course in the case of every future Government nominee. Mrs. Pethick Lawrence, Annie Kenney and Theresa Billington therefore went down to Eye and interviewed Mr. Harold Pearson, the Liberal candidate, but he treated the question of Votes for Women with contempt and ridiculed the idea that women could do anything to hinder his return. Owing to the size of that large county constituency and the pressure of work in London these three members of our Committee then decided to return to London. But at home in Manchester they were exceedingly anxious to see the policy of opposition to the Government at by-elections put into practice.

The funds of the Manchester branch of the Union were entirely depleted, but five pounds was got together, an address to the Electors of Eye from the Women's Social and Political Union was printed and Mrs. Drummond set off to the constituency to fight the election single-handed. Five pounds to fight an election campaign with seems an absurdly small sum when one realises that the candidates spend many hundreds. Nevertheless, though she was entirely friendless and unknown in that part of the country, Mrs. Drummond succeeded in creating a wonderful impression. She could not afford to hire a carriage, it is true, but there was always a friendly farmer or tradesman who would give the cheery little Scotchwoman a lift in his cart, and so active was she that in a short time the impression was spread abroad that not one solitary Suffragette had gone to Eye, but that several were working from different centres. Before the end of the Election the Conservative candidate and even scornful Mr. Harold Pearson, the Liberal, had declared in favour of Votes for Women.

Meanwhile Mr. Keir Hardie had secured a place for a Women's Suffrage Resolution which was to be discussed in the House of Commons on the evening of April 25th. Though a resolution is only an expression of opinion and can have no practical legislative effect, this was considered important because it was realised that if the new Parliament were to show a substantial majority in its support, the women's claim that the Government should deal with the question would be greatly strengthened. Unfortunately only a second place had been obtained for the Resolution. Hence there was every reason to fear that, as so often before, our talkative opponents would succeed in preventing its being voted upon. The situation became more hopeful, however, when the Anti-Vivisectionists, who had obtained the first place for the evening, entered into a compromise by which they agreed to withdraw their resolution early. The way was thus left clear for the Votes for Women Resolution, but we ourselves still thought that the " talkers out " would probably have their way. We were

determined not to allow this to happen without protest.   Therefore, in order to be in readiness for any
emergency, a large number of us had obtained tickets
for the Ladies' Gallery.

Looking down through the brass grille, from behind which women are alone permitted to listen to
the debates in Parliament, we saw that the House
was crowded as is usual only at important crises, and
that both the Government and Opposition front
benches were fully occupied. The Resolution,
" That in the opinion of this House it is desirable
that sex should cease to be a bar to the exercise of
the Parliamentary franchise " was moved and seconded in short speeches in order that the opponents
should have no least excuse for urging that there had
been no time for their own side to be fairly heard.
Then Mr. Cremer rose to speak in opposition.   His
speech was grossly insulting to women and altogether
unworthy of a Member of the People's House of
Representatives.   Both by his words, his voice and
gestures he plainly showed his entire view of women
to be degraded and indeed revolting.   Yet, though
one was angry with him, he was an object for pity
as he stood there, undersized and poorly made, obviously in bad health and with that narrow, grovel-
ling and unimaginative point of view, flaunting
his masculine superiority.   The women found it
very difficult to sit quietly listening to him, and,
though my mother strove to check them, some subdued exclamations caught the Speaker's ear.   He immediately gave orders for the police to be in readiness
to clear the Ladies' Gallery if any further sounds
should issue from it.   But, once Mr. Cremer had finished speaking, absolute quiet was restored.   Mr.

Willie Redmond, brother of John Redmond, the leader of the Irish Party, then indignantly protested against the tone of Mr. Cremer's speech, crying fervently that he himself had always believed in Women's Suffrage because, all his life, he had been opposed to slavery in any form, and declaring that " any of God's creatures who are denied a voice in the Government of their country are more or less slaves," and that " men have no right to assume that they are so superior to women, that they alone have the right to govern."

All through the debate everyone was waiting for a declaration from the Government. At last Mr. Herbert Gladstone, the Home Secretary, rose to speak, but his words were vague and evasive, and whilst not absolutely excluding the possibility of the Government's taking the matter up, he certainly made no promise on their behalf.

At ten minutes to eleven Mr. Samuel Evans rose with the obvious intention of talking the Resolution out and, as eleven o'clock, the hour for closing the debate, drew nearer, whilst spinning out his remarks by means of some very doubtful jokes, he kept turning round, every now and then, to look at the clock. Our eyes were also eagerly fixed upon the timepiece. Every moment one woman or another stretched across and asked Mrs. Pankhurst whether the demonstration of protest should begin, but her answer was always that there was " time yet," and that we must wait.

At last someone looked round and saw that the police were already in the gallery and we realised that we were to be taken away in order that the Resolution might be " talked out " without our having an

opportunity to protest.   Irene Miller could no longer
be restrained.   She called out loudly, " Divide!
Divide! " as they do in the House of Commons,
and " We refuse to have our Resolution talked out."
Then we all followed suit, and Theresa Billington
thrust a little white flag bearing the words, " Votes
for Women " through the historic grille.   It was
a relief to thus give vent to the feelings of indignation which we had been obliged to stifle during the
whole of the evening, and though we were dragged
roughly out of the gallery, it was with a feeling almost of triumph that we cried shame upon the men
who had wasted hours in useless talk and pitiful and
pointless jokes with which to insult our countrywomen.

But the rough usage of the police was not by any
means the hardest part of the experience.   When we
reached the Lobby, we learnt that our action had
been entirely misunderstood.   A number of non-militant Suffragists were present, and most of these believed, as the Members of Parliament were telling
them, that, but for our " injudicious " action, a vote
would have been taken upon the Resolution.   They
met us with bitter reproaches and disdainful glances,
and even those Members of Parliament who had
proved themselves to be absolutely careless of our
question, now took it upon themselves to come up
and scold us.   On all sides we were abused, repudiated and contemptuously ridiculed, but, after
a few days, public opinion began to turn somewhat
in our favour.   It leaked out that the Speaker had
not intended to allow a Resolution calling for the
closure of the debate to be moved, and it therefore
became known that we had judged correctly in think-

ing that the Women's Suffrage motion was to be
talked out.

Writing in the *Sussex Daily News* for May 2nd,
Mr. Spencer Leigh Hughes, well known under his
pen name "Sub Rosa," recalled the account given
in Lady Mary Montague's "Memoirs" of the way
in which the Peeresses of the eighteenth century had
frequently disturbed the serenity of the House of
Lords debates, and how they had triumphed over
the Lord Chancellor Philip Yorke, First Earl of
Hardwicke, who had attempted to exclude them from
the House of Lords. Lady Mary describes the
"thumping," "rapping" and "running kicks" at
the door of the House of Lords, indulged in by the
Duchess of Queensberry and her friends, the strategy
by which they finally obtained an entry, and the way
in which, during the subsequent debate, they "showed
marks of dislike not only by smiles and winks (which
have always been allowed in these cases), but by
noisy laughs and apparent contempts." Mr. Hughes
ended by saying, "After this excellent and pertinent
account of the action of the Peeresses in the House
of Lords, I suppose no one will be so silly as to
complain of what the women did the other day in
the House of Commons."

Mr. Stead in the *Review of Reviews* published an
article by a "Woman's Righter," who said:

Patience has been tried long enough, and what has it
brought? Less than one ten minutes' expression of the
divine impatience that the Suffragists showed in the Ladies'
Gallery that memorable night! . . . "Surely it was
unwomanly?" Pshaw! It was not anything like so unwomanly as it was unmanly to allow a cause admittedly
just to be stifled without a single indignant protest.

Nevertheless, our supporters were still in the minority. Instead of upholding what we had done to rebuke the anti-Suffragists for their mean and cowardly policy of obstruction (a policy which had prevented the enfranchisement of women for so many years), the National Union of Women's Suffrage Societies and some of the members of the Parliamentary Committee, which was at the time engaged in arranging the deputation to the Prime Minister, now urged that the Women's Social and Political Union had disgraced itself too deeply to form part of the deputation. Efforts were made to induce us to withdraw from it, but this we refused to do. At last, both because some Members of Parliament — and it is said Sir Henry Campbell-Bannerman himself — strongly supported our claim to be represented, and because it was well known that if we were not received we should simply agitate for another deputation, the attempt to exclude us had to be abandoned.

On the morning of May 19th our procession started from the Boadicea statue on Westminster Bridge. First came the members of the Deputation to the Prime Minister, amongst whom were to be seen the veteran Suffragist, fragile little Mrs. Wolstenholme Elmy, with her grey curls, Mrs. Pankhurst, Mrs. Pethick Lawrence, Mr. Keir Hardie, and Annie Kenney, wearing the clogs and shawl which she had worn in the Lancashire cotton mill. Amongst the deputation marched a body of women textile workers from Lancashire and Cheshire, who had joined us, carrying the bright banners of their respective trades. Then came the great red banner of the Women's Social and Political Union, inscribed in white letters with the words, " We demand Votes for Women

this Session." The poles of the banner were lashed
to a big forage lorry in which rode a number of
women, who were either too old or too feeble to
walk. After these came the members of the
Women's Social and Political Union and women
members of various other societies and last of all,
a large contingent from the East End of London,
a piteous band, some of them sweated workers themselves, others the wives of unemployed working men,
and many of them carrying half-starved-looking ba-
bies in their arms.

The deputation which assembled at the Foreign
Office was introduced by Sir Charles M'Laren, and
it was arranged that there should be eight women
speakers. The first of these was the aged Miss
Emily Davies, LL.D., one of the two women who
in 1866, more than forty years before, had handed
to John Stuart Mill the first petition for Women's
Suffrage ever presented to Parliament, and whose
part in opening the University examinations to
women, and in founding Girton, the first of the
women's colleges, will be gratefully remembered by
women of all ages. In pleading for the removal
of the sex disability Miss Davies said: "We do not
regard it as a survival which nobody minds. We
look upon it as an offence to those primarily concerned, and an injury to the community." Then
Mrs. Eva M'Laren, Miss Margaret Ashton and
Mrs. Rolland Rainy, representing respectively some
80,000, 99,000 and 14,000 women Liberals in England and Scotland, urged, each in her own way, that
the Party for which these women had done so much
should extend the franchise to them.

Miss Eva Gore Booth and Mrs. Sarah Dickinson,

who had herself been a factory worker for sixteen years and a Trade Union Organiser for a further eleven years, then spoke on behalf of the fifty delegates from the Lancashire and Cheshire Textile and other Workers' Representation Committee. They dwelt on the low wages — often no more than six or seven shillings a week, and the other heavy economic hardships under which the women whom they represented were obliged to labour. They pointed out that these women, millions of whom since leaving school had never eaten a meal which they had not earned, were not only helping to produce the great wealth of the country but were caring for their homes and their children at the same time, and urged that they were every day more gravely conscious of the heavy disadvantage under which they suffered from their absolute lack of political power. Industrial questions were now becoming political questions, they said, and the vast numbers of women workers had their point of view and their interests which ought to be taken into consideration, but which were disregarded because they were without votes.

Next followed Mrs. Gasson, the speaker for 425 branches and 22,000 members of the Women's Co-operative Guild. She said that the Co-operative movement, with its 62,000,000 members and annual trade of £60,000,000, had often been called a " State within a State." In that State women had votes, they attended quarterly business meetings and voted side by side with men on questions of trade, employment and education. Women were elected as directors of Co-operative societies and also on Educational Committees connected with the Co-operative movement. And yet the prosperity of the co-opera-

tive " State " continued to increase, although in many
places the women members outnumbered the men.
The Co-operative Guild Women saw that when questions affecting the Co-operative movement came before Parliament the movement lost much of its power
because the women had no vote.   Unwise or unjust
taxation was injurious to the Co-operative trade, and
women were the chief sufferers by unjust taxation.
Whatever taxes were put upon necessaries men did
not receive larger incomes, and so women had less
to spend.   That very month Mr. Birrell had received
Resolutions from large conferences of the Co-operative Guild members, urging that medical examination
should be made compulsory under the New Education Bill, but the Resolutions were worth nothing
without a vote behind them.   The women who had
sent up these Resolutions felt " like a crying child
outside the door of a locked room, demanding entrance with no one to open it."   Most of the Co-
operators were married working-women.   Their
houses were both their workshops and their homes,
and therefore Housing and public Health questions
were especially important to them.   Their incomes
were affected by laws relating to trades, accidents,
pensions and all industrial legislation that went to
secure the good health of the workers.   Therefore
they appealed that this common right, the right of
a citizen, should be granted to them and to other
women.

Mrs. Watson spoke on behalf of the Scottish
Christian Union of the British Women's Temperance
Association, with a membership of 52,000 women.
Then Mrs. Mary Bateson presented a petition for
the franchise from 1,530 women graduates, amongst

whom were Doctors of Letters, Science and Law in the Universities of the United Kingdom, the British Colonies and the United States.

Mrs. Pankhurst spoke for the Women's Social and Political Union, the militant organisation of which most of the others were half afraid. She urged on its behalf that the women of the country should be enfranchised during that very year, either by a clause in the Plural Voting Bill then before Parliament, or by a separate measure. Assuring the Prime Minister that the members of the Union believed that no business could be more pressing than this, she stated calmly and firmly that a growing number of them felt the question of Votes for Women so deeply that they were prepared, if necessary, to sacrifice for it life itself, or what was perhaps even harder, the means by which they lived. She appealed to the Government to make such sacrifices needless by doing this long-delayed act of justice to women without delay.

Now that the women had all clearly and carefully laid their case before him, Sir Henry Campbell-Bannerman rose to reply. He began as though he had been an earnest and convinced supporter of the Women's cause and dwelt at length not only upon the benefits which the franchise would confer upon them, but also on the enthusiasm which they had shown in working for it, their fitness to exercise it and the good work which they had already done in public affairs. Then, after a long pause, he said: " That is where you and I are all agreed. It has been very nice and pleasant hitherto, but now we come to the question of what I can say to you, not as expressing my own individual convictions, but as speaking for others, and I have only one thing to preach to you and that is the virtue of patience." With hurried hesitating accents he explained that there were members of his Cabinet who were opposed to the principle of giving votes to women, and that, therefore, he must conclude by saying, " It would never do for me to make any statement or pledge under these circumstances." Poor blundering old man, if he really spoke truthfully to the deputation, one may well pity him in that invidious and humiliating position.

During Sir Henry Campbell-Bannerman's last words there had been a strange silence amongst the women, and as he resumed his seat a low murmur of disappointment ran through the room. Mr. Keir Hardie had been asked by those in charge of the arrangements to move the vote of thanks to the Prime Minister for having received the Deputation, and, though he now performed this duty with characteristic graciousness of manner, he plainly said that all present must have suffered great disappointment on hearing the Prime Minister's concluding statement. Nevertheless, they were glad to learn that the leaders of the two great political parties in the House of Commons were now personally committed to the question, by Mr. Balfour, a statement he had made in the House a few evenings before and the Prime Minister by what he had said that afternoon. " With agreement between the leaders of the two great historic parties," Mr. Hardie said gravely, " and with the support of the other sections of the House, it surely does not pass the wit of statesmanship to find ways and means for the enfranchisement of the women of England before this Parliament

comes to a close." At this point Sir Henry Campbell-Bannerman turned and looked at Mr. Keir
Hardie and solemnly shook his head.

After the resolution had been seconded Mrs. Elmy,
whose name had not been placed upon the authorised
list of speakers, interposed, saying that she had
worked in the cause of Women's Suffrage since October, 1865, and that during that period she had seen
the men voters of the country increased from less
than 700,000 to more than 7,000,000. When the
Reform Act of 1884 had been under consideration,
women Suffragists had been full of hope, but Mr.
Gladstone had refused point blank to give them the
franchise. No Parliament had ever offered a greater
insult to womanhood than the Parliament of that
year, for it had actually taken six or seven divisions
on the point as to whether a criminal should continue to be disfranchised for more than a year after
his release from prison, but only one division had
been taken to decide that English women should not
exercise the vote. Every year it had become more
and more difficult to remedy the injustices under
which women suffered. " If I were to tell you of
the work of the last twenty years of my life," she
said, " it would be one long story of the necessity
for the immediate enfranchisement of women."

The vote of thanks to Sir Henry Campbell-Bannerman was then carried with feeble spiritless clapping and some hisses. Then the Prime Minister
made his reply, but he did not in any way strengthen
his previous declaration and ended by saying that
what women had to do was " to go on converting
the country." As he concluded Annie Kenney sud-

denly rose up and cried, " Sir, we are not satisfied,
and the agitation will go on."

Then we dispersed to meet again at three o'clock
in Trafalgar Square. No better meeting place could
have been chosen, for it was here in Trafalgar Square,
that Edmund Beales and the other leaders of the
Reform movement had spoken when the Hyde Park
gates had been closed against them by the authorities
on that historic 23rd of July, 1866, on which the
Park railings were pulled down and the blow struck
which won the Parliamentary vote for the working
men in the towns. It was here, too, that in February, 1886, John Burns had made that speech to the
starving unemployed men of his own class which
caused him to suffer a month's imprisonment and
made him a famous man, and it was here in Trafalgar Square on the 5th of November, 1887, that, in
taking part in the Demonstration against the imprisonment of O'Brien and the other Irish leaders, poor
Alfred Linnell had been trampled to death by the
horses of the police.

On this ground, consecrate to the discontented and
the oppressed, under that tall column topped by the
statue of the fighting Nelson and on that wide plinth,
flanked by the four crouching lions, the first big open-
air Women's Suffrage meeting in London was held.
By three o'clock more than 7,000 people had assembled. I well remember every detail of the scene.
In my mind's eye I can clearly see the Chairman, my
mother, with her pale face, her quiet dark clothes, her
manner, calm as it always is on great occasions, and
her quiet-sounding but far-reaching voice with its
plaintive minor chords. I can see beside her the

strangely diverse group of speakers: Theresa Billington in her bright blue dress, strongly built and up-standing, her bare head crowned with those brown coils of wonderfully abundant hair. I see Keir Hardie, in his rough brown homespun jacket, with his deep-set, honest eyes, and his face full of human kindness, framed by the halo of his silver hair. Then Mrs. Elmy, fragile, delicate, and wonderfully sweet, with her face looking like a tiny bit of finely modelled, finely tinted porcelain, her shining dark-brown eyes and her long grey curls. Standing very close to her is Annie Kenney, whose soft bright hair falls loosely from her vivid sensitive face, and hangs down her back in a long plait, just as she wore it in the cotton mill. Over her head she wears a grey shawl as she did in Lancashire, and pinned to her white blouse is a brilliant red rosette, showing her to be one of the marshals of the procession, whilst her dark-blue serge skirt just shows the steel tips of her clogs. How beautiful they are, these two women, as hand clasped in hand they stand before us! — one rich in the mellow sweetness of a ripe old age which crowns a life of long toil for the common good; the other filled with the ardour of a chivalrous youth; both dedicated to a great reform. But now, Annie Kenney speaks. She stands out, a striking, almost startling, figure, against the blackened stone-work of the plinth and speaks with a voice that cries out for the lost childhood, blighted hopes and weary, overburdened lives of the women workers whom she knows so well.

First Women's Suffrage Demonstration ever held in Trafalgar Square, May 19th, 1906. Mr. Keir Hardie speaking: Mrs. Pankhurst and Mrs. Wolstenholme Elmy in centre of the platform

CHAPTER V

MAY TO AUGUST, 1906

As Sir Henry Campbell-Bannerman had told the deputation that he could not do anything for us because some members of his Cabinet were opposed to Women's Suffrage, we determined to bring special pressure to bear upon the hostile Ministers, the most notorious of whom was Mr. Asquith, the Chancellor of the Exchequer. Strangely enough, just as we had decided upon this course of action, we were virtually advised to adopt it by no less a person than Mr. Lloyd George, at that time, President of the Board of Trade. When interrupted by Suffragettes in Liverpool Mr. George claimed the sympathy of the audience on the ground that he himself was a believer in Votes for Women, and said: "Why do they not go for their enemies? Why do they not go for their greatest enemy?" At once there was a cry of "Asquith! Asquith!" from all parts of the hall, and as Mr. Lloyd George made no attempt to repudiate the suggestion that he had referred to Mr. Asquith, it was very generally assumed that he had done so. An opportunity to "go for" Mr. Asquith soon presented itself on the occasion of his

81

speaking at Northampton on June 14th. A few days before the meeting, Theresa Billington and Annie Kenney visited the town and in a series of open-air meetings took the people of the place entirely into their confidence, with the result that Mr. Asquith was welcomed not by cheering but by hooting crowds.

During the meeting and at the end of his speech Mr. Asquith was questioned by several women, all of whom were ejected with the greatest violence, whilst the audience broke into the now familiar turmoil. The cowardly and unnecessary brutality shown to them by the stewards at recent Liberal meetings, had by this time aroused great indignation amongst the women. Theresa Billington, who was of strong and vigorous physique and whose instinct, like that of every man, was to strike back if she were hit, had come to feel that she could no longer quietly endure the disgraceful treatment to which she had been subjected on several occasions. To this meeting therefore, she had gone armed with a dogwhip, the weapon she felt most suitable to employ against cowardly men. Her intention was not to use it if she were merely dragged out of the meeting, just as a man might have been, but only if her assailants should seek to take advantage of the fact that she was a woman and should behave in a peculiarly objectionable way.[1] Therefore, when the stewards had torn down her hair and treated her with every form of indignity and violence, not merely in drag-

[1] Out of all the many hundreds of women who have taken part in the militant Suffrage movement, and in spite of the many kinds of violence to which they have been subjected, only three women upon three single occasions, have ever made use of any weapon to protect themselves from their assailants.

ging her from the hall but outside in the corridors as well, she had pulled out her whip and made a fairly free use of it.

The general trend of events now made us feel the necessity of securing a personal interview with Mr. Asquith, and we therefore wrote asking him to receive us. He replied that his rule was not to receive any deputation unconnected with his office of Chancellor of the Exchequer, and we then wrote as follows: —

To THE RIGHT HON. H. H. ASQUITH, CHANCELLOR OF THE EXCHEQUER.

Sir:

I am instructed by my Committee to say that the subject of the enfranchisement of women, which they desire to lay before you, is intimately bound up with the duties of your office. Upon no member of the Cabinet have women greater claims than upon the Chancellor of the Exchequer. Your Budget is estimated on a system of taxation which includes women. Women not being exempt from taxation have a right to claim from you a hearing. Women are told that you are mainly responsible for the refusal of the Prime Minister to deal with their claim. But being convinced of the justice of giving votes to women they renew their request that you receive a deputation on an early date in order that their case may be presented to you.

Faithfully yours,

E. SYLVIA PANKHURST.

Hon. Sec. of the London Committee of the Women's Social and Political Union 45, Park Walk, Chelsea, S.W.

Mr. Asquith returned no answer to this our second letter, and therefore, without making any further attempt to obtain his consent, we wrote to him saying that a small deputation would call at his house, No. 20 Cavendish Square, on the morning of Tuesday, June 19th. On the appointed day the women arrived just before 10 o'clock in the morning, but, early as it was, they were told that Mr. Asquith had already gone to the Treasury. They thereupon decided that half their number should wait on the doorstep and that the other half should go to look for him. Those who went to the Treasury were told that Mr. Asquith had not arrived, and those who remained on guard at his house were equally unsuccessful, for whilst they had been standing there waiting, the Chancellor of the Exchequer had escaped through the back door in a closed motor car.

Our determination to meet Mr. Asquith face to face was still strong, and after our failure to see him on the Tuesday we at once wrote to say that we were sending a larger deputation to interview him in two days' time. We had now three flourishing branches of the Union in London, one in the centre and two in the East End, and some thirty or forty representatives, partly drawn from these branches and partly from our central Committee, formed the deputation.

Carrying little white Votes-for-Women flags and headed by Theresa Billington, some thirty of the East End members marched off in procession for Mr. Asquith's house; but on arriving at the edge of Cavendish Square, they were met by a strong force of police who told them that they must at once turn back. The poor women stood still in affright, but would not turn. Then the police fell upon them and began to strike and push them and to snatch their flags away. Theresa Billington tried in vain to prevent

this violence, " We will go forward," she cried.
" You shall not hit our women like that," but a
policeman struck her in the face with his fist and
another pinioned her arms. Then she was seized by
the throat and forced against the railings until, as
was described by an onlooker, " she became blue
in the face." She struggled as hard as she could to
free herself but was dragged away to the police
station with the East End workers following in her
train.

Immediately afterwards Annie Kenney, with a
number of others, most of whom were members of
our Committee, came into the Square. Annie knew
nothing of what had taken place and, preoccupied
and intent on her mission, she walked quickly across
the road, but, as she mounted the steps of Mr.
Asquith's house and stretched out her hand to ring
his bell, a policeman seized her roughly by the arm
and she found herself under arrest. Following
this, Mrs. Knight, one of the East End workers, who,
because she suffered from hip disease had felt that
she could not walk in the procession, came into the
Square and crossed the road. On seeing none of the
other women she concluded that they had already
gone into Mr. Asquith's house. She intended to
join them but, just as she was about to step on to
the pavement opposite No. 20, she was roughly
pushed off the curb-stone by a policeman and arrested as soon as she attempted to take another step
forward. Mrs. Sparborough, a respectable elderly
woman dressed with scrupulous neatness in worn
black garments, who by the work of her needle supported herself and her aged husband, stood watching this scene in deep distress. Noticing that two

maid servants and some ladies at the window of
Mr. Asquith's house were laughing and clapping
their hands, she turned to them protesting gravely:
" Oh, don't do that. Oh, don't do that. It is a
serious matter. That is how *the soldiers were sent
to Featherstone.*" [1] A policeman immediately
pounced upon her and dragged her away.

At the police court afterwards Theresa Billington,
on being charged with an assault upon the police,
refused either to give evidence or to call witnesses in
her defence, saying that she objected to being tried
by a court composed entirely of men and under laws
in the framing of which men alone had been consulted. Her plea was abruptly swept aside and she
was ordered to pay a fine of £10 or in default to go
to prison for two months. [2]

Miss Billington chose imprisonment, but her resolution was balked by " an anonymous reader of the
Daily Mirror," who handed the amount of her fine
to the Governor of Holloway Gaol. [3]

[1] Some years before a trades dispute had taken place at
Featherstone in the course of which Mr. Asquith was said to
have ordered that the military should be called out, and as a
result the soldiers had fired upon the workingmen who were on
strike. In consequence of this Mr. Asquith became so unpopular that he was frequently assailed at Public Meetings by the
cry of "Featherstone Asquith, the Assassin." Mrs. Sparborough, like many other persons had of course read of this.

[2] On a protest being raised in the House, this sentence was
afterwards reduced by half.

[3] In the case of Christabel Pankhurst and Annie Kenney, the
Governor of Strangeways had refused money tendered to him by
outsiders, saying that he was not authorised to accept a fine
paid in this way, but now the Governor of Holloway, after con-
sultation with the Home Office accepted the fine, and told Miss
Billington that she must leave the prison.

The charges of disorderly conduct against the other three women were adjourned until July 14th.

Every charge against the prisoners, except that of being in Cavendish Square with the object of seeing Mr. Asquith broke down, but Mr. Paul Taylor, the magistrate, who seemed quite incapable even of trying to understand their motives, decided that they had created an obstruction and ordered them to enter into their own recognisances in the sum of £50 and to find one surety for the same amount, to be of good behaviour and to keep the peace for twelve months. In the event of their not finding such sureties and consenting to be so bound over he ordered that they should be sent to prison for six weeks.

To agree to be bound over to keep the peace would have been both an admission of wrongdoing and a promise to refrain from similar methods of agitation. Rather than this Annie Kenney preferred to suffer a second imprisonment and the other women, though they had but recently joined the Union and though many friends urged that they had already done good work and might now fairly return to their homes, decided that they too would go to gaol.

In the meantime there were stirring doings in Manchester. On June 23rd there had been a great Liberal Demonstration at the Zoological Gardens, Belle View, on the outskirts of the town, where Mr. Lloyd George, Mr. John Burns and Mr. Churchill had been the principal speakers. Representatives of the Women's Social and Political Union had been present to question the Cabinet Minister and had been thrown out as soon as they had raised their voices. In the scuffle Mr. Morrissey, a Liverpool city councillor, intervened to protect his wife from the violence of the stewards and was very roughly used.   As the Suffragettes were flung by the stewards into the public road outside they were ordered to move on by the police and because Mr. Morrissey, whose leg had been seriously injured by his assailants, was unable to walk away, he was arrested. Seeing this my youngest sister, Adela, then scarcely out of her teens, and only about five feet in height, expostulated with one of the constables and in doing so laid her hand upon his arm, saying, " Surely you can see that Mr. Morrissey cannot walk! "   But at that she was accused of attempting to effect a rescue, and was also taken into custody.   The councillor's wife and a friend, who both offered similar protests, were treated in the same way.   The case of these four people came up in Manchester simultaneously with that of Annie Kenney and her comrades in London, with the result that Adela was committed to prison for a week on refusing to pay a fine [1] of five shillings and costs whilst Mrs. Morrissey and Mrs. Mitchell on refusing to be bound over to keep the peace were imprisoned for three days.   Of course this punishment was for daring to urge an unwelcome question upon Members of the Government, but as this was not a punishable act the charges of disorderly conduct outside in the road had been trumped up.

The question of these trials was raised in the House of Commons by Mr. Keir Hardie, who declared that it was stretching the law too far to for-

[1] Mr. Morrissey, who could not afford to leave his business, was regretfully obliged to pay his fine.

bid a deputation to approach a private house.   He also pointed out that Mr. James Kendall, one of the magistrates who had tried the case of the Manchester Suffragettes, and had been Chief Steward at the Liberal meeting from which they had been ejected, Mr. Cremer and Mr. Maddison both delivered vindictive speeches against the Suffragettes, the former describing the sentence passed upon them as " extremely lenient " and the latter referring to them as " female hooligans."   The more sensational and less reputable of the newspapers adopted a similar line speaking of the women as " Kenney," " Knight " and " Sparborough," calling them " mock martyrs " and " martyrettes " and publishing hideous and libellous drawings of them. Even the staider and more serious periodicals gave one-sided and biassed accounts of what had taken place, rebuking the Suffragettes for what they termed their " disgraceful behaviour," telling them that they were " ruining " their cause, and urging them to save it by returning to " Constitutional " and " orderly " methods of propaganda.

The following interesting and valuable letter to the press from Mr. T. D. Benson, the Treasurer of the Independent Labour Party cleverly exposed the hypocrisy of these strictures: —

Dear Sir:

Having had, through illness, plenty of time on my hands this last week, I have made a calculation of the number of years which the lady Suffragettes have put back their movement.   I find that it amounts to somewhat about 235 years. The realisation therefore, of their aims is, according to this mode of chronology, as far off in the future as the Plague and the Fire of London are in the past.   Nevertheless, I shall not be surprised if they succeed within the next twelve months, or two or three years at the most.

Of course, when men wanted the franchise, they did not behave in the unruly manner of our feminine friends. They were perfectly constitutional in their agitation. In Bristol I find they only burnt the Mansion House, the Custom House, the Bishop's Palace, the Excise Office, three prisons, four toll-houses, and forty-two private dwellings and warehouses, and all in a perfectly constitutional and respectable manner. Numerous constitutional fires took place in the neighbourhoods of Bedford, Cambridge, Canterbury and Devizes. Four men were respectably hanged at Bristol and three in Nottingham. The Bishop of Lichfield was nearly killed, and the Archbishop of Canterbury was insulted, spat upon, and with great difficulty rescued from amongst the yells and execrations of a violent and angry mob. The Suffragists in those days had a constitutional weakness for Bishops, and a savage vandalism towards cathedrals and bishops' palaces. A general strike was proposed, and secret arming and drilling commenced in most of the great Chartist centres. Wales broke out even into active rebellion, and nine men were condemned to death. At London, Bradford, York, Sheffield, Liverpool, Chester, Taunton, Durham and many other towns long sentences of penal servitude were passed. In this way the males set a splendid example of constitutional methods in agitating for the franchise. I think we are well qualified to advise the Suffragettes to follow our example, to be respectable and peaceful in their methods like we were, and then they will have our sympathy and support.

Yours truly,

" The Downs," T. D. Benson.

   Prestwich,

     July 3rd, 1906.

The day after the trial Mrs. Pethick Lawrence received from Annie Kenney a little note hastily scribbled in pencil and posted by some kind-hearted person just as she was being taken away from the Police Court cell. " I am writing this," it read, " before going in the van. I am very happy and I shall keep up and be brave and true, and when I come out I shall be fully prepared to do anything the Union asks of me."

As yet most of us knew little of the interior of a prison, but, on those burning July days, we knew enough to think with sorrow and anxiety of our comrades shut away from the beauty of the summer in the heat of their small, stifling cells. We heard with joy that they were happy and contented to suffer imprisonment for the women's cause.

And now it seemed to us as though the spirit of revolt against oppression were flowing onward and spreading, like some great tide to all the woman-hood of the world. We read of that wonderful Marie Spiridorovna, the Russian girl who after en-during the most incredible and unspeakable tor-ture and dying in the agony of her wounds, was yet upborne by the greatness of the cause for which she suffered, and cried with her last breath, " Mother, I die of joy." The movement towards liberty then springing up amongst the women of the Far East also inspired us. We read of the words of one of the Korean women leaders who said : —

The women of our country are the most pitiable of all civilised humanity. . . . They are enclosed like pris-oners, bottled up like fish. But we must remember that after the cock crows the dawn comes, and after work there is reward. Should we but put forth together our feeble efforts a way will be found of accomplishing our object and women will gradually be able to stand in the shining light of the sun and to breathe the sweet heavenly air freely and happily.

News of the Women's cry for freedom came to us from North, South, East and West, and we felt ourselves part of a Universal movement. We were keyed up to any sacrifice. We felt that the fate of other women depended upon us. We knew that our battle to overcome the first and greatest barrier — to obtain political liberty — was to be a sharp one. We hoped it would be short. We heard that on June 14th, but a month before our women had gone to prison, the women of Finland had gained their vote. We believed then that the franchise would be won for British women within a few months' time.

Very soon after Annie Kenney, Mrs. Knight and Mrs. Sparborough had gone to prison, another opportunity occurred for our Union to strike a blow at the Government, for it was announced that there was to be a by-election; this time at Cockermouth. Christabel was at first the only member of the Union free to take part in the Election. She at once introduced an entirely new departure in electioneering tactics by hiring a stall in the market-place, where she sold Votes-for-Women literature. When, by this means she had collected a sufficient crowd around her, she mounted a stool and addressed the people, explaining to the electors that she wished them to vote against the Liberal candidate in order to show the Government that they did not approve of its refusal to give votes to women. After a time other women joined her and the little band of Suffragettes made a considerable impression upon the people of Cockermouth, who had heard of the imprisonments

in London and Manchester and who were deeply
moved by learning that women were prepared thus
to fight and to suffer for their cause. When on
August 3rd, the poll was declared, it was found
that the Liberals had lost the seat which had long
been held for them by Sir Wilfred Lawson, and that
Sir John Randles, the Unionist candidate had been
returned by a majority of 690. The figures being:

    Sir John Randles (U)................. 4,593
    Hon. F. Guest (L).................... 3,903
    Robert Smillie (Lab.)................ 1,436

The Votes at the General Election had been:

    Sir W. Lawson (L)................... 5,439
    Sir J. Randles (U)................... 4,784

Probably because the Liberal nominee against
whom she was working had been returned to Parliament, and also because she had been single-handed,
Mrs. Drummond's campaign at Eye had passed almost unnoticed outside the constituency itself. At
Cockermouth, on the other hand, the Liberal had
been defeated, and so it naturally followed that all
the influences that had led to his defeat were carefully analysed by the politicians and the Press.
Some of the members of the Women's Social and
Political Union had formerly been Liberals and
though the Liberal leaders steadfastly declared that
the action of women could make no possible difference to the situation, they were very deeply in-
censed by the thought that women should dare to
put the question of their own enfranchisement before every other consideration and, instead of seek-

ing to win the Government's favour as they had
done in the past, should prefer attempting to force
those in power to attend to their claims.

To a man the politicians were surprised. " Who
would have dreamt," they said, " that women could
be so selfish ? " Though their candidate, Mr.
Robert Smillie, had not been attacked, the Labour
men were also discontented, for there were Labour
women in the Women's Social and Political Union,
and they considered that these particular women
ought to have been working directly for the Labour
Party and not to have been subordinating its interests to the getting of votes for themselves. The
Conservatives meanwhile said very little about the
matter, for their candidate had won and having,
therefore, no reason to be aggrieved, they contented themselves with declaring that a glorious
victory had been won for the cause of Tariff Reform.

So much for the politicians. The Party-follow-
ing Press, with scarcely an exception, had been
unanimous from the very first in their hostility to
the Women's Social and Political Union and its
methods. Now, as before, they either shook their
heads at us, expressing sorrow and regret that we
should place ourselves in opposition to the " forces
of progress," or merely professed amusement that
we should be so foolish and conceited as to think
that anything that we could say or do would influence elections.

Timid and half-hearted friends of the Suffrage
movement also condemned the new by-election policy
on the ground that it was unwise for women to thus
oppose the Government that had the power, if it

wished, to give them what they asked. All this, of course, was to be expected, and so was comparatively easy to meet — it is what every true reformer has had to face. But even amongst some of those who had been hitherto the warmest supporters of the Suffragettes and all that they had done, there was much heart-searching and heart-burning because of the independent by-election policy, and it was felt by these that a mistake was being made in thus holding aloof from Men's party organisations and counting as nought the opinions of private Members of Parliament. The W. S. P. U. pointed out to them that a large majority of the private Members in the House of Commons had long been pledged to give their support to Women's Suffrage but that these pledges had been useless. This was due in the first place to the fact that private Members had little power to carry their pledges into effect because practically all the time at the disposal of Parliament was taken up by the Government, and that, as had been done on the 29th of April, a few obstructionists could easily block the question unless the party in power were prepared to find further time for it. Besides this, private members had over and over again shown that they would willingly break the pledges they had made to women at the bidding of their party leaders.

But these explanations failed to reassure many faint-hearted doubters, for though they agreed that in theory the independent policy was well enough, they felt convinced that in practice it was doomed to fail. They freely admitted that the women, by their clever speeches and the undeniable justice of their cause, would be almost certain to convince the

electors that they were in the right, but they urged
that the British elector was a hard-headed individual,
who could never be induced to throw aside his party
politics and to cast his vote on this one issue alone,
especially as this issue was a women's question that
did not directly affect him.

So these critics agreed that the policy would " be
possible with an electorate of heroes, but not with
average men." For this reason it must fail.

But in spite of these gloomy predictions the
Women's Social and Political Union held to its
course, and did not swerve one hair's-breadth from
the plan of campaign that it had laid down.

An Anti-Government election policy has frequently been employed by men politicians; notably
by the Irish under Parnell. In the course of the
agitation for the repeal of the Contagious Diseases
Acts, Mrs. Josephine Butler and her colleagues
fought the Government at many by-elections, but
with that exception an Anti-Government by-election
policy had never been adopted by women. In following it out now, when many members, even of
our own Committee doubted its wisdom, and few
were really enthusiastic in its favour, Christabel
Pankhurst, its originator in this case, gave evidence
of that keen political insight and that indomitable
courage and determination which are so essential to
real leadership, and which have since enabled her to
steer the Suffragette ship through so many dangerous
shoals and quicksands.

On August 14th the three Suffragettes, " Mr.
Asquith's Prisoners," as they had been called, were
released from Holloway. They were all cheerfully

and bravely uncomplaining. Mrs. Knight and
Annie Kenney were both white and feeble-looking
but only spoke of their anxiety to be of service to
the cause, whilst Mrs. Sparborough, though she had
got rheumatism through being made to scrub the
stone floor of her cell without a kneeler, made light
of the imprisonment, saying that she had felt peaceful and happy and had sung hymns to herself to
drive her loneliness away.

And now great meetings of welcome to the prisoners were being held in London and Provincial
campaigns were being organised in various parts of
the country. Everywhere that the fiery torch of
zeal and enthusiasm was carried there was warm
sympathy from the masses of the people and the
slumbering desire for enfranchisement amongst all
classes of women began to awake. Mrs. Lawrence
was holding a series of fine meetings in Yorkshire.
Annie Kenney, after addressing vast and enthusiastic crowds in Lancashire, made her way up to Scotland and with Theresa Billington went on to Mr.
Asquith's constituency of East Fife. Aroused by
their speeches the women here demanded that The
Chancellor of the Exchequer should receive them in
deputation. He judged it wisest to consent, but
protected himself from meeting the two ex-prisoners
by stipulating that only residents in the constituency
should be present. In his reply to this deputation
he declared himself to be still an opponent of their
cause. " Then there is no hope for women? " asked
one of them; but he only answered " Women must
work out their own salvation."

In Wales the flag of the W. S. P. U. was being

hoisted by Mary Gawthorpe,[1] another new recruit, a winsome, merry little creature, with bright hair and laughing hazel eyes, a face fresh and sweet as a flower, the dainty ways of a little bird, and having with all so shrewd a tongue and so sparkling a fund of repartee, that she held dumb with astonished admiration, vast crowds of big, slow-thinking workmen and succeeded in winning to good-tempered appreciation the stubbornist opponents. Whilst she was in his constituency, it was announced that Mr. Samuel Evans who had " talked out " the Votes-for-Women resolution on the twenty-ninth of April, and who was now appointed a Law Officer of the Crown, was coming to speak to his constituents.   Miss Gawthorpe determined to talk him out as he had " talked out " the Women's resolution. She therefore attended two of his meetings and at the first of these was dragged out by the stewards, but at the second a strong force of men gathered round to protect her and insisted that she should be heard.   The Chairman then tried to checkmate her by playing the Welsh National Anthem, but little Mary won all hearts by leading off the singing, and so poor a figure did Mr. Samuel Evans cut

[1] Mary Gawthorpe had become a pupil teacher at the age of thirteen and had worked for her living from that time.   Amongst other distinctions, she had taken a first class King's Scholarship. She had represented the Leeds Labour Church on the Local Labour Representation Committee.   She had been a member of the Leeds Committee for the Feeding of School Children, and the Leeds Committee of the National Union of Teachers.   In 1906 she had been elected as Labour delegate to the University Extension Committee, she was Vice-President of the Leeds Independent Labour Party and Secretary to the Women's Labour League.

that Mrs. Evans was said to have declared that next time there was a Women's Suffrage debate in the House of Commons she should keep her husband at home.

In London the work was being organised by Christabel, who amongst other things was conducting an active campaign in Battersea, the constituency represented by Mr. John Burns, the President of the Local Government Board. The income of the Union was still very small, and everything had to be done with the strictest possible economy. The money for meetings in halls was only forthcoming on very special occasions, and wherever possible the expenses of printing and advertising were curtailed. A large number of meetings were held at street corners, with a chair borrowed from a neighbouring shop as platform, and, in order to collect a crowd, my sister started the custom of ringing a large muffin bell. One of those who had been greatly impressed by the work of our Union was Miss Elizabeth Robins, the novelist, whose impressions of these early days of the movement are so graphically described in her novel, *The Convert.*

The following extract from this book is a very truthful picture of a typical Battersea meeting:

In Battersea you go into some modest little restaurant, and you say, " Will you lend me a chair? " This is a surprise for the restauranteur. . . . Ernestine carries the chair into the road and plants it in front of the fire station. Usually there are two or three helpers. Sometimes Ernestine if you please, carries the meeting entirely on her own shoulders — those same shoulders being about so wide. Yes, she is quite a little thing. If there are helpers she sends them up and down the street sowing a fresh crop of hand-

bills. When Ernestine is ready to begin she stands on
that chair in the open street and, as if she were doing the
most natural thing in the world, she begins ringing that
dinner bell. Naturally people stop and stare and draw
nearer. Ernestine tells me that Battersea has got so used
now to the ding-dong and to associating it with " our meetings," that as far off as they hear it the inhabitants say,
" It's the Suffragettes, come along." And from one street
and another the people emerge laughing and running. Of
course, as soon as there is a little crowd that attracts some
more, and so the snowball grows. . . . Last night she
was wonderful. . . . When she wound up " The motion is carried; the meeting is over!" and climbed down
off her perch, the mob cheered and pressed round her so
close that I had to give up trying to join her. I extricated
myself and crossed the street. She is so little that unless
she is on a chair she is swallowed up. For a long time
I could not see her. I did not know whether she was
taking the names and addresses of the people who wanted
to join the Union, or whether she had slipped away and
gone home, till I saw practically the whole crowd moving
off with her up the street. I followed for some distance
on the off side. She went calmly on her way — a tiny
figure in a long grey coat between two " helpers," a Lancashire cotton spinner and the Cockney working-woman and
that immense tail of boys and men (and a few women)
all following after — quite quiet and well-behaved — just
following because it didn't occur to them to do anything
else. In a way she was still exercising her hold over her
meeting. I saw presently there was one person in front
of her; a great big fellow who looked like a carter. He
was carrying home the chair. . . . Oh, if you could
only see her! Trudging along, apparently quite oblivious
of her quaint following, dinner bell in one hand, leather
case piled high with leaflets on the other arm. Some of
the leafllets sliding off and tumbling onto the pavement.
Then dozens of hands helped her to recover her property. . . .

CHAPTER VI

OCTOBER TO NOVEMBER, 1906

A Protest Meeting in the Lobby of the House of
Commons. Eleven Women go to Prison. What
it is Like in Holloway Gaol.

On October 3d, 1906, Parliament re-assembled
for the Autumn session. A large number of our
women made their way to the House of Commons
on that day, but the government had again given
orders that only twenty women at a time were to be
allowed in the Lobby. All women of the working
class were rigorously excluded. My mother and
Mrs. Pethick Lawrence were among those who succeeded in gaining an entrance. They at once sent in
for the Chief Liberal Whip and requested him to
ask the Prime Minister, on their behalf, whether he
proposed to do anything to enfranchise the women
of the country during the session, either by including
the registration of qualified women in the provisions
of the Plural Voting Bill then before the House, or
by any other means. The Liberal Whip soon returned with a refusal from the Government to hold
out the very faintest hope that the vote would be
given women at any time during their term of
office.

On hearing this, Mrs. Pankhurst and Mrs. Pethick
Lawrence returned to their comrades and consulted

with them. The women had received a direct rebuff, and they felt that they must now act in such a way as to prove that the Suffragettes would no longer quietly submit to this perpetual ignoring of their claims. They therefore decided to hold a meeting of protest, not outside in the street, but just there, in the Lobby of the House of Commons — of all places the most effective one for women to choose for a meeting, because the nearest within their reach to that legislative Chamber which had so frequently refused to grant them the franchise. Once made, the resolution was acted upon without delay. Mary Gawthorpe mounted one of the settees close to the statue of Sir Stafford Northcote and began to address the crowd of visitors who were waiting to interview various Members of Parliament. The other women closed up around her, but in the twinkling of an eye dozens of policemen sprang forward, tore the tiny creature from her post and swiftly rushed her out of the Lobby. Instantly Mrs. Despard, a sister of General French, a tall, ascetic-looking, grey-haired figure, stepped into the breach; but she also was roughly dragged away. Then followed Mrs. Cobden Sanderson, a daughter of Richard Cobden, and many others, but each in her turn was thrust outside and the order was given to clear the Lobby. Mrs. Pankhurst was thrown to the ground in the outer entrance hall and many of the women, thinking that she was seriously hurt, closed round her refusing to leave her side. Crowds were now collecting in the roadway and the women who had been flung out of the House attempted to address them but were hurled away.

Annie Kenney, who had scarcely recovered from

the effects of her last imprisonment, had been told
by the Committee that she must not take any part in
the demonstration for fear that she should be again
arrested. She agreed to run no risks, but she could
not keep entirely away from the scene of action and,
standing on the other side of the road, was now
watching to see what might befall her comrades. In
the midst of the struggle she noticed that Mrs.
Pethick Lawrence was being roughly handled, and
impulsively ran forward to ask her if she were hurt.
Being already well known to the police, she was immediately arrested. Mrs. Lawrence was greatly
distressed and cried out, " You shall not take this
girl; she has done nothing." But the only result
of her protest was that she herself was also taken
into custody. Before long seven women had shared
the same fate, including Miss Irene Miller, my sister
Adela Pankhurst, and Mrs. How Martyn, B.Sc.,
who had recently become Honorary Secretary of the
London Committee of the Women's Social and Political Union.[1]
     Meanwhile, some of the poor women who had
marched from the East End and who had been denied admission to the Lobby, were resting their tired
limbs on the stone benches in the long entrance hall,
and after Mrs. Cobden Sanderson had made her
attempt to speak and had been hustled away, she
seated herself quietly beside these women and began
to talk with them. Shortly afterwards a young policeman came up and abruptly ordered her away and,

[1] The Secretarial duties had now increased so greatly that no
one person could cope with them without giving the whole of
her time to the work. As I was unable to do this, I had been
obliged to resign.

as she did not go he seized her and dragged her to the police station.

The next morning the women were brought up at Rochester Row Police Court before Mr. Horace Smith.   Mrs. Cobden Sanderson's sisters, Mrs. Cobden Unwin and Mrs. Cobden Sickert and several friends and relatives of the other women, had come early in order that they might be sure of obtaining a seat in Court.   Whilst another trial was in progress the Usher had asked them to leave the Court for the present in order to make room for other people, saying, " You shall be allowed in again when your own case comes on."   They at once acceded to his request, but were prevented from returning and were subsequently told that no women would be allowed to enter.   Some twenty or thirty of us had by this time congregated in the large entrance hall, but, though men were constantly passing in and out of the Court where the trial was taking place, admittance was denied to us.   Many of us wished to testify as witnesses, but we were told that we could not go into the Court, and were taken into a side room, where an attempt was made to lock us in.   To prevent this, we insisted upon standing in the doorway.

In the meantime the case against the ten Suffragists was being hurried through.   They were all put into the dock together.   After the police evidence had been heard against them, Mrs. Cobden Sanderson asked leave to make a statement.   You must not picture her to yourself as being either big-boned, plain-looking and aggressive and wearing " mannish " clothes, or as emotional and overstrung.   On the contrary, she is just what Reynolds, Hoppner, Sir Henry Raeburn, or Romney with his softest and ten-

derest touch, would have loved to paint. Not very
tall, she is comfortably and firmly knit and as she
walks she puts her foot down quite firmly, in a dignified and stately way. She is always dressed in low-
toned greys and lilacs, and her clothes are gracefully
and delicately wrought, with all sorts of tiny tuckings
and finishings which give a suggestion of daintiest
detail without any loss of simplicity or breadth. She
has a shower of hair like spun silver that crinkles itself
in the most original and charming way, and which she
binds around with broad ribbon, lest its loose falling
strands should mar the neatness of her aspect. Her
cheeks are tinged with the soft dull rose that one
sees in pastel, and her eyes have the most genial and
benevolent glance.

Speaking now to the Magistrate, she said, quite
quietly, that she had gone to the House of Commons to demand the vote; that so long as women
were deprived of citizen rights and had, therefore, no constitutional means of obtaining redress,
they had a right to be heard in the House of
Commons itself. She wished to take the whole responsibility of the demonstration upon her own
shoulders. "If anyone is guilty," she said, "it is
I. I was arrested as one of the ringleaders, and
being the eldest of these, I was most responsible."
Then she quoted in her defence the words of Mr.
John Burns, who was now the President of the Local
Government Board and who, in circumstances similar to those in which she was placed, had said, " I
am a rebel because I am an outlaw. I am a law-
breaker because I desire to be a law-maker."

At this point the Magistrate, who had repeatedly
interrupted her, refused to hear any more, or to al-

low any statement at all from the other prisoners, although in doing so, he was disregarding every legal precedent. He said that each of the ten defendants must enter into her own recognisances to keep the peace for six months and must find a surety for her good behaviour in £10, and that if she failed to do this, she must go to prison for two months in the second division. The women at once protested against this mockery of a trial, and raising a banner bearing the words " Women should vote for the laws they obey and the taxes they pay " declared that they would not leave the dock until they had been allowed the right to which all prisoners were entitled, namely that of making a statement in their own defence. But Mr. Horace Smith cared nothing for the justice of what they said; he merely called the police and the women were forcibly removed.

The Police Court authorities now announced to those of us who were waiting in the witness room that the case was over and that our friends had been taken to Holloway. I can scarcely express our feelings of indignation. It seemed, indeed, terrible that ten upright, earnest women should have been thus hustled off to prison, without a word from their friends, after a trial lasting less than half an hour.

Some protesting, others filled with silent consternation, the women turned to go, but I, myself, felt that I could not leave without a single word of rebuke to those who had conducted the proceedings against us so shamefully. I therefore returned to the door of the inner court and asked to be admitted. " It is all over," said the doorkeepers, " there is nothing to interest you now; " but I walked quickly past them and entered the court. It was quite a small room; one could easily make oneself heard without raising one's voice, and as shortly as I could, I told the magistrate how women had been refused admittance whilst the trial was in progress, and how some who had actually taken their seats had been tricked into leaving. I pointed out to him that as it was customary to allow the general public, and especially friends of the prisoners, to be present in court, it was grossly unfair to refuse to do so in this case, and likely to destroy confidence in the justice of the trial. I was explaining that even the women who had wished to testify as voluntary witnesses had been kept out of the court, when the magistrate interrupted me saying, " There is no truth in any of your statements. The court was crowded."

I was then seized by two policemen, dragged across the outer lobby and flung into the street. Here a great mass of people had assembled and I felt that I ought not to go away without telling them something of the cause for which we were fighting and of the very scanty justice which had been doled out to our women. I tried to speak to them, though I had been rendered almost breathless by the violent manner of my ejection, and only to those who were near me could I make myself heard. In a moment, I hardly knew how or why, I was again seized by the policeman and dragged back into the court house. Soon afterwards I found myself in the dock before Mr. Horace Smith, and was charged with causing an obstruction and with the use of violent and abusive language. I protested against the latter half of the charge and it was immediately withdrawn. At greater length than on the first occasion, I was then able to describe all that had happened within the precincts of the court. Many of our friends and members, on hearing that all was not over, had returned and from amongst them I called as witnesses to the truth of my statement, Mrs. Cobden Unwin, Mrs. Cobden Sickert and a number of other ladies, but their testimony was ignored and I was found guilty and sentenced either to pay a fine of £1 or to undergo fourteen days' imprisonment in the third and lowest class. Of course I chose the latter alternative, and was taken to join my comrades in the cells. But now, instead of being ordered away as before, our friends were allowed to come up and bring us lunch and talk to us for a little while.

The police court cells were small and dark, furnished only with a wooden seat fastened to the wall and a sanitary convenience. The walls were whitewashed, the floors were of stone, and each of the cells opened into a long stone passage, whose barred windows overlooked the courtyard, beyond which we could see through gaps in the prison buildings, the crowds of people who were assembled in the street beyond. We were not shut up in the cells but allowed to move about from one to another, or to stand in the passage, at the end of which were several stone steps leading up to a strongly-fastened iron gate. This passage, though dimly lit, was lighter than the cells and seemed to us less insanitary, and so as we had many hours to wait before we were to be taken to Holloway in the prison van, " Black Maria," we seated ourselves together on the stone steps. Someone had brought with her a volume of Browning, and Mrs. Lawrence read aloud to us from those of the poems which seemed to apply to our own case.

All too soon the order came for us to go down to the van and, one by one, as our names were called, we walked across the yard, climbed the steps and took our places separately in one of the twelve little compartments which it contained. I was one of the two last to enter, and I had, therefore, a little more of the fresh air than most of the others, and from the small barred window of my compartment, I could see the burly form of the guarding policeman who stood in the passageway between us and, when he moved from time to time, could see past him and out the barred window in the door of the van to the streets through which we drove.

How long the way seemed to Holloway, as the springless van rattled over the stones and constantly bumped us against the narrow wooden pens in which we sat! As it passed down the poor streets, the people cheered — they always cheer the prison van. It was evening when we arrived at our destination, and the darkness was closing in. As we passed in single file through the great gates, we found ourselves at the end of a long corridor with cubicles on either side. A woman officer in holland dress, with a dark blue bonnet, with hanging strings on her head and with a bundle of keys and chains jangling at her waist, called out our names and the length of our sentences and locked each of us separately into one of the cubicles, which were about four feet square and quite dark. In the door of each cubicle was a little round glass spy-hole, which might be closed by a metal flap on the outside. Mine had been left open by mistake, and through it I could see a little of what was going on outside.

Once we had been locked away, the wardress came

from door to door, taking down further particulars
as to the profession, religion, and so on, of each
prisoner — there were many beside ourselves — and
asking if we and they could read and write and sew.
Meanwhile the prisoners called to each other over
the tops of the cubicles in loud, high-pitched voices.
Every now and then the officer protested, but still
the noise continued. Soon another van load of
prisoners arrived and the cubicles being filled, several women together were put into the same compartment,— sometimes as many as five in one of those
tiny places! It was very cold, and the stone floor
made one's feet colder still, yet for a long time —
until I was so tired that I could no longer stand —
I was afraid to sit down because, in the darkness,
one could not see whether, as one feared, everything
might be covered with vermin.

After waiting a long time, the prisoners were sent
to see the doctor, and we Suffragists stood waiting in
a line together. The wardress passed constantly up
and down our ranks saying, " All of you unfasten
your chests." When at last we got into the doctor's
room, he either asked us no questions, or said in a
mechanical way, " Are you all right? " then he
touched us quickly with his stethoscope and we passed
back to our cubicles.

After another long wait we were sent to change
our clothes. In a large room, lined with shelves,
with two or three wardresses hovering about, and
one seated at a table, we were told to undress, three
or four at a time, and given a short cotton chemise
to put on after we had removed our own clothes.
Then we were ordered to hand over our clothes,
hats, dresses, boots and all together, which were

roughly tied up in bundles and placed upon the shelves. Then, barefooted, and wearing only the chemise, we were made to march across to the officer at the table. The officer now told us to deliver to her our money, jewellery, hair pins and hair combs. She gave us back the hair pins and kept everything else, taking down particulars of these and entering them in a book. At the same time she again asked us our names, ages, and the other particulars which we had now given so often. After this we were searched; the officer first telling us to put up our arms, and then feeling us all over and examining our hair to see that we had nothing concealed about us. A wardress then led us through a doorway into the dimly lit bath room.

The baths were separated from each other by partitions, and from the rest of the room by a half door which had no fastening and over which the wardress could look. The baths were of black iron, covered with an old and very dingy coat of white paint, which had worn off in patches and the woodwork which enclosed them was stained and worn. I shrank from entering the bath, but I was shivering with cold, and though I feared it was not clean, there was something comforting about the feel of the warm water. Presently the wardress hung some towels and underclothing over the top of the wooden door, and told me to dress as quickly as I could. I hastened to obey her, and found that the clothes, which were badly sewn and badly cut, were of coarse calico and harsh woollen stuff, and that there were innumerable strings to fasten around one's waist. A strange-looking pair of corsets was supplied to each of us, but these we were not obliged to wear unless

we wished.   The stockings were of harsh thick wool,
and had been badly darned.   They were black with
red stripes going around the legs, and as they were
very wide, and there were no garters or suspenders
to keep them up, they were constantly slipping down
and wrinkling around one's ankles.

On opening my door I found that outside all was
hurry and confusion.   In the dim light the women
were scrambling for the dresses, which were lying in
big heaps on the floor.   The skirts of these dresses,
like the petticoats — of which there were three —
were of the same width at both top and bottom and
they were gathered into wide bands which, though
fastened with tapes were not made to draw up, and
had to be overlapped in the most clumsy fashion in
order to make them fit any but the very stoutest
women.   The bodices were so strangely cut that even
when worn by very thin people they seemed bound
to gape in front, especially as they were fastened
with only one button at the neck.   My bodice, the
only one I could manage to get hold of, had several
large rents, which had been roughly cobbled together
with black cotton.[1]   Every article of clothing was
conspicuously stamped with the broad arrow, which
was painted black on light garments, and white on
those which were dark.

I had scarcely fastened my dress when somebody
called out to us all: " Look sharp and put on your
shoes."   These we had to take for ourselves from
where they were bundled together on a wooden rack.
None of them seemed to be in pairs and they were
heavy and clumsy, with leather laces that, when one

---

[1] Some days afterwards it was condemned and I had a somewhat better one given to me.

attempted to tie them, broke easily in the hand.
Lastly, white cotton caps fastened under the chin
with strings and stamped in black with the broad
arrow, and the blue and white check aprons and handkerchiefs, both of which looked like dusters,[1] were
given to us and we were led off on a long journey
to the cells.

It seemed a sort of skeleton building that we were
taken through — the strangest place in which I had
ever been. In every great oblong ward or block
through which we passed, though there were many
stories, one could see right down to the basement
and up to the lofty roof. The stone floors of the
corridors lined the walls all the way round, jutting
out at the junctions of the stories like shelves some
nine or ten feet apart, being protected on the outer
edge by an iron wire trellis work four or five feet high,
and having on the wall side rows and rows and rows
of numbered doors studded with nails. The various
stories were connected by flights of iron steps bor-
dered by iron trellis work, and reaching in slanting
lines from corridor to corridor. All the walls and
doors were painted stone colour and all the iron
work was painted black.

We clattered up those seemingly endless flights and
shuffled along those mazy corridors in our heavy
shoes and at last stopped at a small office, rather
like one of the pay desks which one sees in drapers'
shops, where our names and the length of our sentences and all the various other particulars were
verified once more, and the sheets for the bed, a
Bible and a number of other little books with black

---

[1] We afterwards learnt that one clean handkerchief was supplied each week. We had no pockets to keep them in.

shiny bindings, were given out to us. Annie Kenney had told us that a tooth brush would be given to us if we asked for it, but that if we neglected to do this, nothing would be said about it, and we might not be allowed to have it later. As we waited in line I noticed that the other women were eating chunks of brown bread,[1] but, though by this time I was very hungry, none had been given to me. I asked Mrs. Baldock, who stood next to me, where she had got her bread, and she told me that one of the wardresses had given it to her, and seeing that I had been overlooked, she broke off half her own small loaf and gave it to me. These were the last words I was to have with my fellow prisoners, for, whilst they had been put into the second class, I had been sentenced to the third, and even in chapel they were hidden from me by a buttress.

After another long march through the prison corridors, a wardress, with her jangling keys, unlocked a number of heavy iron doors and having ordered each of us to enter one of them separately, shut them behind us again with a loud bang. I now found myself in a small whitewashed cell twelve or thirteen feet long by seven feet wide, and about nine feet high. The floor was of stone. The window, which was high up near the ceiling had many little panes, enclosed in a heavy iron frame-work and guarded by strong iron bars outside. The iron door was studded with nails and its round eye-like spyhole was now covered on the outside. On the left-hand side of the door was a small recess, some four

[1] Each prisoner, on the day of entering is according to prison rules to be given a supper consisting of six ounces of meat and one pint of cocoa.

feet from the ground, in which, behind a pane of
thick opaque glass was a flickering gas jet which cast a
dim light into the cell. Under this recess was a
small wooden shelf, somewhere about fourteen or
fifteen inches square, which I afterwards learnt was
called the table, and opposite this was a wooden
stool. By the window, set into the corner of the
room, was another shelf about three feet six inches
high, with one about six inches from the floor immediately under it. The lower shelf was for the
mattress and bedding. The upper one held a
wooden spoon, a pint pot of block tin stamped with
the broad arrow, a wooden saltcellar, a small piece
of hard yellow soap, a red card case containing some
prison rules and a card on which was printed a morning and an evening prayer, a small oval hair brush
without a handle, like a good-sized nail brush, and
a comb between three and four inches long. On
this shelf I was afterwards told to place my books
and tooth brush. These things had all to be kept
in certain never varying positions. On the floor,
leaning against the wall under the window, were arranged a number of utensils made of block tin, these
being a plate, a small water can holding about three
pints of water, a tiny shallow wash-basin less than a
foot in diameter, and a small slop-pail with a lid.
Two little round brushes, in shape rather like those
we use for brushing clothes with, which were intended for sweeping the floor, a little tin dust pan,
and a piece of bath-brick wrapped in some rags for
cleaning the tins. These also were all placed in an
order which, as I soon learnt, was never to be
changed. A small towel and a smaller table cloth,
both of them resembling dish cloths, hung on a nail.

Propped against the right-hand wall was the plank bed, with the pillow balanced on top. The bed is, I think, two feet six inches in width, and when in position for sleeping is raised up by two cross pieces to about two inches from the floor.

As I was examining in wonder all these various things, a wardress opened the door and said sharply, " What, have you not made your bed yet? The light will be put out soon. You had better make haste ! " " Please can I have a nightdress? " [1] I asked, but she answered " No." Then the iron door banged and I was left alone for the night.

After eating my little piece of bread, I did as I was told and tried to sleep. But sleep is one of the hardest things to obtain in Holloway. The bed is so hard, the blankets and sheets are scarcely wide enough to cover one, and the pillow, filled with a kind of herb, seems as if it were made of stone. The window is not made to open. The system of ventilation is exceedingly bad, and though one is usually cold at night one always suffers terribly from the want of air.

I learnt next day that we were as yet only in the admission cells, and as everyone was too busy to set us to work we had nothing to do but examine our books. These I found, in addition to the prayer book, consisted of a Bible, a hymn book, a tract called " The Narrow Way," which was intended to show how easy it is to fall into temptation, and a little book on health and cleanliness, which described the way in which human beings are gradually poi-

[1] Since this time night dresses have been introduced into Holloway, and are given to Suffragettes, and, let us hope, to other prisoners.

soned when they were not able to get enough fresh
air.

The following day we were removed to the cells
which we were to occupy during the remainder of
our imprisonment. Many of the ordinary cells are
exactly like the reception cells, but the cell into which
I was now put was smaller, but better lit than the
reception cell, for it had a larger window and there
was a small electric light bulb attached to the wall
instead of the recessed gas jet. Hanging on a nail
in the wall was a large round badge made of yellow
cloth bearing the number of the cell and the letter
and the number of its block in the prison. I was
told to attach this badge to a button on my bodice,
and henceforth, like the other prisoners, I was called
by the number of my cell, which happened to be
twelve.

.   .   .   .

Suppose yourself to be one of the Third Class
prisoners. Like them you will follow the same routine. Each morning whilst it is still quite dark you
will be awakened by the tramp of heavy feet and
the ringing of bells; then the light is turned on.
You wash in the tiny basin and dress hurriedly.
Soon you hear the rattle of keys and the noise of
iron doors. The sound comes nearer and nearer
until it reaches your own door. The wardress flings
it open and orders sharply, " Empty your slops,
12 ! " You hasten to do so, and return at the word
of command.

Then, just as you have been shown, you roll your
bed. The first sheet is folded in four, then spread
out on the floor, and rolled up from one end, tightly,
like a sausage. The second sheet is rolled round it,

and round this, one by one, the blankets and quilt. You must be careful to do this very neatly or you are certain to be reprimanded.

Next clean your tins. You have three pieces of rag with which to do this. Two of them are frayed scraps of brown serge, like your dress, and the other is a piece of white calico. These rags were probably not new and fresh when you came here, but had been well used by previous occupants of the cell. Folded up in these rags you will find a piece of bath-brick. You have been told to rub this bath-brick on the stone floor until you have scoured off a quantity of its dust. Then you take one of the brown rags and soap this on the yellow cake which you use for your own face. Then with the soapy rag you rub over one of the tins, and this done, dip the rag into the brick-dust which is lying on the floor and rub it on to the soapy tin. Then you rub it again with the second brown rag and polish with the white calico one that remains. You must be sure to make all the tins very bright.

Presently the door opens and shuts again. Some-one has left you a pail of water; with it you must scrub the stool, bed and table, and wash the shelves. Then scrub the floor. All this ought to be done before breakfast, but unless you are already experienced in such matters it will take you very much longer.

Before you have done your task there comes again the jangling of keys and clanging of iron doors. Then, "Where's your pint, 12?" You hand it out, spread your little cloth and set your plate ready. Your pint pot is filled with gruel (oatmeal and water without any seasoning), and six ounces of bread are thrust upon your plate. Then the door closes. Now eat your breakfast, and then, if your cleaning is done, begin to sew. Perhaps it is a sheet you have to do. Of these, with hem top and bottom and mid-seam, the minimum quantity which you must finish, as you will learn from your " Labour Card " is 15 per week.

At half past eight it is time for chapel. The officer watches you take your place in line among the other women. They all wear numbered badges like yours, and are dressed as you are. A few, very few, four or five perhaps, out of all the hundreds in the Third Division, wear red stars on caps and sleeves. This is to show that they are first offenders who have previously borne a good character and have someone to testify to that fact. Every now and then the wardress cries out that someone is speaking, and as you march along there is a running fire of criticism and rebuke. " Tie up your cap string, 27. You look like a cinder-picker. You must learn to dress decently here." " Hold up your head, number 30." " Hurry up, 23." In the chapel it is your turn. " Don't look about you, 12." In comes the clergyman. He reads the lessons and all sing and pray together.

Can they be really criminals, all these poor, sad-faced women? How soft their hearts are! How easily they are moved! If there is a word in the services which touches the experience of their lives, they are in tears at once. Anything about children, home, affection, a word of pity for the sinner, or of striving to do better,— any of these things they feel deeply. Singing and the sound of the organ make them cry. Many of them are old, with shrunken cheeks and scant white hair.   Few seem young.   All are anxious and careworn.   They are broken down by poverty, sorrow and overwork.   Think of them going back to sit, each in her lonely cell, to brood for hours on the causes which brought her here, wondering what is happening to those she loves outside, tortured, perhaps, by the thought that she is needed there.   How can these women bear the slow-going, lonely hours?   Now go back to your cell with their faces in your eyes.

At twelve o'clock comes dinner.   A pint of oatmeal porridge and six ounces of bread three days a week, six ounces of suet pudding and six ounces of bread two days a week, and on two other days eight ounces of potatoes and six ounces of bread.

After dinner you will leave your cell no more that day, except to fetch water between two and three o'clock, unless it be one of the three days a week on which you are sent to exercise.   In that case, having chosen one for yourself from a bundle of drab-coloured capes, and having fastened your badge to it, you follow the other women outside.   There, all march slowly round in single file with a distance of three or four yards between each prisoner.   Two of the very oldest women, who can only totter along, go up and down at one side, passing and repassing each other.

If you came into the prison on Wednesday, the first day for you to exercise will be Saturday.   How long it seems since you were last in the outside world, since you saw the sky and the sunshine and felt the pure fresh air against your cheek!   How vividly everything strikes you now.   Every detail stands out in your mind with never-to-be-forgotten clearness.

Perhaps it is a showery Autumn day. The blue sky is flecked with quickly driving clouds. The sun shines brightly and lights up the puddles on the ground and the raindrops still hanging from the eaves and window ledges. The wind comes in little playful gusts. The free pigeons are flying about in happy confidence. You notice every variation in their glossy plumage. Some are grey with purple throats, some have black markings on their wings, some are a pale brown colour, some nearly white; one is a deep purple, almost black, with shining white bars on his wings and tail. All are varied — no two are alike. The gaunt prison buildings surround everything, but in all this shimmering brightness, in this sweet, free air, they have lost for the moment their gloomy terror.

Now, your eye lights on your fellow prisoners. You are brought back to the dreary truth of prison life. With measured tread, and dull listless step, they shuffle on. Their heads are bent, their eyes cast down. They do not see the sun and the brightness, the precious sky or the hovering birds. They do not even see the ground at their feet, for they pass over sunk stones, through wet and mud, though there be dry ground on either side. The prison system has eaten into their hearts. They have lost hope, and the sight of nature has no power to make them glad. It may be that when next you walk with them you will feel as they do. These gloomy overshadowing walls and the remembrance of your narrow cell, with its endless twilight and dreary, useless tasks may have filled your mind and driven away all other thoughts.

Once inside, the last break in the day will be

supper at five o'clock (like breakfast, six ounces of bread and a pint of gruel), except that just before the light goes out at night, comes a noisy knocking at every door, and the cry, " Are you all right? " Then darkness, a long, sleepless night, and the awakening to another day like yesterday and like to-morrow.

CHAPTER VII

NOVEMBER, 1906, TO FEBRUARY, 1907

FURTHER ARRESTS. THE "MUD MARCH."

WHILST their comrades were in Holloway, the
W. S. P. U. members were putting forth redoubled
efforts to press forward the work outside. A manifesto explaining the objects of our movement and
calling upon the women of the country to stand by
those who had gone to prison and to fight with them
to secure enfranchisement was posted upon the walls
and circulated broadcast as a leaflet. This appeal
met with a far readier response than any that had
yet been made. Amongst people of all parties, there
was a growing feeling that the imprisoned Suffragettes should receive the treatment due to political
offenders. The Liberals, large numbers of whom
knew her personally, found an especial difficulty in
reconciling themselves to the idea that Richard
Cobden's daughter should be thrown into prison and
treated by a Liberal government as though she had
been a drunkard or a pickpocket. Mr. Keir Hardie,
Lord Robert Cecil and others, raised the matter in
the House of Commons, and drew comparisons between our lot and that of the Jameson raiders, Mr.
W. T. Stead and others who had been imprisoned
for political reasons. In reply to this, Mr. Gladstone, the Home Secretary, began by saying that he

had no power to take action. On October 28,
however, Mrs. Pethick Lawrence left Holloway
owing to serious illness. On the following day,
Mrs. Montefiore was also released for the same reason, and a day or two afterwards it became known
that Mrs. How Martyn and Mrs. Baldock had been
removed to the prison hospital. Protests against the
treatment of the Suffragettes daily became more and
more insistent, and at last, on October 31st, Mr.
Herbert Gladstone changed his mind and ordered, [1]
or as he put it, " intimated his desire " that the Suffrage prisoners should be transferred to the first class.

On the eighth day of our imprisonment my cell
door was flung open suddenly and the Matron announced that an order had come from the Home
Office to say that I was to be transferred to the
first class. I was then hurriedly bustled out of my
cell and a few minutes afterwards as, in charge of
a wardress, I was staggering along the passage carrying my brush and comb, the sheets that I was hem-
ming, and all my bed linen, I met my comrades
going in the same direction.

[1] Speaking at Leicester on January 30th, the Home Secretary, Mr. Herbert Gladstone, was proceeding to extoll the
promptitude and care with which, he asserted, the Home Office
inquired into alleged cases of miscarriage of justice, when he
was interrupted by cries of protest from Annie Kenney and a
band of other Suffragettes. Whilst they were being speedily
ejected, Mr. Gladstone tried to curry favour with the audience
by saying that he particularly regretted what had taken place
because his action in regard to the Suffragettes had been to
reduce the sentences passed upon them and to ameliorate their
prison treatment. As we have seen the change was only made
in response to an unmistakable public demand, and after Mr.
Gladstone had begun by saying he had no power to effect it.

We were ushered into a row of rather dark cells adjoining each other in an old part of the prison, which is chiefly occupied by prisoners on remand who have not yet been tried. These women, we were horrified to find, are treated exactly like second class prisoners, except that their dress is blue instead of green, and that some to whom permission has been given are allowed to wear their own clothes, and to have food sent in to them at their own expense. We were now offered the same privileges, but these we declined. On consulting the prison rules, however, I found that first class misdemeanants are entitled to exercise their profession whilst in prison, if their doing so does not interfere with the ordinary prison regulations. I therefore applied to the Governor to be allowed to have pen, pencils, ink and paper, and after a day's waiting my request was granted. For me prison had now lost the worst of its terrors because I had congenial work to do.

We were now able to write and to receive a letter once a fortnight, and to have books and one newspaper a day sent in by our friends. The food served out to us was exactly like that of the second class except that instead of oatmeal gruel, a pint of tea was substituted for breakfast and a pint of cocoa for supper. As the second class is that into which the majority of the Suffragettes have been relegated, it is useful to give the table of dinners here.

Monday, 8 oz. haricot beans, 1 oz. fat bacon, 8 oz. potatoes, 6 oz. bread.

Tuesday, 1 pt. soup, 8 oz. potatoes, 6 oz. bread.

Wednesday, 8 oz. suet pudding (exactly like that served in the third class), 6 oz. bread, 8 oz. potatoes.

Thursday, 6 oz. bread, 8 oz. potatoes, 3 oz. cooked meat — a kind of stew.

Friday, Soup 1 pt., 6 oz bread, 8 oz. potatoes.

Saturday, Suet pudding 8 oz., bread 6 oz., potatoes 8 oz.

Sunday, bread 6 oz., potatoes 8 oz., 3 oz. meat " preserved by heat " *i. e.,* some kind of preserved meat slightly warmed.

The soups or meat for each prisoner was served in a cylindrical quart tin into the top of which, like a lid, was fitted another shallow tin holding the potatoes. One did not clean these tins oneself as one did the other untensils, and probably because the kitchen attendants were overburdened with work, they were always exceedingly dingy and dirty-looking. Everything was as badly cooked and as uninviting as it could be. The cocoa, which was quite unlike any cocoa that I have ever tasted, had little pieces of meat and fat floating about in it. It was evidently made in the same vessel in which the meat was cooked. To cut up our meat, in addition to the wooden spoon, which is common to the second and third classes, we were now provided with " a knife." This knife was made of tin. It was about four inches in length and Mrs. Drummond later on aptly described it as being " hemmed " at the edge. There was no fork.

On November 6th my sentence came to an end, and the newspaper representatives were all eager to hear from me what the inside of Holloway was like. I was thus able to make known exactly what the conditions of imprisonment had been both before and after our transfer to the first division and to show that even under the new conditions, the treatment of the Suffragettes was very much more rigorous than that applied to men political prisoners in this and other countries.

Next day, November 7th, Mr. Keir Hardie introduced a Women's Suffrage Bill into the House of Commons under " the ten minutes rule." It had only two chances of passing into law; the first that the Government should provide time for it and the second that not one single Member of Parliament should oppose it in any of its stages. The Government refused to give the time, and the second chance was destroyed by a Liberal Member, Mr. Julius Bertram.

On November 19th another demonstration was therefore held outside the House of Commons as a result of which Miss Alice Milne of Manchester was arrested, and imprisoned for one week. Public sympathy was still daily turning more and more to the side of the Suffragettes and when a by-election became necessary at Huddersfield, Mr. Herbert Gladstone decided to release Mrs. Cobden Sanderson and her colleagues, though they had served but half their sentences and, on November 24th they were set free after one month's imprisonment. They were not only welcomed with enthusiasm by their fellow militant Suffragettes, but a dinner was given in their honour by the older non-militant Suffragists at the Savoy Hotel.

Believing that it was to the Huddersfield by-election that they owed their unexpected freedom, a number of the released prisoners at once hurried off to the constituency where Mrs. Pankhurst and a band of other women were strenuously working against the Government and had already become the most popular people in the election.

Though the train by which the prisoners arrived was more than two hours late, they were welcomed at the station by cheering crowds, and found that a great meeting of women, which had been called for the due time of their arrival, was still patiently waiting to hear them speak.

The three candidates, Liberal, Unionist and Labour were now, because of its extraordinary popularity, all anxious to be known as supporters of Women's Suffrage and they went about wearing the white Votes for Women buttons of the W. S. P. U. Mr. Sherwell, the Liberal, tried to sidetrack the Suffragettes' appeal to the electors to vote against him because he was the nominee of the Government, by constantly announcing that he was in favour of Women's Suffrage, and that the Liberal Party was the best of all parties for women. The following handbill issued from his committee rooms:

"MEN OF HUDDERSFIELD, DON'T BE MISLED BY SOCIALISTS, SUFFRAGETTES, OR TORIES.

VOTE FOR SHERWELL."

Polling took place on November 28th, and when the votes were counted, it was found that the Liberal poll as recorded at the General Election had been reduced by 540. The figures were:—

Arthur Sherwell (L.) 5,762
T. R. Williams (Lab.) 5,422
J. Foster Fraser (U.) 4,844

Liberal Majority 340

At the General Election the figures had been:—

Sir J. T. Woodhouse (Lib.)............ 6,302
T. R. Williams (Lab.)................ 5,813
J. Foster Fraser (U.)................ 4,391

Liberal Majority................ 489

Meanwhile the Government had been pushing on with its Bill for the abolition of plural voting, to which the Women's Social and Political Union had persistently claimed that a clause providing for the registration of qualified women voters should be added. When the Bill reached the Report stage on November 26th, Lord Robert Cecil moved and Mr. Keir Hardie seconded and Mr. Balfour supported an amendment to postpone the operation of the Bill until after the next General Election, unless in the meantime the franchise had been given to women on the same terms as men. The object was, of course, to call attention to the need of Votes for Women, and this somewhat round-about way had been adopted because it was ruled out of order to simply suggest that votes for Women should be enacted as a part of the Plural Voting Bill. The amendment was opposed by the Government, and defeated by 278 votes to 50.

Our Manchester Members were now anxious to organise a protest on their own account and it was agreed that they should have their way. Accordingly, on December 13th, a valiant little army of some twenty or thirty North Country women came down to London and proceeded straight to Parliament Square, carrying a small wooden packing case which they set down in the gutter opposite the

stranger's entrance.   The box was mounted by Mrs.
Jennie Baines of Stockport, a fragile little woman,
who had begun her strenuous life as a Birmingham
child home-worker, rising early in the morning in
order to help her mother to stitch hooks and eyes
on to cards before going to school, snatching a few
moments for the same task in the dinner hour and
on returning home in the evening, working far into
the night.   In her girlhood she had been a Salvation
Army " Captain."   Later she had married a journeyman bootmaker, and though, in addition to caring for her home and her children, she had been
forced to toil in the factory, in order to keep the
home together, she had still managed to work as a
Police Court Missionary and Temperance and Social
reformer.

Therefore, it was with the knowledge born of
much experience, that Mrs. Baines now pleaded for
the enfranchisement of her sex.   Within a few
moments a strong force of police came hurrying up
and she was roughly dragged down and hustled
away.   Her place was instantly taken by Mrs.
Morrissey of Manchester, whilst the other women
linked arms and pressed closely round to form a
guard, but after a short hard struggle the police
broke through, tore the speaker from the box, and
made five arrests.   One woman was thrown to the
ground and lay unconscious, and Mrs. August Mac-
Dougal, an Australian,[1] knelt on the ground beside
her, raised her head and held a cup of water to her
lips.   Then a heavy hand was laid upon Mrs. Mac-
Dougal's shoulder and a rough voice ordered her to

---

[1] A cultured literary woman, who, with her husband, had recently published two anthologies of music.

go, but she remained to attend to the injured woman. For this offence she was arrested, whilst Mrs. Knight, the woman who had been hurt, was removed to Westminster Hospital.

Next day the five women who had been taken into custody were at Westminster Police Court each ordered by Mr. Horace Smith either to pay a fine of twenty shillings or to go to prison for fourteen days, in the first class. They all chose the latter alternative and were taken to the cells. Two days afterwards some of our members attempted to hold a meeting in the Strangers' Lobby. As a result of this eleven of them were sent off to join their comrades in gaol for fourteen days.

Still the Government refused to withdraw their hostility to votes for women, Parliament remained apathetic, and still the majority of the general public were content to allow things to remain as they were. Therefore we felt that yet another protest must be made before the year 1906 should come to an end, and on December 20th, the eve of Parliament's rising for the Christmas holidays, Mrs. Drummond, who had now settled in London, organised a third attack upon the House. Whilst her followers were attempting to speak in the Lobby, she succeeded in entering the House unobserved and in making her way by the back passages to within a few yards of the sacred chamber of debate itself. Here she was captured by the police, but she resisted their efforts to remove her with so much spirit that she won the sympathy and admiration of the constables; one of whom was heard to say, " I wish the members of Parliament would come here and do their own dirty work ! "

Next day as the evening-paper boys were eagerly crying the news that another five women were gone to join those already in prison and that twenty-one Suffragettes would now be spending Christmas there, Parliament rose for the holidays. As the Members left the House, comrades of the imprisoned women handed each one an envelope inscribed: —" What a woman really wants for a Christmas box," and within was a small slip of paper bearing the words, " A vote."

For the first batch of Suffragettes to be released from prison in January, a Christmas dinner was provided by Mr. and Mrs. Pethick Lawrence at the Holborn Restaurant, and for Mrs. Drummond and those of the Suffragettes who were set free later, the first of the public welcome breakfasts, which have since become an institution, was held at Anderton's Hotel. The released prisoners were able to tell us that Christmas day in Holloway is, except that one goes twice to Chapel, exactly like all the other days of the year and that the Christmas dinner, of which so very much is thought outside, is just the usual one that would naturally fall at any other season to that particular day of the week. But as Mrs. Hillier on their release, said, they went to prison for " a cause that they held dear," and so, as Mrs. Martha Jones added, they regarded having gone there, " not as a sacrifice, but as an honour." What they had seen in Holloway had more than ever convinced them of the pressing need that women should be enfranchised. " The stories that I have heard in the Prison hospital," said Mrs. Baines, " have reached to the bottom of my heart. I have come out with the firm resolve to work on."

So the year 1906, the first year of the Union's
work in London came to an end. In October, the
step of opening a permanent central office had been
decided upon and a large general office having a small
private room opening out of it was taken in Clement's
Inn, Strand. It seemed a big undertaking at first,
but the offices were indispensable. The small room
was considered chiefly as Christabel's office, but all
private business was transacted there, whilst the large
room was used for general clerical work and as a
meeting place. Weekly Monday afternoon and
Thursday evening At Homes, were held there and
all those who had joined the Union in those early
days can remember Mrs. Sparborough making tea
and handing round bread and butter and biscuits, and
Christabel, with a sheaf of newspaper cuttings in her
hand, standing up on one of the chairs to furnish
the latest news of the militant campaign and to explain the next move in the plan of action.

On the following February 4th, Mr. Winston
Churchill spoke in the Free Trade Hall, Manchester,
and he bargained beforehand with the Suffragettes
that they should not interrupt him during his speech,
on condition that he would answer a question on
Women's Suffrage before he left the platform. At
the close of the meeting he accordingly did so by
saying definitely that he would not vote for a Bill to
enfranchise women on the same terms as men. He
added that he greatly regretted that " earnest, good-
hearted women should pursue courses which brought
them suffering and humiliation," but " God forbid "
that he should " mock " them by concealing his opinion. My sister Adela then rose to ask if he had intended to speak for himself alone, or on behalf of

the Government, an exceedingly important point. What followed is best described in the words of an eye witness who wrote at once to Christabel at Clement's Inn: "Last night's affair was terrible. It was a wonder someone was not killed. Your sister was thrown down and kicked by several men. The attack was really unprovoked; the stewards had made up their minds to do it before the meeting. Your sister has a black eye, Mrs. Chatterton's throat was hurt and Miss Gawthorpe would have been seriously handled but that some men came to her rescue."

Many women who had long felt that there was "something wrong" with the position of their sex, but had not realised that the possession of the Parliamentary franchise could do anything to remove the disabilities both of law and custom from which they suffered, were now being awakened by the much-talked-of militant tactics to a knowledge of what the vote could do for them. Moreover, many who for years had been nominal adherents of the Suffrage movement, now began to feel that if some other women cared so passionately for the cause that they were prepared to throw aside all the usual conventions of good manners and to thrust themselves forward to meet ridicule, scandalous abuse, ill usage and imprisonment, it was surely time that they too should make sacrifices. Their hearts smote them that they had not done more for it in the past. But most of them as yet thought only of bolstering up and stirring to new activity the old National Union of Women's Suffrage Societies for they still looked upon the militant women as a rather dreadful body of fanatics who could have no notion either of systematic organisation or the prudent laying-out of money.

Therefore, though the W. S. P. U. was already growing largely, the N. U. W. S. S. was as yet benefiting most largely from its activities. But times had changed and even the most old-fashioned of the Suffragists were now ready to copy the first non-militant doings of the Suffragettes and, in order to prove that they really wanted the franchise, they too determined to march in procession through the London streets. Therefore on February 9th, 1907, three days before the opening of Parliament, a crowd of the non-militants assembled close to the Achilles statue at Hyde Park Corner. It was a dismal wet Saturday afternoon, but in spite of the rain and the muddy streets a procession of women half a mile in length was formed and marched steadily on to attend meetings in Exeter Hall in the Strand and in Trafalgar Square. This procession was afterwards known as the " Mud March."

At the Exeter Hall the principal speakers who had been chosen to address the gathering of women were Mr. Keir Hardie and Mr. Israel Zangwill. Mr. Hardie devoted himself to urging the women to place the question of their enfranchisement before all other party considerations. Meanwhile a most extraordinary scene occurred, for, whilst his remarks were punctuated by volumes of cheers from the great body of the audience, a number of Liberal ladies on the platform set up a hissing chorus.

When Mr. Zangwill came to speak, he, too, declared himself to be a supporter of the militant tactics and the anti-Government policy, and the same Liberal ladies, although they had themselves asked him to speak for them, expressed their dissent and disapproval as audibly as though they had been Suffragettes and he a Cabinet Minister. From Mr. Zangwill's brilliant speech — his maiden speech as a politician as he said it was — which has since been published under the title " One and One are Two," I can but quote an extract to conclude this chapter:

What is it that prevents the Prime Minister bringing in a Bill for Female Suffrage at once, in this very Parliament that is opening? He is in favour of it himself, and so is the majority of the House. The bulk of the representatives of the people are pledged to it. Here, then, is a measure which both parties deem necessary. A sensible woman would think that the first thing a Parliament would do would be to pass those measures about which both parties agree. Simple female! That is not man's way. That is not politics. What is wanted in Parliament is measures about which both parties *disagree,* and which, in consequence, can never be passed at all. I declare I know nothing outside Swift or W. S. Gilbert to equal the present situation of Women's Suffrage. . . . The majority have promised to vote for Women's Suffrage. But *whom* have they promised? Women. And women have no votes. Therefore the M.P.'s do not take them seriously. You see the vicious circle. In order for women to get votes they must have votes already. And so the men will bemock and befool them from session to session. Who can wonder if, tired of these gay deceivers, they begin to take the law into their own hands? And public opinion — I warn the Government — public opinion is with the women. . . . They *are* unwomanly — and therein consists the martyrdom of the pioneers. They have to lower themselves to the manners of men; they have to be unwomanly in order to promote the cause of womanhood. They have to do the dirty work. Let those lady suffragists who sit by their cosey firesides at least give them admiration and encouragement. " Qui veut la fin, veut les moyens." And undoubtedly the means are not the most ladylike. Ladylike means are all very well if you are dealing with gentlemen; but you are dealing with politicians. . . . In politics only force counts, but how is a discredited minority to exercise force? . . . There is a little loophole. Every now and then the party in power has to venture outside its citadel to contest a by-election. The ladies are waiting. The constituency becomes the arena of battle, and every Government candidate, whether he is for female suffrage or not, is opposed tooth and nail. For every Government — Liberal or Conservative — that refuses to grant Female Suffrage is ipso facto the enemy. The cause is to be greater than mere party. Damage the Government — that is the whole secret. Are these tactics sound? In my opinion, absolutely so. They are not only ladylike, they are constitutional. They are the only legitimate way in which woman can bring direct political pressure upon the Government. . . . Far better than to put yourself in prison is to keep a man out of Parliament. . . . What Christianity cannot do, what charity cannot do, what all the thunder of your Carlyles and your Ruskins cannot do, a simple vote does. And so to these myriads of tired women who rise in the raw dawn and troop to their cheerless factories, and who, when the twilight falls, return not to rest but to the labours of a squalid household, to these the thought of Women's Suffrage, which comes as a sneer to the man about town, comes as a hope and a prayer. Who dares leave that hope unillumined, that prayer unanswered? . . . For fifty years now woman has stood crying: "I stand for justice — answer, shall I have it?" And the answer has been a mocking "no" or a still more mocking "yes." With this flabby friendliness, this policy of endless evasion. To-day she cries: "I *fight* for justice and I answer that I *shall* have it."

CHAPTER VIII

FEBRUARY AND MARCH, 1907

THE FIRST WOMAN'S PARLIAMENT IN THE CAXTON HALL AND THE SENDING OUT OF THE MOUNTED POLICE TO DRIVE AWAY THE WOMEN'S DEPUTATION. MR. DICKINSON'S BILL AND THE SECOND WOMEN'S PARLIAMENT.

AND now again the thoughts of all the women who wanted votes were turning towards the opening of Parliament. The old fashioned Suffragists had held their demonstration during the recess but that of the Suffragettes was still to come and it had been announced that on February 13th, 1907, a Parliament of women would sit in the Caxton Hall to consider the provision of the King's speech to be read in the Nation's Parliament on the previous day. It was but a year since Annie Kenney had set off to rouse London and since Mrs. Pankhurst had feared that we should neither fill the Caxton Hall nor induce a body of women to march for the sake of a vote through the London streets, but the tickets were now sold off so rapidly that the Exeter Hall in the Strand was also requisitioned, and we could now firmly rely on hundreds of women who were ready and eager, not merely to walk in procession, but if need be to risk imprisonment for the Cause.

Parliament met on Tuesday the 12th, and we soon learnt that the King's speech had made no mention of

138

Votes for Women. Therefore when the Women's Parliament met at three o'clock next day, it did so ready for decisive action. Mrs. Pankhurst was in the Chair, and throughout the proceedings there were manifestations of an enthusiasm such as the women of our time had before then never learnt to show. A Resolution expressive of indignation that Votes for Women had been omitted from the King's speech and calling upon the House of Commons to insist that precedence should be given to such a measure, was moved in stirring words and carried with every demonstration of fervent eagerness. A motion that the resolution should be taken to the Prime Minister by a deputation from the meeting was greeted with cheering and waving of handkerchiefs. Then the watchword, " Rise up women! " was sounded, and the answer came in a great unanimous shout, " Now," while hundreds of women volunteers ready for Parliament or Prison sprang to their feet.

Mrs. Despard was chosen to lead the deputation, and, as each woman marched out of the Caxton Hall, a copy of the Resolution for the Prime Minister was put into her hand. We formed up in orderly procession, and, amid the cheers of the thousands of men and women who had gathered in sympathy, and with police walking in front of us, we marched into Victoria Street and on towards the House of Commons.

It was cold but a shimmering dainty day, the sky a delicate rain-washed blue and the sunshine gleaming on the fine gilded points on the roof of the tall clock tower. We stepped out smartly and all seemed to be going well, but when those who were in front reached the green in front of the Abbey, a body of police barred their way and an Inspector called to them to turn back, and ordered his men to break up the procession. The police strode through and through our ranks, but the women at once united again and pressed bravely on. A little further we went thus, when suddenly, a body of mounted police came riding up. In an instant Mrs. Despard and several others in the front rank were arrested, and the troopers were urging their horses into the midst of the women behind, scattering them right and left.

Still we strove to reach our destination, and returned again and again. Those of us who rushed from the roadway on to the pavement were pressed by the horses closer and closer against the walls and railings until at last we retreated or were forced away by the constables on foot. Those of us who took refuge in doorways were dragged roughly down the steps and hurled back in front of the horses. When even this failed to banish us, the foot constables rushed at us and, catching us fiercely by the shoulders, turned us round again and then seizing us by the back of the neck and thumping us cruelly between the shoulders forced us at a running pace along the streets until we were far from the House of Commons. They had been told to drive us away and to make as few arrests as possible. Still we returned again, until at last sixty-five women and two men, all of them bruised and dishevelled, had been taken to the police station, and those who had not been arrested were almost fainting from fatigue. Then, after ten o'clock, the police succeeded in clearing the approaches to the House of Commons, and the mounted men were left galloping about in the empty square till midnight, when the House rose.

In spite of the fierce battle to keep them out,

fifteen of the Suffragettes succeeded by strategy in making their way into the Strangers' Lobby of the House of Commons and at about six o'clock attempted to hold a meeting there. The police, of course, rushed to put them out and, in the confusion that ensued one of the women succeeded in getting past the barriers and making her way down the passage leading to the beautiful white inner lobby which opens into the sacred chamber of debate. She had just reached the first set of swing-doors when a Member of Parliament dashed up and slammed them against her with such force that she was thrown to the ground and carried out in a fainting condition.

Members of Parliament could scarcely fail to have been impressed by the extraordinary scenes which had taken place, and when the adjournment of the House was moved that night a Unionist Member, Mr. Claud Hay, asked the Home Secretary whether it had been necessary to inconvenience its Members by surrounding Parliament with a body of police, both upon horse and foot, as great as though it had been a fortress instead of a deliberative assembly. It appeared to him, he said, that Mr. Gladstone was afraid of the women, but they were entitled to make a protest even if it were not agreeable to Members of Parliament, and there was no need to brow-beat them by using force. Mr. Gladstone replied that he had very little knowledge of what had been going on outside the House, but Mr. Claud Hay interrupted him with, " Then you ought to have ! " At that he hesitated and changed his tone, saying that it was the police who were responsible for keeping open the approaches to the House, that

they had only done their duty, and that he hoped
they would continue to do it in the same way.

Next morning all the world was talking of the
mêlée, and in the newspapers there were long accounts and startling headlines describing the scenes
that had taken place.   These were very much more
favourable to the women than any which had been
published hitherto, for, though the Press was still
far from admitting the extreme urgency of the cause
of Women's Suffrage, or the need for the militant
tactics as a means of obtaining the Parliamentary
vote, still a large section of both Press and public
were unanimous in condemning the Government for
the violent measures which it had employed to sup-
press the women's deputation.   Many compared the
sending out of mounted police against a procession
of unarmed women to the employment of Cossacks
in Russia, and the *Liberal Daily Chronicle* published a cartoon called " The London Cossack "
which showed a portly policeman riding off with a
trophy of ladies' hats.

At ten o'clock on Thursday morning, January
14th, the fifty-seven women and the two men who
had been arrested on the previous day appeared at
the Westminster Police Court.   The women were
put in one of the side rooms, and then a band of
policemen filed in and each one identified his prisoner.   For most of the women this was a first visit
to the police court, and, though many of them were
severely bruised by the previous day's encounter,
they were all determined to make the best of the
experience and to dwell, as far as possible, upon the
humorous side of the situation.   Whilst the Suffragettes were ready to forgive, the constables seemed

mostly anxious to forget the violence, and many of the men asked their captives to give them the round white " Votes for Women " buttons which they were wearing as mementoes of the women's famous " raid " on the House of Commons. After waiting until the drunkards and pickpockets had been disposed of, the Suffragettes were taken into the Court one or two at a time. Christabel Pankhurst, as organiser of the Demonstration was, at her own request, the first to be placed in the dock. She explained clearly that many of our members had suffered very seriously, but that the W. S. P. U. wished to fix the blame for what had occurred, not upon the police, but upon the Government that had dictated the use of these measures for clearing the women away. If the Government refused to take " the only just, simple and proper way out of the difficulty — that of giving women their undoubted right to vote," she said, " the responsibility must be theirs, and if lives are lost in this campaign the Liberal Government will be directly responsible. One thing is certain; there can be no going back for us, and more will happen if we do not get justice." Mr. Curtis Bennett, the magistrate, here intervened, saying with what he evidently thought was unanswerable firmness, that the women undoubtedly were responsible for all the trouble, that there were other means of obtaining votes; and that these disorderly scenes in the streets must be stopped. " They can be stopped," she retorted, " but only in one way." He looked at her sternly, and " twenty shillings or fourteen days," was his sole reply. Then she was hurried away, and, in an incredibly short space of time, fifty-four Suffragettes had been tried and sentenced to undergo punishment varying from ten shillings or seven days' imprisonment to forty shillings or one month. Forty shillings or one month's imprisonment had also been imposed on a working man, Mr. Edward Croft, who had been arrested for trying to defend one of the women in Parliament Square. All those who had been convicted refused to pay their fines and decided to go to prison, and whilst Mr. Croft was removed to Pentonville, we Suffragettes were taken away in the van to Holloway Gaol.

On arriving at the prison we found that, as was now the rule, most of our number were to be treated as first class misdemeanants, though some few, without any apparent reason were to be placed in the second division. Those of us who had been there some months before now found that several minor innovations had been introduced since our last visit to Holloway. When we had originally been put in the first class, Mrs. Cobden Sanderson, who was a vegetarian, was daily served with the usual prison diet, and though she was obliged to leave the meat, no extra vegetables were allowed her, and she was obliged to exist on her potatoes and bread. Now a special dietary had been introduced for vegetarians, which consisted at this season of an alternation of carrots and onions, with occasional rather stale eggs as a substitute for meat, and milk, night and morning, instead of cocoa and tea. Butter was sometimes allowed by the doctor's special order. Now that so large a number of us occupied adjoining cells in one corridor and were sent out to exercise together apart from the other prisoners, the authorities found it difficult to enforce the full rigour of

the prison régime. They found it difficult to prevent our speaking to each other occasionally when
we stood together in line waiting to be marched to
exercise or chapel; they could scarcely stop the tap-
ping out conversations on the cell walls which was
carried on by neighbouring Suffragettes.   Sometimes,
when the wardresses were off duty, one of our number would strike up a hymn or march to which words
suitable to our movement had been adapted.   The
others would join in chorus; and when the officers
came hurrying back it would be some moments before silence could be restored.

For one cause or another many of us were sent
to the hospital, some being placed in a ward with
some twenty or thirty other prisoners, others in
separate hospital cells.

With the exception of Mrs. Despard and myself
all the Suffragettes were released at the end of the
first fortnight, but our sentences did not expire until a
week later.   A procession had been organised to welcome our comrades, and a band had played for an
hour outside the prison gates.   It is difficult to describe the effect upon ourselves which was created
by the music.   We knew that it was being played
by our friends.   We felt almost as though they
were speaking to us, and to hospital prisoners who
are not even allowed to attend service in the chapel,
the very sound of the music in that dreary place was
extraordinarily impressive.   It made one's pulses
throb and filled one's eyes with tears.

The poor ordinary prisoners were filled with excitement and delight and when we were out at exercise
with them on the day before our release, woman after
woman contrived to walk for a few moments either

before or after one or other of us in the line and
to ask if we also would be met by a band. " How
splendid for you! " said one of the girls to me wist-
fully. " I only wish I had friends to meet me.
But I am glad for you." " We are looking forward
to the band, but we shall be sorry to lose you," another said.

Whilst so many of us had been in prison, a by-
election had taken place in South Aberdeen, where
Mrs. Pankhurst, at the head of the Suffragettes'
forces, had vigorously opposed the Government candidate whose majority had fallen by more than 4,000
votes.

The figures were : —

    G. B. Esslemont (L.)................. 3,779
    R. McNeill (C.)..................... 3,412
    F. Bramley (Soc.).................... 1,740
                                             367

At the General Election the figures had been : —

    J. Bryce (L.)........................ 6,780
    W. G. Black (U.)................... 2,332
                                             8,448

The Suffragists, too, had not been inactive, for
Mrs. Henry Fawcett, and four of her colleagues,
had written to the Prime Minister asking that they
might be allowed to plead the cause of Woman's Suffrage at the Bar of the House. They pointed out
that in 1688, Anne, the widow of Edward Fitz
Harris, who was executed for treason in 1681, had

been allowed to speak for herself and her children at the Bar, and that Mrs. Clarke, mistress of the Duke of York, had been summoned thither to give evidence in regard to the charges of corruption against the Duke. Nevertheless, Sir Henry Campbell-Bannerman refused to grant their request on the ground that there was no precedent for women to appear at the Bar of the House in support of a petition.

Meanwhile, since the so-called " Raid " on the House that had led to our imprisonment, candid friends had been constantly telling us that we had entirely alienated the sympathy of those who had hitherto supported the enfranchisement of women. Yet, even whilst the " Raid " had been in progress, a very much larger number of Parliamentary representatives were agreeing to give their places in the private Members' ballot to a Woman's Suffrage Bill than had ever done so before. When the result of the ballot became known, it was found, that for the first time in the history of the movement, the fortunate member who had secured the coveted first place out of 670 was willing to devote it to introducing a measure to give votes to women. It was a Liberal member, Mr. Dickinson, who had won the first place and had decided to introduce the Women's Enfranchisement Bill. The Anti-Suffragists at once began to work actively against the measure and the first Women's Anti-Suffrage Society that had ever been formed was inaugurated to oppose it. Two petitions against the Women's Enfranchisement Bill, one of them said to be signed by 21,000 and the other by 16,500 persons, were presented to Parliament on March 5th and March 22nd. They were

heralded by the jubilations of our opponents but
when the petitions came to be examined they were
rejected by the Petitions Committee of Parliament
as " informal." This was because the separate sheets
upon which the signatures had been written were not
each headed by the prayer against the granting of
Women's Suffrage, and there was consequently no
evidence to prove that the signatories had known for
what purpose their names were being collected.
Afterward Mr. J. M. Robertson examined the
Anti-Suffrage Petitions and reported that " whole
batches of signatures had been written in by a single
hand," that " the batch work began on the very first
sheets," and that it appeared as though the petitions
" had been got up wholesale in this fashion." Mr.
J. H. Wilson, M.P., Chairman of the Parliamentary
Committee on Public Petitions, afterwards stated in
the House of Commons, that the names of whole
families of persons had undoubtedly been written in
by the same hand. But even had these petitions
been so evidently authentic as to have been accepted
by Parliament without question, they would still
have been quite insignificant as compared with the
great petitions and memorials in support of Votes
for Women, which had been presented year after
year since 1866. But the days in which women
might have won or lost the Parliamentary vote by
petitioning had long gone by, and all politically
minded women knew this.

For a Member of Parliament to declare himself in open opposition to Votes for Women, rendered him extremely unpopular, many of the anti-
Suffragists, especially of the Liberal Party, now
pretended that their reason for objecting to Mr.

Dickinson's Bill was that they did not consider it to be a democratic measure. They declared that it would " disfranchise married women " would give the vote to women of wealth and property only and would exclude all those who had to work for their own living. So emphatically was this statement made that it was difficult to convince many people that the measure in question was the old equal Women's Enfranchisement Bill, and that there was no intention of introducing some new-fangled, fancy franchise. Yet as a matter of fact, Mr. Dickinson's Bill contained only a slight alteration in the wording, though not in the sense, of the last clause of the original measure. Instead of the phrase " any law or usage to the contrary notwithstanding," which occurred in the original Bill and was intended to strike at the disability of coverture which affects married women, the words, " A woman shall not be disqualified by reason of marriage from being so registered and voting, notwithstanding any law or custom to the contrary," were substituted.

On moving the Second Reading of the Bill, Mr. Dickinson dealt especially with the objections of those who declared that the measure was anti-democratic. He stated, that in 1904, the women electors in his constituency of North St. Pancras had numbered 1,014. Of these women three per cent. had belonged to the wealthy upper class, thirty-seven per cent. to the middle class, and sixty per cent. to the working class; many of the latter being exceedingly poor.

When asked by the Secretary of the Local Women's Suffrage Society in his constituency of Dunfermline, whether he would support the second reading of the Bill, Sir Henry Campbell-Bannerman had replied, " I will with much pleasure give my support to Mr. Dickinson's Bill when it comes before the House of Commons." Now that the moment for fulfiling his promise had arrived, however, the Prime Minister threw cold water upon the measure. " I am not very warmly enamoured of it," he said, and after casting doubt upon the accuracy of Mr. Dickinson's figures he added, that in his opinion, the Bill would merely " enfranchise a small minority of well-to-do women." Where the Prime Minister had led, the rank and file Anti-Suffragist Liberal Members of Parliament followed. Though they had neither facts nor figures of their own to quote in support of their contention, and, in face of both of Mr. Dickinson's figures and Mr. Snowden's reminder that the I. L. P. census of 1904 had shown that eighty-two per cent. of the women on the Municipal Register belonged to the working classes, they still continued to assert that only " a handful of propertied women " could obtain votes under this Bill. At the same time, although they themselves belonged almost exclusively to the middle and upper classes, they persistently stated their belief in the dangerous influence of the women who belonged to those same classes.

As the afternoon wore on attempts were made to move the closure of the debate in order that a vote on the Bill might be taken, but the Speaker refused to accept the resolution, and at five o'clock Mr. Rees, the Liberal Member for Montgomery Burghs talked the measure out after a five hours' debate. There was no protest from the Ladies' Gallery this time as the Suffragettes had all been rigorously excluded, but both Suffragettes and Suffragists combined in urging the Government to give another day for the discussion of the Bill. This they curtly refused, and though the Suffragettes had not agreed to accept the decision as final and intended to renew their demand until it was granted, Mr. Dickinson shortly afterwards withdrew his Bill in order to make way for a Women's Suffrage Resolution, a place for which had been obtained by Sir Charles M'Laren. No sooner had Mr. Dickinson's Bill been withdrawn and Sir Charles M'Laren's Resolution set down in its stead than it was blocked by a discreditable move on the part of a well known Anti-Suffragist, Mr. (afterwards Sir) Maurice Levy. Taking advantage of a rule of the House of Commons by which a Resolution cannot be proceeded with, if a Bill dealing with a similar subject has been introduced, this Liberal member now brought forward a Bill which he never intended to be discussed to give a vote to every adult man and woman. Therefore Sir Charles M'Laren's Resolution was thus entirely shelved. This was not by any means the first time that the trick had been used in the case of a Women's Suffrage motion, but the device was acknowledged to be an unjustifiable abuse of the Procedure rules. Mr. Levy refused even the Speaker's request to withdraw his dummy Bill. Protests were raised on all sides of the House, because it was realised that, if the practice of bringing in dummy Bills to prevent discussion were to become common, the right of private Members to introduce Resolutions would be entirely destroyed. A Resolution embodying this point of view was therefore agreed to, and Mr. Asquith promised that the Government would take action in the matter.[1]   Though the question was raised again three months later, however, the promise was never kept, and though the general feeling was that Mr. Levy had offended against the recognised etiquette of Parliament, it must be remembered, that, as the *Standard* put it "if the Government had chosen to exercise pressure Mr. Levy would have proved complaisant."[2]

But after all this was only a Resolution, and, realis-

[1] When Sir Henry Campbell-Bannerman, introduced a Resolution dealing with the Veto of the House of Lords, three months afterwards, Lord Robert Cecil, introduced a Dummy Bill for the abolition of the House of Lords' Veto in order to prevent Sir Henry Campbell-Bannerman's motion being discussed, and thus to teach the Anti-Suffragists that their own blocking tactics could be used against themselves. As Lord Robert Cecil came forward with his Bill, Sir Henry Campbell-Bannerman, knowing what he was going to do, begged him not to introduce it, in order that the Government's Resolution might not be delayed. If Lord Robert Cecil would not agree, the Prime Minister threatened to call a sitting of the House for the next Saturday — the day which had been fixed for the King's garden party — in order to pass a special motion to allow the Government's Resolution to be proceeded with. Still Lord Robert Cecil protested that the Government must draw up the proposed Standing Order or he would insist upon introducing his Bill and Mr. Balfour supported him saying, "You can cook up a land Bill in three days, yet you cannot draft a Standing Order in three months." In the end the Government again promised to make such action as Mr. Levy's impossible, and Lord Robert Cecil withdrew his Bill, but the promise has not yet been redeemed.

[2] So far from exercising pressure upon Mr. Levy, the Liberal Government shortly afterwards gave him a knighthood. The failure to carry out their pledge, which I have referred to in the previous note, clearly shows that the Government did not in any way disapprove of Mr. Levy's action and were anxious that the possibility of its being repeated should remain.

ing that the Government, with practically all the time of Parliament at its disposal, could easily provide the few days necessary for carrying into Law a Woman's Suffrage measure, the Women's Social and Political Union were now preparing for further militant action.

On the day of the talking out of Mr. Dickinson's Bill a meeting had been held by the Union in the Exeter Hall at which Mrs. Pethick Lawrence had called for subscriptions to inaugurate a £20,000 campaign fund, and over £1,400 had been sent up to the platform during the meeting. On March 20, 1907, the second Women's Parliament assembled in the Caxton Hall.[1] This Parliament was specially characterised by the large numbers of delegates from the provinces, amongst whom was a contingent of Lancashire Cotton Operatives, led by Annie Kenney and wearing their clogs and shawls. As before, the decision to carry a resolution to the Prime Minister was heralded with an enthusiasm that was almost fiercely overwhelming. Then, when Christabel Pankhurst called out from the platform, " Who will lead the deputation? " Lady Harberton, for many years a Suffragist of the old school, eagerly answered " I," and at once hundreds of women sprang up to follow her. As soon as the deputation gained the street the police began to push

[1] Shortly after this Second Women's Parliament, a proposal was raised that the Westminster City Council should prevent the Hall being let to the Women's Social and Political Union. The Chairman of the General Purposes Committee then stated that this course would be adopted if any damage were done to the hall itself. Up to the present time no further attempt has been made to prevent the holding of the Women's Parliament in the Hall.

and hustle them, but though overwhelmingly outnumbered, they bravely strove hour after hour to
carry out their purpose.   Rigid lines of police drawn
up across the approaches to the House prevented
their even getting near to it, and though at one point
a number of Lancashire mill hands drove up in a
couple of waggonettes, and, being mistaken for sight-
seers, succeeded in reaching the Strangers' Entrance,
they were discovered and beaten back.

Meanwhile Caxton Hall was kept open all the
afternoon and on into the evening, and the disabled
women were constantly returning thither.   They
brought with them the news that numbers of women
had been arrested, and that though Lady Harberton had at last got into the House of Commons, her
petition had been ignored.   Christabel Pankhurst
then advised any who might succeed in entering
Parliament to take sterner measures,— to rush, if
they could, into the sacred Chamber of debate itself,
to seat themselves upon the Government bench
and demand a hearing.   "If possible," she cried,
"seize the mace, and you will be the Cromwells of
the twentieth century!"   The women rushed back
with renewed zeal.

It was now dark, and, as the crowds grew denser
and denser and the police turned on them more
angrily, many Members of Parliament, including
Mr. Herbert Gladstone and Mr. Lloyd George,
came out to watch the scene.   Some showed distress
at the way in which the women were being treated,
but others regarded it as a joke.   Many of the
women were roughly handled and some were seriously hurt, but, speaking generally, the violence used
against them was not so great as on the previous

February 13th. It was said that no fewer than a thousand extra police were especially drafted into Parliament Square to guard the House of Commons.

Amongst those who had been arrested were Dr. Mabel Hardy, Miss Naici Peters, a Norwegian painter and a friend of Ibsen. Miss Cemino Folliero, a portrait painter from Rome and Miss Constance Clyde, a well known Australian journalist and novelist.

Next day when the women were brought up before Mr. Horace Smith at the Westminster Police Court, Mr. Muskett, who appeared to prosecute on behalf of the police, protested that the Suffragettes had hitherto been treated with " the utmost indulgence," and begged that they should in future be dealt with " as ordinary lawbreakers." Therefore the magistrate gave to most of the women exactly the same sentences — varying from twenty shillings or fourteen days to forty shillings or one month's imprisonment — that had been meted out to their comrades on the last occasion. Miss Patricia Woodlock and Mrs. Ada Chatterton, the former having only left Holloway on the expiration of her previous month's imprisonment one week before, were, as " old offenders," sentenced to one month's imprisonment without the option of a fine. Mrs. Mary Leigh though this was her first arrest, also received a month's imprisonment because, by hanging a Votes for Women banner over the edge of the dock, she annoyed the magistrate, who said that he did not think it " a decent thing to wave a flag in a court of justice."

Thus as a result of two attempts within the short space of five weeks to carry Resolutions to the Prime Minister from meetings of women held in the Caxton

Hall, one hundred and thirty women, who were agitating for an eminently just and absolutely simple reform, had been imprisoned. Even to the next generation this state of things will appear monstrous, how much more so to those that are to follow in the dim future.

CHAPTER IX

A CROP OF BY-ELECTIONS, MARCH TO MAY, 1907

No sooner had the second Women's Parliament been concluded than Mrs. Pankhurst had hurried off by the night train to take command of the Suffragette forces against the Government at a by-election at Hexham in Northumberland, where the Liberal majority was reduced by more than a thousand votes. This election was scarcely over when it was followed, with scarcely a week's intermission, by no fewer than seven others, at six of which the Suffragettes were to the fore.

From Hexham our militant army was transferred to Stepney and then to Rutland, the smallest English County.

Writing at the beginning of the Rutland contest, the *Daily News* correspondent said: "Each of the three parties (the third being the Women's Social and Political Union) opened its campaign with meetings in the Rutland Division to-night." Thus recognised from the start as one of the three forces to be reckoned with in the Election, the W. S. P. U. kept its important position right through until the end. In every hamlet and village the women speakers were cordially received and their speeches were listened to with earnest attention and respect. After the meetings, men and women clustered round to ask questions and tell how, before the passing of the 1884 Reform Act which had enfranchised the agricultural labourers, in the days when voters were scarce, widows and daughters whose fathers were dead, had been frequently turned out of their farms, not because they could not pay the rent, but because they could not vote. Even to-day the people said that a woman tenant was sometimes looked upon with disfavour on that account. Though the wages of the agricultural labourers in this district were exceedingly low, there was hardly a single member of the audience who did not buy at least one badge or penny pamphlet, whilst the free leaflets were eagerly seized upon, and labourers would come hurrying across the fields to the roadside in order to secure them.

As the days went by the journeyings of the Suffragettes from meeting place to meeting place throughout the constituency became a sort of triumphal progress. We were cheerily hailed from afar by distant workers amongst the crops and by drivers of passing carts. Men, women and children ran to the cottage doors to see us pass, and everywhere we were greeted with smiles and kindly words.

Only in the towns, at Oakham, the capital, and at Uppingham, did we meet with any opposition, but here most of the working men were deeply anxious that the Liberal should be returned. Rightly or wrongly they believed in the Liberal Party, believed it to be the party of progress and the one that would stand by the poor man. Nevertheless the majority listened courteously to our arguments, and admitting at last that our policy was logical and right for us, although inconvenient to them. Many of the

staunchest Liberals were even won over to go all
the way with us and to help us to " keep the Liberal
out."

But, whilst the majority were thus willing to listen
and anxious to understand, there was also a bitterly
hostile element which was inflamed by an absolutely
unreasoning spirit of party antagonism, and it was
well known, and quite openly stated in Oakham, that
a certain well-to-do Liberal was paying a gang of
youths to shout down the Suffragettes at their nightly
meetings in the market place.   It is always found by
those who take part in political warfare that the
roughest and least civilised members of society are
invariably opposed to the pioneer and the reformer
and usually support the Government in power, to
whatever party it may belong, just as they try to
" back the winner " in a race.   With the additional
monetary incentive to create a disturbance, this element soon rendered our market place meetings un-
pleasantly turbulent, with the result that the local
police were kept busier than they had been for a
generation, and reinforcements had to be sent in
from Leicestershire in order to keep the peace.
The tradesman from whom we hired the lorry
that we used as a platform, now announced that he
dared not let us have it in future because he had
been warned, not only that the vehicle itself would
be damaged, but that his windows would be broken
and his shop looted.   Not until we had tried without success every lorry owner in Oakham, did a man,
who was storing a waggon for a farmer living many
miles outside the constituency, at last come to us and
say that, if we would go to the barn in the field
where it was kept and fetch it out for ourselves, we

might have the use of this waggon on promising to make good any damage that might be done. We agreed to this and were able to hold our meetings right on until the end of the contest, though on the last two nights very little that we said could be heard, owing to the number of horns, bells and rattles that were loudly sounded by our opponents. After these stormy meetings the police and hosts of sympathisers always escorted us home to protect us from the rowdies. Just as we reached our door there was generally a little scuffle with a band of youths who waited there to pelt us with sand and gravel as we passed in. Once inside the house, the rest of the evening was always taken up with interviewing the host of previously unknown callers, who came to ask whether we had arrived home safely, to apologise for the roughs, to express sympathy with " Votes for Women," to buy literature, badges and buttons, or to ask us to inscribe our names in autograph albums. At Uppingham, the second largest town, the hostile element was smaller than at Oakham, but its methods were more dangerous. Whilst Mary Gawthorpe was holding an open-air meeting there one evening, a crowd of noisy youths began to throw up peppermint " bull's eyes " and other hard-boiled sweets. " Sweets to the sweet," said little Mary, smiling, and continued her argument, but a pot-egg, thrown from the crowd behind, struck her on the head and she fell unconscious. She was carried away, but next day appeared again, like a true Suffragette, quite undaunted, and the incident and her plucky spirit, made her the heroine of the Election. Polling took place on June 11th, and instead of the great increase in the Government vote that had been expected the Conservative majority was nearly doubled. The figures were:

J. Gretton (C.)...................... 2,213
W. F. Lyon (L.)..................... 1,362
                                     ─────
                                       851

The figures at the General Election had been:

H. G. Finch (C.).................... 2,047
Harold Pearson (L.)................ 1,564
                                     ─────
                                       483

The campaign in Rutland was not yet over, when Mrs. Pankhurst and part of our forces were obliged to go north to Jarrow, where there was a Government majority of nearly three thousand votes to pull down. The Conservatives, the Labour Party, the Irish Nationalists, and, of course, the Liberals themselves had each put a candidate into the field, and every one of this bevy of candidates was " in favour " of Votes for Women.

Whether the majority of these who came in contact with the Suffragettes during these by-Election Campaigns understood the workings of the Party machinery, which controls the Government of our country, well enough to realise that by voting against the Government they would help the Votes for Women cause may perhaps be doubted by some, though the Suffragettes were constantly receiving both written and verbal assurances from electors who declared that their votes had turned upon this question; but that the hearts of the people were stirred by the Suffragettes' appeal is absolutely sure. In the leafy lanes and tiny villages of Rutland great interest and sympathy had been evoked, but in smoky struggling Jarrow, with its coal mines, shipbuilding yards and engineering works, with its dingy slums where overcrowding and infant mortality are, in common with the rest of this district, more rife than in any other part of the country, the message of the Suffragettes came to the overburdened women as a wonderful ray of hope that had burst in upon the squalor of their lives.

On the first night of their arrival in Jarrow, Mrs. Pankhurst and Annie Kenney held the largest open-air meeting that had ever been seen in that town, and the numberless subsequent gatherings, whether for men and women, or for women only, which were held in halls, in open spaces, at work gates, and at the collieries, were, in every case, larger and more orderly than those held by any of the other parties. A systematic canvass was made of the women householders, who numbered more than one thousand, and a Committee of Local Women who had come forward with offers of help sprang almost spontaneously into being.

Three days before the end of the contest it was suggested that a women's procession should march to the various polling booths, in order to remind the men to vote against the nominee of the Government that had refused to allow women to become voters too. The idea was eagerly caught up, banners were quickly made by voluntary helpers, the news was carried throughout the district, and on polling day great crowds of women came flocking to the Mechanics' Hall, where they were to assemble. They came early, but found that a well dressed mob of men and youths, wearing the Liberal Colours, had already gathered to bar the doorway, and the women were literally obliged to fight their way both in and out of their own meeting. As soon as the procession had got fairly out into the main road, however, everything went well, for though at no time did the police put in an appearance, either to keep order or to clear the way for them, the women were protected from obstruction by the sympathy and good will of the populace. As they passed onward, greater and greater numbers joined their ranks until it seemed as though all the women of Jarrow were marching along the road.

The men whom they met coming from the polling booths greeted them with cheers and cries of " We have voted for the women this time. We have kept the Liberal out." They spoke truly, for when the votes were counted, it was found that the Government candidate was third on the list, and that the Liberal vote at the General Election had been reduced by more than half. The figures were:

Pete Curran (Lab.)................... 4,698
P. Rose Innes (C.).................... 3,930
Spencer Leigh Hughes (L.)............ 3,474
J. O'Hanlon (N.).................... 2,124

The figures at the General Election had been:

Sir C. M. Palmer (L.)................ 8,047
Pete Curran (Lab.).................. 5,093

Before the Jarrow election was over came another in the Colne Valley, in Yorkshire, and here again an old Liberal stronghold was wrested from the Government. After the declaration of the poll, Mr.

Grayson, the successful candidate, publicly admitted that his return was largely due to the heavily damaging effect of the Suffragettes' attack upon his Liberal opponent. An article [1] on this election headed " Votes for Women, but Fair Play for Liberals," which appeared in the Liberal *Tribune,* condemning the anti-Government by-election policy of the Suffragettes, was an admission of the great influence which they had been able to exercise at this and other recent by-elections.

A more gracious tribute to the electioneering capabilities of the Suffragettes by the special correspond-

[1] If Mr. Stanley is the saint and Mr. Twyford the hero, the Suffragettes are the politicians of the Election. . . . I confess that until I had seen the Suffragette Ironsides at work I thought the Tariff Reform Ruperts unsurpassed. The organization of the Suffragettes is as good as their political insight. They adopt the " fan " formation. They usually have three or four local centres in a scattered constituency. The members of each group in each centre live together irrespective of class differences. It is a pleasure to see the fan opened, controlled and set by the controlling hand at the centre. Early in the morning while men are sleeping or at the Committee Rooms a group of women will walk up the street of their centre. . . . At the crossroads of each centre each single group becomes a fan itself. Each member takes a different road. Chalk in hand, each woman whilst, going to one meeting, makes the announcement of another. The men usually hunt in couples. They do not care to face these hostile audiences single-handed, but each of these women, as often as not, tackles an audience alone. If combined hammering is necessary the central hand sends to the rescue. Their staying power, judging them by the standard of men, is extraordinary. By taking afternoon as well as evening meetings they have worked twice as hard as the men. They are up earlier, they retire just as late. Women against men, they are better speakers, more logical, better informed, better phrased, with a surer insight for the telling argument.

ent of the *Morning Post* appeared in that paper on August 1st, 1909, during the North West Stafford-shire by-election,

The next Election was at Bury St. Edmunds in Suffolk. Here the Liberal vote was greatly reduced, and that of the Conservative more than doubled. The figures were:

The Hon. W. Guinness (U.)	1,631
W. B. Yates (L.)	741
Unionist majority	890

The figures at the General Election had been:

Capt. F. W. Harvey (U.)	1,481
W. B. Yates (L.)	1,047
Unionist Majority	434

When, after the declaration of the poll, the successful candidate, the Hon. W. Guinness, appeared at the window of the Angel Hotel to thank his supporters and to speak to the people in the customary way, he asked, " What has been the cause of this great and glorious victory? " He was interrupted by cries of " Votes for Women ! " and by " Three cheers for the Suffragettes ! " vigorously given from the assembled crowd. " No doubt the ladies had something to do with it," he was constrained to agree.

During this first year of by-election work since the anti-Government campaign had been started at Eye and Cockermouth in 1906, the Suffragette forces had grown very largely, and instead of the one or two workers who had gone to the first contests there were now upwards of thirty regular by-election campaigners, who could always be relied upon, at head-quarters. During each contest from sixteen to twenty meetings were held by the union each day. At all these gatherings collections were taken and admission was charged for many of the election meetings held in halls, though both practices were unexampled at Election times. A fine answer to the Liberal cry that they were fighting with " Tory Gold," and a striking proof of the Suffragette speakers' popularity with the audiences were thus provided. At every contest in which the Suffragettes had fought hitherto, there had been a fall in the Government vote, which had been reduced at Cockermouth by 1,446; at Huddersfield by 540; in North West Derbyshire by 1,021; in South Aberdeen by 3,001; at Hexham by 231; at Stepney by 503; at Rutland by 202; at Jarrow by 4,573; at Colne Valley by 2,204; in North West Staffordshire by 271, and at Bury St. Edmunds by 306; making in all a total loss of votes to the Government of 13,300. In spite of the denials of Party wire-pullers a part of this loss was certainly due to the Suffragettes.

At some of the later election contests, beginning at Hexham, a new complication had been introduced. During all the years of its existence the old non-militant National Union of Women's Suffrage Societies had held entirely aloof from all election warfare but, seeing that the Suffragettes during the first year of their anti-Government by-election campaigning had rapidly grown not only in surface popularity but in real influence with the electorate, the older Suffragists now came to the conclusion that they, too, must adopt a by-election policy. Unfortunately, however, the older Suffragists had not the courage to make common cause with the Suffragettes who had raised the question of Women's Suffrage from the position of a stale, old-fashioned joke to that of a living, moving force in practical politics. They decided, instead, not to oppose the Government, but to support any Parliamentary candidate who should declare himself to be favourable to Woman Suffrage. If, as generally happened nowadays, all the candidates should claim to be favourable, the N. U. S. S. should either support the most favourable, or remain neutral. In the event of no candidate being favourable, a special Women's Suffrage candidate might be run.

Thus, rather than boldly oppose a Government that had only too clearly shown that it would never give women the vote until it was forced to do so, these old-fashioned Suffragists preferred to ignore entirely the dominating principle of the politics of their own time, namely, government by party. They preferred to go on working for the return of a few more of the Private Members of Parliament who, though they already formed a majority of more than two-thirds of the House of Commons, had themselves, for the hundredth time, been proved to be incapable of doing anything to prevent the wrecking of a Women's Suffrage Bill, when, in that very March in which this futile election policy was decided upon, Mr. Dickinson's Bill had been " talked out."

It is always more difficult to carry out a weak policy than a strong one, and the adoption of this particular policy not only failed to advance the Suffrage cause, but also failed in one object for which it primarily was designed, namely, to prevent dissension in the ranks of the National Union of Women's Suffrage Societies itself. Many members at once seceded and joined the Women's Social and Political Union, and many of those who did not actually resign their membership of the old society now threw all their energy into working for the younger, more active and courageous body.   On the other hand, there were still those Liberal women who cared more for party than for principle to be reckoned with, and one of these, Lady Carlisle, resigned the Vice Presidentship of the N. U. W. S. S., which she had accepted but a few days before the new by-election policy had been announced, because, in her party-ridden opinion, to oppose a Liberal candidate who was opposed to their enfranchisement, seemed too " drastic " and " extreme " a course for women to adopt.

When the by-election policy of the N. U. W. S. S. came to be put into practice its unworkable character was immediately demonstrated.   The candidates at Hexham were interviewed, with the result that the Unionist, Colonel Bates, returned what was considered to be a favourable answer, whilst the reply of Mr. R. D. Holt, the Liberal, was said to be unsatisfactory.   The National Union of Women's Suffrage Societies was therefore, according to the newly framed policy, obliged to support the Conservative candidate, but, when they proceeded to do so, many of the Liberal members of the organisation objected, and some even went so far as to work for the Liberal candidate in opposition to their Secretary, Miss Edith Palliser, and the rest of the Society.   To make matters even more embarrassing for those who were endeavouring to carry out the policy the Liberal candidate now veered round a point or two — as candidates so often will — and stated that he had always been in favour of women's enfranchisement and that his only fear was that women were not asking for their votes upon a sufficiently democratic basis. He was therefore proclaimed by his supporters to be a staunch and devoted friend of the Women's Suffrage Cause.

Meanwhile the Suffragettes foresaw very clearly that this new policy which would sometimes cause the Suffragists to support the Government candidate whom they themselves were strenuously working against would confuse the electors and increase the difficulty of explaining the anti-Government policy, and, though the anti-Government policy was a very simple one, even simple things are difficult to explain when hosts of people are striving to misrepresent them.

In May, the National Union of Suffrage Societies decided to run a Parliamentary candidate of their own, at a by-election in Wimbledon, and had chosen as their nominee a well known Liberal, the Hon. Bertrand Russell. The crushing defeat which resulted has unfortunately been quoted as a proof that the majority of the Parliamentary voters in that constituency were opposed to the principle of women's enfranchisement, but an impartial examination into the facts shows clearly that they do not in any way justify this conclusion.

The Wimbledon seat had always been held by the Conservatives, and their majority at the General Election, in spite of the then great Liberal revival, had numbered more than 2,000 votes. Now, with the well known and typical old Conservative, Mr. Henry Chaplin, in the field, the Liberal Party considered it wisest not to fight. Therefore, but for the intervention of the National Union of Suffrage Societies, who opposed him because of his anti-Suffragist views, Mr. Chaplin would have been returned without a contest. Opinions may reasonably be divided as to whether the game of running Parliamentary candidates would possibly be worth the candle to a Women's Suffrage Society, but everyone will surely agree that if Suffrage candidates were to be run at all, the chief object of the Suffragists ought to have been to efface as far as possible all other points of political difference between the rival candidates in order that upon the question of Votes for Women, and upon that question alone, the electors might have decided how to vote. To ensure that the single issue should predominate, it might have been well to choose as the Suffragist nominee a candidate whose views upon general political questions were, either similar to those of his anti-Suffrage opponent, or altogether colourless and obscure. In any case it was essential that the Suffragist candidate should be willing to subordinate all his other political opinions and to concentrate his attention absolutely upon the question of Votes for Women. In this Election, however, though it was well known that Liberalism was unpopular, the Suffragists chose to represent them a strong Liberal who was determined to make the election contest an opportunity for propagating his Liberal principles. That Mr. Bertrand Russell cared very much more for Liberalism than he did for Women's Votes was at once apparent. With the news that he had consented to stand as the Suffrage candidate came the announcement that he would not in any circum-

stances have agreed to do so had an official Liberal
been nominated, and he showed clearly that he had
no intention of standing out against the wishes of
his party leaders in order to press forward the
Women's Cause. Right from the outset the record
of the Liberal Government, and the general principles of Liberalism were the points constantly put
before the electors, and it was upon these points that
the Election was really fought. Mr. Russell's Election Address, which was in fact the manifesto of
the Suffragists, advocated Free Trade, the Taxation
of Land Values and other questions quite unconnected with their cause. In his last message to the
electors he said:

I ask for the Liberal vote because I am a Liberal through
and through. I am just as much a Liberal as dozens of the
Ministerialists in the House of Commons, who are as keen
as ever I can be upon the Women's Suffrage question. To
those who waver about giving me their vote because they
have doubts on the women's question, I would ask, " Do you
prefer Mr. Chaplin, the protectionist and crusted Tory, to
one who is at least a Free Trader and Progressive?" Such
persons should remember that every vote not given to me is
given to my opponent!

The Conservatives eagerly seized the opportunity
of fighting Mr. Russell on the ground of his Liber-
alism and scouted the idea of his being considered a
Women's Suffrage candidate. At the same time the
Liberals dissociated themselves from his candidature.
It was no great matter for surprise, therefore, that
Mr. Russell was defeated by more than 6,000 votes.
The figures were:

H. Chaplin (U.)..................... 10,263
B. Russell (L.)..................... 3,299

                                    ──────
                                    6,964

The figures at the General Election had been:

C. E. Hambro (U.).................. 9,523
Mr. Lane Fox Pitt (L.).............. 7,409

                                    ──────
                                    2,114

It is interesting to note that in the six elections which had taken place since 1885 the Liberals had only thought it worth their while to contest the seat on three occasions, and on one of these the Liberal vote had fallen below that recorded for Mr. Bertrand Russell.

Perhaps the most unfortunate feature of the contest was that those of the Suffragist women who genuinely wished to further the interests of the women's cause without respect to party, instead of taking command of the situation, leading their candidate aright, and showing that they were determined that Woman Suffrage should be the only feature of the election, allowed the contest to be dominated by Mr. Russell and his Liberal opinions. Herein lay the great point of difference between the Suffragists and the Suffragettes. The Suffragists were ever prone to look upon their cause as a side issue and to apologise for any impatient attempt to press it to the front. The Suffragettes, on the other hand, were ready to stake their all upon it and constantly proclaimed it to be the highest and greatest in the world.

CHAPTER X

THE FORMATION OF THE WOMEN'S FREEDOM LEAGUE. REVIVAL OF MILITANT TACTICS

In spite of its unprecedented growth the Women's Social and Political Union was now approaching a very difficult crisis in its history; little by little, differences of opinion in regard to questions of organisation and policy had begun to show themselves amongst the members of its governing body and finally, in September, 1907, a reconstruction of the Committee and Constitution of the Union took place. Now, although every one of the original founders of the Union remained, a number of those who had for some time belonged to the Central Committee left to form a new militant society called the Women's Freedom League which opened offices at 18 Buckingham Street, Strand,[1] and of which Mrs. Despard became Honorary Treasurer, Mrs. Billington Grieg, Honorary Organiser, and Mrs. Edith How Martyn, Honorary Secretary. At the same time a reconstruction of the organising basis of the Women's Social and Political Union itself was effected, and it became obligatory for all members of the Union to sign the following pledge:

I endorse the objects and methods of the Women's Social and Political Union and hereby undertake not to support

[1] They afterwards moved to Robert Street, Strand.

the candidate of any political party at Parliamentary elections until women have obtained the Parliamentary vote.

All the prominent members of the W. S. P. U. who had not already done so now formally severed their connexion with the political parties to which they had at one time belonged. During the past year a useful little weekly paper entitled *Women's Franchise* had been started by Mr. and Mrs. Francis as the joint organ of the various Suffrage Societies, and in the month of October, 1907, *Votes for Women,* the organ of the Women's Social and Political Union, was first issued as a monthy paper, by Mr. and Mrs. Pethick Lawrence. Our members at once volunteered to sell it in the streets, and were soon turning themselves into sandwich women and parading about with its contents bills slung from their shoulders, riding on horseback through Piccadilly with its posters hanging from the saddle, selling it from decorated busses and carriages, canvassing for subscribers and advertisers for it and evolving a hundred and one devices to increase its sale. As a result of these efforts both its size and circulation increased rapidly. In May, 1908, it became a penny weekly paper, and in the beginning of the year 1909 its circulation had risen to between 30,000 and 50,000 copies weekly, and it was handed over by Mr. and Mrs. Lawrence to the Union itself as a paying concern.

On October 5th a Woman's Suffrage procession was organised in Edinburgh by the Militant and Non-Militant Women's Suffragist Societies, and some four thousand women from all parts of Scotland assembled under the shadow of Arthur's Seat

Selling and advertising " Votes for Women " in Kingsway

and, cheered by upwards of a hundred thousand people who had gathered to see them, marched thence to the Synod Hall, where there was held a crowded demonstration which overflowed into the Pillar Hall.

Sir Henry Campbell-Bannerman was in Edinburgh at the time, and was asked to receive a deputation from the processionists, but, though this was backed by many influential Scotswomen, he refused. When on October 22nd, he spoke at Dunfermline, in his own constituency, the Premier was obliged, as Scotch " heckling " is a recognised institution, to reply to the questioning of women as well as of men. He was asked: " As the Prime Minister believes in Women's Suffrage, would he suggest some fresh methods which we could adopt in order to gain our enfranchisement? "

He replied: " I think women ought to go on agitating, holding meetings and pestering as much as they can, as all other men and women who are interested in public questions have to do." Whatever this piece of advice may have been intended to suggest, it certainly sounded very much like a justification of the policy of " pestering " members of the Government at their meetings.

For six months the Suffragettes had devoted themselves to strengthening and extending their organisation, electioneering, the distribution of literature and the holding of propaganda meetings of which, between May and October, some 3,000 had taken place, including a demonstration in Boggart Hole Clough, Manchester, attended by 15,000 people, another in Stevenson Square, Manchester, attended by 20,000 people, and meetings in Hyde Park each

Sunday at many of which the audiences had numbered upwards of 12,000. Nevertheless the question of Votes for Women, which had bulked so largely in the papers whilst the militant tactics had been in full swing, had almost entirely disappeared from the Press during these latter months and anyone who judged from the newspapers alone might well have imagined that the agitation had died down. This fact, together with the Government's continued refusal even to consider the question of granting Votes to Women, was enough, without the Prime Minister's curiously provocative statement, to convince the Suffragettes that the time had come to recommence an active militant campaign, and from this time onward a Cabinet Minister's Meeting was invaded on almost every day until Parliament met in the new year. Again and again members of our Union, with a courage and perseverance which too few people have ever recognised, presented themselves at these meetings, and, having asked their question or made their protest, were rudely set upon by crowds of stewards and flung fiercely and violently out into the street.

Many outsiders preferred to look upon the women who faced this violence as being harder and less sensitive or as differing in some other way from the rest of their sex, but this was not by any means the case. Many of those who bore the worst brunt of the battle were women who had hitherto taken no part in politics, and had always led quiet and sheltered lives. Others had had to fight hard for their livelihood. Indeed they were of all ages and of all classes. Week by week greater numbers of them were join-

ing the Union and coming forward to take a part in
this work; but young and old, rich and poor, were
treated in the same way.   Meanwhile Cabinet Ministers either expressed surprised and horrified disapproval of their behaviour or sought instead to
cover them with ridicule.   Mr. Sidney Buxton, at
his meeting at Poplar on October 12th cynically
called to his women questioners, whom the stewards
were maltreating, to " behave decorously like men."
That old self-styled " friend " of Women's Suffrage,
Mr. Haldane, addressing a meeting of women
Liberals in Glasgow on January 8, 1908, devoted
the greater part of his speech to condemning the
Suffragettes, saying that men did not like to be
fought with " pin pricks," and that, though women
might " wage war," he should advise them " not to
do it with bodkins."   At a meeting in his own constituency, shortly afterwards, he insisted that the
women who interrupted him should be ejected by the
police, and when finally, with bruised and aching
limbs and torn and dishevelled clothing, they had
all been thrown out of the hall, he treated the whole
matter as a joke saying that he was " bachelor-proof
against these belles."   Mr. Asquith, like the Prime
Minister, was forced to reply to a question put to
him in his own Scotch constituency, at Tayport, on
October 29th.   There he said that, if the vote were
granted to women it would do " more harm than
good," and that in any case, the House of Commons is not elected on a basis of Universal Suffrage,
for " children are not represented there."   At several meetings, notably those of Mr. Asquith at
Nuneaton on November 16th, and of Mr. Winston

Churchill in the historic Free Trade Hall, the stewards behaved with so much brutality that the police intervened to protect the women.

But though at these gatherings of Liberal partisans the women were usually flung outside without delay, there were still some occasions on which the audience rallied round them. Incidents of this kind occurred when Mr. Herbert Gladstone, now frequently nick-named " the prison Secretary," spoke in his constituency in Leeds on November 21st and 22nd. On the first night the audience prevented the ejection of women questioners, and on the second Mr. Gladstone was howled down by both men and women, and next morning the papers stated in startling headlines that the Home Secretary had been " put to flight." Mr. Lewis Harcourt, the first Commissioner of Works, had a similar experience in his constituency, the Rossendale Valley, on October 28th. During the day he declared to a deputation of women that he was opposed to their cause " because he was." At his evening meeting women protested again so vigorously and in such numbers that it was broken up, and his departing audience flocked to hear Mrs. Pankhurst, who was speaking from a waggon outside the hall. On November 22nd Mr. Lloyd George stated to a deputation of the Members of the old non-Militant Glasgow and West of Scotland Association for Women's Suffrage that votes could not be granted to women until the subject of their enfranchisement had been made a test question at a General Election, and disposed of the contention that this had already been done, because over four hundred Members of Parliament out of 670 returned at the last General Election had been pledged

to support Women's Suffrage, by saying that these
pledges did not count because they had not been
made to constituents. As unenfranchised women
were no man's constituents, Mr. Lloyd George, therefore, evidently saw no harm in the breaking of
promises that had been made to them, and he gave
no indication as to how, whilst neither political party
was prepared to put votes for women upon its
programme, women were to make their franchise a
test question at election times, except either by obtaining pledges from individual members or by at-
tacking the Government in power as the Suffragettes
were doing. He yet went on to say that he should
oppose " very strenuously any legislation that excluded any class of women from its scope, and any
measure to enfranchise women that would not give
to the working man's wife as much voice in the making of the laws of the country as her husband possessed." This meant, of course, that Mr. Lloyd
George would " strenuously oppose " the Women's
Enfranchisement Bill to give women the vote on the
same terms as those upon which it had already been
or might in the future be granted to men, but he did
not seem to realise that if he meant what he said and
wished to act with honesty, fairness and consistency
towards this great question, he ought strenuously to
oppose the status quo, which not only refused a
voice in the making of the laws which governed her
to the wife of the working man but to every other
woman beside.

On December 19th a strange drama was played
out in Aberdeen. The Liberal officials of the town,
had succeeded in inducing the Suffragettes to promise not to interrupt Mr. Asquith, if he would an-

swer the question of one woman, and they had begged Mrs. Black, the President of the local Women's Liberal Federation, to be the woman. Mrs. Black had agreed " in the interests of peace," as she said. When she rose up to comply with the Liberal official's request, however, she was howled at by their enthusiastic followers in the audience, threatened by the stewards of the meeting, and told by the chairman that she was " out of order," almost as though she had been a real Suffragette. Though at last she succeeded in putting her question, Mr. Asquith replied in snappish and hostile manner. Mr. Alexander Webster, a Unitarian Minister and well known citizen of Aberdeen, a slender, elderly figure, with long grey hair and the face of a saint, was afterwards violently handled for trying to move a women's suffrage rider to the official resolution. Finally Mrs. Pankhurst, who was seated at the back of the hall, rose to explain the situation to the curious and excited audience, and was immediately thrown out of the hall. Then the meeting broke up in disorder. As the *Aberdeen Free Press* put it, " Many a Liberal left the meeting with the uneasy feeling that the Suffragettes had had the best of it." Nevertheless the Suffragettes were loudly censured for these incidents especially by those who had consistently boycotted the Suffrage question when women had worked quietly for it in the old days. In reply to the critics Dr. George Cooper, an honest Radical and Member of Parliament for Bermondsey, in the course of a letter to the *Daily News* said:

My political life began as a member of the Reform League. It is within my recollection that in 1867 and also in 1884

very few public speakers who were opposed to the extension
of the Parliamentary franchise to men, whether members of
the Cabinet or otherwise, could utter a single word at a
public meeting. Meetings were broken up, platforms
stormed and their occupants had to escape the best way they
could. In 1884 every Tory speaker used against the extension of the franchise the same arguments now used by some
Liberal speakers and newspapers against the extension of the
Parliamentary franchise to women. . . . Why should
women be condemned for using the same weapons men
found so useful when demanding the vote for themselves?
. . . Cabinet Ministers do not recognise antagonists using
any other. There is one fact which cannot be denied. The
activity of the Suffragettes has lifted the Women's franchise
Bill out of the category of amusing and frivolous debate into
that of a serious political question.

Meanwhile the Suffragettes were fighting at two
more by-elections. The first of these was at Hull,
where polling took place on November 29th, the
result being that the Liberal vote was reduced from
8,652 to 5,623, and the Liberal majority from 2,247
to 241. The second of these contests, one of the
most striking at which the W. S. P. U. has ever
fought, was at Mid-Devon. In each of the seven
elections that had occurred in this constituency since
its creation in 1885 a Liberal candidate had been
returned, the majority on the last occasion having
numbered 1,289 votes. The Suffragettes at once
opened Committee Rooms in the main street of
Newton Abbott, the principal town in the division,
and published a manifesto calling upon every elector
who wished to see fair play for women to vote
against the Liberal candidate, and concluding " We
want votes for women this year. Defeat the Gov-

ernment in Mid-Devon as a message that women are to have votes in 1908."

The contest was a very trying one for the workers, for, in addition to the extensive area covered by the constituency, it took place in a season of heavy snow falls and bitter winds which came driving in from the sea. Besides this there was a most turbulent variety of human nature to contend with. The Mid-Devon Elections had always been notorious for their violent character and the roughs of Newton Abbott had long been a byword in the district. Early in the campaign the speakers representing both candidates were frequently howled down and were unable to continue their meetings, and, though on the whole we fared very much better, we ourselves had some similar experiences. On one occasion some of the Conservatives had arranged to speak at a place called Bovey Tracey, but they fled away on being told that the Liberals of the town were not only preparing to break up the meetings of their opponents but had even built a cage in which to imprison them. On the same day three young members of our Union had also appeared in Bovey Tracey. They too were warned of the terrible cage, but decided to hold their meetings in spite of it. All went well and they were told by the men who met to hear them that they had no desire to injure those who trusted them, and that the cage had only been built for cowards. On one occasion it happened that Mr. Buxton, the Liberal candidate, and the Suffragettes held simultaneous school-room meetings in the same village. The Liberal meetings had been advertised several days beforehand, but though ours was arranged on the spur of the moment,

all the people came to our meeting and not a single
person turned up to hear him.

As time went on the state of the district became
more and more turbulent and the great party newspapers, the London *Tribune, Daily News,* and others,
sought to stir up the wildest and most unrestrained
element in the constituency. The *Daily News*
hailed with enthusiasm the formation of what was
known as the " League of Young Liberals," which
was in reality a gang of young roughs whose first
act was to push a policeman through the plate glass
window of the shop which served as our Committee
Rooms. This and other violent acts were described
by the *Daily News* as " diverting incidents with the
Suffragettes," but the special correspondent of the
Daily Mail, said:

Miss Mary Gawthorpe, who usually has no difficulty in
maintaining good-humoured relations with audiences of every
class, was not only compelled to hear language from some of
the Newton Abbot Liberal partisans that brought a flush
to her face and tears into her eyes, but had to resist by
force the efforts of one man to mount the waggon from which
she and several other ladies were speaking. And the most
pitiful part of the business was that the language and the
conduct seemed to be regarded by their perpetrators as engaging little gallantries, appropriate to be offered to a lady.

A few days later the roughs dragged the lorry in
which our women were speaking round and round
with such violence that it was feared that it would
be overturned, and they only stopped when a little
boy had been run over and trampled upon and seriously injured. Still the Liberal politicians made
no protest. Mr. Buxton's reply to a newspaper cor-

respondent who asked him what he thought of the disorder was: " You must remember that they are keen politicians down here. From the fact that Mid-Devon has had three elections within the space of four years the people have necessarily heard a great deal about politics."

So the contest went on — Liberals and Conservatives smashing up each other's meetings, howling each other down, pelting each other with vegetables from the market and snowballing each other on Dartmoor. The *Daily Telegraph* for January 10th, writing in regard to a Liberal meeting, threatened that, if the Unionists were not admitted, the building would be stormed.

When on January 17th the poll was declared it was found that the Liberal candidate had been defeated. Everyone was surprised except the Suffragettes. The figures were:

        Captain Morrison Bell (U.)............ 5,191
        Mr. C. R. Buxton (L.)................ 4,632
                                           ─────
                Unionist majority............... 559

At the General Election the figures had been:

        Mr. H. T. Eve, K.C. (L.)............. 5,079
        Captain Morrison Bell (U.)........... 3,790
                                           ─────
                Liberal Majority............... 1,280

After the declaration of the poll Mrs. Pankhurst and Mrs. Martel, the only members of the Suffragette band left in the storm centre of Newton Abbott, saw Captain Morrison Bell escorted from the Market Square by a strong force of police, and were themselves urged to hurry away and leave the town at once. The warning seemed to them absurd, and Mrs. Pankhurst laughingly said that she had never yet been afraid to trust herself in a crowd. Immediately afterwards she and her companion met a procession of young men and boys wearing the Liberal colours, who were hurrying from their work in the clay pits. As soon as they heard that the Liberal had been defeated, one of them pointed to Mrs. Pankhurst and Mrs. Martel: "Those women have done it." Then the whole crowd of them started running and from somewhere or other there came a shower of rotten eggs. The two women were completely taken by surprise, and, more anxious to avoid the eggs than the angry crowd, they rushed into a grocer's shop, whilst a big brewer's drayman, who had been standing by jumped into the doorway and fought their assailants off until they were safe. The men and boys outside howled as their prey escaped them, and the people to whom the shop belonged, though anxious to protect the women, cried out despairingly that the windows would be broken in. Mrs. Pankhurst at once said that she could not bear to be the cause of loss to those who had sheltered her, and at her own request she and Mrs. Martel were led through a back door and across a yard leading to a narrow lane behind, whence it was thought that they would be able to escape. As soon as the door had been shut upon them, their assailants who had guessed their movements came rushing up. Mrs. Martel was seized by one who caught her by the throat and began to beat her about the head, but in a flash the shopkeeper's wife had heard the noise and had opened the door again and, somehow

or other, she and Mrs. Pankhurst had rescued Mrs.
Martel and had dragged her into the yard. The
door was shut and safely bolted in all haste, but just
as it closed, a man struck Mrs. Pankhurst a heavy
blow on the back of the head, and, as she staggered
on the threshold, pulled her back and she was left
outside. Then the men gave an angry shout, and
one of them, seizing her by the collar of her coat and
by her wrists, flung her to the ground. She caught
a glimpse of them all rushing on her, then for a time
she knew nothing until she felt the wet mud soaking
through her clothes. There was a pause. As she
lay there looking at them, she saw that they had all
closed round her in a ring, and that in the centre
was an empty barrel. " Are they going to put me
into it? " The thought flashed through her mind.
Hours seemed to pass as she watched them, all
dressed in drab-coloured clothes, smeared with yellow clay, and every one wearing a red Liberal
rosette. They all seemed to be puny half-grown
youths, and without knowing why she did so, she
asked, " Are there no men here? " For an instant
they still stood. Then one of them came forward,
and she felt that whatever was to be done to her was
about to begin, but suddenly there was a shout, and
the police came galloping up with a crowd of res-
cuers at their heels. Her assailants turned tail, and
she was lifted up and carried back through the yard
into the shop. A large force of police now surrounded the premises, but a great crowd had assembled, and it was two hours before a motor car
could be brought through it and the women were
able to get away. The disorder did not end here,
for the rowdies flocked thence to the Conserva-

tive Club, smashed every one of its windows, and kept its members besieged there all through the night. Next morning the body of Sergeant Major Rendall of the Royal Marines, an ex-Instructor of the Newton Abbot College, was found in the mill race. Foul play was suspected, as he had been severely bruised about the head. Throughout this violent disturbance not a single arrest was made. During the whole course of the election but one man was fined five shillings and costs for assaulting one of his political opponents. Well indeed might the Suffragettes say that the treatment meted out to them was very different from that extended to men who were fighting on the Government side.

As a result of the attack which had been made upon her, Mrs. Pankhurst was unable to walk for some considerable time, and her ankle was so severely injured that it gave her trouble for more than a year, whilst owing to the treatment she received Mrs. Martel will probably always bear a scar upon her neck. Scarcely a word of regret for the violence which had been done to these two women ever appeared in the Liberal newspapers, who were so largely to blame for what had occurred. After the election was over the Conservative politicians claimed that they alone had kept out the Liberal and the Liberals also preferred to attribute their defeat to the Tariff Reformers rather than to the Suffragettes. Only one of the Liberal newspapers, the *Manchester Guardian* admitted both during and after the election that the woman's question had played a decisive part. The Special Correspondent of this paper, in the issue of January 20th, said:

I think there can be no doubt that the Suffragettes did influence votes. Their activity, the interest shown in their meetings, the success of their persuasive methods in enlisting the popular sympathy, the large number of working women who acted with them as volunteers, these were features of the election which, although strangely ignored by most of the newspapers, must have struck most visitors to the constituency.

An amusing proof that the Liberals in the district had considered the Suffragettes to be very formidable opponents came to light in the following mock mourning card which had been got out in expectation of the Liberal victory.

In Fond and Loving Memory
of the
TARIFF REFORMERS AND SUFFRAGETTES
Who fell asleep at Mid-Devon on January 17th, 1908.

The Suffragettes and Tariff Reformers are now very sore,
And should see it's no use contesting Mid-Devon any more;
And the Hooligans of Shaldon you can send over and tell,
That a strong and Buxton Liberal has broken their Bell.

R.I.P.

Meanwhile the Suffragettes were fighting the Government at three other elections — at South Hereford (Ross), Worcester, and South Leeds. The result of the Poll at Ross was that the Liberal majority of 312 was turned into a Conservative majority of over 1,000. The figures were:

Captain Clive (U.)..................... 4,945
Mr. Whitely Thompson (L.).......... 3,928

Unionist majority............... 1,019

The figures at the general election had been:

Lieut.-Col. Alan C. Gardner (L.)....... 4,497
Capt. Percy A. Clive (U.).............. 4,185

Liberal majority................ 312

CHAPTER XI

THE THIRD WOMEN'S PARLIAMENT, AND MORE MILITANT TACTICS

Calls Upon Cabinet Ministers. The Third Women's Parliament. The Pantechnicon Van Stratagem. Mrs. Pankhurst's First Arrest. Mr. Dickinson's Bill, the First Albert Hall Meeting and the By-Election at Peckham.

Incidents in the Votes for Women campaign now followed each other with such rapidity that they defy the chronicler who wishes to note them down. Because vigorous militancy was the order of the day, the Press teemed with articles upon the abstract question of Votes for Women and with notices of the doings of the Suffragettes. "SUFFRAGETTES IN DOWNING STREET," "CABINET BAITING AS THE LATEST RUSE," "SUFFRAGETTES IN CHAINS." These and others of the same nature, were the startling headlines that one saw in the evening papers on January 17th and in the morning papers of the following day. It was merely that Mrs.. Drummond and a number of other members of our Union, knowing that the Cabinet was sitting to decide upon the questions which should find a place in the legislative programme of the forthcoming session had made an attempt to urge upon them the necessity of dealing with the women's claim.

Whilst Press representatives were congregating in Downing Street, to snapshot the Ministers and to gain material for foolish paragraphs describing their appearance and manner of arrival at the first Cabinet Council of the Season, and whilst police were assembling to dance attendance upon the Prime Minister and his colleagues, three or four of the Women appeared to demand an interview. The police pulled them aside and the Cabinet Ministers brushed past as they tried to speak, and when they applied at the door of the official residence, no notice was taken. Then Miss New, well knowing that her words would be heard both inside the House and by the crowd that was collecting in the street, began to make a speech explaining what she and her friends had come for. Before beginning, she chained herself to the railings beside the Prime Minister's front door, both symbolically to express the political bondage of womanhood, and for the very practical reason that this device would prevent her being dragged speedily away. Her example was followed by Nurse Olivia Smith and, whilst the police were struggling to break the double set of chains, a taxi-cab drove up and stopped on the opposite side of the street. Suspecting more Suffragettes, some of the constables rushed to the door of the cab which opened on to the pavement. At the same moment, Mrs. Drummond (for it was she who had devised this stratagem), opened the cab door on the road side and bounded across to the sacred Residence, where, as there was no one to bar her progress and as she now possessed the secret of the little knob in the centre of the door, she was inside and very near to the Council Chamber itself, before a number of men, some of whom she believed to be Cabinet Ministers, though owing to the violent and hurried nature of her ejection it was impossible to make quite sure, rushed upon her, and she was flung out and hurled· down the steps. She was then arrested, and shortly afterwards she and four of her comrades found themselves before Sir Albert de Rutzen at Bow Street Police Court, charged with disorderly conduct. They were found guilty and on refusing to be bound, were sent to prison for three weeks. Instead of placing them in the first division, as had been done in the case of all the Suffragettes since the transfer of Mrs. Cobden Sanderson and the rest of us had taken place in October, 1906, the authorities reverted to the old plan of putting them in the second class.

On January 29th the King opened Parliament in great state, and four members of the Women's Freedom League rushed in to the Royal Procession and attempted to present him with a Petition, but were dragged back and hustled aside by the soldiery and police. The King's speech did not contain any mention of Votes for Women, and the Women's Social and Political Union was already preparing to confer upon the subject at a Women's Parliament to be held in the Caxton Hall on February 11th, 12th, and 13th. In the meantime the Members of the Women's Freedom League had determined to make an immediate protest, and the day after the opening of Parliament they set out to interview six members of the Cabinet. Three of the ladies, Dr. Helen Bourchier, Mrs. Kennindale Cook, a well known novelist, and

Miss Munro, a Scotch woman from Sir Henry Campbell-Bannerman's constituency, visited Mr. Haldane at his house at Queen Anne's Gate at 9:30. They agreed with the butler to wait outside until Mr. Haldane could see them, but the Secretary of State for War telephoned to the police, who soon appeared in force and placed the women under arrest. The same sort of thing happened at the houses of Sir Edward Grey, Mr. Harcourt and Captain Sinclair. Altogether seven women were arrested and sentenced to terms of imprisonment varying from two to six weeks.

In the afternoon of the same day Mr. Asquith received a deputation from the National Union of Women's Suffrage Societies. He then definitely said that the Government would not introduce a Vote for Women measure on their own account and also refused to hold out any hope that the Government would allow of the passage of a private Member's Bill. As they left the Treasury offices the so-called "Constitutional" Suffragists agreed that Mr. Asquith's remarks would merely serve *to incite the Suffragettes to further militancy*.

They judged rightly, for the next day nine members of the Women's Freedom League called at Mr. Asquith's house at No. 20, Cavendish Square, and, on being refused an interview with him, decorated his area railings with "Votes for Women" banners and bills, and, using his topmost doorstep as a platform, proceeded to address a crowd of some seventy persons that had collected. Four arrests were the result. The women were brought up before Mr. Plowden at Marylebone Police Court and claimed the right to speak in their own defence, but Dr. Helen Bourchier, the first who uttered a word, was stopped by the would-be witty Mr. Plowden, who said rudely " Behave yourself! You are the bell-weather of the flock." He then declared all the women guilty of obstruction, and ordered them either to pay fines of forty shillings or to undergo one month's imprisonment in the Second Division, saying that he wanted them to understand that if they thought the punishment light, it was because it was all that the Law allowed him to give them, and adding " I do not consider it by any means a fair measure of your deserts."

Meanwhile the reversion to the policy of treating the Suffragettes as ordinary criminals instead of according to them the treatment usually meted out to political prisoners, was being raised in both Houses of Parliament. Earl Russell and others urged the government that " the blood of the martyrs is the seed of the Church," but the Government were deaf alike to appeal and warning.

The Women's Social and Political Union had long realised this, and when the third Women's Parliament met in the Caxton Hall on February 11th, 1908, it did so with all the splendid courage and enthusiasm for militant action that had characterised its predecessors. It was now known that an excellent place in the private Members ballot had been won, and on the Women's Bill, by Mr. Stanger, a Liberal, and it was realised that before February 28th, when the Bill was to come up for second reading, strong pressure must be brought to bear upon the Government to prevent this Bill being wrecked as that of Mr. Dickinson had been in the previous year. It was therefore with an added sense

of immediate pressing necessity that the women set
out unflinchingly for the old hard fight with overwhelming force. The motion to carry the usual
resolution to the Prime Minister was moved by Miss
Marie Naylor and Miss Florence Haig both London
Members of the Union and both Chelsea portrait
painters, and then the whole Hall seemed to rock
with the noise of the cheers as the majority of the
women present sprang up to form a deputation.

Meanwhile an extraordinary scene had taken place
close to the Strangers' Entrance to the House of
Commons. It had been anticipated, of course, that
the Suffragettes would make an attempt to lay their
Resolution before the Prime Minister and a great
force of Police was massed in readiness before the
House. Just about four o'clock as the long lines of
men in their dark-blue uniform waited there, two
furniture removal vans slowly approached, coming up
Victoria Street and round by the green which sur-
rounds the Abbey and St. Margaret's Church, as
though they were about to make their way past the
House of Commons and along Millbank towards the
Tate Gallery and Westminster Embankment. The
first van went slowly by the House, the second
crawled leisurely in its wake and along the back ledge
of the second van lay a sleepy-looking boy, his eyes
idly fixed upon a little man sauntering along the
pavement some distance away. Just as this van
was passing the Strangers' Entrance the little man
dropped a handkerchief, then suddenly the boy
sprang from the ledge, the back doors of the van
flew open wide, and one-and-twenty women plunged
out and made a rush for the House of Commons.
They were blinded by the broad daylight after their

long ride in the darkness of the van, and as they jumped, many of them fell on their knees and groping helplessly, ran the wrong way. Nevertheless there were some who headed straight for the door-way and two of them managed to get inside, only to be flung back instantly, whilst the police closed round and several arrests were made.

Meanwhile the body of women who had engaged to carry the Resolution to the Prime Minister, had emerged from the Caxton Hall, and having formed up four abreast in orderly procession, had begun to move quietly forward towards the House of Commons. Large crowds had gathered to see them whilst the police were drawn up on either side of the road, and at one point formed a line across the thoroughfare. The constables pushed and jostled the women for some time without altogether preventing their passage, but at Broad Sanctuary, a large contingent of police entirely blocked the way. Undaunted, the women pressed forward, and the crowds, some with the idea of helping the Suffragettes, others from curiosity, pressed forward too. The police charged again and again, and there was grave danger that someone would be trampled under foot. When at last the streets were cleared, it was found that some fifty women had been arrested, amongst these Miss Marie Naylor and Miss Florence Haig, Georgina and Marie Brackenbury, both of them painters, and nieces of General Sir Henry Brackenbury, and Miss Maud Joachim, niece of the great violinist.

The Suffragette cases came on next morning before Mr. Horace Smith at the Westminster Police Court, Mr. Muskett, who prosecuted on behalf of

the police, then announced that on this occasion
the authorities had decided as before to prosecute
under the Prevention of Crimes Amendment Act of
1885, which enabled the Magistrate to inflict a fine
of £5 or, in default, to order imprisonment with
or without hard labour for two months. Throwing down a remarkable challenge to the women, he
added that there were greater and stronger powers
in reserve which could be enforced to put down disorder, for there was still upon the Statute Book
an Act passed in the reign of Charles II which dealt
with " Tumultuous Petitions either to the Crown or
Parliament." He recalled the fact that it had
been stated by the judge at the time of the Lord
George Gordon riots that that Act was still good
law, and, he said, that the dictum still applied. The
Act of Charles II provided that

No person whatever shall repair to His Majesty or both
or either of the Houses of Parliament upon pretence of presenting or delivering any petition, complaint, remonstrance
or declaration or other address accompanied with an excessive number of people, nor at any one time with above the
number of twelve persons.

Penalties might be enforced under this Act up to
a fine of £100 or three months' imprisonment. In
holding forth this threat to women who might
demonstrate in the future, Mr. Muskett again appealed to the Magistrate to deal with those who
were now charged with all the rigour which he
would apply to ordinary law-breakers.

The prisoners were then one by one brought in.
Georgina Brackenbury, tall, fair, and well featured,
was the first to be put into the dock. The Magistrate affected to take scant interest in the case, and

in spite of her own splendid courtesy of manner, addressed her with pettish rudeness, and finally interrupted her statement with " That is all nonsense." The whole of the proceedings were conducted in the same spirit. But two women out of the fifty had been imprisoned before, and these two, Mrs. Rigby, the wife of a doctor in Preston, and Mrs. Titterington, as " old offenders," were ordered either to pay fines of £5 or to suffer one month's imprisonment in the third and lowest class. The other forty-seven women were ordered to be bound over in two sureties of £20 to keep the peace for twelve months or to serve six weeks' imprisonment in the second Division. With the exception of two, whose absence from home was found to be impossible owing to the serious illness of relatives, all the women chose imprisonment.

All these things were of course largely discussed in the Press. The furniture van incident attracted the greatest attention, and the van itself was likened by almost every newspaper to the wooden horse of Troy. The *Daily Chronicle* said:

> The Suffragettes are essentially heroic. First they lash themselves to the Premier's railings; now borrowing an idea from the Trojan horse, they burst forth from a pantechnicon van. . . . A high standard of artifice has been set and it should be maintained. The Trojan horse would have been of no use if it had remained outside the walls, and though curiosity could never be expected to prompt Members to drag a deserted pantechnicon into the House, there must be occasions when a large-sized packing case is taken into St. Stephen's.

The *Glasgow Evening Times* called for a poet of Hudibrastic gifts to rise and embody in heroic

verse the deeds of the Suffragettes, and asserted that
" The daring attack yesterday evening on that
citadel of democratic liberty, the House of Commons, is of itself sufficient to inspire a Homer, or
at least a Peter Pindar." The *Evening News* said
that until the Suffragettes had outwitted the policemen by the use of the furniture van, they had never
believed in the story of the Trojan horse, now they
knew it to be quite possible after all.

In the Women's Parliament it was the more serious side of the case that appealed to us. We saw
that the Government were preparing still further to
resist our just and moderate demands, and rather
than concede them were even ready to revive ancient coercive Statutes which the customs and principles of modern times had caused to fall into disuse.
This Act of Charles II, with which they had threatened us, had originally been passed to obstruct
the growth of the Liberal Party, which first
came into existence in Stuart times. It was the
political descendants of those very Liberals who
would now use this coercive Statute against their
countrywomen. Well might Christabel Pankhurst
ask in the Women's Parliament, " What would have
been said if a Tory Government had done this
thing ? " " This takes us back to stirring times,
ladies," she told the women. " At last it is realised
that women are fighting for freedom as their fathers
fought. . . . If they want twelve women, aye,
and more than twelve, if a hundred women are
wanted to be tried under that Act and to be sent
to prison for three months they can be found."

There was no militant demonstration on that day,
but everyone knew that something more was to

happen, and on Thursday afternoon, the 13th of February, when the Women's Parliament met for its concluding session, a feeling of most extraordinary excitement prevailed. Mrs. Pankhurst had just returned from the by-election at South Leeds, and the audience listened eagerly to her account of the campaign, and especially to the story of the torchlight procession and the wonderful meeting of 100,000 people on Hunslett Moor. In spite of the fact that police protection had been refused at the last moment, there had been no disorder, only sympathy and enthusiasm all along the route, whilst the vast crowds that parted to let the procession through had joined on to it and added to its numbers from behind, and some of the women had constantly called out in broad Yorkshire: "Shall us have the vote?" to be answered by others with cries of "we shall."

I have come to London, Mrs. Pankhurst concluded, feeling, as I have never felt before, the seriousness of this struggle. I feel that the time has come when I must act, and I wish to volunteer to be one of those to carry our Resolution to Parliament this afternoon. My experience in the country and especially in South Leeds has taught me things that Cabinet Ministers who have not that experience do not know, and has made me feel that I must make one final attempt to see them and to urge them to reconsider their position before some terrible disaster has occurred.

Then, amid some emotional excitement and cries of "Mrs Pankhurst must not go," "We cannot spare our leader"— cries which were calmly set aside by practical business-like Christabel, who announced that the deputation was definitely chosen and that its thirteen members were all prepared to be arrested and tried under the Charles II Act — the

Resolution was carried and Mrs. Pankhurst, Annie
Kenney, and eleven other women marched out of
the hall, whilst almost the whole of the audience
flocked into the corridor and stood around the doorway to watch them go.

Mrs. Pankhurst had been lamed in the cowardly
attack that had been made upon her at Mid-Devon,
and had not yet recovered. Seeing this Mrs. Drummond ran forward to get a conveyance. She saw
none for hire, but called to a man in a private dog-
cart and asked him if he would drive Mrs. Pankhurst to the House of Commons. He agreed, and
the other women formed up on foot behind the
vehicle two and two abreast. The police were already massed around in great force and the little
procession had moved but a few slow steps when
a Police Inspector came forward and insisted that
Mrs. Pankhurst should dismount. She instantly
obeyed the order, signing to her companions not to
protest. The twelve women of the deputation at
the same time hurried forward to re-form in double
line behind their leader, but the Inspector and his
men dragged them apart. Then the deputation,
hemmed in by men, women and police on every side,
proceeded in single file as far as Chapel Street.
There the Inspector said they must not walk in procession. They therefore broke into twos and threes,
but when they came to the entrance of Victoria
Street the police entirely barred the way, and it was
only after a considerable struggle that they were
able to gain the main thoroughfare. There a
vast concourse of people had assembled and right
in the midst of it one saw Mrs. Pankhurst wearing a long loose cloak whose light grey colour

made her figure stand out from the darkly clad men around. She came forward with Mrs. Baldock clinging to her arm, and tall, pretty, smiling young Gladice Keevil, her face a little flushed and her soft hair blowing a little in the wind, walking on the other side, and with the great crowd following and filling the whole street around.

Scattered amongst the people behind and moving forward either singly or in twos, the rest of the deputation followed. Close to Westminster Palace Hotel Mrs. Pankhurst, who up to this point had followed in the wake of a Police Inspector and carefully obeyed all the instructions of the police, was arrested and taken through Parliament Square on the side furthest from the House in the strong grip of two burly policemen. Clad in her heavy travelling cloak, her face had grown white with exhaustion, and she was evidently in pain, but no heed was paid to her lameness, and she was hurried along at a brisk trot, and at last disappeared down the narrow lane at the top of Bridge Street which leads to Canon Row Police Station. Mrs. Baldock and Gladice Keevil, who had refused to leave her, had for this cause been arrested and almost immediately afterwards Annie Kenney was also taken into custody. Later on the same fate befell Mrs. Kerwood of Birmingham and five others, some of whom were not members of the deputation.

Whilst this was happening, the Women's Parliament was still in session, and every now and then someone returned from the battle to describe how events were going. Before the meeting closed our ever thoughtful Treasurer, Mrs. Pethick Lawrence, urged all not on the fighting line to subscribe to the

Mrs. Pankhurst carrying a petition from the Third Women's Parliament to the Prime Minister on February 13th, 1908

war chest. More than £400 had been raised when the prisoners came back to us on bail at the rising of Parliament.

In the House of Commons itself the Government's hostile attitude towards the Suffragettes was raised as a matter of urgency on the motion for the adjournment, by Sir William Bull, the Unionist member for Hammersmith, who showed genuine concern at the news of Mrs. Pankhurst's arrest. Other members of the same Party followed by jeering at the Government for the marked difference between their treatment of the Suffragist women and the men who had been arrested for cattle driving and similar offences in Ireland. Why was Mr. Ginnell, the Nationalist Member for Westmeath, to receive the privileges of a first class misdemeanant, they asked, whilst Mrs. Pankhurst and her comrades were to be treated as ordinary criminals. Lord Robert Cecil raised a laugh against the President of the Local Government Board, by pointing out that when he, Mr. John Burns, had been in prison for inciting to riot, the Government of the day had intervened to secure preferential treatment for him. In reply to all this Mr. Gladstone refused to take any action, saying that the women could come out of prison whenever they liked.

When Mrs. Pankhurst and her comrades were brought up at Westminster Police Court before Mr. Horace Smith, next day, it was found that the authorities, who were perhaps disappointed at the way in which their challenge had been accepted, had changed their minds and instead of prosecuting the women as they had threatened under the Charles II Act, had decided to revert to the old method of stigmatising the whole affair as a mere vulgar brawl with the Police. Probably thinking the true facts would arouse too much public sympathy, the prosecution put forward as evidence an absolute tissue of falsehood, in which it was stated that the deputation had set out from the Caxton Hall singing and shouting in the noisest manner and that they had knocked off the helmets of the police and had assaulted them right and left. As we have seen everything had been done most quietly, and Mrs. Pankhurst herself had carefully complied with every order from the police short of abandoning her intention to reach the House of Commons. Our rebutting evidence was disregarded and Mrs. Pankhurst's own statement in the dock was cut short by Mr. Horace Smith's saying, " I have nothing to do with that. It only amounts to another threat to break the law, and it is in no way relevant here. You, like the others, must find sureties in £20 for twelve months' good behaviour or be imprisoned for six weeks in the Second Division."

Then as usual the women were hurried off in the van to prison, the Holloway gates were closed upon them, and the Government settled down to forget them as far as it could until next time.

February 28th was the day for the discussion of the Women's Enfranchisement Bill, in moving its second reading, Mr. H. Y. Stanger, whilst he carefully dissociated himself from the methods of the Suffragettes, reminded the House that, if in the course of a political agitation, excesses were committed, the authorities should search for the cause of the discontent and apply an appropriate remedy. Mr. Cathcart Wason, another Liberal member, but

an anti-Suffragist, declared on the other hand that
the Suffragette movement was founded on riot, and
that the House should not " yield to clamour "; yet
with an entire lack of consistency, he went on to
extol physical force, saying that because in his opinion women could make no contribution to this, they
ought not to be allowed to vote. Evidently he forgot that, whilst the whole trend of civilisation has
been in the direction of mental rather than physical
dominance, in the age when physical force was the
governing power, women were actually members of
the legislature and, that they retained the right to
vote for Members of Parliament throughout the
ages when its possession was looked upon as a burden
and until, having become a privilege, it was wrested
from them. But all this talk was mere word spinning. It was a pronouncement from the Government
benches, that was eagerly awaited. As last time,
it was Mr. Herbert Gladstone who spoke, and for
the Ministry, and he soon disclosed the fact that the
Government was still determined to make no move.
It was the old story of opposition in the Cabinet and
the old excuse that no party in the House was united
either for or against the question. As for the Bill
he himself intended to vote for it, for, he said, making an important admission which his colleagues
might well have taken to heart, " It may be im-
perfect, but at any rate *it removes a disqualification
and an inequality which have been for so long a deep
source of complaint with great masses of the people
of this country.*" Then Mr. Gladstone went on to
make some very remarkable statements, of which
both he and the Government were afterwards to be
reminded. He said amongst other things:

Men have had to struggle for centuries for their political rights. . . . On the question of Women's Suffrage, experience shows that predominance of argument alone — and I believe that that has been attained — is not enough to win the political day.

In any reform movement, he went on to explain, various stages had to be gone through; first there was the stage of " academic discussion," and the ventilation of " pious opinions " unaccompanied by " effective action," but after this, he continued, becoming perhaps a little carried away by his own words;

Comes the time when political dynamics are far more important than political argument. You have to move a great inert mass of opinion which, in the early stages, always exists in the country in regard to questions of the first magnitude. . . . Men have learned this lesson and know the necessity for demonstrating the greatness of their movement and for establishing that *force majeure* which actuates and arms a Government for effective work. That is the task before the supporters of this great movement. . . . Looking back at the great political crises in the thirties, the sixties and the eighties, it will be found that people did not go about in small crowds, nor were they content with enthusiastic meetings in large halls; they assembled in their tens of thousands all over the country.

" But," said Mr. Gladstone, " of course it is not to be expected that women can assemble in such masses," but, " power belongs to the masses and through this power a Government can be influenced into more effective action than a Government will be likely to take under present conditions."

Mr. Rees (Liberal) then made an attempt to talk out this Bill as he had done that of Mr. Dickinson

the year before, and, after firing off all the jokes that
he could think of, he fell back upon the Scriptures,
saying, " Jerusalem is ruined and Judah has fallen.
As for my people, children are their oppressors and
women   rule   over   them. . . . Because   the
daughters of Zion are haughty and walk with
stretched-forth necks, therefore the Lord will smite
with a scab the crown of the head of the daughters
of Zion and in that day the Lord will take away
the bravery of their tinkling ornaments."

But at this point he was interrupted by Lord Robert Cecil who moved the closure of the debate, and,
on the Speaker's accepting the motion and its being
agreed to without a division, a vote was taken upon
the Bill itself, in which 271 members voted for the
Bill and only ninety-two against. There was therefore a favourable majority of 179, the largest that
had ever been cast in support of Women's Suffrage.

Unfortunately it now appeared that Mr. Stanger
had been informed beforehand that the closure resolution, which would prevent the talking out of the
Bill, would only be accepted on condition that he,
as the Bill's sponsor, would move that it be referred
to a Committee of the whole House instead of passing automatically to one of the Grand Committees.
Mr. Stanger had agreed to the condition and now
fulfiled the promise that had been exacted, and the
result was that nothing further could be done with
the Bill unless the Government would provide time
for its discussion.

Had the Cabinet been prepared to act honourably
and to stand by the statement of their spokesman,
Mr. Gladstone, the position would now have been
that, if the women who wanted votes could organise

a series of demonstrations which could compare with those held by men in support of the various extensions of the franchise that had already taken place, the Government would concede their demands and would either provide time for the passage into law of Mr. Stanger's Bill or introduce and put through its various stages a measure of their own framing. The Women's Social and Political Union were prepared to accept Mr. Gladstone's challenge.

When Mrs. Pankhurst and the other women had gone to prison, their comrades of the W. S. P. U., at Mrs. Pethick Lawrence's suggestion, had entered upon a week of self-denial in order to raise funds for the campaign. The thought of those who were in prison spurred on every member of the Union to renewed zeal. Some went canvassing from house to house for money. Others stood with collecting boxes at regular pitches in the street. At the Kensington High Street District Railway Station, for instance, four well known women writers, Miss Evelyn Sharpe, Miss May Sinclair, Miss Violet Hunt, and Miss Clemence Housman, were gathering in pennies all through those wintry days. Some women sold flowers, swept crossings, became pavement artists and played barrel organs. Poorer members obliged to work continuously for a living, denied themselves sugar and milk in their tea, butter on their bread, and walked to and from their work, in order to be able to give something to the funds. The result of this week of earnest effort was to be announced at a great meeting at the Albert Hall on March 19th, to advertise which a great box kite, with a flag attached, was hanging over the Houses of Parliament for a fortnight, whilst a similar flag floated over Holloway Gaol to cheer the prisoners within.

Every seat in the great Albert Hall was sold long before the day of the meeting, and hundreds of people were turned away at the doors. The vast audience was composed almost entirely of women, and there were 200 women stewards in white dresses. The platform was decorated with flowers and thronged with ex-prisoners and the officials of the Union, but as the sentences of Mrs. Pankhurst and eight of her comrades were not to expire until the following morning, the Chairman's seat which the founder of the Union should have occupied, was left vacant and in it was placed a large white card bearing the inscription " Mrs. Pankhurst's chair."

Throughout that great gathering there was a wonderful spirit of unity and not one woman there could wish in her heart, as so many millions have done, " if I had only been a man." No, they were rather like to pity those who were not women and so could not join in this great fight, for to-day it was the woman's battle. The time was gone when she must always play a minor part, applauding, ministering, comforting, performing useful functions if you will, incurring risks, too, and making sacrifices, but always being treated and always thinking of herself as a mere incident of the struggle outside the wide main stream of life. To-day this battle of theirs seemed to the women to be the greatest in the world, all other conflicts appeared minor to it. A great wave of enthusiasm had caught them up and they were ready to break out into cheers and clapping at the least excuse. Fate, in the person of the Government, had provided an incident entirely in keeping with their mood, for Christabel immediately announced that Mrs. Pankhurst and the remaining prisoners had been unexpectedly released, and Mrs. Pankhurst herself walked quietly on to the platform to take possession of the vacant chair.

Then it was a wonderful sight to see the up-springing of those thousands of women from those rows and rows of seats and tiers and tiers of boxes and galleries sloping to the roof of the great circular hall. There was a sea of waving arms and handkerchiefs and a long chorus of cheers,— with no greater welcome could any leader have been met. The founder of the Union stood there quite still in her dark grey dress, and her face, usually pale, had that strangely blanched look, which comes to prisoners. When, as the applause subsided, she stepped forward to speak to the assembled women, it was evident that she was deeply moved by their greeting, and as she told how the chief wardress had come to her cell at two o'clock that afternoon to tell her that an order had come for her immediate release, one felt that she was very tired and almost overwhelmed by the sharp contrast between that great brightly lighted hall, with its vast seething throng of human beings, and the still silence of the prison cell. She had heard, she told the women,—" for these things filter even into prison "— that the Bill had successfully passed its second reading, but she said, and all present knew that she spoke rightly, that if ever the Bill were to become an Act, women must do ten times more yet than they had ever done in the past.

" I for one, friends," Mrs. Pankhurst cried, and we knew that she was thinking of the women she

had seen in prison, " I for one, looking round on
the sweated and decrepit members of my sex, say
that men have had control of these things long
enough and that no woman with any spark of
womanliness in her will consent to allow this state of
things to go on any longer. We are tired of it, we
want to be of use and to have the power to make
the world a better place both for men and women
than it is to-day. She paused then and went on to
express quietly but with deep feeling her joy in this
great woman's movement that a few years before
she had thought she would never live to see. The
old cry had been, " You will never rouse women," but
she said, " we have done what they thought, and
what they hoped, to be impossible; we women are
roused." At those words they stopped her with their
cheers.

Then Annie Kenney rose to tell the story of her
first and only other visit to the Royal Albert Hall,
when she had gone there to ask of the newly elected
and triumphant Liberal Ministry, a pledge for the enfranchisement of her sex. That night, two years
before, she had been received with cries of abuse and
howled down by an audience of angry men. " There
seemed to be thousands against one," she said, " but
I did not mind because I knew that our action that
night was like summer rain on a drooping flower; it
would give new life to the woman's movement."

And now Mrs. Pethick Lawrence, our Treasurer,
was to come forward to give yet one more proof
that Annie Kenney's words were true. When the
treasurer had imagined that Mrs. Pankhurst's chair
was to be an empty one, she had planned that those
present should place in it an offering of money for

the cause, but now she would be able to place that offering in the founder's hands. Towards the sum that was collected there was already the £2,382 11s. 7d, which had been raised by the devotion and sacrifice of members of the Union during the week of self denial; a promise of £1,000 a year till women were enfranchised, from a lady who wished to remain anonymous, and a second £1,000 which Mrs. Lawrence herself, in conjunction with her husband, wished to give. And now it was for the audience to do their part.

Whilst the treasurer had been speaking, Mr. Lawrence had been arranging a scoring apparatus. Then, one by one, twelve women rose up in the hall and each promised to give £100. Their example was followed by numbers of others. At the same time, promise cards, filled up by members of the audience, were constantly being handed to the platform, where Mrs. Lawrence read them out. At last the sum of £7,000 had been set up, and, with a stirring call from Christabel to work at the by-elections at Peckham and Hastings in which the Union was then engaging, the meeting closed.

As it was in London, the Peckham election was of course most noticed by the Press and, because it was so near its headquarters, the Women's Social and Political Union was able to put up the biggest fight there.

On Peckham Rye, a stretch of common land where hosts of preachers and speakers of all kinds are to be heard on every holiday, each of the parties in the election, including the Suffragettes, began by holding a meeting on the first Sunday of the contest. There was a good deal of rather dangerous horse-

play which ominously recalled the Mid-Devon election, the Suffragettes being chief target of the
disturbers. But before many days were over the situation had entirely changed. Peckham, as every
Londoner knows, is one of that great forest of sub-
urbs of mushroom growth on the south side of the
river. Its miles and miles of dingy streets are lined
with monotonous rows of ugly little houses which the
jerry builder tries to convert into villa residences
by disfiguring with heavy over-ornamented stone
work and by planting a useless pillar on either side
of the narrow doorway. A large proportion of
these little dwellings are tenanted by at least two
families, and the district is given over to small shop-
keepers and clerks, shop assistants, teachers and those
who belong more frankly to the working classes.
No one who can afford to live elsewhere chooses
to live in Peckham; it is full of honest worthy people, but there is nothing romantic or attractive about
it.

The Suffragettes opened their Committee Rooms
in the High Street and soon seemed to be everywhere. They were riding up and down on the noisy
electric tram cars and dashing along Rye Lane,
where the cheap shops are and where on Saturday
nights you can buy everything for half the usual
price at the costermongers' stalls, chalking the pavements, giving out handbills, and speaking at the street
corners, and soon it was found that these busy, active
women had not only converted almost everyone in the
district to the justice of their claims, but had captured the heart of the constituency. How had it
happened? Partly, it may be, because of the romance and colour that they had brought into the

humdrum Peckham life, but perhaps the following impressions of " An Enthusiast " which appeared in the *Daily Mail* in the midst of the election will best explain the mystery:

Three happy girls, eyes laughter-lit, breezy, buoyant, joyous, arm in arm, talking like three cascades, are making a royal progress down " the lane that leads to Rye." Such is the head of the comet. Just a glance at the tail. A heterogeneous nebula of human life — all ranks and ages, both sexes and all professions, following, jostling, bustling, hustling. Miss Christabel Pankhurst shakes herself free from one of her supporters, and takes under her wing a barefoot, ragged urchin, whose eyes are dancing with glee and pride, for his pals are envious. Who is he that that gloved hand should rest caressingly upon his shoulder? The girl and the gamin trudge along together. " Oh, ain't she just sweet? " says a factory girl, " and fancy 'er abeen to prison! " " Carn't she tork — my word? " chimes in her mate. " Why, she just shut up them blokes as arsked the questions just like a man, she did! "

Her magnetism lies in her complexity, her bafflingness, her buoyance, her radiant health, her colouring — that of the inside of a seashell. She is so every inch alive — the very exuberance of life, body and mind. Not the racked intensity that comes of nerves high strung and over-active brain, but just that finger-tip aliveness which comes of perfect health and perfect happiness in engrossing occupation.

This girl orator and organiser, martyr and crusader, holds and sways her crowds by a very network of antithesis, and her rosy face is the index of her complexity. Defiance chases demureness; she flings a madcap word and then lectures you like a schoolmistress.

One moment reticent, grave, and serious, then simmering with mischief, as she lays a Cabinet Minister or a man in the crowd safely upon his back — O rash questioner! Then her wilfulness — that puckered chin tells a tale — yet her

willingness to listen and to learn. Her melting, compre-
hending sympathy for the sorrowful and heavy-laden — her
rapier wit and repartee, but ever smothered in the white
sugar of good humour. All these you see — some, when
sitting in the background of the trolly, she seeks to hide
from the public stare, which she shrinks from with a maid-
en's modesty when not actually engaged in speaking —
others, when with lissome figure swaying, in rhythmic sympathy with the outpouring words, she fastens her mind and
yours upon the point at issue.

And then her unconscious petulance. That green veil of
hers tied under her chin that would for ever get awry.
Yes, she is very, very feminine, and that is what will win
the vote for women.

With a voice that never tires (nor ever tires the listener),
she is born to charm the ear with an ebb and flow of sweet
sound — sound so clear, so silver, so bell-like, now rising,
now falling, now rushing and tumultuous, now measured
and tempered and austere — earnest and grave — impetuous,
a very volley, ardent, burning, scathing, denunciatory —
then sinking to appeal to low notes and something near to
sadness.

Shall I speak of her logic? It is inexorable. It is not on
mere smart retort that she depends when heckled — she has
a good case and relies on it. She is saturated with facts,
and the hecklers find themselves heckled, twitted, tripped,
floored. I think they like it. She does, and shows it. She
flings herself into the fray, and literally pants for the next
question to tear to shreds. Her questioners are for the most
part earthenware, and this bit of porcelain does them in the
eye, quaintly, daintily, intellectually, glibly.

Look to it, Mr. Gautrey, or the witchery of Christabel
will " do you in the eye."

No, the electors of Peckham agreed, these Suffragettes were not the sort of women they had read of.
They were neither the " disorderly," " shouting,"

" abusive," " unsexed," " violent " creatures, nor the " soured," " dry," and " disappointed " women they had been led to expect.

It was not merely the " enthusiast " in the *Daily Mail* who testified to the work that the Suffragettes were doing. Conservative newspapers, though they generally preferred to ignore the Suffragettes because, though opposing the Government, they were not supporting either the Conservative candidates or their proposals, nevertheless they allowed some of the truths that the special correspondent told them about the women's campaign to filter into their columns.

The *Standard* said: " These women are prepared to kill themselves with fatigue and exposure, not for the vote but for what the vote means." The *By-Stander* said: " The ladies' tongues have been tireless and their brains inexhaustible. Of all the assembled bodies, and their name was legion, who thronged Peckham, theirs has been the most persistent." The *Pall Mall Gazette* said: " Everybody seems agreed that the best speeches in the election are being made by the lady Suffragists," whilst the *Daily Mail* asserted that " in no contest have the Suffragettes figured so largely or done such harm to the Radical candidate."

There is a type of man who will sometimes ask a woman's advice about politics and may even admit that she is not only a better speaker than he is but knows more about public questions than he will ever know, and who yet thinks it quite tolerable that she should be forever debarred from voting, though he has had that privilege since he was twenty-one. Men of this type are usually great followers of Party, and allow their ideas of right and wrong in politics to be almost entirely dictated by the actions of the very fallible gentlemen who happen to be their Party leaders. Liberals of this type, whether editors of newspapers, journalists, Members of Parliament, or merely rank and file, had always condemned the Suffragettes because the Liberal party happened to be attacked by them.

The Suffragette opposition at Peckham caused them to be more indignant than ever, for Peckham was a Liberal seat that had been held at the last election by the great majority of 2,339 votes, and if this big majority were to be pulled down they feared that the House of Lords would be emboldened to throw out the Government's Licensing Bill which was then being debated in Parliament. It was true that, though the Liberals now spoke of this Bill as being of paramount importance, they had themselves been just as keen upon a host of other questions and had over and over again before this called upon the Suffragettes to stand aside and refrain from pressing their claim at what on each occasion they assured them was *the crisis* of all crises. First it had been that the Liberal Government might come safely into power that they had charged the women to wait, then that Free Trade might be put out of danger, then for the passage of the Education Bill, the Plural Voting Bill and every measure put forward. In every case they assumed that the proposal advanced by the Liberal Cabinet was the only possible solution of the problem and in spite of the differences of opinion amongst men, they maintained that no right-minded woman could conscientiously wish for any other.

When it came to the question of the Licensing Bill, the Liberal politicians declared that the sole issue of the election was between the Licensing Bill on the one hand and intemperance on the other. This was absurd, for if the Liberals wished to be rid of the Suffragette opposition, they had only to remove their veto from the Woman's Bill.

On the morning after their release from Holloway, Mrs. Pankhurst and the other ex-prisoners drove off to Peckham in brakes and paraded the constituency holding meetings at various points, and worked there incessantly until the end. A procession of their own ex-prisoners was also organised by the Suffragettes of the Women's Freedom League who were also helping to fight the Government in this election. The Liberals retorted by displaying a big stocking, blue, the Peckham Liberals colour, labelled, " since my wife turned Suffragette I can't get my stockings darned! " but this fell very flat. On polling day the *Star* showed its belief in the strong influence which women were exerting in the election, by making its final appeal on behalf of the Government candidate, not to the men voters but to the women of Peckham. The Suffragettes were stationed at every polling booth, and, as the voters passed in, many of those who had hitherto voted for the Liberal party handed their colours and polling cards to the women with a promise to vote against the Government on this occasion. On seeing this one of the Liberal officials became so angry that he threatened to prosecute a member of the Freedom League under the Corrupt Practices Act.

In the evening after the poll closed, Mrs. Drummond, upon whom the organisation of the Suffra-

gettes' campaign had chiefly fallen, and who had
been too busy all day even to get a meal, repaired
to the Town Hall where the votes were being
counted. As she stood waiting on the steps, weariness showing at last in every line of her bonnie round
face and sturdy little figure, the door-keeper, invited
her to rest in the entrance hall until the result was
known. Presently she heard a loud burst of shouting, and a number of men, in the midst of whom was
Mr. Winston Churchill, came running down the
stairs from the count. She started up, eager to learn
the news, but was swept out into the street in the
midst of those who were impetuously rushing on. At
that moment there flared out a magnesium light —
red, the Conservative colour. It was known that
the Government candidate had been defeated,[1] and
the huge crowd outside broke into cheers. Mr.
Churchill was pushed about like anyone else, and
had to work his way out of the throng, but the working men seeing Mrs. Drummond there, a worker
like themselves, who had been labouring strenuously
amongst them during the past week, and whom they
all thoroughly respected, crowded round her cheering, and as her husband's constituents did to little
Scotch Maggie in Mr. Barrie's play " What Every
Woman Knows," they lifted her shoulder-high, and
bore her in triumph down the street. But Mrs.

---

[1] The figures were Mr. C. A. Gooch (C)............. 6,970
Mr. T. Gautrey (L).............. 4,476

Majority............... 2,494

The figures at the General Election had been:
Mr. Charles G. Clarke (L)........ 5,903
Sir F. G. Banbury (C)........... 3,564

Drummond felt exceedingly uncomfortable in this exalted state, and, asking to be released, hurriedly sped away.

Now that their late majority of 2,339 had been turned into a majority for the Conservatives of 2,494, the Liberals proceeded to heap abuse upon the electors and to assert that the contest had been disgraced by unprecedented corruption and insobriety. But the experience of the Suffragettes was that the election was one of the most sober and orderly that they had ever attended, and their feeling was that the defeat of the Liberal candidate was very much more largely due to the Government's refusal to grant votes to women and to its coercive treatment of the women's movement than to any other cause. This opinion was shared by many others. Dr. Robert Esler, the Divisional Surgeon for Peckham, wrote to the *Daily Telegraph* as follows:

Sir:

The statement was advanced several times that the new member was floated into the House on beer. . . . Lest others should infer from the words that the electors constitute a drunken community, may I, being in a position to know the facts, indicate them. . . . During the ten days of intense tension in canvassing and speaking, there was literally no insobriety. . . . The charges at the police station fell much below the usual low average, . . . and there was not a single assault case. . . . In my opinion a high moral tone was imparted at the beginning by the presence on the Rye of the ladies who took part in the proceedings. Their dignified demeanour and cultured oratory made a profound impression, and I think this should not be overlooked when considering the result.

Mr. St. John G. Ervine wrote to the Liberal organ, *The Nation,* on March 28th, saying:

There is not a man in the National Liberal Club to-day who does not know that Mid-Devon was lost to the Liberals because of the adverse action of the militant suffragists, a fact which was patent even to the rowdy mob who rolled Mrs. Pankhurst in the mud when the result of that poll was declared. There is not a Liberal member to-day who does not dread the prospect of a General Election with the absolute certainty that he will have to fight, not only the usual enemy, but also a very determined body, which, at the present time, has no political creed other than that expressed in the three words "Votes for Women." I am wrong, there is one man who does not seem to realise all this, to whom Mid-Devon was not a warning, to whom Peckham will convey no sign of further trouble, the Premier elect, Mr. Asquith. . . . This Peckham election has been a revelation to me of the perfectly wonderful forces which the Women's Social and Political union are bringing to bear on by-elections. . . . As a purely impartial observer of the Peckham election I submit to you, Sir, and to the Liberal party, that it is time they started doing something for the women. The mandate might not have been there in 1906, but it most certainly is there now.

Mr. Gooch, the successful candidate, stated: "A great feature of this election has been the activity of the supporters of women's suffrage." And even the *Daily News,* which published a correspondence from its readers dealing with the Liberal defeat at Peckham, stated in its issue of March 31st, that the majority of the letters received referred to the action taken by the Suffragettes.

CHAPTER XII

APRIL AND MAY, 1908

Mr. Asquith Becomes Prime Minister. Defeat of
Mr. Winston Churchill in North West Man-
chester and His Election at Dundee; Mr.
Asquith's Offer and the Women's Reply.

Owing to Sir Henry Campbell-Bannerman's continued illness, Mr. Asquith had been acting as his
deputy for many months past, and the Easter Holidays were scarcely over when it was announced that
he had become Prime Minister in fact, for the state
of Sir Henry's health had compelled him to resign.
The Ex-Premier did not live long afterwards.
Though he had been converted to Women's Suffrage
late in life when his fighting powers were always
seriously impaired, there is little doubt that he spoke
truly when he declared his disappointment at not being able to do anything for the Suffragists when they
waited upon him in deputation on the 19th of May,
1906; and, if ever the secret history of the Government during that time comes to be written, we shall
probably learn that, had he possessed the strength
to enforce his will upon his colleagues, votes would
have been granted to women that very year. Once
when Annie Kenney and Mary Gawthorpe were travelling with Mr. and Mrs. Pethick Lawrence to Bor-
dighera, Sir Henry Campbell-Bannerman and they
chanced to enter the same train and afterwards Sir

Henry happened to seat himself at the very table where Annie and Mary were taking tea. They at once introduced themselves to him and all three had a long talk together in the course of which Annie naïvely assured him, " You have no one in the Cabinet so clever as Miss Christabel Pankhurst." Other things, too, she must have told him out of her loyal, earnest heart for, as she explained to us later, " he looked *so* much happier afterwards," and we have been told by some who knew him that, when criticisms of the Suffragettes were subsequently made in his hearing, he would invariably protest, " Oh, you must not say anything against my little friend, Annie Kenney."

Mr. Asquith who had come to take his place, was a man of very different metal. He was one whom nobody seemed to like and the only reason for his having become Prime Minister appeared to be that he had the reputation of being what is *called* " a strong man," and what generally turns out to *be* an obstinate one. It was a significant fact that it was whilst he had held the reins of power during Sir Henry Campbell-Bannerman's illness, that the practice of treating the Suffragettes as first class misdemeanants had been abandoned. On the promotion of Mr. Asquith, a general move up to better paid and more important posts took place in the Cabinet. According to the Constitutional Law of the country, the newcomers into the Cabinet were obliged to vacate their seats and to offer themselves for reëlection. At the same time there were three elevations from the lower to the upper House, curtailing a choice of new representatives in the Commons by the constituencies for which the new peers had sat. Two va-

cancies also occurred owing to deaths, and Sir Henry
Campbell-Bannerman's own seat at Stirling Burghs
was soon vacant.   Something almost like a miniature
General Election was therefore sprung upon the country, and the Suffragettes were compelled to marshal
their forces simultaneously in no fewer than nine constituencies.

The election at North West Manchester, where a
vigorous campaign was organised in opposition to
Mr. Winston Churchill, who was endeavouring to
obtain the people's sanction to his appointment as
President of the Board of Trade, was the most
hardly fought, and aroused the greatest interest.   It
was the scene of the first anti-Government struggle
during which Mr. Churchill had angrily declared
that he was being " hen-pecked "; but the women
had no need to go round to his meetings now, as they
had done then, in order to attract public attention to
their cause, for all Manchester was now wanting to
hear about it.   The Suffragettes had but to arrange
their own meetings and the *Manchester Guardian* itself was ready to publish a detailed list of them in its
columns.

Mr. Churchill himself, Cabinet Minister though
he was to be, could not obtain such crowded audiences as the Suffragettes.

At the same time many Liberal women, dissatisfied
with the behaviour of the Government and pro-
foundly distrustful of Mr. Asquith, held almost entirely aloof from the contest while Miss Margaret
Ashton, one of the most prominent, publicly stated
that she would work no more for the Liberal Party
until the Liberal Party were prepared to give her a
vote.   The *Manchester Guardian* wofully deplored

these defections; declaring that " the Women's Liberal Associations were deprived in a large measure of their natural leaders " and tended " to become as sheep without a shepherd," and Mr. Churchill now began to realise that the women's opposition was a serious matter. Therefore, asked at an election meeting on April 15th, what he intended to do to help women to obtain the Parliamentary franchise, Mr. Churchill made the following statement: " I will try my best as and when occasion offers, because I do think sincerely that the women have always had a logical case *and they have now got behind them a great popular demand amongst women.* It is no longer a movement of a few extravagant and excitable people, but one which is gradually spreading to all classes of women, and, that being so, *it assumes the same character as franchise movements have previously assumed.*"

Some people thought that the Suffragettes would be satisfied with Mr. Churchill's promise to use his influence, and would accordingly withdraw their opposition to his return, but Christabel Pankhurst at once addressed a letter to the Manchester press explaining that the W. S. P. U. would be satisfied with nothing less than a definite understanding from the Prime Minister, and the Government as a whole, that the equal Women's Enfranchisement Bill would be carried into law without delay.

When polling began at eight o'clock on the morning of April 25th the Suffragettes took their places at the entrance to the booths in the midst of a heavy snow storm and remained there is spite of it, throughout the day. The excitement which had been growing as the contest progressed was not confined to the poorer members of the electorate, but spread in all its force to the candidates themselves, and one of the Suffragettes was able to tell that when Mr. Churchill drove past the polling booth at which she was stationed, he stood up in his open carriage, shouting and shaking his fist at her.

During the counting of the votes, huge crowds assembled in Albert Square outside the Town Hall, and inside there was a large gathering of the more favoured persons. With pallid face the future Cabinet Minister walked feverishly up and down the room and when the figures were announced and it was known that Mr. Joynson-Hicks had defeated him by a majority of 429 votes, the Suffragettes, although they were his opponents, could not refrain from pitying him, for he burst into tears and hid his face on his mother's breast. As he passed out of the room, Mrs. Drummond, always eager and impulsive, darted up to him and, laying her hand on his arm, said: "It is the women that have done this, Mr. Churchill. You will understand now that we must have our vote." But he shook her off petulantly saying, "Get away, woman!" Meanwhile, Mr. Joynson-Hicks was outside thanking the electors who had returned him to Parliament, and in the course of his remarks he said: "I acknowledge the assistance I have received from those ladies who are sometimes laughed at, but who, I think, will now be feared by Mr. Churchill,— the Suffragists." These words were received with cheers. Next day all the newspapers were discussing Mr. Churchill's defeat and amongst others, the *Manchester Guardian* (L), the *Daily News* (L), the *Morning Leader* (L), the *Daily Mirror* (C), the *Daily Telegraph* (C), the

Daily Chronicle (L), and the *Standard* (C), admitted that this was largely due to the opposition of the Suffragettes, whilst the *Daily News* now called upon the Liberal Party to bring this state of affairs to an end by granting the suffrage to women.

Of course it was a foregone conclusion that a safe seat would now be found for Mr. Churchill, and that of Dundee, which happened to be vacant, was immediately offered to him. On his accepting the invitation, the Suffragettes' armies hastened North to oppose him, and Mrs. Pankhurst held a great meeting in the Kinnaird Hall on the evening before his arrival. One of Mr. Churchill's first acts on reaching the constituency was to address a gathering of Liberal women, for he was determined to make every effort to secure their help in counteracting the influence of the Suffragettes. Instead of expatiating on the greatness of the general principles of his party, and calling upon his hearers to support him on those grounds, as politicians had been wont to do in the past, he dealt almost entirely with votes for women, saying that there was a " general demand " for the suffrage on the part of " a very large body of women throughout the country," and that the question had " now come into the arena of practical politics." He asked to be considered as a friend of the movement, and added, " No one can be blind to the fact that at the next General Election, Women's Suffrage will be a real *practical issue and the next Parliament, I think, ought to see the gratification of the women's claims. I do not exclude the possibility of the suffrage being dealt with in this Parliament."* He refused, however, to give any pledge that those in power would take action.

He went on to describe the Suffragettes, as " hornets," and presumably referring to the by-election at Peckham, he said: " I have seen with regret, some of the most earnest advocates of the cause allying themselves with the forces of drink and reaction carried shoulder high, so I am informed, by the rowdy elements which are always to be found at the tail of a public-house made agitation."

Mr. Churchill's slanderous innuendoes in regard to the Women's Campaign at Peckham were not considered worthy of notice by the W. S. P. U., but Miss Maloney, a high spirited young member of the Women's Freedom League who had also taken part in that particular by-election, determined that she would force him to withdraw what he had said. At his next open air meeting she appeared brandishing a large muffin bell and warned him that unless he would apologise to the women, she would not let him speak. As he refused to do so, she carried out her threat. The Women's Social and Political Union regretted this action, because at by-elections they preferred to fight the Government with argument alone, but the Freedom League upheld Miss Maloney, and she continued to make it impossible for Mr. Churchill to speak in the open. On the eve of the poll it came to a pitched battle between them in which Miss Maloney triumphed. It had been arranged that Mr. Churchill should address a meeting at the Gas Works and " la Belle Maloney," as she was afterwards nicknamed, was speaking at the gates when he appeared. As before she at once called upon him to apologise, but, without answering, he passed on to enter the gates. She followed and though Mr. Churchill's friends strove to prevent her entering, the crowd swept her into the yard. She had lost her bell in the rush but, quite undaunted, she darted into the shed where the meeting was to take place, and, whilst Mr. Churchill mounted a bench to address the workmen, Miss Maloney climbed up on to a pile of boxes directly opposite to him. Again she called for the apology, but he remained silent and the crowd burst into shouts and yells. At last, as the noise grew, the Manager of the Gas Works, a supporter of the Government, shouted out, " hands up all those who want to hear Mr. Churchill." A few hands, half a dozen or so, were all that were raised, and seeing this Miss Maloney cried, " Now, friends, who wants to hear me? " and when a great forest of hands shot up, in answer, she pressed home her advantage saying, " Gentlemen, the resolution has been put to the meeting and by a large majority it has been decided in my favour." Then she went on to explain what she had come for, but in the midst of her words, Mr. Churchill jumped up and repeated his earlier statement in a modified form. For some time she and the future Cabinet Minister continued shouting at each other through the uproar of the crowd. At last, white with rage, he turned tail and left the meeting to her. Thus, as the papers said, " the amazing episode concluded."

Meanwhile the Women's Social and Political Union had been holding some two hundred large and enthusiastic meetings in the constituency each week, and on the eve of the poll they wound up with five monster demonstrations, four of which were in the open air and the fifth in the Drill Hall. Though the bulk of the Press throughout the country pre-ferred to give greater space to the account of the incident between Mr. Churchill and Miss Maloney with her bell, glowing accounts of these W. S. P. U. meetings appeared in the Dundee papers. The *Referee* for May 3rd also said:

> The women are doing wonderful election work and not getting half the credit for it that they deserve. Our wayward Winnie does not underestimate them as a fighting force. The War Song of the conquering Christabel to the worsted Churchill is " Bonnie Dundee."

> " And Tremble, false Whig, in the midst of your glee,
> You have not seen the last of my bonnet and me."

It was perhaps to guard against any falling off in the Liberal Majority that on May 7th, two days before the Dundee poll, Mr. Asquith announced in the House of Commons that the establishment of Old Age Pensions was to be the outstanding feature of the forthcoming Budget. On polling day, May 9th, Liberal men and women stood beside the Suffragettes at the polling booths with handbills which were adapted from those of the Suffragettes, and read " Vote for Churchill, and never mind the women," and " Put Churchill in and keep the Women out."

As had been a foregone conclusion, Mr. Churchill was returned by a large majority, but he received more than 2,000 votes fewer than Mr. Robertson, his predecessor, had done at the last election, and, whilst fifty-eight per cent. of the recorded votes had been cast for Mr. Robertson, Mr. Churchill only received forty-four per cent. of the total, and therefore represented a minority of the electors.

The figures were: [1]

[1] At the General Election there were two seats to be con-

Mr. Winston Churchill, Liberal......... 7,079
Sir G. Baxter, Unionist............... 4,370
Mr. G. H. Stewart, Labour............ 4,014
Mr. E. Scrymageour, Prohibitionist...... 655

At the General Election the figures had been:

Mr. E. Robertson, Liberal.............. 9,276
Mr. Alex. Wilkie, Labour.............. 6,833
Mr. Henry Robson, Liberal............ 6,122
Mr. E. Shackleton, Unionist.......... 3,865
Mr. A. D. Smith, Conservative........ 3,185

The results of the other elections which had been fought meanwhile, were as follows:
Dewsbury, polling day, April 23rd.

Mr. W. Runciman (L.).............. 5,594
Mr. W. B. Carpenter (C.)........... 4,078
Mr. B. Turner (Lab.)............... 2,446
_____
Liberal majority 1,516

The figures at the General Election had been:

Mr. W. Runciman (L.).............. 6,764
Mr. W. B. Carpenter (C.)........... 2,954
Mr. B. Turner (Lab.)............... 2,629
_____
Liberal majority 3,810

Kincardineshire, polling, April 25th.

The Hon. A. Murray (L.)........... 3,661
Mr. S. G. Gannell (C.).............. 1,963
_____
Liberal majority 1,698

tested, and every elector had two votes but he might only give one vote to each candidate.

At the General Election the figures had been:

Mr. W. J. Crombie (L.)............... 3,877
Mr. S. J. Gannell (C.)............... 1,524
_____
Liberal majority 2,353

Wolverhampton (E), polling day, May 5th.

Mr. G. Thorne (L.)................. 4,514
Mr. L. S. Amery (C.)............... 4,506
_____
Liberal majority 8

At the General Election the figures had been:

Sir H. Fowler (L.)................... 5,610
Mr. L. S. Amery (C.)............... 2,745
_____
Liberal majority 2,865

Montrose Boroughs, polling day, May 12th.

Mr. R. V. Harcourt (L.).............. 3,083
Mr. Burgess (Lab.)................... 1,937
Mr. A. H. B. Constable (C.).......... 1,576
_____
Liberal majority 1,146

At the General Election the figures had been:

Mr. J. Morley (L.)................. 4,416
Col. Sprott (C.)..................... 1,922
_____
Liberal majority 2,494

In the batch of by-elections which had occurred since Mr. Asquith had become Prime Minister, most of them as a consequence of the change in the ministerial leadership, the Government had therefore suffered a reduction of 6,663 votes or more than eighteen per cent. of the total Liberal poll recorded in the same constituencies at the General Election of 1906. Though the party leaders denied that the Suffragette campaign had affected any of the election results, there were few who had really worked in the elections who believed this and only Cabinet Ministers, newspaper editors and the Suffragettes themselves could form any impression of the large number of influential people who were writing to one or other of those three agencies to say so. At the same time a growing spirit of disaffection towards the Government was showing itself amongst Liberal women and Miss Florence Balgarnie's declaration that they had been " hewers of wood and the drawers of water for the Liberal Party too long, and that they must now look out for themselves," found a wide echo.

An ominous resolution had now been set down on the agenda for the Women's Liberal Federation Conference on behalf of the Cuckfield Association which stated that " Unless Women's Suffrage is granted before the dissolution of Parliament, the time will have arrived for a definite refusal on the part of Liberal women to work at Parliamentary elections." These things, doubtless, led Mr. Asquith to receive on May 20th, a deputation of Liberal Members of Parliament who urged him to grant the few days required for the carrying into law of Mr. Stanger's Women's Enfranchisement Bill, which earlier in the Session had already passed its second reading by so large a majority. In reply Mr. Asquith said that he himself did not wish to see women enfranchised, and that it was impossible for the Government to give any time for Mr. Stanger's Bill, but he added, " barring accidents, I regard it as a duty, indeed a binding obligation on this Government, before the present Parliament comes to an end, to bring in a really effective scheme for the reform of our electoral system." Having referred to what he considered to be the defects in the existing electoral provisions, dwelling especially on that of plural voting, he explained that, though the Government intended to introduce a Reform Bill, Woman's Suffrage was to have no place in it, but that when the Bill had been laid before the House, those Members of Parliament who believed in giving Votes to Women might move an amendment to that effect. If this were done, he did not consider it would be any of the Government's duty to oppose such an amendment, because two-thirds of the Cabinet were of the opinion that women should vote. But though Mr. Asquith began by stating that the Government would not oppose the amendment if it were approved by the House of Commons, he went on to attach certain conditions to this promise. These were, that any proposed Women's Suffrage amendment " must be on democratic lines," and " it must clearly have behind it the support — the strong and undoubted support — of the women of the country as well as of the present electorate."

Christabel Pankhurst at once exposed the unsatisfactory nature of Mr. Asquith's statement through the medium of the Press. She pointed out that he had not shown sufficient reason for his refusal to give facilities for the discussion of the Women's Enfranchisement Bill, and recalled the fact that after the second reading of the Women's Bill had been carried, a London Electoral Reform Bill had been introduced by a private Member, and that the Government had promised to carry this latter Bill into law, if it should pass the second reading. The House had, however, rejected the London Electoral Bill, and the time which the Government had designed to give that measure might therefore be handed over to the Votes for Women Bill. In regard to the details of Mr. Asquith's promise, she explained that women could not wait contentedly for the introduction of the proposed Reform Bill, because, as Mr. Asquith had himself foreshadowed, in his words " barring accidents," some unforeseen turn of events might precipitate a General Election before it had been introduced. Even if the Reform Bill were actually laid before Parliament the position of the Government with regard to Women's Enfranchisement was far from satisfactory. Apart from the fact that their refusal to make this question a part of the original Reform Bill was certainly insulting to women, the promise not to oppose an amendment moved by a private Member and carried by the House of Commons could not be relied on, because two conditions had been attached to it. The first condition was that it should be framed on " democratic lines." But Mr. Asquith had not defined the term " democratic " and there was reason to fear that the Government intended to resist the proposal to enfranchise women on the terms applying to men voters to which a majority of the House of Commons had pledged itself. Mr. Asquith was an anti-suffragist, and, according to the vague form of his statement, it was open to him to object to any and every amendment except one that was of so broad a nature that it could scarcely pass the House of Commons and would certainly be thrown out by the House of Lords.

The second condition was that the women of the country and the present electorate should show their strong and undoubted desire for a measure of women's enfranchisement, but Mr. Asquith had neglected to indicate how this desire should be expressed. The Women's Social and Political Union contended that the women had already, by demonstrating, petitioning, and going to prison for their cause, shown a very strong and very earnest desire for the franchise, and that the electors in the by-elections had also shown their belief in the justice of Votes for Women. But Mr. Asquith had hitherto refused to admit that such a desire had been manifested, and it was possible that he would always refuse to recognise its existence. Even if, in spite of all obstacles, the Woman's Suffrage amendment were safely carried and secured a place in the Reform Bill, the Bill itself was certain to prove a highly controversial measure. It was to deal with many other electoral questions besides that of Women's Suffrage, and if, as was only too probable, it were shipwrecked upon one of these, the Woman's claim to vote would go down with the rest.

The opinion of Christabel Pankhurst and that of the other leaders of the Women's Social and Political Union appeared in the Press next morning and in the Conservative papers there were other warnings; the *Standard* plainly said, " Of course Mr. Asquith does not intend to carry such a change." But most of the Liberal papers upheld Mr. Asquith.

BERNARD PARTRIDGE (after SIR EDWARD BURNE-JONES).

KING COPHETUA AND THE BEGGAR-MAID.

THE KING (MR. ASQUITH). "'THIS BEGGAR-MAID SHALL BE MY QUEEN'—THAT IS, IF THERE'S A GENERAL FEELING IN THE COUNTRY TO THAT EFFECT."

Cartoon from *Punch* on Mr. Asquith's false promise.

The *Daily News* called for a cessation of the militant tactics of the Suffragettes and referring to Christabel's objections said, " A more mature and experienced leader than Miss Christabel Pankhurst would have understood that the pledge which Mr. Asquith has given is quite exceptionally definite and binding." The *Star* said, " The meaning of Mr. Asquith's pledge is plain: Women's Suffrage will be passed through the House of Commons before the present Government goes to the country."

Events have already proved how rightly Christabel and the other Suffragette leaders had summed up the situation, for two General Elections have since come and gone and still women remain unenfranchised and the promised Reform Bill has not yet been introduced. But at the time only too many women were deceived by Mr. Asquith's false promise. Lady Carlisle presided over the Liberal Women's Conference which met next morning. " This is a glorious day of rejoicing," she cried. " Our great Prime Minister, all honour to him, has opened a way to us by which we can enter into that inheritance from which we have been too long debarred." She swept the majority of the women onward with her. A resolution of deepest gratitude to Mr. Asquith and the Cabinet was carried with every sign of enthusiastic joy, and the Cuckfield resolution was lost by an overwhelming majority.

Whilst the Liberal women were thus thanking the Prime Minister for his worthless " pledge," another body of women were striving to expose his insincerity, for, before ten o'clock that morning, the members of the Women's Freedom League were at the door of number ten Downing Street armed with a petition asking for an assurance either that the Government would give facilities for the passing of a Women's Suffrage measure or would promise to include Women's Suffrage in a general Government Reform Bill to be introduced before the end of the Parliament.

Mr. Asquith refused to give an answer and sent out police to clear the women away. Eventually they were arrested and sent to prison for from seven to twenty-one days.

Meanwhile at Stirling Burghs, the last of the recent series of by-elections, the Liberals were using Mr. Asquith's false promise to counteract the influence of the Suffragettes. The Women's Freedom League had wasted no time in making their protest to expose it and the Women's Social and Political Union had also proclaimed it to be worthless, but polling was already taking place, and on every newspaper placard appeared the words: " Premier's great Reform Bill, Votes for Women," and there was no time for the Suffragettes to undeceive the people.

When the result of the poll was declared, it was found that the Liberal majority of 630, that had been cast for the late Prime Minister in the General Election, had been more than doubled. The actual Liberal poll had also increased from 2,715 to 3,873. Thus the constant falling off in the Liberal vote which had manifested itself through so many elections was suddenly checked.

Mr. Asquith's promise had done its work at the Stirling by-election and had secured the loyalty of the Liberal Women for another year.

On Wednesday, May 27th, just a week after the

day on which it had been given to the deputation of Liberal members who supported Woman's Suffrage, Mr. Asquith was questioned in the House of Commons by Mr. Alfred Hutton, a Liberal Member, who was opposed to it. Mr. Hutton asked whether he considered himself pledged to introduce the proposed Reform Bill during the present Parliament, whether in that event he would give an opportunity for raising the question of Woman's Suffrage, and whether, if a Woman's Suffrage amendment to the Government Reform Bill were carried, it would then become part of the Government policy in relation to the franchise. After some close cross-questioning, in which he had tried hard to evade the point, Mr. Asquith finally replied, " My Honourable Friend has asked me a contingent question with regard to a remote and speculative future." Thus was the hollowness of the vaunted pledge exposed.

The Liberal papers still called upon the women to support the Cabinet, but in spite of this they showed that they found it difficult to uphold the trickery of their leader, and it was the Liberal *Daily Chronicle* that said " the skill and dexterity of the Prime Minister in parrying embarrassing questions was much admired, but not a few loyal supporters of the Government felt that the occasion was one that demanded candour rather than adroitness."

CHAPTER XIII

JUNE, 1908

THE time was now approaching when the women were to take up Mr. Gladstone's challenge to them to show that they could rival the great franchise demonstrations which men had held in demanding the three Reform Acts of 1832, 1867 and 1885. In the Autumn of 1907, long before the challenge had been made, the Women's Social and Political Union had determined to hold a record meeting in Hyde Park on Sunday, June 21st, 1908. The greatest meeting that had ever yet been held there was said to have numbered 72,000, but it was determined that at the Women's demonstration there must be gathered at least a quarter of a million people. The organisation of this great project was the work of many months and a large part of this fell to the share of our devoted Treasurer, Mrs. Pethick Lawrence, her husband, and Mrs. Drummond who now began to be called our " general." Mr. Lawrence carefully thought out the scheme for the seven great processions which were to march into Hyde Park by seven separate gates. To Mrs. Pethick

240

Lawrence was primarily due the introduction of the colours, purple, white and green, which the Union now adopted for its own. The colours at once secured a most amazing popular success for, although they were not even thought of until the middle of May, before the month of June arrived they were known throughout the length and breadth of the land.[1]

As Treasurer of the Union, Mrs. Lawrence bore upon her shoulders the special responsibility of meeting the very heavy cost of the demonstration as well as the other great expenses which were now being incurred; but that magnetic power of hers which had hitherto proved so invaluable to the movement was as infallible as ever. Whatever the sum she asked, it was immediately paid down. To make the forthcoming demonstrations known to everyone an immense poster, measuring thirteen feet by ten feet, containing the photographs of the twenty women who were to preside at the twenty platforms from which the audience was to be addressed, as well as a map showing the route of each of the seven processions and a plan of the meeting place in Hyde Park was displayed upon the hoardings in London and all the principal provincial towns at a cost to the Union of more than £1,000. Our organisers stationed in various parts of the country arranged for thirty special trains to run from seventy different towns in order to carry contingents of women demonstrators from the various provincial centres. At the same

[1] Other suffrage societies soon afterwards also adopted colours. The Women's Freedom League chose yellow, white and green, and the National Union of Women's Suffrage Societies red, white and green.

time London itself was systematically organised for the demonstration. My experiences as organiser of the Chelsea district which included also Fulham and Wandsworth, are vividly present with me as I write. At many of the open air pitches from which we then spoke, no Women's Suffrage meetings had ever been held before, but wherever we went our experiences were, in their main essentials, always the same. Our first meeting was, usually, almost wholly a fight to subdue a continued uproar. On more than one occasion the little box or the chair used as a platform was overturned by a gang of hooligan youths, and the meeting had to be abandoned. But, whatever may have happened at the first meeting in a fresh place, we always found that at the second meeting the majority of the audience were sympathetic. At the third meeting all was harmony, and we were generally seen to our homeward trams or busses by cheering crowds.

Those splendid people, the Suffragettes of Kensington, not only contrived to carry on a constant campaign of meetings but at the same time to make all their own banners and bannerettes.

In the meantime the National Union of Women's Suffrage Societies, in conjunction with a number of other organisations, had decided to organise a women's procession, and on June 13th, a week and a day before the Hyde Park demonstration, some 13,000 Suffragists assembled on the Embankment and marched to the Albert Hall where a meeting was held. It was a striking pageant with its many gorgeous banners, richly embroidered and fashioned of velvets, silks and every kind of beautiful material and the small bannerettes showing as innumerable

patches of brilliant and lovely colour, each one varying both in shape and hue.   Seventy of the large banners had been prepared by the Artists League for
Women's Suffrage.   Some were blazoned with the figures of women great in history, amongst them, Boadicea, Joan of Arc and Queen Elizabeth; others
bore emblems commemorating women's heroic deeds,
or reforming achievements,— Elizabeth Fry, Lydia
Becker, and Mary Wollstonecraft, being amongst
those recalled.   Walking in the procession were many
of Lydia Becker's comrades and contemporaries, including the aged Miss Emily Davies, Dr. Garrett Anderson, and her sister, Mrs. Fawcett, the President of
the National Union of Suffrage Societies.   After
these came a contingent of international Suffragists;
Australians, Americans with their Stars and Stripes
headed by Dr. Anna Shaw, and representatives from
Hungary, Russia, South Africa, and other countries,
each with their national flags and colours.   The professional women were led by Mrs. Ayrton and other
scientists and a great band of medical women in their
splendid robes of crimson and black, with hoods of
purple, red and blue.   Other graduates followed and
the representatives of Newnham and Girton were in
great force.   Amongst the women writers, headed
by the Scrivener's banner, were Beatrice Harraden,
Elizabeth Robins and Evelyn Sharpe.   Then came
the artists, the actresses.   Next, the nurses, all in
uniform, and, after these, a host of others, garden-
ers, pharmacists, physical trainers, typists and shorthand writers, shop assistants, factory workers, and
home-makers.   Next came the militant Women's
Freedom League, the Women's Co-operative Guild,
the National Union of Women Workers, and the

members of various women's organisations connected with the political parties including the Women's Liberal Associations, and the women of the Independent Labour Party and the Fabian Society. Altogether the procession was acknowledged to be the most picturesque and effective political pageant that had ever been seen in this country, and every newspaper spoke of its impressive dignity and beauty.

Now the Women's Social and Political Union and all whom they could press into the service were busily engaged on a ten days' crusade for the winding up of the Hyde Park Demonstration campaign. How the women worked! They held innumerable meetings; they went out canvassing from door to door; they stood in the streets with flags and posters; they distributed handbills broadcast; chalked announcements upon the pavements and met the workmen's trains to give out little purple, white and green mock railway tickets, a million of which had been printed. On the Thursday evening before the Demonstration, Mrs. Drummond and a dozen other members of the Union set sail for the Houses of Parliament in a steam launch decorated with banners and posters announcing the Demonstration. At the little tables on the terrace many members, including Mr. Lloyd George, were entertaining their lady friends at afternoon tea, when the sound of a band playing heralded the Suffragettes' arrival. Everyone crowded to the water's edge as the boat stopped, and Mrs. Drummond began to speak. She invited all Members of Parliament, and especially Cabinet Ministers, to join the womens' procession to Hyde Park on the twenty-first of June, assuring them that it was their duty to inform themselves as to the feelings of the people.

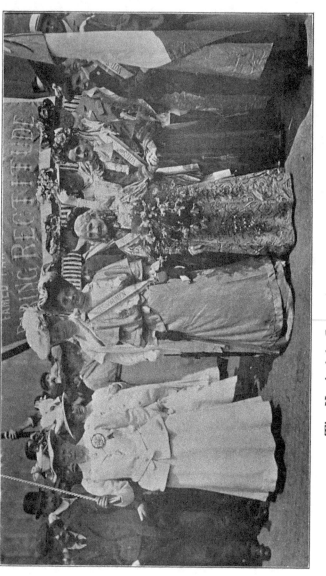

The Head of the Procession to Hyde Park, June 21st, 1908

She twitted the Government who were supposed to
be democratic with remaining always behind barred
gates under the protection of the police, and urged,
" Come to the Park on Sunday; you shall have police
protection there also, and we promise you that there
shall be no arrests." The Members appeared both
pleased and interested and many more came flocking
out to listen, but somebody, a waiter it was said, hurriedly telephoned to the police and in a few moments
Inspector Scantlebury with a number of officers appeared on the Terrace, whilst at the same time one of
the police boats hove in sight. Seeing this, the Suffragettes steamed away.

On Sunday, the 21st, we were busy early in the
morning for the processions were to start between one
and two; the people were expected to begin to assemble at least a couple of hours before that time. All
London seemed to have turned out to see us, and all
along the Chelsea Embankment, which was thronged
with people, were coffee stands, costermongers, and
hawkers selling badges and programmes in the purple, white and green. When the moment for start-
ing came our Chelsea procession numbered some seven
thousand people, but the dense crowds of by-standers
marched with us too, and grew in a countless number
as we moved along, so that, instead of one procession
we had formed three — the central one being composed
almost entirely of women, wearing white dresses and
scarfs of purple, white and green, and carrying banners in the same colours. The whole road was filled
with people moving with us, and from balconies, windows and tops of busses people cheered and waved.
The same thing was happening in each of the other
six districts. At the head of each procession rode

policemen on horseback and numbers of constables walked on either side of the ranks in order to keep the way clear. Six thousand police in all accompanied the seven processions, the police authorities being most helpful and courteous toward us throughout the arrangements.

In Hyde Park the railings for over a quarter of a square mile had been taken up for us in order to add a further open space to that which is usually open in the neighbourhood of the Reformer's Tree. In the centre of this meeting-ground a furniture van was stationed to serve as an impromptu Conning Tower. Those who stood there watching saw, first the fine procession from Marylebone with great crowds marching in on either side sweep into the quiet grassy space, and then, one after another, from the seven different gates, the rest of the seven processions with their accompanying armies come streaming in. Before we arrived from Chelsea the whole ground was a surging mass of people, and it was with difficulty that we made our way to the platform which had been reserved for us. Once we gained it we clambered hastily on to our lorry and looked around with wondering and astonished gaze. As far as the eye could reach was one vast mass of human beings — not black, as crowds usually are,— but coloured, like a great bed of flowers because of the thousands and thousands of women all dressed in the lightest and daintiest of summer garments, whilst even the men had most of them come out in cool greys and were wearing straw hats. Over the whole of the area there was to be seen not a single blade of grass. Who could attempt to estimate the number of peo-

A Section of the great " Votes for Women " meeting in Hyde Park on June 21st, 1908

ple that were present? They were innumerable;
they defied calculation and there was no one of us
who had ever imagined that we should see so many
people gathered together. The sky was a perfect
blue; the sun poured down on us; everyone seemed
to be in holiday mood, just as they were in holiday
dress, and during the time in which the people
waited for the speakers to begin, perfect good humour reigned. Then bugles were sounded from the
Conning Tower and the speeches at each of the
twenty platforms began.

Probably less than half the people could hear the
speakers, but that was of small account. They had
come there to show their sympathy with Votes for
Women and to take part in the greatest demonstration the world had ever seen, and if they stood there
the whole of the afternoon without catching a single
sentence, they had been well rewarded. At most of
the platforms there was nothing but the kindliest
sympathy, except at the platforms of Mrs. Pankhurst and Christabel, where a number of rowdy and
ignorant young men attempted to prevent the speakers from being heard.

At five o'clock the bugle sounded and the Resolution calling upon the Government to give votes to
women without delay was put and carried at every
platform, in most cases without dissent. Then the
bugle was heard again and the cry, "One, two,
three!" and the assembled multitude, as they had
been asked to do, shouted, "Votes for Women!"
three times, and then that great and wonderful gathering began slowly to disperse.

Next morning every newspaper devoted long columns to the demonstration. In the course of a long descriptive account the Special Correspondent of the *Times* said:

Its organisers had counted on an audience of 250,000. That expectation was certainly fulfilled and probably it was doubled, and it would be difficult to contradict anyone who asserted that it was trebled. Like the distances and numbers of the stars, the facts were beyond the threshold of perception.

The *Standard* said:

From first to last, it was a great meeting, daringly conceived, splendidly stage-managed, and successfully carried out. Hyde park has probably never seen a greater crowd of people.

The *Daily News* said:

There is no combination of words which will convey an adequate idea of the immensity of the crowd around the platforms.

The *Daily Express:*

The Women Suffragists provided London yesterday with one of the most wonderful and astonishing sights that have ever been seen since the days of Boadicea. . . . It is probable that so many people never before stood in one square mass anywhere in England. Men who saw the great Gladstone meeting years ago said that compared with yesterday's multitude it was as nothing.

The *Daily Chronicle* said:

Never, on the admission of the most experienced observers, has so vast a throng gathered in London to witness an outlay of political force.

Lord Rosebery and other Members of both Houses watching the Suffragettes' struggle in Parliament Square, June 30th, 1908

After the great meeting was over, its organisers returned to Clement's Inn and Christabel Pankhurst immediately wrote to the Prime Minister forwarding the Resolution: " That this meeting calls upon the Government to grant votes to women without delay," which had just been carried by that great gathering. At the same time she asked " what action the Government would take in response to the demand."

Mr. Asquith replied that he had nothing to add to the statement — the so-called promise of a Reform Bill, which he had made to the deputation of Members of Parliament on May 20th.

The wonderful Hyde Park Demonstration, the greatest meeting that had ever been held, and the impressive procession of the Women's Societies both of which had been held within a few days' space had therefore, it seemed, made no impression upon the Government. Seeing, therefore, that to argue further would be mere waste of time, the Women's Social and Political Union immediately decided to take action. Hitherto, through all the hard battles which the Suffragettes had fought outside the House of Commons, they had never asked the general public to come to their aid, but, now that the great peoples' demonstration in Hyde Park had been thus contemptuously ignored, it was decided to call upon both men and women to attend another monster meeting on June 30th, to be held this time in Parliament Square, in order that the Government could not fail to see.

The Commissioner of Police replied by issuing a warning to the public not to meet in Parliament Square, on the ground that danger would necessarily arise from the assembling of a large number of persons in that restricted area, through which the way must be kept for Members of Parliament.

Meanwhile, the W. S. P. U. again and again urged Mr. Asquith to receive a deputation, but he still refused, and at last he was informed that the deputation would start from the Women's Parliament on June 30th, and would wait upon him at the House of Commons at half past four that afternoon. Once more he returned a refusal to see the women, but Mrs. Pankhurst herself replied, as their leader, that the deputation would arrive at the appointed hour. Next day Mrs. Pankhurst, Mrs. Pethick Lawrence and eleven other women set out from the Caxton Hall. At the main entrance of the building Superintendent Wells was waiting with a body of some twenty constables and, at his orders, as soon as the thirteen women had emerged, the doors were locked and even the Pressmen begged in vain to be released. Then the Superintendent constituted himself the leader and protector of the deputation and led them quickly through the cheering crowds who pressed forward pushing and struggling to catch a glimpse of the little band of women. Straight up Victoria Street he led them and right to the door of the Stranger's Entrance where they were met by the burly and familiar form of Inspector Scantlebury surrounded by his minions. He stepped forward and addressed Mrs. Pankhurst gravely, " Are you Mrs. Pankhurst, and is this your deputation? " he asked. She answered, " Yes," and he said, " I have orders to exclude you from the House of Commons." " Has Mr. Asquith received my letter? " she questioned him in turn, and, replying, " Yes," the Inspector drew the document from his pocket, adding in response to a further inquiry, that Mr. Asquith had sent no message of any kind by way of reply. Then Inspector Scantlebury turned away and walked into the House, leaving behind him a strong force of police to guard the door. For an instant or two the women stood there baffled, but they had to remember the resolve that this effort to interview the Prime Minister should be entirely peaceful. Moreover, there was the Mass Meeting of the evening. They therefore merely turned and made their way back to the Caxton Hall. Meanwhile larger and larger crowds were flocking towards Parliament from every direction, and long before eight o'clock, the time at which they had been asked to assemble, it was estimated by the newspapers that more than 100,000 people had collected in Parliament Square. The police had made most extensive preparations to prevent any meeting being held and it was said that more than 5,000 ordinary constables and upwards of fifty mounted men had been requisitioned for this purpose.

When, at eight o'clock, the women sallied forth in groups from the Caxton Hall to speak to the great multitude that had assembled in response to their appeal, the scene was already becoming turbulent. There were no platforms to speak from, and it would have been useless to provide them, for the police would instantly have dragged them from the ground. But it is possible to hold a meeting without official sanction and to make speeches without platforms and the women bravely essayed the task. Some of them clung to the railings of Palace Yard to raise themselves above the crowd, others mounted the steps of the offices in Broad Sanctuary, others the steps of the Government buildings at the top of Parliament Street opposite the Abbey, whilst others again merely spoke from the pavement wherever and whenever the police would cease for an instant from driving them along. Every woman who attempted to speak was torn by the harrying constables from the spot where she had found a foothold and was either hurled aside and flung into the dense masses that were being kept constantly on the move or placed under arrest. Meanwhile, the crowd was always surging and swaying forward shouting out mingled cheers and jeers.

Some groups of the men stood with linked arms around the women who were striving to make speeches, bodies of others pushed little band of Suffragettes forward against the rows of constables with cries of " Votes of Women," " we'll get you to the House of Commons," and " back up the women and push them through ! " Again and again the police lines were broken and again and again the mounted men charged and beat the people back. Mr. Lloyd George, Mr. Winston Churchill, Mr. Herbert Gladstone, Lord Rosebery and other members of both Houses stood in Palace Yard, and near the Strangers' entrance watching the scene. As it became dark the disorder grew, and gangs of roughs who supported neither the government nor the women kept making concerted rushes, sweeping the rest of the people on before them, absolutely heedless of trampling others under foot. In some cases isolated women were surrounded by them and with difficulty rescued from their ill treatment by the soberer and more respectable members of the gathering. But, undaunted

either by violence from the roughs or from the police, the Suffragettes, though their slight frames were
bruised and almost worn out by the constant batter-
ing of those who were so much heavier, stronger and
more numerous than themselves, still continued to
address the throng. Every woman who was arrested was followed to the police station by a stream
of cheering people and was saluted with raised hats
and waving handkerchiefs.

As Mr. Asquith passed from the House of
Commons to Downing Street in his motor-car he was
hooted by the crowd. He arrived home to find his
windows broken, for Mrs. Leigh and Mrs. New had
driven swiftly past the guardian policemen at the
entrance to the street in a taxicab and had each
thrown two small stones through two of the lower
windows of Number 10 before an arm of the Law
had been stretched out to drag them away to Canon
Row. Meanwhile Miss Mary Phillips had endeavoured to dash into the House of Commons by way
of Palace Yard in the midst of a little company of
Parliamentary waitresses but half way across the
Yard had been seized and dragged back. Miss
Lena Lambert had chartered a little rowing boat
and had set off in the darkness to reach the House
from the river side. Crowds of Members were
lounging on the lighted terrace that hot summer's
night when she and her little craft appeared out of
the darkness, to urge them to determine that the simple measure of justice, which was being so hardly
fought for, should be carried into law. But not
many words had she spoken, when the police boats
swooped down on her and she was towed away, lest
she should irritate and annoy the people's representa-

tives by telling them of the battle whose dull roar nothing could shut out.

So the night wore on and that weary fight continued. Not until twelve o'clock did the police at last succeed in clearing the streets, and it was then found that twenty-nine women had been arrested.

Next morning twenty-seven of the women were brought up at Westminster Police Court before the Magistrate, Mr. Francis, and were charged with obstructing the police in the execution of their duty. With the usual callous haste their trial was hurried through. The magistrate had always had all the political rights that he cared to use and would not trouble to imagine what it is like to be without them. He testily brushed aside the defence of the women that the Government had driven them to adopt these methods of obtaining the franchise and that Mr. Asquith by his ignoring of the Great Hyde Park Demonstration had taught them once and for all the uselessness of peaceful propaganda. The sentences ranged from one to three months' imprisonment in the second division. Mrs. Leigh and Miss New were dealt with separately at Bow Street but, as this was not generally expected, very few people were present. In the dimly lighted Court, with the magistrate in his high backed chair regarding them sternly from deep cavernous eyes, the two little women in the great dock with its heavy iron railings looked strangely forlorn. What dreadful sentence, we wondered, was in store for these, the first of the Suffragettes to deliberately throw stones! Mr. Muskett in prosecuting them for doing wilful damage to the value of ten shillings at the Prime Minister's residence, spoke of them with extreme harsh-

Christabel Pankhurst inviting the public to " rush " the House of Commons at a meeting in Trafalgar Square, Sunday, October 11th, 1908

ness, urging that they should be sent to prison without the option of a fine. Though the Magistrate rebuked the women for the methods they had adopted, we felt that he was impressed by their demeanour and that he was loth to sentence them. He ordered that they should go to prison for two months in the third division without the option of a fine. The sentence was heavy enough, but lighter than we had feared in view of the fact that many of the other women were to remain in prison for three months.

When the House of Commons met on the same afternoon, several members of every party in the House asked, as they had done on previous occasions, that the women should be treated as political offenders. As before, however, Mr. Gladstone sheltered himself behind the statement, which nobody believed, that the Magistrate was alone responsible for placing the women in the second and third divisions and that he himself had no power to interfere.

On the morning after the " raid " the newspapers had mostly contented themselves with rebuking the women' for what they had done, but in a few days there came a reaction of feeling which was accelerated both by the harshness of the sentences imposed and by Mr. Gladstone's refusal to mitigate the rigours of the prison treatment.

The country was now overwhelmed by one of those terribly oppressive heat waves which come upon us suddenly from time to time and are borne with such difficulty in our usually temperate climate, and there gradually leaked out from Holloway accounts of the Suffragist women fainting in the exercise yards [1] and being seized with illness in their cells. There happened to be some cases of measles in the prison hospital, and Miss Elsie Howey, having contracted the disease there, was exceedingly ill for many weeks.

All these things combined to focus public attention upon the harsh treatment of the Suffragette prisoners. On July 10th the *Manchester Guardian* in a leading Article said:

It demands considerable obtuseness to believe, as some persons apparently do, that close confinement in the heat of Summer or the cold of Winter within a solitary and unwholesome cell, deprival of exercise for twenty-three hours out of the twenty-four, subjection to menial authority, ignorance of the welfare of one's friends, the performing of dull and alien tasks, deprivation of writing materials, partial suffocation and the wearing of ugly, ill-fitting clothing that has already been worn by the vilest criminals, are for delicate and sensitive women the elements of a comedy. They compose a great and terrible torture. . . . Because they are suffering for an idea their stringent imprisonment is indefensible. It violates the public conscience and the law and the courts cannot wage war on the public conscience without forfeiting respect and authority.   .

[1] The efforts of Dr. Mary Gordon (the first lady Inspector of Prisons, who had been appointed during the previous April, admittedly owing to the publicity given to the condition of women in prison by the Suffragettes) now secured that when exercising in the future the women should be provided with cotton sunbonnets. By her advice the prisoners were also supplied with notebooks and pencils, but the latter privilege was afterwards withdrawn. Eventually she succeeded in abolishing the unsanitary wooden spoon — at any rate, for Suffragette use.

Mrs. Pankhurst and Christabel hiding from the police in
the roof garden at Clement's Inn, October 12th, 1908

CHAPTER XIV

JULY TO OCTOBER, 1908

Great Demonstrations in the Provinces: Mr. Lloyd George Accuses Women of Being Paid to Interrupt Him. Arrest of the Three Leaders and the Fifth Women's Parliament.

MEANWHILE, in spite of the fact that the Union had thought it necessary to again resort to militant tactics the campaign of great provincial demonstrations was proceeded with, and included gatherings of 100,000 people in Shipley Glen, Bradford, on May 31st, 15,000 at Heaton Park, Manchester, on July 19th, of 100,000 on Woodhouse Moor, Leeds, on July 26th, of many thousands, also, on the Durdham Downs Clifton, near Bristol, on September 19th, in Nottingham Forest, on July 18th, at Huddersfield, on September 27th, at Rawtenstall, on September 3rd, and in the Market Square Leicester on July 30th.

During these months, by-elections had been fought in Pembrokeshire, Haggerston and Newcastle. At the first of these the Liberal majority was reduced. At the second a Liberal majority of 1,401 was turned to a Conservative majority of 1,143. At Newcastle, the Suffragettes swept all before them, and, when Mrs. Pankhurst announced to a great meeting on the Town Moor that five of the released prisoners were shortly to arrive, an immense procession was

formed to do them honour, and the railway authorities placed the entrance usually reserved for Royalty
at the disposal of the Suffragettes.   Almost the
whole population turned out to cheer the women.
There seemed no doubt the Government nominee
would be defeated, and so it proved, for a Liberal
majority of no fewer than 6,481 votes was turned
into a majority of 2,143 for the Conservatives.

After the poll, Mr. Renwick, the successful candidate said: " I must express admiration for those
who have addressed meetings on behalf of Women's
Suffrage.   They have taught us a lesson as to how
to speak and conduct a campaign.   I am sure we all
wish that they may realise their hopes."   The defeated Liberal candidate also expressed the hope that
the women would be voting at the next election.

Meanwhile, at almost every meeting addressed
by a Cabinet Minister throughout the length and
breadth of the land, the Suffragettes had been in evidence, and when they had been unable to secure admission to the halls, they had held meetings outside.

At some of Mr. Lloyd George's meetings the
women hecklers were treated with special brutality,
and this was certainly increased by the exclamations
of the Cabinet Minister on the platform.   He
called his interrupters " sorry specimens of womanhood," and added, " I think a gag ought to be tried."
So calculated to aggravate the already savage behaviour of the stewards were his remarks, that quite
a storm of protest was raised and Mr. Lloyd George
found it necessary to write to the *Times,* saying:

Owing to the constant interruptions to which I was subjected, it was doubtless difficult for me to make myself clearly

and fully understood, and the difficulty which I found in speaking was no doubt shared by the Press in reporting. Under these circumstances I am not surprised that some misunderstanding may have arisen, and I appeal to the courtesy of your columns to remove it.

Nevertheless, when he spoke at Swansea, his remarks were even more unguarded, and he urged on the stewards with such cries as, " By and by we shall have to order sacks for them, and the first to interrupt shall disappear," and " fling them ruthlessly out." At that there were shouts of laughter from Liberals on the platform mingled with cries of " frog march them ! " Then he taunted the women. " I wonder how much she has been paid for coming here," he called as one was being dragged away. His supporters responded with cheers and shouts of " Tory money," and he added " I am sorry to say this business is becoming a profession."

On hearing of this remark, Mrs. Pethick Lawrence wrote to Mr. Lloyd George as Treasurer of the Women's Social and Political Union to protest against his suggestion that the women who interrupted Cabinet Ministers did so as a " profession." In doing so she forwarded him a copy of our Annual Report. He replied by repeating his insinuations and calling attention to the fact that the Report showed considerable sums of money to have been dispensed in " salaries," " travelling expenses," and " special board and lodging." Mrs. Lawrence then stated that whilst, like every other political organisation, the Women's Social and Political Union had its paid staff and organisers and that whilst these organisers were occasionally present at Cabinet Ministers' meetings, the protests were almost entirely made by members of the Union who gave their time and work freely. Thus, of the thirty women who had interrupted Mr. George at the Queen's Hall on July 28th and had been ejected, twenty-nine had never at any time been in receipt of any salary from the Union, and of the five women who had taken part in the protest made at Swansea, four had never been in receipt of any salary from the Union and the fifth was not receiving any salary at the time.

The eyes of all Suffragettes were now fixed upon the opening of Parliament for the autumn session, which was to take place on October 12th. The Prime Minister was again asked that facilities should be given for the House of Commons to proceed with the Women's Enfranchisement Bill, but he again refused and the W. S. P. U. then determined that a fifth Parliament of Women must be called together on October 13th, and that a deputation from it must again seek an interview with the Prime Minister. It was thought desirable that, as on the last occasion, the general public should be present, both that they might see what actually happened between the women and the authorities, and also that it might be shown to the Government that many thousands of men and women were prepared to support the Suffragettes and to answer to their call. Knowing well the difficulty of bringing anything prominently before the public in these modern days of crowded interests except with the aid of the advertisement afforded by notices in the Press, and knowing also that in this epoch of Press sensationalism that nothing, even if it be as serious as a struggle between life and death, is reported except when it is new, the Committee of the Union cast about in their minds

for some racy and attractive means of drawing public attention to the forthcoming deputation. At last
the phrase, " Help the Suffragettes to rush the House
of Commons " was hit upon, because of its double
suggestion and echo of the oft heard but almost always ridiculously unfounded complaint that legislation is being " rushed " through our too talkative
and dilatory Parliament. The words were at once
embodied in a handbill of which the accompanying
illustration is a facsimile.

Meanwhile another body of agitators who had
become impatient with the Government's treatment
of their own particular question, were preparing to
take similar steps. Even in the early summer, there
had been signs that the forthcoming winter was to
be one of exceptional hardship for the working
classes, and the Labour Members of Parliament had
then begun to urge upon the President of the Local
Government Board the need for making extensive
preparations for helping the great numbers of persons whom they foresaw would fall out of employment. The distress that had been foreshadowed
was now upon the country, a feeling of general discontent prevailed, and rumours of all sorts of wild
doings were beginning to spread. Bodies of unemployed came marching up to London from the provincial towns and held meetings on the Embankment
and Tower Hill at which it was announced that
there was to be a great gathering of the unemployed
in Parliament Square on Monday, October 12th, and
that an attempt was then to be made to see the
Prime Minister, the President of the Local Government Board and the President of the Board of
Trade. On Sunday, October 4th, a meeting for the

unemployed was held under the auspices of the Social Democratic Federation in Trafalgar Square,
and some very inflammatory speeches were delivered.[1] The words of Mr. Will Thorne, M.P. for
West Ham, were milder than those of some others.
In the course of his remarks he said:

Next Tuesday the Suffragettes admit that they are going
to " rush " the House. There is nothing there. If you
want to " rush " anything, you rush where there is something to be rushed; not the House. I say that if you are
in earnest, the first thing that you ought to do is to rush
the bakers' shops. You ought to rush every bally bakers'
shop in London rather than starve. I suppose it means that
a few of you will get locked up. You would be better off
in prison.

He added that until the unemployed struck " the
fear of man " into the hearts of the Government,
the Government would do nothing for them. After
the unemployed meeting was over, there was some
disorder in the neighbourhood of Charing Cross and
two or three men were arrested.

On Sunday, October 11th, the Women's Social
and Political Union held a meeting in Trafalgar
Square at which Mrs. Pankhurst, Christabel Pankhurst, and Mrs. Drummond spoke from the plinth
of the Nelson column, whilst the police who were
present in great numbers, took notes of all that was
said.

On Monday, October 12th, came the day of the
unemployed demonstration, but, though much had
been feared and expected of it, little happened.

[1] My authorities in these cases are the report in the *Times*
and the evidence given in the witness box at Bow Street.

WOMEN'S SOCIAL AND POLITICAL UNION,
4, CLEMENTS INN.

VOTES FOR WOMEN

MEN & WOMEN

HELP THE SUFFRAGETTES

TO RUSH

THE HOUSE OF COMMONS

ON

TUESDAY Evening, 13th October,

At 7.30.

Printed by St Clements Press, Ltd., Newspaper Buildings, Portugal Street, W.C.

Small groups of unemployed began to arrive in the Square at an early hour, but a pacificatory attitude was adopted by the authorities and though the police kept the crowd moving in the thoroughfares they did not prevent the assemblage of a number of people in the centre of the green in front of Westminster Abbey. Many of the men were allowed to enter the House, where Mr. John Burns assured them that within a few days the Prime Minister would make a pronouncement in the House of Commons pledging the Government to provide some measure of relief.

During the week that had passed, the last before their demonstration, the Suffragettes had been working strenuously. The " rush " hand-bills had been circulated broadcast, a " Votes for Women " kite had floated constantly over the House of Commons, and a steam launch, decorated with banners and posters announcing the deputation had steamed up and down the river. Everything had gone on without let or hindrance and new recruits, anxious to take part in the demonstration had been eagerly presenting themselves. Yet from day to day there grew the knowledge that the authorities were lying in wait to take some sudden step against the Union and the women began to notice that the police were shadowing all the prominent members of the Committee and were constantly hanging about the offices at Clement's Inn. The blow came in the shape of the following document, a copy of which was served upon Mrs. Pankhurst, Mrs. Drummond, and Christabel Pankhurst about mid-day on Monday, October 12th:

Information has been laid this day by the Commissioner of Police for that you, in the month of October, in the year 1908, were guilty of conduct likely to provoke a breach of the peace by initiating and causing to be initiated, by publishing and causing to be published, a certain handbill, calling upon and inciting the public to do a certain wrongful and illegal act, viz., to rush the House of Commons at 7 :30 P. M. on October 13th inst.

You are therefore hereby summoned to appear before the Court of Summary Jurisdiction now sitting at the Bow Street Police Station on Monday, October 12th, at the hour of 3 :30, to answer to the said information and to shew cause why you and each of you shall not be ordered to find sureties of good behaviour.

(Signed)   H. CURTIS BENNETT.

It was felt that the summons had been issued to withdraw public attention from the deputation to Mr. Asquith which was to go from the Caxton Hall next evening. Therefore it was decided to disregard it for the present, but at the crowded At Home in the Queen's Hall that afternoon the members of the Union were informed that it had been received. The devotion and loyalty to leaders, always so strong in the Union, was now at fever heat. Numbers of constables were posted at the doors, official police reporters were present and it was momentarily expected that the police would force their way on to the platform and arrest the three. The excitement culminated when someone said that a police inspector was entering the building. Then hundreds of women leapt to their feet and cried out that the officers should not be allowed to enter and that they would never let them take their leaders. But this proved to be a false alarm, for it was only a

messenger to say that the summonses had been adjourned until the following morning. Mrs. Pankhurst, Christabel and Mrs. Drummond decided not
to give themselves up till evening and they accordingly sent the following note to the Court:

We shall not be at the offices at 4, Clement's Inn until
six o'clock to-day, but at that hour we shall all three be
entirely at your disposal.

This did not appease the authorities in any way
and a warrant for their arrest was immediately issued with an order to Inspector Jarvis to execute it
without delay. Having guessed that this might
happen Mrs. Drummond had quietly arranged to
spend her last day of liberty with friends whilst my
mother and sister had merely made their way to one
of the upper flats in Clement's Inn, No. 119, which
was rented by Mr. and Mrs. Pethick Lawrence and
to which a roof garden was attached. This had
scarcely been done when the police swooped down
upon our offices to demand the three, and on no information being forthcoming they remained roaming
about the passages and standing in the doorways,
trying to get information from postmen, porters and
tradesmen, all day long.

At six o'clock, Mrs. Drummond returned,
promptly to the moment, and the two other prisoners walked calmly downstairs and into the offices.
Inspector Jarvis and a detective in plain clothes were
already waiting and, after the warrant for their arrest had been read out to them, they were taken in a
cab to Bow Street. The Court having risen, it was
impossible for the trial to be proceeded with that
evening and when they applied to be allowed out on

bail until the next morning their application was refused and they were hurried away to the cells. The
police court cells are about five feet wide by seven
feet long, exceedingly badly lit and furnished only with
a wooden bench attached to the wall and a sanitary
convenience. There are neither washing utensils
nor bed of any kind, but each prisoner is given a
dark and dirty-looking rug in which to wrap herself during the night. Mrs. Pankhurst at once
claimed her right as an untried prisoner to communicate with the outside world and immediately de-
spached telegrams to several Members of Parliament. A weary hour or two went by. Then the
door of Mrs. Pankhurst's cell was thrown wide
open, and the tall, breezy presence of Mr. Murray,
Liberal Member of Parliament for East Aberdeenshire, appeared. He was horrified to find the three
ladies in these unpleasant surroundings and, promising to return soon, he hurried to the Savoy Hotel,
and there arranged for various comforts to be sent
in to the prison. Then he prevailed upon the
authorities to allow the three Suffragettes to take their
evening meal together and, in an incredibly short
space of time, they were ushered into the matron's
room.

The bare little place with its dingy walls, its
wooden chairs and two deal tables, had been wonderfully transformed. Numbers of tall wax candles
had been lighted, the tables were laid with silver,
flowers and brightly coloured fruit, and three wait-
ers were ready to serve the prisoners with a most
elaborate meal. At the same time, Mr. Murray,
with his face wreathed in smiles, was superintend-
ing the carrying in to the cells of three comfortable

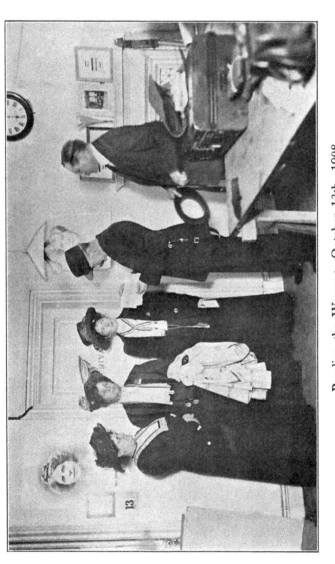

Reading the Warrant, October 13th, 1908

beds. The management of the Savoy had thrown themselves into the enterprise with the greatest eagerness and, having acted throughout with almost overwhelming kindness and courtesy, ended by refusing to charge anything at all for what they had provided. As well may be imagined, the three comrades were in no haste to finish the meal and return to the dark and solitary cells.

Meanwhile there were stirring doings at Westminster. All police leave had been stopped for the day in the whole of the metropolitan area, and every mounted policeman had been called up to headquarters. Parliament Square itself was cut off from the rest of London as though it were in a state of siege, by double cordons of foot police, each of them five deep, which were drawn up across all the streets leading to it. Within these barriers the great area, usually thronged with vehicles of all kinds and hurrying passers-by, was emptied of all but the few mounted police who rode about in it, the ring of their horses' hoofs sounding strangely sharp and loud, and an occasional wheeled vehicle carrying some Member to the House of Commons.

Outside the massed ranks of police the whole population of London seemed to have gathered. The newspapers said that it was just like Mafeking night without the disorder. Members of Parliament came out from time to time to watch the scene, amongst the spectators being Mr. John Burns, Mr. Haldane, Mr. Walter Long and Mr. Lloyd George, who came with his little daughter, a fair haired child of six years old. Soon a deputation of eleven women with Miss Wallace Dunlop a descendant of the great William Wallace, as their leader,

marched out of the Caxton Hall with Mrs. Lawrence's instructions to oppose with spiritual force
the physical force which the authorities had arrayed
in such strength against them, ringing in their ears.

A cheer from the waiting crowd greeted them as
they gained the street, and though some fifty constables attempted to bar their passage into Victoria
Street, the people swept them through. At last
near the end of Victoria Street, they were met by a
body of police and the Inspector in Charge asked
Miss Wallace Dunlop that the deputation should
wait for a few moments in order that he might bring
up some mounted police to clear a way to the House
of Commons. She agreed to wait until eight o'clock
but when that time came the Inspector returned and
said the deputation could not pass. Then, faithful
to their trust, the little band of women pressed
bravely forward and commenced their hopelessly
unequal struggle with the police. In a moment
their ranks were broken and they were scattered
hopelessly amongst the crowd of constables and sight-
seers. Before long a number had been arrested and
the others were swept far away from their destination. When the news of the first deputation's fate
reached the Caxton Hall a second body of women
numbering some thirty or forty, marched out to take
their place. Like their predecessors, they too
reached the top of Victoria Street where the
mounted police were still waiting. Then suddenly,
Mrs. Leigh, a slight agile figure in white, dashed
forward from their midst and threw herself into the
mounted line, seizing a police horse by the bridle
with either hand. The horses reared and kicked
furiously, the constables closed upon her and she was

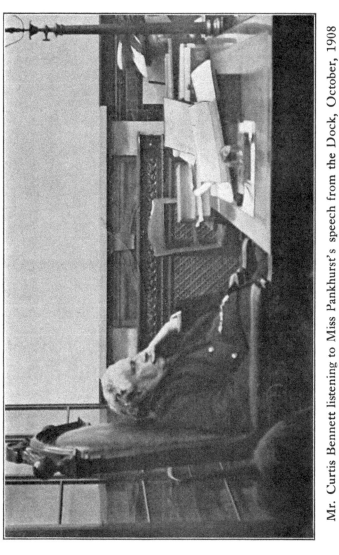

Mr. Curtis Bennett listening to Miss Pankhurst's speech from the Dock, October, 1908

flung to the ground. From time to time several isolated women succeeded by strategy in getting quite
close to the House of Commons and one even found
her way into one of the underground passages used
by Members of Parliament. In every case they
were captured by the police and either placed under
arrest or dragged away and pushed outside the
guarding cordons into the crowd. At last so fearful did the authorities become that the women might
be concealed at other strategic points that they proceeded to thoroughly search every corner of Westminster Abbey and with their lanterns were to be
seen amongst the buttresses and pinnacles of St. Margaret's Church, searching for Suffragettes. Yet
with all their vigilance they were circumvented, for
one woman succeeded in outwitting everyone and
entered the sacred chamber itself. The lady in
question was Mrs. Margaret Travers Simons, Mr.
Keir Hardie's Parliamentary Secretary, who, whilst
a believer in the Votes for Women Movement, had
never taken any active part in it. On her way to
the House that evening she had been deeply moved
by the violent scenes. As she sat thinking of them
in the Lobby, and realising that the Suffragettes,
struggle as they might, would never reach the House,
the thought suddenly flashed across her mind that
she herself had the power to make the appeal and
protest which was impossible to them. Seized by
an irresistible impulse, she sent in for Mr. T. H. W.
Idris, the Liberal Member for Flint Boroughs, and
asked him to take her to look through a little window, known as the " peep hole," which is situated on
the left side of the glass doors leading into the
House of Commons, and to which Members of

Parliament had the privilege of taking their lady friends. He agreed, and, on reaching the window, she mounted a seat, which is in front of it in order that she might get a clear view of the chamber. After a moment or two she descended and Mr. Idris turned towards the outer Lobby thinking that she was about to accompany him. In that instant, she pushed open the double glass doors and, before anyone could prevent her, darted into the Chamber and rushed up the central aisle towards the Speaker's chair, calling upon the House to " attend to the women's question! " She was seized by one of the attendants at the Bar, a big, powerful man who carried her back into the lobby, and in a very short space of time she had been handed over to a police inspector, conducted out of the House of Commons, and allowed to go free.

Outside in the street the conflict still continued and went on until midnight when it was found that ten persons had been injured and treated at Westminster Hospital, and that twenty-one women and a number of men had been arrested.

CHAPTER XV

OCTOBER, 1908

ON the morning of October 14th began the trial both of the three leaders who had been arrested by warrant and the twenty-one women whom they were said to have incited to break the peace. Excited crowds early assembled in Bow Street, and besieged the doors of the Police Court, begging the unyielding custodians for admission. In the dark passageways and lobbies of the Court were numbers of women, imploring the officials to allow them to pass into the Court itself. The public enter by a door at the back of the room and here there is a space where visitors may stand. This space was now crowded with women, pressing closely against the wooden barrier which cut them from off the narrow rows of equally crowded wooden seats, where the friends and relatives of the prisoners, who could obtain the ear of some kindly officer, were allowed to sit. In front of these seats is the dock itself — a wooden bench some six feet long, empty as yet, and surrounded by a heavy iron railing on three sides, the fourth to be guarded by a policeman when the prisoners arrive. In front and at one side of the dock are the benches for the Press, which that morning

271

contained representatives from all the leading newspapers. In front of this again, divided by a barrier
and on a lower level so that one sees little more than
the heads of its occupants, was another bench where
Mr. Muskett, the solicitor for the Prosecution who
had so often appeared against the Suffragettes, and
other minions of the law now sat. In front again
and placed at right angles to this bench is the witness box — a little wooden pen with a foolish
wooden canopy which looks as though it were meant
for keeping out the rain. On the right, opposite
the witness box, are two rows of seats, each entered
by a little wooden door, like church pews, where
counsel and distinguished strangers sit. In the well
between the witness box and these seats sit the re-
cording clerks and other officials, and opposite to
them, and facing the whole court is the Magistrate's
high-backed chair and his table. Mr. Curtis Bennett, the Magistrate who was to try the case, sat
there now, handsome and dignified, and looking the
picture of a high-bred eighteenth-century squire.

The familiar figures of Mrs. Pankhurst, Christabel and Mrs. Drummond were soon ushered into
the dock, and then Christabel began by asking the
Magistrate not to deal with the case in that Court,
but to send it for trial by Judge and Jury, her object
being to secure that Suffragette cases should no
longer be decided by a body of Police Court officials,
whom we had every reason to believe were acting
under the direct instructions of the Government
against whom our agitation was directed, but should
instead be submitted to a body of ordinary citizens.
She urged that, under section seventeen of the Summary Jurisdiction Act of 1879, she and her co-de-

fendants were entitled to the option of being tried
where they desired, and she wished now to state that
they desired that the case should go before a jury.
Mr. Curtis Bennett bent his head and smiled, saying,
" Yes, yes, but we will go on with the case now."
She pressed him to at once give an answer to the
point which she had raised, but he replied that he
could not do so until he had heard the case.

Mr. Muskett, then rose to prosecute. Speaking
quickly in a low voice and showing considerable irritation, he began by complaining that the defendants
had failed to obey a summons to appear, firstly on
Monday and secondly on Tuesday morning, to answer to the charge of having been guilty of conduct
likely to provoke a breach of the peace. Then in
the most fastidious manner and with clearly expressed disgust, he proceeded to set forth the details
of the case. He explained that, on October 8th, Inspector Jarvis had visited the offices of the Women's
Social and Political Union and had there seen Mrs.
Drummond with Miss Christabel Pankhurst. Miss
Pankhurst had said, " What about the 13th? Have
you seen our new bills?" and had produced the
hand-bill which formed the foundation of the present
charge. It was worded: " Votes for Women.
Men and women help the Suffragettes to rush the
House of Commons on Tuesday, October 13th, at
7:30 P. M." In showing this to Inspector Jarvis,
Miss Pankhurst had said that the words " to rush "
were not in sufficiently large type and that they were
to be made much more distinct.

On Sunday, October 11th, the Defendants had
held a meeting in Trafalgar Square, to which Mr.
Muskett objected, because it had caused " an enor-

mous amount of additional labour to be thrown upon the shoulders of the police." At this meeting, he asserted gravely, speeches had been delivered by the defendants inciting those present to carry out the programme of rushing the House of Commons. "You will agree sir," said Mr. Muskett, "that such conduct as that cannot be tolerated in this country." Finally he asked on behalf of the Commissioner of Police that the defendants should be ordered to be bound over to keep the peace.

Stout, red-faced Superintendent Wells, whom we usually found most friendly and obliging, now, looking very cross and uncomfortable, lumbered into the witness box. After taking the oath he gave evidence in regard to a visit of his own to the offices at Clement's Inn. He said that Mrs. Pankhurst had then shown him a copy of a letter which had been sent by the Women's Social and Political Union to Mr. Asquith. This document pointed out that at many large demonstrations all over the country, resolutions had been carried, calling upon the Government to adopt the Women's Enfranchisement Bill and also that, at a succession of by-elections, the voters had shown unmistakably their desire that the Government should deal with the question without further delay. It concluded by asking the Prime Minister to inform the Union as to whether the Government would carry the Bill into law during the autumn session.

After the Superintendent had read the letter, Mrs. Pankhurst had told him that, if Mr. Asquith returned a satisfactory reply to it, nothing would take place on October 13th save a great cheer for the Government, but that, if he did not, there would be

a demonstration and the women would get into the
House of Commons. " I said, ' You cannot get there
for the police will not let you unless you come with
cannon,' " the Superintendent went on, looking very
imposing, and explained that Mrs. Pankhurst had
then stated that " no lethal weapons " would be used.
She had also said, " Mr. Asquith will be responsible
if there is any disorder and accident."

Superintendent Wells next described the meeting
in Trafalgar Square where he had seen Mrs. Drummond distributing the " rush " hand-bills. He said
that he looked upon her as a " very active leader of
the Suffragettes " and that she frequently wore a
" uniform " with the word " general " or " general-
issimo " on the cap. He had told her that she and
Mrs. Pankhurst would be prosecuted. When questioned by Mr. Muskett as to the happenings of, the
previous evenings, Superintendent Wells said that
traffic had been " wholly disorganised " in the vicinity of the House of Commons for four hours and
that for three hours the streets had been in " great
disorder "; that a very large body of police indeed
had been required to maintain the peace, that ten
persons had been treated at Westminster Hospital
and that seven or eight constables and sergeants had
been more or less injured.

It was now Christabel Pankhurst's turn to cross-
examine the Superintendent and he looked across the
dock at her very nervously. She first questioned
him as to the statement that had been made that she
and her companions in the dock had broken their
promise to appear at the court either on the Monday
or Tuesday morning, and drew from him the admission that he had not received any undertaking " in

actual words." She then changed the subject and brightly asked him whether he was in the habit of reading the official organ of the Union "Votes for Women," to which he replied in the negative. "You are not aware, then," she said, "that Mrs. Pankhurst wrote the following words:

On October 13th in Parliament Square there will be many thousands of people to see fair play between the women and the Government. Let us keep their support and co-operation by showing them, as we have done before, with what quiet courage, self-restraint and determination, women are fighting against tyranny and oppression on the part of a Government which has been called the strongest of modern times. It is by the exercise of courage and self-restraint and persistent effort that we shall win in this unequal contest.

"There is nothing very inflammatory in those words," she urged. "Does it really occur to you that those words were circulated to incite a riot?" But Mr. Wells shrugged his shoulders and answered gruffly, "I am not complaining of that article, I am complaining of those bills."

Then she asked whether the crowd in Trafalgar Square was a disorderly one. He admitted that it was not, but at the question "are you aware that any member of the Government was there?" he looked round at the Magistrate cautiously and said, "I do not know that I should answer that." "You can say yes or no," said Mr. Curtis Bennett, and when the query was repeated the reply came, "I saw one there." "Was it Mr. Lloyd George?" said Miss Pankhurst with a smile, and at this there was laughter in court, and even the Magistrate plainly showed

amusement. Mr. Wells flushed redder still and remained silent. She next questioned the Superintendent as to the nature of the speeches in Trafalgar
Square and the exact meaning of the word "rush,"
but he frequently took refuge in silence, and refused
to be drawn. It was plain that Mr. Wells was not
accustomed to being cross-examined by a prisoner in
the dock and that he did not at all like it. Just as
he began to hope that it was nearly over, she suddenly changed the subject, and asked him whether
he had been present when Mr. John Burns had made
the famous speech which led to his arrest. "I was
not," he answered, and she asked, "Are you aware
that the words he used at that time were very much
more calculated to lead to destruction and damage
to property than anything that we have said?" "I
am not aware of it," said Mr. Wells looking appealingly across to Mr. Muskett. "You are aware
however that John Burns is a member of the present
Government and is responsible jointly with his colleagues, for the action which has been taken against
us?" "Yes," he answered, almost without thinking. "You are aware of that, you are aware that
the law-breaker is now sitting in judgment upon those
who have done far less than he did himself?" she
said, pressing home her advantage. "You are
aware of *that?*" she repeated after a pause. But
there was no reply.

Next she asked whether the Superintendent had
heard the Trafalgar Square speech of Mr. Will
Thorne, M.P. in which he had advised the people
to rush the bakers' shops? Mr. Wells felt on
safer ground now, for this did not concern a Cabinet
Minister. "I did not hear it," he ventured to an-

swer, " but it was reported to me." " Well, does it occur to you that his language was far more dangerous to the public peace than the language that we have used? " " I am not complaining of your language," he again answered doggedly, " I am complaining of the bills." " Well, the language that was used on the bills, he *spoke, he used the word 'rush,'* moreover he incited people to riot and violence," she urged. " Does it occur to you that his action is more reprehensible than ours? " " It occurs to me," said Mr. Wells sulkily, " that he might be prosecuted the same as you are." " You are not aware whether proceedings will be taken? " she asked with an air of pleased interest — but Mr. Curtis Bennett interposed to say that that question could not be allowed. Then she asked the Superintendent whether he knew that Mr. Gladstone had stated in the House of Commons that the proceedings against herself and her colleagues had not been instituted by the Government, but by the police. He tried to evade her, saying, " You have kept me so busily engaged that I have not had time to look at the papers this morning," but before he left the box he had virtually admitted that, in spite of Mr. Gladstone's denial, the Government was responsible for the prosecution.

The next witness was our old friend, Inspector Jarvis with whom we had had negotiations in all sorts of matters connected both with our peaceful and militant propaganda ever since our campaign in London had been started. He is a tall thin man with a pale, thoughtful face and is not at all like the typical police officer. As a rule he has the most kindly and courteous manners, but to-day he seemed thoroughly ill-tempered and refused to look directly at any of us. He was called upon by Mr. Muskett to read the notes which he had taken of Christabel's speech at the Sunday meeting in Trafalgar Square and he did so in halting and expressionless tones:

I wish you all to be there on the evening of the 13th and I hope that this will be the end of this movement. On June 30th we succeeded in driving Mr. Asquith underground; he is afraid of us and so are the Government. Years ago John Bright told the people that it was only by lining the streets from Charing Cross to Westminster that they could impress the Government. Well, we are only taking a leaf out of his book. We want you to help the women to rush their way into the House of Commons. You won't get locked up because you have the vote. If you are afraid, we will take the lead, and you will follow us. We know we shall win because we are in the right.

Then, just as a child at school who does not understand the words, he read an extract also from Mrs. Pankhurst's speech:

On Tuesday evening at Caxton Hall we shall ask those who support the women to come to Parliament Square. There will be a deputation of women who have no right in the House of Commons to a seat [1] there such as men have. The Government — does not know — its own mind — it — changes — so, but we do know — that we want the vote — and mean to have it. When the people in Parliament Square —

But Mr. Muskett interrupted, he had heard enough. He went on to ask if it were not a fact

[1] This, as Mr. Jarvis afterwards admitted, was a mistake; Mrs. Pankhurst really said that women had no representation in the House of Commons.

that, on Monday morning, Inspector Jarvis had himself served a summons upon the defendants to appear in court on the afternoon of the same day and on the Inspector assenting, he said, " I want to know about this question as to whether they promised to attend here or not." Inspector Jarvis hesitated, " Well, Miss Christabel," he began, " I saw her alone, and she said, ' We are not afraid, we shall be there.' " " Then," said Mr. Muskett, " I believe they were served with a summons to appear on the following morning at eleven o'clock." " Yes." " And as they did not put in an appearance then, a warrant was issued? " " Yes." " And you had to wait there for them until they surrendered to you? " Again the Inspector assented, looking very much aggrieved.

Christabel Pankhurst began her cross-examination by closely questioning Mr. Jarvis on this very point and soon drew from him the admission that no definite promise had been made. As she was speaking to him his face cleared visibly and he generously owned that he had been mistaken. Similar evidence from a third Inspector closed the case for the prosecution.

Christabel then applied for an adjournment and the Magistrate agreed to allow the case to stand over for a week. The three prisoners being released on bail for the time being.

As soon as this had been decided Mr. Curtis Bennett said that he would deal with the cases of the women who had been arrested in Trafalgar Square, and seven of these were soon ordered to undergo from one to two months' imprisonment in default of being bound over for twelve months. As each woman was asked if she had anything to say for herself, she replied, " I demand a trial by jury." This seemed to annoy Mr. Curtis Bennett considerably and he became more and more irate until the fifth woman had spoken. Then he laughed and said, " I see this has evidently been arranged beforehand." It was unfortunate for the fourth woman that he had not recovered his temper earlier for, though a first offender arrested for doing practically nothing, she received a sentence of two months' imprisonment, whilst one month only was served out to others of the same class. Mrs. Leigh, as this was the third time that she had been charged, received a sentence of three months. Thirteen of the Suffragettes pleaded that they wished to obtain legal advice, and were remanded for a week, at the end of which time milder methods obtained, for their sentences ranged merely from three weeks to one month.

Next day, Thursday, October 15th, a summons was issued against Mr. Will Thorne, M.P. for inciting the unemployed to rush the bakers' shops, and when his case came up on the 21st, he expressed the belief that no summons would have been issued against him but for the remarks made by Christabel Pankhurst during the Suffragette trial. He declared that in speaking as he had done his object had been to persuade the unemployed not to take part in the Women's Demonstration in Parliament Square, because he felt sure that they would get into trouble if they did so, and urged that his speech had been taken too literally. Mr. Curtis Bennett, however, ordered him to be bound over in his own recognisances of £200 and two sureties of £100 each to be of good behaviour for twelve months or in default to go to prison for six months. Mr. Thorne agreed to be bound over.

On Wednesday, October 21st, the trial of the Suffragette leaders again came on and, whilst the Court was just as crowded, the Press seats were even fuller than before. Mr. Curtis Bennett seemed more than ever dignified and magisterial. Everyone waited with impatience and presently there was a stir in the court, and, with much ceremony, some of the officers opened the door by which the prisoners usually enter and ushered in a group of gentlemen, who seated themselves in the pew-like benches reserved for counsel and distinguished persons. Then, preceded by a stout, black-bearded gaoler, and with three or four police on either side of them, the three Suffragettes made their way into the dock. As soon as they had seated themselves, Mr. Muskett rose and said in his usual rather peevish and very indistinct tones that the case for the Prosecution had been concluded on the previous Wednesday.

After a short preliminary argument as to legal forms between Christabel and the Magistrate and a pledge that she should be allowed to submit her objections later, there was a slight scuffling in those important side benches, the pew doors were opened, two of the gentlemen who had accompanied him stepped aside and Mr. Lloyd George, Chancellor of the Exchequer, came forward and passed across the court into the witness box.

Seen for the first time, he is totally unlike what one has been led to expect. Instead of the romantic-looking Welsh bard, with black and very curly hair, portrayed by the newspaper cartoons and drawings, there stood, cooped up in the little witness box,

with its useless-looking wooden canopy, a plain little
man, with a pale face, a long untidy moustache and
hair which, though he wears it somewhat long, as
it is in the pictures, has not the least suspicion of a
curl but lies limp and scanty and is a dull dingy
brown. At first he leant his arm on the front of the
witness box and looked across at the three prisoners
in the dock. He regarded Christabel Pankhurst
curiously, as well he might, for, in her fresh white
muslin dress whose one note of colour was the broad
band of purple white and green stripes around her
waist, with her soft brown hair uncovered, the little
silky curls with just a hint of gold in them clustering
about her neck, and, in this dingy place, her skin
looking even more brilliantly white and those rose
petal cheeks of hers even more exquisitely and vividly flushed with purest pink than usual, she was as
bright and dainty as a newly opened flower, and with
all her look of perfect health and vigour, appeared
so slender and so delicately knit as to have little
more of substance in her than a briar rose. But
she was to triumph over her opponent in the witness
box, not by her grace and freshness and by the outer
aspect of her vivid glowing personality, but by her
sparkling wit, her biting sarcasm and by the force
and depth of her arguments. And these went home,
not merely as they can be set down here in cold dull
print, but far more truly, because they were en-
hanced by the everchanging eloquence of gesture,
voice, and facial expression — by a lift of the
eyebrows, a turn of the head, a heightening of the
lovely rose colour that flooded sometimes as far as
the white throat and as quickly ebbed again, a sweep
of the slender hand or a turn of that slight virile

frame.   All these, because so perfectly they echoed
and expressed her thoughts, could lend to even the
baldest and tritest words, a fanciful humour, a delicate irony, or an inexorable force.

As she rose to examine Mr. Lloyd George, she
began quite formally, but with a cheerful and pleasant manner asking whether he had been present at
the Trafalgar Square meetings on October 11th?
and whether he had seen a copy of the bills which
were being distributed?   "Yes," he replied, with
just the least suspicion of a smile, " a young lady
gave one to me the moment I arrived.   It invited
me to rush the House of Commons."   "How did
you interpret the invitation conveyed to you as a
member of the audience?" she asked next with a
brisk business-like air.   "What did you think we
wanted you to do?"   He replied pompously, " I
really should not like to place an interpretation upon
the document.   I do not think it is quite my func-
tion."   "Well, I am speaking to you as a member
of the general public," she urged, refusing to be put
off.   "Imagine you were not at the meeting at all,
but were walking up the Strand, and someone gave
you a copy of this Bill, and you read it —' Help the
Suffragettes to rush the House of Commons.'   And
suppose you forgot you were a member of the Government and regarded yourself just as an ordinary
person like myself — quite unofficial," she added,
smiling, and with a little quick shake of her shoulders.   "What would you think you were called
upon to do?"   "Really, I should not like to be
called upon to undertake so difficult a task as to interpret that document," was the tart reply, but
Christabel went on persuasively, "Now this word

Miss Christabel Pankhurst questioning
Mr. Herbert Gladstone

'rush,' which seems to be at the bottom of it all, what does it mean?" She waited with parted lips and raised eyebrows for a reply. It came unwillingly. "I understood the invitation from Mrs. Pankhurst was to force an entrance to the House of Commons." "No, no, I want you to keep your mind concentrated on the bill," she corrected. "Let us forget what Mrs. Pankhurst said. What did the Bill say?" "I really forget what the Bill said," he snapped out sharply. She repeated the phrase to him graciously —"Help the Suffragettes to rush the House of Commons." "Yes, that is it," he assented, and she said, "I want you to define the word 'rush.'" "I cannot undertake to do that." "You cannot?" she asked incredulously. "No, Miss Pankhurst, I cannot." "Well," she replied, I will suggest some definitions to you. "I find that in 'Chambers' English Dictionary' one of the meanings of the word is 'an eager demand.' Now, what do you think of that?" "I cannot enter into competition with 'Chambers' Dictionary.' I am prepared to accept it," he said stolidly.

Mr. Lloyd George was beginning to turn his head away from her and to show every sign of unwillingness to continue answering. Her imperturbable good humour made the situation harder for him to bear. As Max Beerbohm in the *Saturday Review* said, "His Celtic fire burned very low; and the contrast between the buoyancy of the girl and the depression of the statesman was almost painful. Youth and an ideal, on the one hand, and on the other, middle age and no illusions left over."

But Christabel appeared not to notice his discomfiture: "'Urgent pressure of business.' That is another meaning. Now, if you were asked to help the Suffragettes to make an eager demand to the House of Commons that they should give votes to women, would you feel that we were calling upon you to do an illegal act?" "That is not for me to say." Here Mr. Curtis Bennett interposed. "The witness is perfectly right. This is for me to say on the evidence. I have not interfered so far," but Christabel went on unheedingly and continued gravely reading from her list of definitions. "There is another sense in which the word 'rush' is used and I think it will be of some interest to you. We use it in this connexion, to 'rush' Bills through Parliament." Mr. Lloyd George smiled in spite of himself. "Yes, I think I have some experience of that!" he said. "'On the rush' we are told in another dictionary means 'in a hurry.' There is nothing unlawful in being in a hurry." Mr. Lloyd George shook himself impatiently, and the Magistrate again interposed; this time with more severity. "I have already said you must address those remarks to me afterwards." But quite impassively she held to her point and with her eyes upon the witness continued, "Did you understand you were asked to go in a hurry to the House of Commons to make this eager demand for enfranchisement? Was that the meaning which the Bill conveyed to you?"

In spite of his remonstrances Mr. Curtis Bennett was evidently enjoying the scene, and his eyes twinkled as he listened to the quickly and pleasantly directed questions and to the slow, grudging replies. Mr. George kept glancing at him angrily, and again looking severe he said at last, "Miss Pankhurst, you must take my ruling, please."

At this she changed her tack a little, questioning
Mr. Lloyd George as to the speeches he had heard
in Trafalgar Square and the demeanour of the crowd
and always making her inquiries with a polite air
of expectation that valuable information would be
forthcoming. When Mr. Lloyd George admitted
that he had heard some part of Miss Pankhurst's
speech, Christabel gravely inquired whether her
mother had threatened violence to any member of
the Government. "She did not invite the audience
to attack you in any way?" she asked. Then gradually, through his fear of being made to appear ridiculous, she brought him to admit that he had thought
that, if the public responded to the invitation to
"rush" the House of Commons, the consequences
would not be formidable and that there had been no
suggestion either that public or private property
should be damaged or that any personal violence
should be done.

Then she suddenly asked, "There were no words
used so likely to incite to violence as the advice you
gave at Swansea, that the women should be ruthlessly flung out of your meeting?" This was unexpected. Mr. Lloyd George frowned and remained
silent. Mr. Muskett stood up and appealed to the
Magistrate who interposed as was expected of him.
"This is quite irrelevant. That was a private
meeting, and not of the same character," he said re-
provingly. Christabel shook her head. "It was a
public meeting," she insisted. The Magistrate
waved his hand. "Well, private *in a sense.*"
"They *are* private now-a-days, that is quite true,"
she said pointedly, and obviously referring to the fact
that ticket meetings only were now addressed by

Cabinet Ministers, all women with a few selected exceptions being rigidly excluded. Then she went on to question Mr. Lloyd George as to the reason for which the " rush " had been planned, but he obstinately refused to answer.

Turning to the events during the so-called " rush " on October 13th, she elicited the fact that Mr. Lloyd George had taken his little six-year-old daughter with him to watch the scene. " She was very amused," he said with a malicious air. " You thought it was quite safe for a child of those tender years to be amongst the crowd? " asked Christabel, and this time it was her turn to be a little severe. " I was not amongst the crowd," he snapped, and later, as if anxious to justify himself, added, " You see, I only brought her from Downing Street to the House, and I think that was clear." " The Prosecution asserts that a serious breach of the peace took place," was her next question. " Do you agree with that statement? "

The Magistrate interrupted, " The Chancellor of the Exchequer would have nothing to do with that," he said. " I believe you are a lawyer? " with a quick change of front, she asked, turning politely to Mr. Lloyd George. " Well, I hope I am," he answered with a surly air. " Don't you think the offence alleged against us would be more properly described as ' Unlawful Assembly '? " " There again, I was not put in the witness box to express an opinion of that sort," he objected and the Magistrate again supported him. She made another attempt: " You have seen the form of summons against us? " but he protested that he had not and did not know with what offence the prisoners were charged. She explained to him the form of the summons and explained that, owing to this, the defendants were denied the right of trial by jury. He merely replied, " I take it from you, Miss Pankhurst, but I do not know."

An awkward question for Mr. Lloyd George was: " Do you think that coercion is the right way of dealing with political disorders? " He remained silent, and the Magistrate tried to help him out, saying, " It is not for the witness to express an opinion." Christabel looked full at Mr. Lloyd George, asking, " You refuse to answer? " " I do not refuse to answer," he said, not very honestly, " but I must obey the decision of the Bench that I cannot express an opinion about things in the witness box." " Am I to understand that an answer must not be given to that? " she appealed to the Magistrate. He replied, " No." " Not even if the witness would like to do it? " " No," he said, but she tried again. " Well, is it likely to be a successful way of dealing with political disturbances? " But the Magistrate said, " That again, is not admissible." " But for these restrictions, your Worship — she broke out with some heat, but he waved her aside and she understood that he was implacable, so she turned cheerfully to the witness and said, " Can you tell me whether any interference with public order took place in connexion with previous movements for franchise reform? " " I should have thought that that was an historical fact, Miss Pankhurst," he replied. Again the Magistrate interposed to save him. " That is cross-examination. The witness

19

cannot go into that." "In a *sense* he is my wit-ness," she said, but though Mr. Curtis Bennett smiled, he replied, "In *every sense* at present."

Nevertheless he had evidently seen the justice of the remark and he did not object when a similar question was now put. It was: "Have we not re-ceived encouragement from you, or if not from you, from your colleagues to take action of this kind?" "I should be very much surprised to hear that, Miss Pankhurst." Mr. George gave his answer pom-pously. "You deny that we have been encouraged by Liberal statesmen to take action of this kind?" she said eagerly. "I simply express astonishment at the statement," he said casting up his eyes with an exaggerated, but not very convincing air of indigna-tion. "Have you ever heard these words spoken by us at Trafalgar Square or by any Liberal statesman:

I am sorry to say that if no instructions had ever been addressed in political crises to the people of this country except to remember to hate violence, to love order, and to exercise patience, the liberties of this country would never have been attained.

"Have you ever heard those words before?" "I cannot call them to mind." At this reply there was a sensation in the court, silent, but clearly felt. "Those were the words of William Ewart Glad-stone," said Christabel. "I accept your statement, Miss Pankhurst," was Mr. Lloyd George's reply, and when asked whether he was aware that in 1884 Mr. Chamberlain had threatened to march 100,000 men on London, he again replied, "I do not know." Christabel's next question carried the war fur-ther into the enemy's country. "Is it not a fact that

you yourself have set us an example of revolt?"
she asked, but Mr. Curtis Bennett interposed to say
that the Chancellor need not answer that question,
and that she must not attack her own witness.
Whilst they were arguing, Mr. Lloyd George himself burst in. "I never incited a crowd to violence,"
he said hotly, as though this form of defence had
only just occurred to him. "Not in the Welsh
Grave Yard case?" she asked. "No!" he said.
"You did not tell them to break down a wall and
disinter a body?" "I gave advice which was
found by the Court of Appeal to be sound legal advice," he said snappishly, and again almost turning
his back upon her. "*We* think that *we* are giving
sound advice too," she said.

After this Mr. Lloyd George became less and less
ready to give any reply, and his angry eyes were con-
tinually calling for the Magistrate's intervention.

Miss Pankhurst then cited passages from "Taylor
on Evidence," to show that more latitude could be
allowed in questioning a witness who obviously appeared to be hostile or interested for the other party,
or unwilling to give evidence, but Mr. Curtis Bennett declared that none of these descriptions could
be applied to Mr. Lloyd George. So, with a gesture of protest, Christabel said, "I think I need not
trouble him with any further questions."

After some questioning by Mrs. Pankhurst to which
Mr. Lloyd George returned the scantiest and most
surly of replies, Mrs. Drummond said earnestly but
with a touch of humour in her voice.

"I should like to ask Mr. Lloyd George this question; many times he has refused to answer me.
When do you intend to put a stop to these things by

giving us the vote?" Shrugging his shoulders, Mr. Lloyd George turned to the Magistrate who gave the desired reply: "That is not a question for the witness." Mrs. Drummond added, after a pause, quietly and reproachfully: "You and your colleagues are much to blame for this agitation." "You must not make a statement," said the Magistrate." "You see, we never get a chance at other times," said Mrs. Drummond appealingly. At this Mr. George smiled broadly, but not very pleasantly, and shaking his head said, "Indeed you do!" as he left the box.

Mr. Curtis Bennett now told Christabel that he wished her to call Mr. Herbert Gladstone in order that the Home Secretary might not be detained from his duties in the House unnecessarily but she declared that it was absolutely essential that she should first call one other witness. Mr. Curtis Bennett protested and she said, "I have only one question to put to this lady." "Very well then, one question," he said smiling as though he scarcely believed her, and one could plainly see, determining to hold her to her word. Christabel then called "Miss Marie Brackenbury," who stepped quietly into the box. Christabel gently asked her whether it were true that she had suffered six weeks' imprisonment in connexion with this agitation and as soon as she had assented said quickly, but in a clear, penetrating voice, "Did Mr. Horace Smith tell you in sentencing you to that term he was doing what he was told?" "You must not put that question!" almost shouted the Magistrate. But the witness had already replied, "He did." "The witness has said

' yes,' upon oath," said Miss Pankhurst triumphantly turning to the place where the Cabinet Ministers sat. There was a strange stir in the court, those present feeling that belief in the inviolability of British Justice was slipping from their grasp. For a moment or two there was an unpleasant pause and Mr. Curtis Bennett sat flushed and angry.

Mr. Herbert Gladstone, the Home Secretary, was then called and took his place in the witness box. With his shiny bald forehead, ruddy face, prominent eyes and corpulent figure, he formed not only a striking contrast to his colleague who had just been examined, but was as far removed from the impressive dignity of his own distinguished father. Altogether his general appearance was that which the romantic idealist would associate rather with a comfortable and prosperous shopkeeper than with a Cabinet Minister. As soon as he had been sworn, he placed his elbows on the ledge in front of him and looked smilingly around the court, as much as to say, " Nothing of this kind can disturb me, I intend to enjoy myself."

Miss Pankhurst began by endeavouring to fix upon him as Home Secretary the responsibility for the proceedings against herself and her colleagues which he had denied in the House of Commons. She succeeded in forcing him to admit, " I am at the head of the responsible department." But when she put the questions more plainly, saying, " Did you not, as a matter of fact, instruct the Commissioner of Police to take the present proceedings? " and " Are the Government as a whole responsible for these proceedings? " Mr. Muskett jumped up, in each case, shouting, " I object to that! " and the Magistrate also said that the questions could not be answered.

They were also determined that no more unpleasant disclosures were to be made, but she would not leave the subject. " Did you instruct Mr. Horace Smith to decide against Miss Brackenbury and to send her to prison for six weeks? " she asked. " You cannot put that question either," said Mr. Curtis Bennett in a slightly raised tone. " It is a pity that the public interest should suffer on that account," was her severe reply, and turning to Mr. Gladstone, she said, " Did you offer any instructions to Mr. Horace Smith? "   " I object to this; it is contempt of court to continue putting these questions! " indignantly cried Mr. Muskett again springing to his feet, but with a broad sweep of her hand she declared, " The public will answer them."   Then turning to Mr. Gladstone, whose enjoyment of the situation had now entirely vanished, she persisted, " What do you suggest is the meaning of what Mr. Horace Smith has said? " but again the Magistrate intervened.

She next asked Mr. Gladstone to define the word " rush."   " I can hardly give any definition of it, but a rush implies force," he said, growing more comfortable again.   " Do you deny that it involves speed rather than force? " she asked, and he replied smiling and putting his head knowingly on one side, " Speed generally involves force."   This argument continued   for   some   time.   Then   she   asked: " Were you anticipating that you would be in bodily danger as a consequence of the issue of this Bill? " " I did not think of it at all. I did not think whether the possibility existed or not," he answered, squaring his shoulders and throwing out his chest. She waved her hand. " You are like us, above these considerations. You were not in fear? " " No, not at all," he answered, looking pleased with himself. " Did you ever think that public property was in danger as a consequence of this bill having been issued? " " I thought it quite possible," he said a little more seriously, " I thought there would be danger from the crowds." " Then you were agreeably disappointed on the morning of the 14th, when you found no harm had been done? " " No, I was not. The police measures were sufficient to stop any serious accident or danger," he said proudly and magisterially.

She kept putting questions of this kind, first in one form then in another until he began to grow tired and puzzled, and was evidently in fear of making some unwise admission. " Did you feel that but for the line of police protecting you, the crowd would have rushed upon you and attacked you? " she asked at last with expressive emphasis. " The police were not protecting me," he answered with an air of offended dignity; " I felt no personal fear." " Did any other person seem in danger of attack? " " The police gave them very little chance." " What made you think them a dangerous or hostile crowd? " " Of course, I am quite accustomed to seeing these crowds. I know what has happened before." " What has happened? " " Disorderly scenes." Mr. Gladstone was standing up now and looking quite severe. " What harm have they done? " " Very little, as it happened." " What harm have they attempted to do? " " That is not for me to answer." "Have they attempted to do more than secure an interview with the Prime Minister?" Mr. Gladstone turned to the Magistrate, who said, "That is not a question for him to answer."

"We will go back to the 13th," she said. "Do you think anyone was obstructed in their passage to the House of Commons?" "I cannot speak for other people." "You saw no attempt to waylay Members of Parliament or Cabinet Ministers?" Her questions continued thick and fast. He admitted that he had seen no one waylaid or injured and no harm done, but took refuge in the assertion: "There was a great crowd." "But a crowd assembles when the King goes to open Parliament," she said. He answered crossly, "Presumably, they were waiting to 'rush' the House of Commons," and added later that he had heard that certain police constables had been injured, and that there had been thirty-seven arrests and over forty complaints of losses of purses and watches. "Comparing that with the net result of a Lord Mayor's Show crowd or any sort of procession, really less harm resulted?" she asked, but he gave no reply and her questioning as to how many policemen were on duty and what the cost had been to the country were suppressed by Mr. Curtis Bennett.

Presently Christabel asked, "How do you define a political offence?" Mr. Gladstone leant over the edge of the box and smiled again. "I wish you would give me a good definition," he said, in friendly confidential tones, "I am often asked that question in the House of Commons." "Well, with the Magistrate's permission, I will," she answered. "A political offence is one committed in connexion

with political disturbances and with a political motive." " I do not think that a sufficient explanation," he said with a challenging air. " If I am at
liberty after this day's proceedings are over, I shall
have pleasure in sending you a fuller account."
Then she asked, " Do you remember that when a
deputation of women went to the House of Commons to see the Prime Minister, instead of being allowed to enter, they were arrested?" " I have no
immediate recollection of that, only a general recollection," was the Home Secretary's reply given with a
lofty manner. When the question was put again in
a slightly different form, the Magistrate interrupted:
" That does not arise on the issue." " It throws a
light on it though," said Miss Pankhurst. " Please
do obey; otherwise I shall have to stop it altogether,"
said Mr. Curtis Bennett, and one heard a note of
regret in his voice. He evidently enjoyed the dis-
comfort of the Cabinet Ministers and the spectacle
of their professing blankest ignorance on well-known
points. " I have given you much more licence than
I should give Counsel," he urged.

" In the action we took on the 13th is it within
your knowledge that we were acting on advice given
by yourself?" Christabel asked. " I wish you
would take my advice," Mr. Gladstone answered.
" We are trying to take it," she said quietly.
" What did you mean when you said that men had
used *force majeure* in demanding the vote?" " If
you hand me the speech, I daresay I can tell you."
She held out a copy of it towards him but Mr.
Curtis Bennett interposed. " How is this material
to what Mr. Gladstone saw? You are cross-exam-
ining your own witness, Miss Pankhurst, and you

must not do that." " May I not ask any explanation whatsoever as to the counsel given to us?" she
asked with a persuasive air. " No, you may not,"
the Magistrate replied sternly. " We never have
any opportunity. May I ask whether he made certain statements?" Mr. Curtis Bennett smiled and
pretended not to notice, and Christabel eagerly
turned to Mr. Gladstone, reading from the printed
copy of his speech. " Did you say it was impossible
not to sympathise with the eagerness and passion
which have actuated so many women on this subject?" " Yes," he replied. " Did you say men
had had to struggle for centuries for their political
rights?" " Yes." " Did you say that they had to
fight from the time of Cromwell and that for the last
130 years the warfare had been perpetual?" His
smile was growing broader and broader. " Yes,"
he said. " Did you say that on this question experience showed that predominance of argument alone
— and you believed that that had been attained —
was not enough to win the political day? Did you
say that?" " Yes." " Did you say that we are in
the stage of what is called ' academic discussion,'
which serves for the ventilation of pious opinions
and is accompanied, you admit, by no effective action
on the part of the Government, or of political parties or of voters throughout the country?" " Yes."
" Did you say that members of the House of Commons reflect the opinion of the country, not only in
regard to the number of people outside, but in regard to the intensity of the feeling in support of a
movement, and that the Government must necessarily be a reflex of the party which brought it into
being?" " Yes." " Did you say this: ' There

comes a time when political dynamics are far more important than political arguments?' You said that?" "Yes." "And that 'men had learned this lesson?'" "Yes." "And that they know the necessity for 'demonstrating that *force majeure* which actuates and arms a Government for effective work'?" "Yes, I think it was a most excellent speech!" he said nodding his head and smiling up at the prisoner evidently regarding the whole affair as a very good joke. The court laughed too, but for a different reason, and the Magistrate raised no objection.

"I agree with you," said Christabel, smiling demurely, "Did you say that this was the task before the leaders of this great movement?" "Yes." "Did you speak of people assembled in tens of thousands in the 'thirties, 'sixties and 'eighties, and do you know that we have done it in Hyde Park, and on Woodhouse Moor and other places?" "Yes." "Why don't you give us the vote then?" she said with quick emphasis, and the court laughed again. "Are you aware of the words your distinguished father spoke on the matter?" she continued. "I heard the quotation." "Do you assent to the proposition he laid down?" "Yes." "Then you cannot condemn our methods any more," she said triumphantly. "That is hardly a matter for my opinion," he said, suddenly remembering that he must preserve his dignity. "It is a very interesting question, though. I need not trouble you further," she concluded.

Now Mrs. Pankhurst rose and the witness turned to her quite cheerfully. "I want to ask Mr. Gladstone," she said, "if he is aware that the consequence of our being ordered to be bound over is that we cannot consent and that we shall go to prison?" "That is a matter of law, and not for the witness," interposed the Magistrate. "If that happens to us, if we go to prison, I hope that Mr. Gladstone will see that we go as political offenders," she said, but again the Magistrate intervened. "Do you think we should be likely to break the law if we had the same means of representation as men?" she then asked, and Mr. Gladstone replied with pompous amiability. "I am sure your motive is excellent, but that is a hypothetical question which I cannot answer."

Mrs. Pankhurst was irritated. "I will ask Mr. Gladstone," she said, "whether, in his opinion we should be treated as ordinary criminals, searched, stripped and put into cells as though we were drunkards and pickpockets?" "You must not put that question," said the Magistrate. The case amused him, but he did not like the unpleasant side of it put forward.

This concluded the evidence of the Cabinet Ministers, and as they were about to leave the court, Christabel graciously said, "May we tender our warm thanks to these two gentlemen who have done us the favour of coming forward to give evidence?" She then called a number of witnesses in support of her contention that the crowd on the night of the 13th was an orderly one and that no violence was done. Amongst these were Colonel Massy, formerly of the Sixth Dragoon Guards, Lady Constance Lytton, and Mr. Nevinson, a well-known leader-writer, and war correspondent. Mrs. May, another witness, said that in her opinion the word "rush"

Mr. Herbert Gladstone in the witness-box being examined by Miss Christabel Pankhurst, October, 1908

had been used on the famous handbill in a sense similar to that conveyed by the expression " A dash to
the North Pole," explaining, that though an attempt
to reach the North Pole is described as a " dash," it
is, in reality, the slowest possible mode of travel.   In
the same way she imagined that the public had been
asked to " rush " the House of Commons into passing a Votes for Women measure.

Then came Miss Evelyn Sharp, well known as
a writer of delightful stories for children, one of
those frail wan-faced little people, who, whilst looking always as though a puff of strong wind would
carry them away, yet manage to accomplish such
quantities of work as fill the strongest with amaze,
and at the same time have ever ready a fund of the
brightest and cheeriest good humour.   Now she told
in the funniest and most winning way, that she had
taken the fateful handbill as an invitation to go to
the House of Commons and, if possible, not to turn
back, and how, when she had found the police were
determined to bar the way up Victoria Street, she
had stooped and dodged between them in the middle
of a scene which she described as being " like a rush
at hockey."

Miss F. E. Macaulay, an historical student, then
gave several instances of women having gone to the
House of Commons for the purpose of presenting
petitions in ancient days and said she considered that
the Suffragettes were only reviving an ancient custom.

Meanwhile the day had passed; the case had begun at ten and it was now seven o'clock.   Except
for half an hour at lunch time, there had been no in-
terval and during all these hours, but for an occa-

sional brief five minutes or so when Mrs. Pankhurst
or Mrs. Drummond had taken a turn, Christabel
had been constantly examining witnesses, remaining
always eager, alert, and full of energy and resource.
Several times she had applied for an adjournment,
but Mr. Curtis Bennett was just as anxious to tire
her out and thus finish the trial, as she was to prolong it. At last, at half past seven, he asked how
many further witnesses she proposed to put into the
box. She replied, " About fifty. We are sorry to
take up the time of the court, but we are fighting for ·
our liberty." On hearing this, Mr. Curtis Bennett
decided to adjourn the hearing of the case until the
following Saturday, ordering that the defendants
should be released on bail as before.

So Christabel had won for the time being. Whatever the final result might be the defendants had
three more days of freedom before them, and the
case which by the long accounts of it that were ap-
pearing in every newspaper was interesting thousands of people in the Votes for Women movement,
was to be carried on for another day. Criminal
cases, many of them dealing with the foulest and
most sordid crimes, are allowed to drag on for weeks
and even months, whilst public time, public money,
and public interest is lavishly expended upon them;
we felt that we need not scruple then to prolong, as
far as we possibly could, a trial dealing with great
political issues. Moreover, our second Albert Hall
meeting had been fixed for October 29th and we
hoped that the defendants might be free to speak
that night.

When Saturday morning at length came round
and the prisoners again took their places in the dock,

it was at once evident that Mr. Curtis Bennett was determined to bring the case to an abrupt conclusion. Speaking in sharper and harsher tones than any we had heard from him before, he announced that he had decided only to hear two or three more witnesses whom the defendants might specially select, unless there were others who could give evidence relevant to the case in regard to a set of facts entirely different from any that had been raised. As this decision might take the defendants by surprise he would allow an adjournment of half an hour in which they might consider which of their witnesses they would prefer to call. Requests to state what class of evidence he would consider relevant, both from Christabel and Mrs. Pankhurst, the Magistrate met with a curt refusal to say anything further, and Christabel was not in form to overcome his objections as she had been on the previous days. Indeed we now saw with anxiety that the excitement and extra pressure of work of the last few weeks, coupled with the constant heavy routine entailed by her position in the Union and the great strain of conducting this case, had begun to tell on her and, for the first time in her life, we began to fear that she might break down. But even now she would not abandon the fight to prolong the case. It was impossible in half an hour to examine individually the hundreds of persons who had by this time offered to testify as witnesses, in order to find out which of them would prove most valuable to our case. The only thing to be done was to choose a few, almost at random, who possessed some special position or influence, and whom we also knew personally to be particularly sympathetic and observant.

When the half hour had elapsed and the prisoners had again taken their places, Christabel first called Mr. James Murray, the Liberal Member of Parliament for East Aberdeenshire, who had so kindly come to the rescue when bail had been refused at Bow Street. He stepped into the box, a huge figure immaculately dressed and faultlessly groomed, and turned his big ruddy, good humoured face towards the three prisoners with a kindly smile. When asked by Christabel if he were present at the meeting in Trafalgar Square on Sunday, October 11th, he replied: " I was going into the National Gallery and saw a collection of well dressed people in the Square. I think your mother was speaking, but I could not hear anything. What struck me was that the crowd listening to her was composed of exactly the type of people who go to Church on Sunday in Scotland." " Then they must have been very respectable," said Christabel. " Did you get a copy of the Bill?" " No." " I daresay you saw it in the papers?" " I saw a statement in the papers." " How did you understand the word ' rush '?" " I did not take the matter seriously at all." Here Mr. Curtis Bennett interrupted curtly, " That really is for me, Miss Pankhurst, as I have told you." " Did you resolve to accept the invitation?" Christabel asked. " I could not very well, you see," said Mr. Murray smiling broadly, " because I was inside the citadel." " He has the right of entry," said Mr. Curtis Bennett with mock solemnity, and for the first time that morning with a twinkle in his eyes. " Were you near Westminster on the 13th?" was the next question. " I was in the House and sitting down to dinner when I got a telegram from your mother sent from the neighbourhood of Bow Street, asking me to go across there." "This cannot be relevant," said Mr. Curtis Bennett sharply, but Mr. Murray merely looked amused, and went on: "In coming here I drove in a hansom up Parliament Street. The whole place was like a besieged city except that we had police officers instead of soldiers. A little beyond Dover House the crowd was held back by a cordon, but I had not the slightest difficulty in getting through in a hansom. Afterwards I returned to the House by the Strand and the Embankment and had very little trouble in getting back." "Was it a disorderly crowd?" "No, I think you could say an ordinary London crowd."

"Did you come to the conclusion that the persons who had called the meeting had done so with a desire to incite the crowd to disorder or damage?" It was Mrs. Pankhurst who spoke now. "No," answered Mr. Murray, "I thought that if it were for any purpose at all it was to advertise the cause." "You know something of the women who are conducting this agitation?" was Mrs. Pankhurst's next question, and Mr. Murray said gallantly: "Yes, I have the greatest admiration for them; for their earnestness of purpose, ability, and general management of the whole scheme. "You know they have tried every other political method?" "Yes, and if they had been men instead of women they would not have been in the dock now — judging by the past." "Do you agree with Mr. Lloyd George when he said that if the Government would give us what we are asking for this agitation would cease?" "I have no doubt it would. I go further than Mr. Lloyd George and I say you are entitled to it," said the witness with fervour, and then, with a genial motion of farewell to the prisoners he withdrew.

After Dr. Miller Macquire, the well known Army coach, a stout little man with a black moustache and a strong Irish brogue, and Miss Agnes Murphy, an Australian, a quiet-voiced, pale-faced lady had also given evidence, Mr. Curtis Bennett said that he would hear no more witnesses. Every attempt to overcome his decision failed and Christabel then applied for an adjournment in order that she and her companions might be in a position to do themselves full justice when they addressed the court. Everyone present anxiously hoped that this request would be granted, for it was evident that the woman who had hitherto conducted the defence so brilliantly, was almost worn out. The Magistrate, however, was determined to bring the case to an end, and he said, " You have had a long time to take this matter into consideration, you must either address me now, or not at all." She protested that the case was being *" rushed "* through the court, and at this there was laughter and applause, for everyone recognised the play on the word " rush." But Mr. Curtis Bennett said hotly, " Are you going to address me or not ? " With a gesture of protest, Christabel Pankhurst then began to speak in her own defence. She held in her hand a sheaf of type-written notes, containing dates and quotations, but every word of her brilliant speech was extemporised. She spoke quickly, and with a passionate emotion which is usually foreign to her. When she referred to the nature of the prosecution and to the conduct of the Government in having denied the women the trial by jury to which the nature of their alleged defence entitled them and in having preferred to hustle their case through the police court where the drunkards and pickpockets are tried, it was with a thrill of indignation that spread through the court.

She began by declaring that these proceedings had been taken " out of malice and for vexation," and " in order to lame, in an illegitimate way, a political enemy." In proof of this she cited the attitude of the Government towards the present women's movement from its very beginning three years before. She drew attention to the fact, which had been sworn to in the witness box, that Mr. Horace Smith had allowed himself to be coerced by the Government into settling, in conjunction with them, whether a certain lady charged in connection with this agitation, was guilty, and even the term of imprisonment which was to be inflicted upon her before the evidence had been heard.

" Now, this policy of the Government of weighting the scales against us," Christabel declared, " is not of interest merely to us, but to the whole community. In the course of British history we have seen many struggles for the purification of our judicial system. . . . It has been left to the twentieth century — to these so-called democratic days — to see our judicial system corrupted for party ends. I am glad that we have been able to perform the public duty and service of doing something to attack this evil while it is in the bud. . . ."

Dealing with the form of the summons, she urged that, if she and her colleagues were guilty of any offence, it was that of illegal assembly, but the Government had not charged them with this offence, because they had wished to keep their trial in the police court and to prevent it from coming before a jury. " They believe, that by this means," she said, " they will succeed in prejudicing the public against us. We know perfectly well that up till recently the general public shunned the police court as a disgraceful place. Well, I think that by our presence here we have done something to relieve the police court of that unenviable reputation. We have done something to raise its status in the public eye.

" The authorities dare not see this case come before a jury," she continued, " because they knew perfectly well that if it were heard before a jury of our countrymen we should be acquitted, just as John Burns was acquitted years ago for taking action far more serious, far more dangerous to the public peace than anything we have done. Yes, I say they are afraid of sending us before a jury, and I am quite sure that this will be obvious to the public, and that the Government will suffer from the underhand, the unworthy and the disgraceful subterfuge by which they have removed this case to what we can only call a Star Chamber of the twentieth century. Yes, this is a Star Chamber. . . . We are deprived of trial by jury. We are also deprived of the right of appeal against the magistrate's decision. Very, very carefully has this procedure been thought out; very, very cunningly has it been thought to hedge us in on every side, and to deprive us of our rights in the matter! Though we are rendered liable to six months' imprisonment, we are yet denied the privileges in making our defence that people liable to three months' imprisonment enjoy. We shall be told in the House of Commons no doubt — we have been told the same thing before now — that we are only bound over, we need not go to prison, if we go to prison we have only ourselves to thank.   .   .   . If the case is decided against us, if we are called upon to be bound over, it must be remembered that that amounts to imprisoning us, and that therefore the authorities cannot possibly escape their responsibility in sending us to prison by saying that we could be at liberty if we liked.   Magna Charta has been practically torn up by the present Government. .   .   .   We consider that it is not we who ought to be in the dock to-day, but the people who are responsible for such a monstrous state of affairs."

Then she went on to deal with the reasons for issuing the bill: "We do not deny at all that we issued this bill; none of us three have wished to deny responsibility.   We did issue the bill; we did cause it to be circulated; we did put upon it the words ' Come and help the Suffragettes to rush the House of Commons.'   For these words we do not apologise. .   .   .   It is very well known that we took this action in order to press forward a claim, which, according to the British Constitution, we are well entitled to make.   After all, we are seeking only to enforce the observance of the law of the land that taxation and representation must go together, and that one who obeys the laws must have a share in making them.   Therefore, when we claim the Parliamentary vote, we are asking the Government to abandon the illegal practice of denying representation to those who have a perfect right to it.

"I want here to insist," she said, "upon the legality of the action which we have taken.   We have a perfectly constitutional right to go ourselves in person to lay our grievances before the House of Commons, and as one witness — an expert student of history — pointed out to you, we are but pursuing a legitimate course which in the old days women pursued without the smallest interference by the authorities."

In regard to the meaning of the word " rush," she pointed out that a large number of witnesses had been examined, and that all these witnesses had testified that, according to their interpretation of the word " rush," no violence was counselled.

" The word ' rush,' " Christabel said, " appears to be very much the rage just now. We find that at a meeting of the League for the Preservation of Swiss Scenery, Mr. Richard Whiteing, discussing the question of Swiss railways, suggested that a general ' rush ' to the Italian Alps might induce the Swiss to listen to reason. Well, I do not think that anyone here would suggest that Mr. Whiteing meant to offer any violence to the Swiss in his use of the word ' rush.' He meant to imply that a speedy advance should be made to the Italian Alps. Then we have Mr. McKinnon Wood counselling the electors to ' rush ' the County Council, and get a lady elected to that body.

" I want to submit that ' rush ' as a transitive verb cannot mean ' attack,' ' assail,' ' make a raid upon,' or anything of that kind."

In support of her contentions, Christabel quoted the definitions given by many dictionaries, including *The Century Dictionary, Chambers' English Dictionary,* and *Farmer and Henley's Dictionary of Slang* which gave amongst other meanings of the word " rush " " an eager demand," " urgent pressure of business," " hurry or hasten,— it may be unduly," " to go forward over hastily; for example a number of Bills are ' rushed ' through Parliament or a case is

' rushed ' through a law court." One of the definitions ran, " A ' rusher,' a go-ahead person," whilst
" on the rush " was said to mean " in a hurry," and
" with a rush, with spirit or energetically."

Christabel also displayed a little label which had
been sent to her during the progress of the case. It
stated, " Rush by first train leaving," and was used
in America for parcels required to reach their destination early. She reminded the magistrate of Mrs.
May's comparison of the phrase " rush the House
of Commons " with " a dash for the Pole," saying:

" Everyone knows that you cannot get to the Pole
in a hurry, but you can try to get there in a hurry,
and that is what ' a dash to the Pole ' means.
Everyone knows that with a timid Government like
the present, having at its service the entire Metropolitan Police Force, if one woman says she is going
to rush the House of Commons, there will be an
immense number of police to prevent her doing it.
Nobody, then, having regard to the facts I have
mentioned, thought the women would rush the
House of Commons, but they knew that the women
would be there to show their indignation against the
Government, and I am glad to say that they were
there. It may mean six months' imprisonment, but
I think it is worth it.

" We are anxious to know by what statute it is
illegal to go to the House of Commons, walk up the
steps and make our way to the Strangers' Entrance?
We should like to know whether that is an illegal
thing to do, and, if it is not illegal to go at a slow
pace, we should like to know whether it is illegal to
go at a quick pace, because that is what the word
' rush ' means. ' To rush the House of Commons '

is to go with all possible speed inside the House of Commons, and I hope that we shall be told what statute we have contravened by doing it ourselves, or by sending or inviting others to do it."

Miss Pankhurst next referred to the speeches made in Trafalgar Square on October 11th. She was glad that the prosecution had raised this point because it was all in the defendant's favor. The speeches made at that meeting were made in interpretation of the famous handbill and all the witnesses who had heard those speeches, not excepting Mr. Lloyd George himself, were agreed that they contained nothing inflammatory and no incitement to violence whatsoever. Christabel continued:

" It is not because of anything serious that occurred on October 13th, or was expected to occur, that we are here; we are here in order that we may be kept out of the way for some months, and may cease from troubling the Government for as long a period as they can find it in them, or for which the public will allow them, to deprive us of our liberty."

Whilst hosts of witnesses had testified to the orderly character of the crowd, she pointed out that two police officers only had been put forward on the other side. The prosecution had been unable to bring forward a single impartial person. But police evidence appeared to be all that was considered in the Police Court, and she cried out passionately:

It seems to me that the Prosecution, the witnesses, the authorities, the magistrates, are all on one side, they are all in the same box, and the prisoner charged with an offence is absolutely helpless whatever facts he may bring forward. It is indeed a waste of time to bring evidence. Over the doors of this court ought to be the motto, " Abandon hope, all ye who enter here." We do not care for ourselves, because imprisonment is nothing to us; but when we think of the thousands of helpless creatures who come into this monstrous place with nobody to help them, nobody to plead for them, and we know perfectly well that they are found guilty before they have a chance of defending themselves, the injustice that is done in these courts is almost too terrible to contemplate.

We saw then those helpless creatures, as we had done so often, and as Christabel called up their image, her voice broke and there were tears on her face. " I am thankful to think," she said triumphantly, " that we have been able, by submitting ourselves to the absurd proceedings that are conducted here, to ventilate this fearful wrong."

Christabel next developed the contention that in the course which they had taken the women had followed historical precedent and had been encouraged by statesmen and especially by Liberal statesmen. The Reform Acts had been obtained by disorder. Prior to 1832, the Mansion House, the Custom House, the Bishop's Palace, the Excise Office, three prisons, four toll-houses, and forty-two private dwellings and warehouses had been burnt. Amongst other things, the breaking-down of the Hyde Park railings won the Reform Act of 1867. In 1884 there were the Aston Park riots. John Bright threatened to crowd the streets from Westminster Bridge to Charing Cross. Lord Randolph Churchill advised the voters of Ulster — and voters have other means of urging their opinions — to resort " to the supreme arbitrament of force." He said, " Ulster will fight and Ulster will be right," and as a result of his words dangerous riots almost amounting to warfare occurred, yet he was never prosecuted. Joseph Chamberlain threatened to march one hundred thousand men on London, but no proceedings were taken against him. " The Gladstone of those days," Christabel declared, " was less absurd, hesitating, and cowardly than the present Gladstone and his colleagues, and therefore he took the statesmanlike action of pressing forward the Reform Bill instead of taking proceedings against Mr. Chamberlain. Even a vote of censure moved upon Mr. Chamberlain in the House of Commons, was defeated." John Burns, whose language was far more violent than any that the women had used, was tried at the Old Bailey and acquitted. He said in his speech that he was a rebel, because he was an outlaw. Well, that fact will support us in all we have done. If we go to far greater lengths than we have done yet, we shall only be following in the footsteps of a man who is now a member of the Government. Following out this line of thought, Christabel went on:

Mr. Herbert Gladstone has told us in the speech I read to him that the victory of argument alone is not enough. As we cannot hope to win by force of argument alone, it is necessary to overcome the savage resistance of the Government to our claim for citizenship by other means. He says: " Go on. Fight as the men did." And then, when we show our power and get the people to help us, he takes proceedings against us in a manner which would have been disgraceful even in the old days of coercion, and which would be thought disgraceful if it were practised in Russia.

Then there is Mr. Lloyd George, who, if any man has done so, has set us an example. His whole career has been a series of revolts. . . . He has said that if we do not get the vote — mark these words — we should be justified in adopting the methods which men had to adopt, namely, in pulling down the Hyde Park railings.

Then, as a sign of the way in which men politicians deal with men's interests, we have heard Lord Morley saying: "We are in India in the presence of a living movement, and a movement for what? For objects which we ourselves have taught them to think are desirable objects, and unless we can somehow reconcile order with satisfaction of those ideas and aspirations, the fault will not be theirs; it will be ours — it will mark the breakdown of British statesmanship." Apply those words to our case. Remember that we are demanding of Liberal statesmen that which for us is the greatest boon and the most essential right. Remember that we are asking for votes, that we are demanding the franchise, and if the present Government cannot reconcile order with our demand for the vote without delay, it will mark the breakdown of their statesmanship. Yes, their statesmanship has broken down already. They are disgraced. It is only in this Court that they have the smallest hope of getting bolstered up.

Turning finally from the Magistrate to the great world of public opinion outside, she finished on a defiant note, caring nothing whether the abuse which she had heaped upon his petty court and its unworthy procedure should cause him to increase her sentence ten or even a hundred fold. Mr. Curtis Bennett sat with brows knit and an angry flush on his face, and the whole court was wrought up to the most intense excitement. But now it was Mrs. Pankhurst's turn to speak and her clear even tones and absolute calm of manner created if possible an even deeper impression.

Sir, I want to endorse what my daughter has said, that in my opinion we are proceeded against in this Court by malice on the part of the Government.   [She began quietly and firmly.]   I want to protest as strongly as she has done. I want to put before you that the very nature of your duties in this Court — although I wish to say nothing disrespectful to you — render you unfitted to deal with a question which is a political question, as a body of jurymen could do. We are not women who would come into this court as ordinary law-breakers.

Mrs. Drummond here is a woman of very great public spirit; she is an admirable wife and mother; she has very great business ability, and, although a married woman, she has maintained herself for many years, and has acquired for herself the admiration and respect of all the people with whom she has had business relations.   I do not think I need speak about my daughter.   Her abilities and earnestness of purpose are very well known to you.   They are young women.   I am not, Sir.   You and I are older, and have both had very great and very wide experience of life under different conditions.   Before you decide what is to be done with us, I should like you to hear from me a statement of what has brought me into this dock this morning.

I was brought up by a father who taught me that his children, boys and girls alike, had a duty towards their country; they must be good citizens.   I married a man, whose wife I was, but also his comrade in all his public life.   He was, as you know, a distinguished member of your own profession, but he felt it his duty, in addition, to do political work, to interest himself in the welfare of his fellow countrymen and countrywomen.   Throughout the whole of my marriage I was associated with him in his public work.   In addition to that, as soon as my children were of an age to permit me to leave them, I took to public duties.   I was for many years a Guardian of the Poor.   For many years I was a member of the School Board, and when that was abolished I was elected to the Educational Committee.   My experience in doing that work brought me in contact with many of my own sex, who, in my opinion, found themselves in deplorable positions because of the state of the English law as it affects women. You in this court must have had experience of women who would never have come here if married women were afforded by law that claim for maintenance by their husbands which I think in justice should be given them when they give up their economic independence and are unable to earn a subsistence for themselves. You know how inadequate are the marriage laws to women. You must know, Sir, as I have found out in my experience of public life, how abominable, atrocious, and unjust are the divorce laws as they affect women. You know very well that the married woman has no legal right to the guardianship of her children. Then, too, the illegitimacy laws; you know that a woman sometimes commits the dreadful crime of infanticide, while her partner, the man, who should share her punishment, gets off scot free.

Ever since my girlhood, a period of about thirty years, I have belonged to organisations to secure for women that political power which I have felt essential to bringing about those reforms which women need. We have tried to be what you call womanly, we have tried to use " feminine influence," and we have seen that it is of no use. Men who have been impatient have invariably got reforms.

I have seen that men are encouraged by law to take advantage of the helplessness of women. Many women have thought as I have and for many, many years have tried by that influence of which we have so often been reminded to alter these laws, but have found that that influence counts for nothing. When we went to the House of Commons we used to be told, when we were persistent, that Members of Parliament were not responsible to women, they were responsible only to voters, and that their time was too fully occupied to reform those laws, although they agreed that they needed reforming.

We women have presented larger petitions in support of our enfranchisement than were ever presented for any other reform, we have succeeded in holding greater public meet-

ings than men have ever held for any reform, in spite of
the difficulty which women have in throwing off their natural diffidence, that desire to escape publicity which we have
inherited from generations of our foremothers; we have
broken through that. We have faced hostile mobs at street
corners, because we were told that we could not have that
representation for our taxes which men have won unless we
converted the whole of the country to our side. Because
we have done this, we have been misrepresented, we have
been ridiculed, we have had contempt poured upon us, and
the ignorant mob incited to offer us violence, which we have
faced unarmed and unprotected by the safeguards which
Cabinet Ministers have.

I am here to take upon myself now, Sir, as I wish the
Prosecution had put upon me, the full responsibility for
this agitation in its present phase. I want to address you
as a woman who has performed the duties of a woman,
and, in addition, has performed the duties which ordinary
men have to perform, by earning a living for her children,
and educating them.

I want to make you realise that it is a point of honour
that if you decide — as I hope you will not decide — to
bind us over, that we shall not sign any undertaking, as
the Member of Parliament did who was before you yesterday. Perhaps his reason for signing that undertaking may
have been that the Prime Minister had given some assurance
to the people he claimed to represent that something should
be done for them. We have had no such assurance. So,
Sir, if you decide against us to-day, to prison we must go,
because we feel that we should be going back to the hopeless condition this movement was in three years ago if we
consented to be bound over to keep the peace which we have
never broken. If you decide to bind us over, although the
Government have admitted that we are political offenders,
we shall be treated as pickpockets and drunkards and I want
you, if you can, as a man, to realise what that means to

Members of the Women's Freedom League attempting to enter the House after the taking down of the grille, October 28th, 1908.

women like us. We are driven to do this, we are determined to go on with this agitation, because we feel in honour bound. Just as it was the duty of your forefathers, it is our duty to make this world a better place for women than it is to-day.

Now, Sir, we have not wished to waste your time in any way; we have wished to make you realise that there is another side to the case than that put before you by the Prosecution. We want you to use your power — I do not know what value there is in the legal claims that have been put before you as to your power to decide this case — but we want you, Sir, if you will, to send us to be tried in some place more suitable for the trial of political offenders than an ordinary police court. You must realise how futile it is to attempt to settle this question by binding us over to keep the peace. You have tried it; it has failed. Others have tried to do it, and have failed. If you had power to send us to prison, not for six months, but for six years, for sixteen years, or for the whole of our lives, the Government must not think that they could stop this agitation. It would go on.

Lastly, I want to draw your attention to the self-restraint which was shown by our followers on the night of the 13th, after we had been arrested. It only shows that our influence over them is very great, because I think if they had yielded to their natural impulses, there might have been a breach of the peace. They were very indignant, but our words have always been, be patient, exercise self-restraint, show our so-called superiors that the criticism of women being hysterical is not true; use no violence, offer yourselves to the violence of others. We are going to win. Our women have taken that advice; if we are in prison they will continue to take that advice.

Well, Sir, that is all I have to say to you. We are here, not because we are law-breakers; we are here in our efforts to become law-makers.

The angry red had faded from Mr. Curtis Bennett's face, and whilst Mrs. Pankhurst was speaking he kept his hand up to it, and at one point we saw it quiver and for a moment he hid his eyes. Some of the big burly policemen whom we knew so well and who, except in the " raids," when they were obliged to do their duty, were always so kind and jovial towards us, were openly in tears. Then Mrs. Drummond, looking paler and more serious than is her wont, rose up to speak in her turn. Her voice was a few notes thinner and higher pitched and like her words, it seemed to be stripped of all emotion and to be instinct with the clearest and most logical commonsense. Not only what she said, but her whole personality was so honest, sincere and unaffected that she seemed to add the one thing lacking to the completeness of that presentment of the great unanswerable case for Woman's Suffrage. Her concluding words were an assurance that the agitation, which was spreading and growing all over the country, would go on as before. " I can speak on good authority," she said, " for we have left everything in working order and we shall find the movement stronger than when we left it because the action which the Government have taken has fired the bosoms of women, who are determined to take up the flag that we have had to lay down to-day."

When Mrs. Drummond had finished, Mr. Curtis Bennett began speaking quite cheerfully and as though the whole affair were an amusing discussion between friends and had no unpleasant side to it. During the first part of his speech he reviewed the arguments on both sides of the case, and as he referred meanwhile to the pages on which he had taken

his notes he so frequently smiled as though they recalled amusing and rather pleasant memories to him,
that many people made up their minds that he was
either about to state a case for a higher court, as the
defendants wished, or to discharge them altogether.
All at once, however, his tone changed and he began to speak hurriedly, with lowered voice and increased severity of manner, and went on to say that
there could be no doubt that it was for that court
and that court alone to deal with the offence for
which the defendants had been summoned; and that
there could be no doubt but that the handbill which
the defendants circulated was liable to cause something to occur which might and probably would, end
in a breach of the peace.   The Chief Commissioner
of Police was bound to keep Parliament Square and
the vicinity free and open, and the Commissioner of
Police had felt that it would be impossible to do that
if crowds assembled together in order to help and to
see the women " rush " the House of Commons.
Therefore each of the two older defendants would
be bound over in their own recognisances of £100,
and, they must find two sureties in £50 each to keep
the peace for twelve months, or in default must
undergo three months' imprisonment.   In the case
of the younger defendant, her own recognisances
would be £50, with two sureties of £25 each, the alternative being ten weeks' imprisonment.

CHAPTER XVII

OCTOBER TO THE END OF 1908

MRS. DRUMMOND was right, for though she and
her companions had left a great blank in the work
of the Union, as she had predicted at the dock at
Bow Street, other women eagerly volunteered to
raise up the flag that they had been compelled to lay
down.   In addition to the newcomers, every member of the staff cheerfully undertook some extra task,
and the movement grew like a living flame.   The
office at Clement's Inn was indeed fortunate in its
abundance of willing and able workers.   Beside
Mrs. Pethick Lawrence and her husband, and
charming Mrs. Tuke, Mrs. Pankhurst's co-secretary,
there were a host of others, amongst them dignified,
business-like Miss Kerr, with her rosy face and
pretty white hair, thoughtful, reliable Miss Ham-
bling, Mrs. Drummond's secretary, and Mrs. San-
ders, who, though financial secretary, was now finding time to keep a list of Cabinet Minister's engage-
ments for us.   There was also Jessie, the London
organiser, earnest and serious like all the Kenneys,
who, showing a grasp of the political situation and
an organising capacity indeed remarkable in a girl
of twenty-two, marshalled the force of women to

322

ask of members of the Government those constant questions.

The very greatest difficulty was now experienced in getting into Cabinet Ministers' meetings, for women were now almost entirely excluded. The expedient of issuing a limited number of special women's tickets, the recipients of which were obliged to sign both name and address to a pledge neither to disturb the meeting nor to transfer the ticket, was first resorted to for Mr. Haldane's meeting at Sheffield, on November 20th, 1907. The practice had now become general and in some cases the women's tickets had also to be countersigned by a Liberal official to whom the applicants were personally known. But in spite of such precautions the Suffragettes frequently still succeeded in getting into the meetings and that without having given any promise, and when they could not get inside, they invariably raised a protest in the street.

When Cabinet Ministers, cast as they were in unheroic mould, discarded, to a large extent, the custom of delivering their pronouncements to great public gatherings where all might come, and instead frequently made their weighty utterances at bazaars, private or semi-private banquets and receptions and meetings of a few tried and trusted friends, the Suffragettes were always there even though the world and Mrs. Grundy might be shocked. On November 5th, for instance, a well-known Liberal hostess, Mrs. Godfrey Benson, gave a reception in honour of the Prime Minister. As they stood together at the head of the stairs receiving the guests, there came amongst the ladies and gentlemen in evening dress, streaming upward towards them, one strikingly tall and handsome lady in white satin with abundant dark hair, who said as she took the Prime Minister by the hand, " Can I do anything to persuade you to give votes to women ? " Then, still holding his hand in hers, she proceeded to read out to him some clauses of Magna Charta, explaining that these had been intended to apply to women as well as to men. Mrs. Godfrey Benson did not for some moments notice Mr. Asquith's dilemma, but as soon as she did so, she seized a police whistle which was attached to a ribbon at her waist, and, by blowing loudly, summoned an officer of the law, who conducted the lady out of the house.

Very great precautions were taken to prevent the Suffragettes approaching Mr. Asquith when he visited Leeds to speak at the Coliseum on the afternoon of Saturday, October 10th. From 7 o'clock in the morning the police had been massed around the hall and cordons, both of foot and mounted men were drawn up outside the railway station and along the road by which the Prime Minister was to pass. But, in spite of all the force to guard him, as Mr. Asquith emerged, Mrs. Baines, a little fragile figure, with face ashen white and dark, blazing eyes, a creature compounded of zeal and passion, threw herself in front of him, crying, " Votes for Women, and down with tyranny ! " and the crowd cheered her, though she was at once rudely hurled aside by the police. Then, followed by thousands of people, she made her way to Cockridge Street outside the Coliseum, where she had already announced that she would hold an open air meeting simultaneously with that of Mr. Asquith, inside. A great crowd had gathered there to hear her and when she put to them a resolution that she and her Suffragette comrades should go to the Coliseum to demand an interview with the Prime Minister, a forest of hands shot up in favour. Then declaring, " If these tyrants won't come to us, we must go to them and compel a hearing," she jumped down from the carriage which had served her as a platform, and, followed by a number of other women and more slowly by the crowd itself, she moved on towards the Coliseum. Half way across the road the police barred the way and an inspector asked her where she was going. " Don't be foolish, Mrs. Baines," he said when she told him, but she was not to be deterred and, running round one of the mounted police, was arrested by a constable on foot. The other women still pressed forward and one by one five of them were arrested and taken to the Town Hall, where they were charged with disorderly conduct, whilst Mr. Asquith left the meeting by a back exit amid the hisses and groans of the crowd.

On Monday morning the others were each sent to prison for five days on refusing to be bound over to keep the peace, but the case against Mrs. Baines was held over until the following Wednesday. She was then charged with inciting to riot and unlawful assembly. Her case was to be held over until the Assizes, in November, and the opportunity of being tried by Judge and Jury which Mrs. Pankhurst, Christabel Pankhurst, and Mrs. Drummond had claimed in vain was thus to fall to her lot. The Grand Jury, having returned a True Bill against Mrs. Baines, Mr. Pethick Lawrence, who was defending her, served subpœnas to give evidence at the trial upon Mr. Asquith and Mr. Herbert Gladstone; but the Cabinet Ministers had no intention of allowing themselves to be examined by the Suffragettes and to be made into a Suffragette advertisement a second time. They applied to the Divisional Court for a Rule to set aside the subpœnas, and did not scruple to take advantage of their position as members of the Government to employ both the Attorney General, Sir William Robson, K. C., and the Solicitor General, Sir Samuel Evans, K. C., to plead their case in opposition to Mr. Pethick Lawrence. Though no precedent for setting aside a subpœna in criminal cases could be found, it was decided that neither Mr. Asquith nor Mr. Gladstone should be called upon to give evidence.

On Thursday and Friday, November 19th and 20th, the actual trial took place in the Leeds Town Hall. Mrs. Baines freely admitted that she had used the words, " if these tyrants will not come to us, we must go to them and compel a hearing," and that her intention had been to get into the meeting and secure an interview with the Prime Minister, but she protested that she had had no intention of injuring him or anyone and when Mr. Bairstow, K. C., the Counsel for the prosecution, asked if she had carried any weapons, she replied, " Oh, my tongue is weapon enough ! " When asked to give an account of her life, she said that she was the daughter of a working man and had begun to help in earning the family living at eleven years of age. After her marriage she had continued to be a wage-earner, though she was the mother of five children, because her husband, who was a shoemaker, was only able to earn 25 shillings a week. Nevertheless she had done much public and social work as she had been a

Salvation Army lieutenant, an evangelist to a working-men's mission, a member of the Stockport unemployed committee and committee for the feeding of school children, and a worker in the temperance cause. When asked to give some account of her speech to the crowd on the 10th of October, she said, " I wanted the men and women of Leeds to understand why we were there to protest against Mr. Asquith's refusal to give us the vote. I said that that afternoon Mr. Asquith would be dealing with the Licensing question; that this was more a woman's question than it was a man's, because we women suffered most through intemperance, and that no real temperance reform would ever be brought about until women had a voice in the matter. The unemployed question was also more a woman's question than it was a man's, because it was the women who really suffered most. Mr. Asquith had never known what it was, as I have done, to go without food or to go to school hungry. We wanted to see Mr. Asquith and we wanted to know when we were going to have access to Mr. Asquith."

After the evidence on both sides had been heard Mr. Lawrence made an eloquent speech for the defence, but it was nevertheless decided that Mrs. Baines was guilty of unlawful assembly. The Judge then asked her to enter into her own recognisances to be of good behaviour, explaining that if she agreed she would merely be promising not to use violence or to incite to violence in future. Mrs. Baines steadfastly maintained that she had had no intention of using violence, but felt that she could not conscientiously agree to be bound over to keep the peace. Mr. Justice Pickford then said that though he was reluctant to do so, he must pass sentence upon her and ordered that she should be imprisoned for six weeks in the Second Division. In the result, however, she was only kept in prison for three weeks because, though she had gone free meanwhile, the fortnight during which she had awaited her trial at the Assizes was counted as part of her sentence, and in addition she was entitled to one week's remission of sentence for good behaviour.

Amid all the whirl of militancy that had been going on the work of educative peaceful propaganda was never allowed to flag and beside the hundreds of uncounted smaller meetings a series of great indoor demonstrations calling for votes for women and the release of the prisoners was held in the Free Trade Hall, Manchester, the Town Hall, Birmingham, the St. George's Hall, Bradford, the Guild Hall, Plymouth, the Town Hall, Huddersfield, the Town Hall, Battersea, the Town Hall, Chelsea, the King's Theatre, Hammersmith, and in many other places, and culminated in a second great demonstration in the Albert Hall on October 29th at which £3,000 was collected. Then, in declaring the £20,000 campaign fund to be complete, Mrs. Pethick Lawrence appealed for it to be carried on to £50,000, and that the half way house of £25,000 should be reached before the founder of the Union should be released from prison.

Whilst the W. S. P. U. had been thus active, the Women's Freedom League had startled London by a cleverly organised and smartly executed demonstration in the Ladies' Gallery of the House of Commons, on October 28th. That morning all the world had awakened to find that little placards, headed " A Proclamation containing a demand for Votes for Women," had been posted on every hoarding. At 8:30 in the evening, whilst Parliament was discussing the Licensing Bill, and Mr. Remnant, one of the Conservative Members, was speaking, a woman in the Ladies' Gallery suddenly thrust through the brass grille one of these proclamations with a cry of " Votes for Women! " Instantly Miss Muriel Matters darted to the front of the Gallery and proceeded to deliver a Suffrage speech, two attendants at once came rushing in, tumbling over the ladies' trains and pushing unceremoniously past them in haste to drag her from her place, only to find that they could not do so, for, by means of a padlock and chain around her waist, she had attached herself to the grille. Whilst some of the men struggled to break the chains, others gagged her by holding their hands over her mouth, but a second woman, also chained, took up the tale with " we demand the vote," and, after she had been stifled in the same impromptu and objectionable fashion, a third cried, " We have remained behind this insulting grille too long."

Members of Parliament were meanwhile pouring into the House to see the show, and though Mr. Remnant spoke on without pausing, but little notice was taken of anything that he said. The attendants in the Gallery now discovered that the chains around the women's waists had been wrapped in wool to prevent their clanking and were secured by strong Yale padlocks, that, on being snapped together, had locked automatically without a key, and after vainly dragging and pulling at the women (who, in spite of the gagging, still managed to articulate a word or two occasionally), and after tugging again and again at both locks and chains, the men came to the conclusion that it would be necessary to remove bodily those parts of the grille to which the three disturbers were attached. Then all the women in the Gallery, Suffragettes, Suffragists and even anti-Suffragists were alike quickly bundled out. Next screwdrivers were brought and the attendants set to work to dismember the grille, and when this had been done the women and the great pieces of wrought brass work, to which they were still attached, were hauled out by the attendants and taken to Committee Room 15, where they were kept until a smith arrived to file through the chains.

By this time the House had resumed its ordinary, humdrum appearance, and the Members who had come in during the disturbance had all drifted away, but, as the Division bell rang and they came trooping back to vote, a man in the Strangers' Gallery shouted, " Why don't you do justice to women? " and was dragged out by a number of policemen, and within ten minutes afterwards a second man shouted, " Why don't you give votes to women? " and flung a shower of leaflets down amongst the Members.

At the same time several women were attempting to hold a meeting in the Lobby. The police flung them outside but they immediately climbed up to speak from the pedestal of the Richard Cœur de Lion statue, and whilst the constables clambered up after them, pulled them down and placed them under arrest, other Suffragettes made dash after dash to re-enter the House. Crowds quickly gathered and the confusion grew and fourteen women and one

Mrs. Pankhurst in Prison

man had been taken into custody before the people were dispersed.

Next morning the prisoners were brought up at the Westminster Police Court before Mr. Hopkins. The first to be charged was Mr. Arnold Cutler, the man who had been arrested in the fray, and it was alleged that he had protested against the action of the police, crying, " Shame! Leave the Women alone! " and that when dragged away he had taken off his belt and " assumed a threatening attitude." He was fined 25 shillings. The women were more heavily punished, being each fined £5, and on refusing to pay were sent to Holloway for one month.

Meanwhile, both in and out of Parliament, day after day, and week after week, Mr. Herbert Gladstone was being urged to extend to the Suffragist prisoners, the treatment that his own father and every Liberal statesman had declared to be due to political offenders, and the protests were rendered the more pointed because at this very time there were a number of men political prisoners, serving sentences in Ireland, who were actually receiving all the privileges which were being demanded on behalf of the Suffragettes. These men were convicted of boycotting and cattle driving. They were allowed to provide their own clothing, furniture, food and malted liquor and to have their own medical attendant and medicines sent in to them at any time. They were allowed to smoke and to have books, newspapers and other means of occupation, to carry on their profession, if that were possible. They were allowed to correspond freely with their friends and to receive visitors every day, and were exempted from prison tasks. Their imprisonment, in fact, entailed little more than the loss of freedom to come and go as they wished. The case of Mr. Farrell, M. P., who, whilst the Suffragette leaders were in Holloway gaol, was convicted of inciting to cattle driving, was technically parallel to that of Mrs. Pankhurst, Christabel Pankhurst, and Mrs. Drummond; but whilst both he and they were alike ordered to be bound over to keep the peace and to find sureties for their good behaviour; on their common refusal, he was committed to prison in the First Division, whilst they were put in the second class.

Meanwhile, news of the prisoners in Holloway had gradually filtered out to us, and the first messenger from them was Mrs. Drummond herself, who nine days after her imprisonment had begun, was suddenly and unexpectedly released. She then told us that on arriving in Holloway, Mrs. Pankhurst had at once announced to the authorities that the time had come when the Suffragettes would no longer submit to the degrading prison regulations which had hitherto been enforced upon them, and that she and her comrades would begin by refusing either to allow themselves to be searched or to change their clothes in the general public dressing room. She further stated that for her own part she was determined to speak with her fellow political prisoners, both at exercise, and at any other time when they might happen to be together, for this was a right to which she considered all political prisoners were entitled. Seeing that it would be both difficult and troublesome to turn her from her purpose, the Governor gave way upon the first point, and agreed that the Suffragist prisoners should be allowed to undress

Ejection of a woman questioner from Birrell's meeting in the City Temple
November 12th, 1908

privately in separate cells; but in regard to any other matters he declared that the Home Secretary must be communicated with. Mrs. Pankhurst and Christabel, therefore, at once addressed petitions to Mr. Herbert Gladstone, claiming that as political prisoners both they and the other Suffragettes should be permitted to write and receive letters; to associate with their fellow political prisoners; to receive visits from their friends; to attend to business matters as far as possible; to have books and newspapers sent in to them; to wear their own clothing, and to provide their own food. Mr. Gladstone refused to comply with any of the requests, and the prison rules were enforced with all their accustomed vigour, except that for the first week Mrs. Pankhurst was allowed, without challenge, to speak to her fellow prisoners. On Sunday, November 1st, however, the wardress suddenly called her out of the ranks, sharply reprimanded her for speaking and, when she refused to give a promise never to do so again, ordered her to return to her cell. Hearing this, the other Suffragettes came running across the yard and clustered around, giving three cheers for Mrs. Pankhurst, whilst the wardress blew her whistle and dozens of others appeared to drive the Suffragettes inside.

It happened that on that same morning, she never could tell why, Mrs. Drummond's cell had not been unlocked at the time for exercise, and she had been left behind whilst the others had gone out into the yard. She was sitting wondering what had happened, when she suddenly heard the sound of cheers. At once she hastily dragged her plank bed to the window and, clambering up, saw the Suffragettes in their prison dress, with numbers of wardresses after them, running across the yard in all directions. Then they disappeared and all was quiet. When next she was let out into the corridor and when she was taken to the chapel, she saw no sign of her comrades, and though she asked the wardress for news of them, no answer was returned. It was on the same evening that a sense of growing weakness that had been upon her since her entrance into prison, overcame her and she must have fainted suddenly, for she was found by the wardress lying unconscious on the floor. She was carried to a hospital cell and put to bed, and as she begged for more air, the outer door was thrown open, and only the gate with which hospital cells are also provided, was closed. Soon afterwards, Mrs. Pankhurst, who occupied the next cell, passed along the corridor to fill her water can and through the bars was able to tell Mrs. Drummond briefly what had happened — that she herself was to remain under punishment, and to be deprived of both exercise and chapel until she would promise not to attempt to speak again. By the doctor's orders, Mrs. Drummond remained in bed until Tuesday, when the Governor and the Matron came to her and told her that the Home Secretary had given orders for her release. As soon as the officers had left her, she sprang up and rushed to the gate of her cell, calling out loudly to Mrs. Pankhurst, "The Home Secretary has ordered me out." "I am glad," was the reply, as the wardress came hurrying back to expostulate.

On hearing Mrs. Drummond's story we at once decided that a demonstration of encouragement to our imprisoned comrades and of protest against their treatment by the authorities, must be held outside the gaol, and on the following Saturday evening a long procession of women, headed by a brass band and a little carriage, in which rode Mrs. Drummond and those of us who were to speak, and a brake filled with ex-prisoners in prison dress, assembled in Kingsway and set off for Holloway gaol. All along the route cheering crowds gathered, and our procession grew as we marched, and when we reached Holloway all the roads that encircle the prison were densely crowded with human beings. We stopped outside the main entrance to hold a meeting, but the masses of people were far too great for our voices to reach them and our horses, startled by the vast crowds which pressed closer and closer, showed signs of becoming restive. Mrs. Drummond therefore led off a cheer for the Suffragette prisoners inside and the crowd raised their voices with her again and again. Then we slowly encircled the prison three times, alternately cheering and singing the Women's Marseillaise: [1]

> Arise! Though pain or loss betide,
> Grudge naught of Freedom's toll,
> For what they loved the martyrs died
> Are we of meaner soul?
> Are we of meaner soul?
>
> Our comrades greatly daring
> Through prison bars have led the way,
> Who would not follow to the fray,
> Their glorious struggle proudly sharing?

[1] By Miss F. E. M. Macaulay.

To Freedom's Cause till death
We swear our fealty,
March on! March on!
Face to the dawn,
The dawn of liberty.

During the ensuing week two batches of our prisoners were released and each one carried out to us further disquieting news. Mrs. Pankhurst, who was still being punished, had been characterised by the authorities as a " dangerous criminal," and, because she still refused to pledge herself to perpetual silence, a wardress was constantly stationed outside her door to prevent any attempt at communication with her. It was rumoured also that she was very ill and this was confirmed by Mr. Gladstone in reply to questions by Members of Parliament, but my request, either to be allowed to see her for myself, or to send in her own medical attendant to interview her, was denied. Again, on the following Saturday, we marched around the prison but this time accompanied by crowds even greater than before. In the meantime, whilst many questions had been put in the House by Members of Parliament, the Suffragettes who had just been released had paid many visits to the Stranger's Lobby and eventually Mr. Gladstone agreed that Christabel and Mrs. Pankhurst should be allowed to spend one hour of each day together. At the same time he refused to allow Christabel to write a book upon the Women's Suffrage question for a firm of London publishers, to be published after her release, though it was well known that Mr. Ginnell during his imprisonment for inciting to cattle driving, had been allowed to write his book entitled *Life and Liberty*.

On Saturday, November 19th, thirteen more prisoners were released and we learnt that a fortnight before there had been another so-called " mutiny " in Holloway. Mrs. Leigh had been falsely accused of inciting the other Suffragette prisoners to mutiny, and as a punishment had been deprived of exercise and chapel for three days, and Miss Wallace-Dunlop determined to prove her innocence. Every prisoner has the right to lay a complaint before the Governor, but the application to see him is supposed to be made when the cell doors are first opened at six o'clock in the morning, and he afterwards visits the prisoner when and where he may think fit and usually in her own cell. It was necessary for Miss Wallace-Dunlop's purpose that he should come to her when all her fellow prisoners were together in order that each might give her testimony. She accordingly chose to make her application during the associated labour which Dr. Mary Gordon, the new lady Inspector, had instituted that summer. So at half past three that afternoon when the Suffragettes with a space of a yard between each other had seated themselves at a number of deal tables in one of the corridors and had settled down to make shirts and mail bags, she asked the wardress in charge to send for the Governor.

By 5 :30, when the time for associated labour was at an end, the Governor had sent no reply and the wardress gave the order, " Return to your cells," but Miss Wallace-Dunlop gave a counter command:

" Do not return to your cells." There had been no
previous understanding between them, but the women
sat firm, and when the order to leave was repeated
they still did not move, leaving it to their leader to
again explain that they would remain where they
were until the Governor or his deputy should arrive.
The wardress then sharply blew her whistle, where-
upon crowds of tall wardresses appeared from all directions and lined the corridor in long rows. Then
Miss Wallace-Dunlop rose. Those of us who know
her can well imagine the scene. She has one of those
faces that, when we recall them to our minds, we always see as though lit up, turned towards a full light
that streams upon them, and at the same time illu-
mined from within. The spirit that glows within
them is intensely vibrant with sympathy for others,
yet though the sadness of others' sorrow finds instant
reflection in them and we know that their hearts
throb with the bitter pain of other hearts, a quiet
gaiety is habitual to them and we think of them always as brightly and serenely happy; it seems not
possible for a shadow to fall across the clear purity
of their minds. So we can plainly picture for ourselves her tall, slight, erect figure standing forth, and
hear her gentle light-toned voice say to the women:
" Set your backs against the wall and all link arms."
Instantly they obeyed and stood where she had told
them, looking firm and immovable though the officials outnumbered them by more than ten to one.
Then there was silence, and the wardresses made no
move. At last steps were heard coming from a long
distance — one always hears them away off in Holloway. Gradually they came nearer and nearer until
the Governor arrived. Then the Suffragette leader

stepped forward. " We have sent for you," she said gravely, " because we have a statement to make. One of our comrades has been unjustly punished." " You know I am always willing to listen to your statements," the Governor replied, " but I can do nothing to-night unless you return to your cells." Then, on his promising to enquire into the whole matter, Miss Wallace-Dunlop was satisfied and she and her comrades quietly obeyed.

But, when the Governor came round the cells next morning, he ordered that every Suffragette who had been present should appear before the visiting magistrates to answer to a charge of mutiny, and on the following day, they were each sentenced to from three to five days' solitary confinement and the associated labour, about which there had always been more labour than association, as the prisoners were forbidden to communicate, was abandoned altogether. Mrs. Leigh was still deprived both of Chapel and exercise, and the others who had caught an occasional glimpse of her, as she passed to fill her water can, stated that she appeared to be suffering very greatly from this close solitary confinement.

Again on the next Saturday we marched to Holloway, carrying before us a white banner inscribed with the text of the Women's Enfranchisement Bill. There we found the police on horse and foot mustered against us a thousand strong, barring the nearest approaches to the prison so that, although we again circled it, it was at so great a distance that only once, through a gap in the surrounding buildings, could we see its walls, and we doubted whether our voices, loud and numerous as they were, could be heard by the prisoners inside.

CHAPTER XVIII

NOVEMBER TO THE END OF 1908

Mrs. Birrell at City Temple. Mr. Lloyd George at Albert Hall. Release of Mrs. Pankhurst, Christabel Pankhurst, and Mrs. Leigh.

During the autumn whilst Mr. Birrell had been visiting his constituency of North Bristol, Annie Kenney, the centre of whose flourishing West of England organising district, was in that town, had prevailed upon him to receive a women's deputation. In reply to this deputation Mr. Birrell had said that the Government did not intend to carry the Women's Enfranchisement Bill during that session; that many members of the Cabinet were strongly opposed to the idea of giving the women the vote on any terms; that, in his opinion, the matter was not ripe for settlement, and also that he would not endanger his position in the Cabinet by pressing the question forward. He added that he was in favour of the enfranchisement of rate-paying widows and spinsters on the Municipal basis, but that he disapproved of qualified married women voting and that he would not support a measure to give adult Suffrage to women. This last point was exceedingly interesting. It clearly demonstrated the cynical character of the suggestion, made by Mr. Lloyd George and others, that to give votes to women on the same terms as men was not sufficiently democratic to be supported by a Liberal Government, for here was a Liberal Cabinet Minister declaring opposition to any wider measure.

On November 12th, Mr. Birrell spoke at the City Temple, the church of Mr. R. J. Campbell, the well-known initiator of the so-called " New Theology." It was well known that the Suffragettes were present to heckle him, and the chairman tried to deter them by stating that Mr. Birrell had promised to give his " influential support to any measure giving a liberal extension of the franchise to women." The Suffragettes considered that this meant absolutely nothing at all, and continued to protest as earnestly as they could. The result was a terrible scene of violence, in which large numbers of women were flung out of the church and dragged down the steps. The W. S. P. U. afterwards wrote to Mr. Birrell to ask what his statement had really meant. His answer, given through his Secretary, was simply and solely that he had " nothing to add to the reply which he gave recently to a deputation introduced by Miss Kenney."

Meanwhile, though the militant tactics were being condemned as vigorously as ever, sympathy for the militants and a desire for the franchise were rapidly spreading amongst women of all shades of opinion. The Women's Conservative and Unionist Franchise Society was formed about this time, and the Margate and the Wallasey Women's Liberal Associations passed Resolutions dissolving themselves until women were enfranchised, whilst the Secretaries and Committee members of other associations resigned their posts on the same ground.

At this point Mr. Lloyd George wrote to the ex-

ecutive of the Women's Liberal Federation offering
to speak for them on Women's Suffrage in the Albert
Hall. They agreed to his suggestion and it was
announced that he would make a Government pronouncement. On this ground the organisers of the
meeting approached the Committee of the W. S.
P. U., asking that the Chancellor of the Exchequer
should not be heckled, but we replied that unless we
had an assurance that Mr. Lloyd George's pronouncement was to contain a Government promise to
act, we could not comply with this request. As requests that we would alter our decision continued to
pour in, Mrs. Tuke, our Honorary Secretary, wrote
to Mr. Lloyd George on November 30th, stating
that we would gladly ask our women not to interrupt
him if he could assure us that the Government were
really prepared to do something for the Suffrage
Cause, and that, if he wished, we would pledge ourselves not to divulge his reply until after his speech
had been delivered. Mr. George's only answer was
a curt note stating that anything that he had to say
in regard to the Government's attitude would be said
in the course of his speech in the Albert Hall.

There was no hint in the letter of any great
Government pronouncement, but indeed everyone
knew, the leaders of the Liberal women themselves
knew, and in fact had admitted to us, that Mr.
Lloyd George had nothing of importance to say.
His speech was merely intended to pacify those
women who were beginning to falter in their loyalty
to the Liberal Party and to take the wind as far as
possible out of the Suffragette sails. Mr. Lloyd
George was as much responsible as any of his colleagues for the present warfare. His own personal

record in regard to the women's movement was not
a good one. Therefore there was absolutely no
reason for modifying, in his favour, the rule that
all Cabinet Ministers must be heckled. Indeed his
coming forward at this juncture to curry favour by
offering empty platitudes was felt to be in the nature
of adding insult to injury. When, on Saturday, December 5th, the day of the Liberal Women's meeting
arrived, the Albert Hall was girt by an army of
mounted police. There was a general feeling of
uneasy expectancy and everyone seemed suspicious of
what his or her neighbour might be going to do.
Bands of men stewards, known by their yellow
badges, were massed in the corridors and stationed
in groups at the end of every row of seats. Nevertheless, in spite of the fact that these men had been
obviously engaged for the forcible ejection of interrupters, in order to protect the promoters of the
meeting from subsequent charges of brutality, "Officials' Orders of the Day" were prominently displayed, in which the stewards were counselled to "do
no violence to any person," and the members of the
Women's Liberal Federation were asked, whatever
happened, to "act as though they were soldiers,
silent and steady under fire."

Lady M'Laren, who presided over the meeting,
rose to speak with obvious uneasiness, which was increased, when she suddenly realised that all the
women in the front row of the arena, who had suddenly removed their cloaks, were clothed as second
division prisoners in dresses of green serge, blue and
white check aprons and white caps, all stamped with
the broad arrow. For sometime, however, all was
quiet and it was not until Mr. Lloyd George had

been speaking for some moments, and was proceeding to give various reasons why women were entitled to the franchise, that he was interrupted by a tall, graceful woman in one of the boxes. She declared that all present were agreed as to the justice of the cause and that a Government pledge to take action was alone required. The speaker was Helen Ogston, B.Sc., of St. Andrew's University, and the daughter of Professor Ogston of Aberdeen. Her words were no sooner uttered than a man in the next box leapt over the barrier and struck her a blow in the chest, whilst several stewards sprang upon her from behind. She protested that she was prepared to leave the hall at once, but the men did not heed her and continued to pummel her in the most savage way. At this the audience were astonished to see her draw a whip from under her cloak and strike at one of her assailants. Immediately afterwards she was knocked down and disappeared.[1]

Now the whole hall was in uproar. Mr. Lloyd George strove to continue, weakly protesting that he was in favour of Women's Suffrage, but, " Then why don't you do something? " and " Deeds not words! Deeds not words! " came a clear bell-like cry. Again he went on to urge that he really was in favour, but was met by, " Why don't you resign from a Cabinet that is hostile to women? " " Our women are in prison." " You run with the hare and

[1] Miss Ogston acted upon her own initiative in using the dog whip, and her intention was not known to the committee of the W. S. P. U. who felt, however, that they could not condemn her for seeking to protect herself. She employed the whip as a protest, not against ejection, but against the unnecessary violence to which she herself and other women had been subjected.

hunt with hounds." Only one woman spoke at one time and each one merely fired a short, sharp, pertinent interjection; but there were many of them, and, more than that, the raising of each woman's voice was the signal for a wild outburst of fury on the part of the stewards, who sprang upon the interrupter, silenced her by a blow under the chin or an impromptu gag and, after flinging her either to the ground or across the seats, dragged her out head foremost, hitting her again and again. Some members of the audience struck with fists and umbrellas at the women who were being carried past. Others tried to protect them, but the latter were always set upon by the officials and speedily bundled out.

Even outside in the numerous passages that surround the circular hall the ejectors, some of whom were heard to say that the affair was more amusing to them than a night at the Music Hall, would not allow their captives to escape and still continued to ill-treat them until they had finally flung them down the steps and out of the building. At last Mr. Lloyd George stopped — the scene was becoming too much even for him. He declared that he would rather sit down than be the cause of so much violence. "Yes, do sit down and stop it," a chorus of distressed voices rose, but after a moment he went on again with the stale old reasons why women should have the vote. "We have known those for forty years," "We want your message," still the women's voices called, and each interruption meant an ejection. "We shall get peace presently by this process of elimination," he said. "Yes, fling them ruthlessly out," his own words at Swansea were repeated, and, "You will never eliminate the Suffragettes from

practical politics." For more than an hour the scene
continued. Again and again Lady M'Laren intervened and secured a few moments' peace for Mr.
Lloyd George to make his statement and again and
again he himself promised to give the Government
message but failed to do so, floundering back instead
into a maze of arguments for and against the vote.
" If Queen Elizabeth had been alive to-day," he
ventured once, but, " She would have been in Holloway " came the retort, and then the protesting voices
broke out afresh. Then at last, after a flight of
oratory on the excellence and the importance to
women of the measures already introduced by the
Liberal Government, the declaration came. It was
nothing but Mr. Asquith's old worn-out promise to
introduce a Reform Bill and not to oppose a
Women's Suffrage Amendment to it on certain conditions. The women reminded the Chancellor that
the Prime Minister had relegated the introduction
of the Reform Bill to " the dim and speculative future," but he protested that it would be introduced
before the Parliament came to an end. He was asked
how women were to prove the " demand " for their
enfranchisement which was one of the conditions
of the promise and his reply was, " as the men
showed their desire," but the women answered: —
" Men burnt down buildings, they shed blood," and,
" the Government has ignored our demonstrations."
He was questioned as to the second condition that
the Votes for Women amendment must be drafted on
" democratic lines," but though asked again and
again " What is democratic? " he vouchsafed no reply and at last the cry, " Where is the message? "
broke out once more and a great white banner, with

the inscription, " Be honest," was hung out from one of the boxes.

Of course the W. S. P. U. was, as usual, much blamed for what had taken place. The heckling of Mr. Lloyd George was declared to be both foolish and wrong; nevertheless many newspapers protested strongly against the behaviour of the stewards of the meeting. The Liberal *Manchester Guardian* said that the ejections were effected " with a promptness that gave the chairman no opportunity for intervening," and in many instances " with a brutality that was almost nauseating." The Special Correspondent of the *Standard* spoke of the " grossly brutal conduct " of the stewards, declaring that " some of the worst acts of unnecessary violence took place within ten yards of the chairman's table, and therefore right under the eyes of Lady M'Laren and Mr. Lloyd George. The men responsible for the acts were stewards wearing the official yellow rosette. That I am prepared to swear to." At the same time the *Manchester Guardian,* in its leading article, though it condemned our action, admitted that Mr. Lloyd George's repetition of Mr. Asquith's promise was entirely unsatisfactory from the Votes for Women point of view. Many others took the same line, and the Conservative *Globe* said, " We see very genuine grounds for the impatience displayed by the Suffragettes at the Albert Hall. Mr. Lloyd George must have known that the declaration he had to make would have infuriated any body of men." But the matter did not end with newspaper discussions. We had realised from the first time that we should be made to suffer in many ways. Again and again attempts had been made to break up meetings addressed both by Suffragettes and Suffragists, but the women were hardly ever afforded the protection of the police and, as their meetings were almost entirely officered by women stewards they were obliged to rely upon their own powers of persuasion and magnetic force of will to control their audiences.   This the Suffragettes have always been prepared to do, but it was not always done without difficulty.

Already, at a meeting in Birmingham, Christabel had been assaulted with the bodies of dead mice and, on live mice being let loose at one of our meetings, a well-known Glasgow daily paper had suggested that rats or even ferrets might suitably be employed.

After Mr. Lloyd George's Albert Hall meeting, such outbreaks of violence against us became for a time exceedingly frequent.   At a meeting which I addressed just then for a Women's Suffrage society in Ipswich there was abundant evidence to prove that well-known Liberals in the town had bought shilling tickets of admission for a number of men whom they paid a further shilling each to create a disturbance and, as soon as I rose to speak, I was assailed by shouts and yells, the singing of a song especially composed and printed with this object, which had been distributed broadcast throughout the town, the rattle of tin cans and the ringing of bells.   During my speech several free fights took place in the hall. Walking sticks and other missiles were sent flying through the air and an offensive smell of sulphuretted hydrogen was let out.   The women who had promoted the meeting, whilst anxious that I should stand my ground, were in despair at the damage which they saw was being done to the hall, but, when

The Chelmsford Bye-Election

they sent for the police to quell the disturbance the Chief Constable of the town declared that he had no power to act. His statement sounded strangely to Suffragettes who had seen the police always massed around the meetings of Cabinet Ministers, and had also frequently seen them brought in to eject women interrupters.

A few days after the Albert Hall meeting Helen Ogston herself spoke at Maidenhead, where a gang of men, some of them made up as guys and dressed in women's clothes, waved whips at her and finally drove the speakers from the platform. The only thing that the police could suggest was that the women should fly.

At this time a by-election was in progress at Chelmsford and, in organising our campaign there, we had at first to contend with great disorder. On the opening night of the election the members of the National Union of Women's Suffrage Societies were entirely swept from their platform in the Market Square, whilst a mob of hooligans surrounded the lorry from which we were speaking and dragged it down a hill into the darkness away from the street lamps. Though, aided by steadier sections of the audience, we still succeeded in maintaining a semblance of order, as soon as we descended from the cart the rowdies crushed and jostled us so unmercifully that had it not been for some men who fought for us and who were seriously bruised in the struggle, we should have been trampled under foot. We were at last dragged for safety into the entrance hall of the Municipal buildings where a banquet was being held. The head waiter, who stood at the door, was exceedingly anxious to get rid both of us and the noisy crowd that remained clamouring outside, and we were therefore taken by an underground passage to the Police Court, and kept waiting there for an hour.

This sort of thing did not continue long in Chelmsford, for, as has invariably been the case, as soon as the Suffragettes became known to the people, the hostility which was at first manifested towards them entirely disappeared. Mrs. Drummond was the heroine of this election, for the W. S. P. U. campaign was entirely organised by her. In the illustration she is shown distributing leaflets to the farmers in the Chelmsford Market Place at the close of her speech to them. The result of the poll was a fall of nearly twenty per cent. in the Liberal vote, and a piling-up of one hostile majority against them from 454 to 2,565, which was generally acknowledged in the constituency to be largely due to the Suffragettes.

The violence of the rowdies met with little rebuke from political leader writers and under the heading, " Sparrows for Suffragettes," the *Westminster Gazette* stated, " Essex has just provided two amusing Suffragist Incidents," and described in the same spirit the letting loose of a flight of sparrows inside a hall where the women were speaking and the breaking up of a Suffragist meeting by boys who had rushed the speakers, and cast carbide on the wet roads.

Consider the action of a body of women who, in order to obtain a share in the constitution, deliberately decide to attend the meetings addressed by the members of a Government that has the power to grant them what they desire but withholds it. Consider also that these women are deprived by their

The human letters dispatched by Miss Jessie Kenney to
Mr. Asquith at No. 10 Downing Street, Jan. 23, 1909

sex of the principal constitutional means of pressing their claim and that their action is taken at great personal risk. Then contrast the action of these women with that of a crowd of men who, absolutely careless of injuring either persons or property, and merely because they imagine that their victims are unpopular or opposed to those whom they believe to be their own political friends, deliberately set out with the intention of breaking up the meetings of women who are withholding no man's rights from him and who have no power to give rights to anyone, but who are merely struggling to obtain the franchise which their assailants themselves possess. Surely no one with an unprejudiced mind could consider that there is a parallel between the case of those particular women and those particular men. Party politicians had before them frequent examples of the two cases and they decided that there was no parallel. They decided that the action of the men was excusable, but that the action of the women must be condemned in the most emphatic terms and must be sternly repressed at any cost.

A measure called the Public Meeting Bill providing that any person who acted in a disorderly manner in order to prevent the transaction of the business for which a meeting had been called together should be rendered liable to a fine not exceeding £5 or to imprisonment for a period not exceeding one month, was therefore laid before Parliament by Lord Robert Cecil. As the slightest interjection or the most pertinent question by a Suffragette had now become the signal for a scene of disturbance, it was clearly apparent that they would not be able to raise their voices at the meetings of Cabinet Ministers without rendering themselves liable to the suggested penalties. Though the Bill was introduced but a few days before the end of the Session, the Government at once provided for it the facilities which had been denied to that equally short measure to enfranchise the women of the country, and it was quickly rushed through the two Houses and became law before the end of the year.

Party feeling on the one hand, and public indifference on the other, veiled for the time being the serious and revolutionary nature of this measure and allowed it to be placed on the statute book with scarcely a word of discussion or protest. Nevertheless it struck at one of our most ancient and fundamental national customs. Describing the ancient governmental assemblies of the Saxon peoples Tacitus explains that though, as a rule, only the more distinguished members of the community put forward new proposals, all had a right to be present and the bystanders at once expressed their opinion in regard to all suggestions. He says:

> The eldest opens the proceedings, then each man speaks according as distinguished by age, family, renown in war or eloquence. No one commands, only the personal dignity residing in him exercises its influence. No distinction of rank exists; the Assembly determines and its determination is law. Proposals, when deemed acceptable, are hailed with loud acclaim and clash of arms. A loud shout of dissent rejects what appears to be unacceptable.

Our present system of Government is, after all, the direct descendant of these ancient assemblies. Largely owing to the distinctions of class which have sprung up and have grown more and more complex

Procession to welcome Mrs. Pankhurst, Christabel and Mrs. Leigh on their release from prison,

and at the same time more deeply marked because of the constant struggling of those who already possess advantages of property and of education to add to these advantages a greater political power than their fellows by restricting the rights of those who are poorer and weaker than themselves many changes have been wrought. It has come about that our modern Parliament is elected by only a section of the people; and that almost the whole of the business transacted by Parliament is carried on by a small Cabinet of persons nominated by one man, himself pitch-forked into power by a possibly transient wave of popularity. Moreover, our existing system of party Government renders this small Cabinet almost all-powerful during its term of office and the strong party prejudice, obtaining both amongst Private Members of Parliament and the Press of the country, secures that the Cabinet shall remain almost exempt from criticism, except by the followers of the opposing party. This criticism loses in influence and value because, for party purposes, it is directed almost without exception against every act of the Cabinet, whether the act be in itself worthy or unworthy. The section of the people who are entitled to vote and who elect the majority that makes the power of the Cabinet possible may, it is true, dismiss them at the next general election if they disapprove of the way in which their stewardship has been fulfilled; but they cannot insist upon an election when they will and they have no power to decide that their representatives have done well in one respect and badly in another. It is only possible either entirely to accept what the representatives have done or to reject them altogether.

23

There exists also the right of every section of the people to carry resolutions embodying their opinion in regard to matters of Government, which may either be published broadcast or presented in the form of petitions for redress of grievances to those in power.   But what usually happens to resolutions and petitions put forward by those who have no political power is aptly expressed in the words of Mr. Serjeant Hullock, the Counsel who spoke for the Coercionist Government in one of the cases arising out of the massacre of Peterloo, which took place in 1819, prior to the passing of the first reform Act. " If deliberation had been their object," he said, " could they not have settled their petition in a private room and then have sent it to the House of Commons, where it would have been laid on the table and never heard of again? "   Nevertheless the old right of the by-standers, the right of the whole people to express their opinion in regard to suggestions put forward by powerful folk and to receive them either with shouts of approval or equally loud cries of dissent still exists and it exists — if it has not been altogether destroyed by the Public Meeting Bill — not merely for men, but for women.   This right is constantly exercised when a member of the Government, and, to a lesser extent, a private Member of Parliament appears before a public meeting of the people to make proposals for fresh legislation and to give an account of his stewardship in the past. When he comes forward thus, the people, women as well as men, have the right to express assent or dissent with what he has done or with what he has left undone, with what he proposes and what he has omitted to propose.   They have the right to question him and to demand an answer, to heckle him during his speech if they will, and if they will to cry out and refuse to let him speak until he has dealt with the thing which they have at heart, and if they believe that he has not dealt justly with that thing they have the right to decide that he shall not be heard. How else can he know the mind of the country? How else can those who are without the Parliamentary franchise express their will? There is no other way and this right is one of those upon which the people of these Islands have always insisted. Those who have said that if this right be exercised the right of free speech will be endangered do not realise what the right of free speech is. The right of free speech is the right of everyone to speak publicly and without penalty or restraint, of what seems important, and this old right to question and to express assent and dissent is included in it. It is the only refuge of those who have no political power. The right of members of the Government to speak freely can never be endangered, for they have Parliament to speak from, the police and military at their beck and call to protect them and enforce their wishes, and the Press of the country all waiting to note down their words and publish them broadcast throughout the land. The right of poor and voteless people to be heard has been endangered by this Bill and so long as it remains on the Statute Book it is a standing menace to our ancient popular liberties.

Happily, up to now, the Bill has been practically a dead letter, but none can be sure that an instrument of coercion which exists will not be put into force. Had the movement for Women's Enfran-

chisement been a movement solely of poor women
with others dependent upon them, as might have been
the case, the new Bill might have proved a serious
menace to the movement, but, as it happened, there
was fortunately no lack of women who were able and
willing to risk imprisonment.   Therefore this Bill
could make no difference to us.

Nevertheless, though our members might not have
left a crowd of starving children behind them, we
well knew that their going to prison entailed many
sacrifices and we always waited impatiently for their
release and welcomed them back amongst us with
the greatest joy.   During the summer and autumn
bands of women in white dresses had flocked to the
gaol gates, had unhorsed the carriages provided to
carry the prisoners to breakfast, and with purple,
white and green ribbons had drawn them in triumph
through the streets.   With Scotch tartans and Scotch
heather the Scotch women had been welcomed; four
Irish colleens and an Irish piper and a jaunting car
met Mrs. Tanner, an Irish woman, and women in
prison dress marched from the station with Mrs.
Baines on her return to London.   When Mrs. Pankhurst, Mrs. Leigh and Christabel were released,
earlier than had been expected, on December 19th,
women on white horses drew their carriage, and
behind and before there marched long lines of W. S.
P. U. members wearing white jerseys, purple skirts,
and gaiters, green caps, and " votes for women "
regalia.

In the evening a meeting of welcome was held in
Queen's Hall, and as Mrs. Pankhurst, Christabel,
and Mrs. Leigh appeared all the organisers of the

Union in their white dresses lined up and saluted them with tricolour flags, whilst the great audience of women sprang to their feet and cheered and waved and cheered again as few but Suffragette audiences can. Then Annie Kenney stepped forward holding in her hand a purple, white and green silk standard with an aluminum staff, bearing a gilt shield inscribed with the great dates in Christabel's career.

When Christabel spoke she recalled the many thousands of Women's Suffrage meetings that had been held in this country and the work of the pioneers who had begun the agitation more than forty years before. These women had laboured well and devotedly, yet they had not succeeded in gaining for women the Parliamentary vote. She believed the reason for this to be that they had relied too much upon the justice of their cause and not enough upon their strong right arm, for an idea had only life and power in it when it was backed up by deeds. What had been wanted was action and it was for this reason that the militant tactics had achieved so much already and would in the end succeed. The old methods of asking for the vote had proved futile, and not only were they futile, but they were humiliating and unworthy of women. " I say to you," she said, " that any woman here who is content to appeal for the vote instead of demanding and fighting for it is dishonouring herself." The women who came into the militant movement did not fear suffering and sacrifice; they felt, not that they gave up anything for the movement, but that they gained everything by it. " Why," she cried, " the women of this Union are the happiest people in the world. We have the glorious pride of being made an instrument of those great forces that are working towards progress and liberty."

That note was struck again and again, and it was upon that note that the whole meeting rested. Loyalty, enthusiasm, courage, belief in a great cause, the joy of fighting for it, these things filled the air. No one could fail to be impressed by them. When Mrs. Pankhurst rose to speak some-one stepped forward and pressed into her hand a replica of a medal struck to commemorate the fall of the Paris Bastille in the French Revolution, because she had been born on the anniversary of that day. She was weakened and worn by her imprisonment, but her speech, brief and somewhat hesitating as it was, contained a pronouncement heralding important events, for it foreshadowed the hardest and bitterest struggle to secure the rights of Political Offenders to British women political prisoners that had yet been fought.

Two further events must be chronicled before closing the story of the year 1908. The first is the fight of the Scottish women graduates for the recognition of their claim to vote under the Scottish University Franchise which they carried right through to the House of Lords. Though they failed to establish their claim, they yet brought to light many valuable new facts in regard to the rights and privileges of their countrywomen in ancient times. One of their contentions was that the question as to whether they might vote should be decided according to the actual wording of the University Franchise Act and not according to the known, or supposed, intentions of Parliament, for that is the rule which the British Courts have agreed to be always the just and proper one to adopt. There was nothing in the words of the Act to prevent women graduates from voting on equal terms with men, and even if it were held that this had happened because when the Act was passed the legislature had not foreseen the possibility of there ever being women graduates, the right course to pursue (because it was the accepted course when such questions in regard to Acts of Parliament arose) was for the women to be allowed to vote until Parliament, if it chose to do so, should carry an amending statute. The graduates pointed out that this had been done in the case of the first woman who had graduated in medicine, in the Netherlands where, as in England, graduation carried with it the right to vote. This lady had claimed her right and not being allowed to exercise it had taken her case to the Courts. For technical reasons the case had been postponed and during the postponement the Legislature had brought in a repealing enactment to prevent women graduates voting and had succeeded in carrying it. The reason for the refusal of the English authorities to take this course is clearly apparent, for it would have been difficult indeed for our Parliament to carry such a repealing measure in the face of the tremendous Suffragette and Suffragist agitation.

The second of these two important happenings and perhaps the most auspicious one of the whole year, was the granting of votes to women in Victoria where, after struggling for many years, the Suffragists had at length succeeded in inducing their Government to take the matter up and had secured their enfranchisement on November 18th, 1908.

CHAPTER XIX

JANUARY TO MARCH, 1909

SPEAKING in December, 1908, on the policy of his Government in the New Year, Mr. Asquith had declared that the stream of advice as to what he should do next session was pouring in upon him " both night and day," and that he was constantly receiving deputations who came to him " from all quarters and in all causes, on an average of something like two hours on three days in every week." These deputations all asked for different things, but were all agreed that " their measure must be mentioned in the King's Speech, and that the best hours, or at all events some of the best hours, of the session must be given to its special consideration. And the worst of it is," he went on, " that I am disposed myself to agree with them all, for, as each group in their turn come to me, I recognise in them some of our most loyal and fervent supporters."

Thus Mr. Asquith was constantly receiving deputations of men and, as he here admitted, the deputa-

Mrs. Pethick Lawrence's release, April 17th.

tions were helping him to decide what measures he must include in the next King's Speech, but he again refused to receive a deputation of the women. Therefore, when the first Cabinet Council of the season met on January 25th, members of the Women's Social and Political Union called at No. 10 Downing Street to urge their claims again as they had done last year. For knocking at the door, four of them were arrested, and at Bow Street, where for administrative reasons all Suffragette cases were in future to be tried, they were ordered to go to prison for one month. They went cheerfully, for Mrs. Clark, a sister of Mrs. Pankhurst, voiced the feelings of all when, during her trial, she said, " I felt that it was not I who was knocking at the Prime Minister's door, but the great need of women knocking at the conscience of the nation, and demanding that justice shall be done."

Next day it was the members of the Women's Freedom League who strove to obtain an interview with Mr. Asquith, and, in consequence, six of their number were arrested in Victoria Street, on their way to the Official residence; sixteen at the entrance to Downing Street; and six, including Mrs. Despard and Mr. Joseph Clayton, a journalist, who protested on their behalf, at the door of the Stranger's Entrance to the House of Commons. The resulting sentences varied from one month to fourteen days' imprisonment.

Little notice was given of these imprisonments, the Press evidently thinking such sensations stale; but those active inventive brains at Clement's Inn were determined not to be check-mated and were ever devising new stratagems and new surprises as

a means of pushing the cause forward.   When Mr.
Churchill visited Newcastle to inspect a battleship,
on December 4th and 5th, he was approached on the
first of these days no fewer than fifteen times, and
on the second almost constantly, by women who met
him at the station, at the door of his hotel, at a reception held in his honour, on the pier, on the launch,
on the ship itself, and again at every turn on land-
ing, and who presented him with copies of " Votes
for Women," urged the cause upon him in brief
hurried reminders, and made speeches to him from
neighbouring boats.   Every other Minister was
similarly waylaid.

When Parliament met, and the King's Speech was
found to contain no mention of " Votes for Women,"
the W. S. P. U. decided that another Woman's
Parliament must be held and another deputation of
women must be sent out from it.   Then again something that had never been done before had to be
contrived for focussing public attention upon this
event.   Quite opportunely the Post Master General
happened to issue new regulations making it possible to post " human letters."   Of course it was
at once determined to post some Suffragettes as letters to Mr. Asquith in Downing Street.   Accordingly, on Tuesday morning, January 23rd, Jessie
Kenney dispatched Miss Solomon and Miss Mc-
Clellan from the Strand post office.   Then, in
charge of a little messenger boy, one carrying a
placard inscribed *" Votes for Women, Deputation to
the House of Commons, Wednesday,"* and the other,
to the *Right Hon. H. H. Asquith, 10, Downing
Street, S. W.,* the two ladies marched off to the official residence.   When they arrived the messenger

The arrest of Miss Dora Marsden, the Standard Bearer,
March 30th, 1909

boy was invited inside, and the door was shut, but, after a few moments, it was opened again and an official appeared, saying to the women, " You must be returned." " But we have been paid for," they protested, and he replied, " The Post Office must deliver you somewhere else, you cannot be received here." " An express letter is an official document," they persisted, " and must be signed for according to the regulations." But the official replied, " You cannot be signed for; you must be returned; you are dead letters." So there was nothing for it but to go back to Clement's Inn.

Another day a facsimile of " Black Maria," the van which takes the prisoners to Holloway, was seen driving through the town. It bore the inscription E. P. for Emmeline Pankhurst, instead of E. R., Edward Rex, and a man dressed almost exactly like a policeman rode on the back step. When the van reached Regent Street a body of women in imitation prison dress emerged and proceeded to distribute handbills to the passers-by and to chalk announcements of the forthcoming deputation to Mr. Asquith upon the pavement. The members of the Women's Freedom League also hit upon a new and striking advertisement, for Miss Matters, the heroine of the Grille scene, floated over the House of Commons in a cigar-shaped dirigible balloon painted with the fateful words, " Votes for Women."

Ridiculous, petty, even unworthy of serious people, you may think, were some of these methods of propaganda and advertisement, but the Suffragettes knew only too well that the cause which does not advance cannot remain stationary, but slips back into the limbo of forgotten things. On February 24th, the seventh Women's Parliament met in the Caxton Hall. Mrs. Pethick Lawrence sallied forth from it with a number of women in her train, but she and twenty-eight of her comrades, including Lady Constance Lytton and Miss Daisy D. Solomon, the daughter of the Late Prime Minister of the Cape, were soon arrested. Their trial took place before Sir Albert de Rutzen at Bow Street next day, and on refusing to be bound over to keep the peace they received sentences of from one to two months' imprisonment.

There were now many members, both of the Women's Social and Political Union and of the Women's Freedom League, in Holloway, and one day, whilst they were exercising together, a member of the latter organisation, Mrs. Meredith Mac-Donald, a lady in middle life, fell on the frosty stones. Two of her fellow prisoners ran to help her, but the wardress forced them away and, though she said she believed her thigh to be injured, she was forced to drag herself unaided to her cell. Her request to see her own doctor was refused and not until she became unable even to turn in her bed was she removed to the prison hospital. When, at last, the ex-rays were applied, it was found that her thigh was fractured, and that, owing to the long delay and lack of proper treatment, she would be lame for life. The matter was reported to the Home Secretary with a demand for redress, but no result followed until June, 1910, more than a year afterwards, when, legal proceedings having been instituted, the authorities at last agreed to pay Mrs. MacDonald £500 damages and her legal costs, amounting to an equal sum.

Meanwhile a place for a Women's Suffrage meas-

Elsie Howey as Joan of Arc, who rode at the head of the
procession formed to celebrate Mrs. Pethick
Lawrence's release from prison

ure had been won in the private Members' ballot by
Mr. Geoffrey Howard, a Liberal Member of Parliament and son of the Countess of Carlisle. Mr.
Howard and the Women's Suffrage Committee of
Liberal Members with whom he was working, decided to abandon the old equal Bill and to introduce
a complicated Reform measure, on the lines of that
foreshadowed by Mr. Asquith in his famous promise
of the previous year, except that, in this case, Votes
for Women was to form part of the original measure,
instead of being left to come in as an amendment.
Under this Private Members' Reform Bill the only
condition required for registration as a Parliamentary voter was to be that the person registered,
whether man or woman, should be of·full age and
have resided for not less than three months within
the same constituency. It was estimated that the
Bill would qualify some fifteen million new voters,
twelve million of whom would be women,[1] and
would thus nearly treble the number at present entitled to exercise the franchise. It would at the
same time abolish plural voting. The professed object of bringing forward this measure was to meet
the stipulation put forward by Mr. Asquith and Mr.
Lloyd George that votes should not be given to
women except on " democratic lines."

On Friday, March 19th, the Bill came up for
Second Reading and Mr. Howard, in explaining its
provisions, said that he had no hope of carrying it
into law, but merely wished to " clear the air " for
the Reform Bill promised by the Government. Sir
Charles M'Laren said that he hoped this Bill might

[1] Estimate given by the Liberal *Daily Chronicle.*

help the Government to come to some decision as to the manner in which they would deal with the Women's Suffrage question next year, but when Mr. Asquith arose to make the expected Government pronouncement, he declared that the opinion of the Government was unchanged and entirely unaffected by the introduction of this Bill. He added, however, that there were certain proposals contained in the measure of which he approved, but carefully explained that his approval only extended so far as the Bill referred to men. Though he was aware that the measure would not be pressed beyond a Second Reading, he stated that the members of the Government would abstain from voting either for or against it. The whole debate, therefore, ended in fiasco, and had been merely a wasted opportunity. After Mr. Asquith's pronouncement the House divided and there voted,

For the Bill............................	157
Against the Bill........................	122
Majority for the Bill................	35

It will be thus seen that this Bill of Mr. Howard's secured a very much smaller measure of support than that which had been accorded to the equal Women's Enfranchisement Bill in the previous year, for the figures had then been: For the Bill 271, against 92. Majority for the Bill 179.

The Women's Social and Political Union now decided that another deputation should attempt to obtain an interview with Mr. Asquith, and an eighth Women's Parliament was held on March 30th. Mrs. Saul Solomon, widow of the Governor General

of South Africa, an elderly, motherly figure, volunteered to lead its deputation of thirty women who
were to carry the usual resolution to the House,
whilst Miss Dora Marsden, B.A., of Manchester,
looking exactly like a Florentine angel, marched before with a purple-white-and-green standard announcing the arrival of the deputation. As soon as
the women reached the street, the usual pushing and
hustling by the police began, and after an hour's
brave struggle, eleven of them were arrested. Next
day nine of those who had not been taken again
returned to the charge, and eventually the twenty
women were sent to prison at Sir Albert de Rutzen's
orders, nineteen of them for one month and Patricia
Woodlock, because she had served several sentences
already, for three.

On April 16th, Mrs. Pethick Lawrence, our dear
treasurer, was released, and we were able to tell her
that no less than £8,000 had been collected by the
sacrifice of our members during self-denial week. A
great procession was formed in her honour and
marched from the Marble Arch to the Aldwych
Theatre, where she was to speak. What a day it
was to welcome anyone from prison! The trees
were just bursting into leaf, and the brilliant April
sunshine glistened on the silver armour of Elsie
Howey, who represented Joan of Arc, the warrior
maid, whose Beatification was taking place that very
day, and rode at the head of the procession, astride
her great white charger, with the brisk wind blowing
back her fair hair, and gaily fluttering the purple-
white-and-green standard which she bore. Then
came women and girls with flowers and banners, and
Mrs. Lawrence's own carriage covered with flags,

and everywhere were the purple-white-and-green colours, except at one point where the American delegates to the International Women's Suffrage Congress, then sitting in London, rode in a carriage draped with their own stars and stripes. Inside the theatre the platform was covered with flowers sent by hundreds of members and friends, and there too the American delegates had added their tribute, a little silk copy of their national flag.

It was a wonderful speech that Mrs. Lawrence then delivered, full, not only of enthusiasm and deep feeling, but of logic and common sense, and of unanswerable arguments for the women's cause. She reminded us that she and her fellow Suffragists had gone to prison in support of the old English Constitutional maxim that taxation and representation should go together. Before she had gone to prison, she told us, a birthday book had been shown to her that had been got out for a Church bazaar. In that book Mr. Asquith had been asked to write his favourite quotation with his signature, and this favourite quotation of Mr. Asquith's had turned out to be, "Taxation without representation is tyranny." Many stories she told us of what she had seen and heard in prison. One morning the Chaplain had come into the hospital where she was, and had called up an old woman to speak to him. Everyone there had heard the conversation that passed between them, and had learnt in reply to his peremptory questioning her name, her age, the length of her sentence, and so on. She was seventy-six, unmarried, and for the first time in her long life she was now imprisoned because she could not pay her rent and taxes £3 16s. "I keep a lodging house for workingmen," she said.

A part of the decoration of the Exhibition held in the
Prince's Skating Rink, May, 1909

" It has been a very bad winter for my lodgers, and they have not been able to pay me." " This woman was quite good enough to pay taxes," said Mrs. Lawrence, " this old woman of seventy-six, and to go to prison when she could not meet the taxes, and yet she was not counted fit to exercise a vote."

Mrs. Lawrence also told us of a conversation between herself and the chaplain. " I have heard a great deal of you, Mrs. Lawrence," he had said. " You have started holiday homes for girls. I wish you would start a holiday home for wardresses. You see they work very hard — twelve hours a day. They very often break down, and then they have not enough money to go away for a holiday." " I looked at him in amazement," Mrs. Lawrence told us, " to think that a Government servant should come to me, a voteless woman, and suggest that I should supply a deficiency created because our legislators do not pay their women servants enough." So argument followed argument, and there were many Suffragettes who joined the Union on that day.

Ever since the night on which the members of the Freedom League had chained themselves to the grille and pieces of that historic monument of prejudice had been taken down, whilst two men in the Stranger's Gallery had loudly demanded votes for women, the galleries had been closed and though Press representatives had still leave to come and go, as far as the general public was concerned, the House had sat in secret conclave for six months. Members of Parliament found the exclusion of all visitors to the House to be exceedingly inconvenient, and at last the Government introduced what it called

24

a " Brawling Bill " which was to settle the question
by providing that: —

Any person, not being a member of either House of Parliament, while present in the Palace of Westminster during
the sitting of either House who is guilty of disorderly conduct or acts in contravention of any rule or order of the
House in respect of the admission of strangers, shall be guilty
of misdemeanour and liable to summary conviction and imprisonment for a term not exceeding six months or to a fine
not exceeding £100.

In bringing the Bill forward the Attorney General urged that though the House could already
punish strangers who broke its rules by committing
them to Newgate prison, their imprisonment there
could only last whilst the House was sitting, so that
those who committed an offence towards the close of
the session would be too easily let off.   Moreover the
House had not the power to punish offenders without
debate and for it to suspend its consideration of
" high matters " in order to discuss the cases of persons, who, though he declared that no offence could
be more serious than theirs, he yet characterised as
unworthy in themselves of " further consideration
than any ordinary police magistrate could give them,"
was to play the game of the disturbers and to give
them the maximum of advertisement with the minimum of punishment.   When someone pointed out
that all accused persons liable to six months' imprisonment were entitled to trial by jury, he at once
stated that he should prefer to reduce the proposed
term of imprisonment to three months.   Finally he
recommended the Bill to the House as one that would
" save its time and safeguard its dignity."

Lord Balcarres urged that anyone charged under the Bill would have the right to subpœna the Speaker or the Chairman of Committee who had witnessed the occurrence complained of to give evidence at the trial. It would be impossible, he said, to say that Mr. Speaker must not be summoned because he represented " the quintessence of the collective wisdom of the House of Commons," and " it would be a most deplorable thing if the Speaker and other officials and Members of the House were to be hauled into court for no other reason than to draw public attention to the Police Court proceedings, and to make sensational paragraphs in the evening papers." Mr. Mooney, an Irish member, said amid great laughter, that he thought the Bill must have been drafted in the neighbourhood of Clement's Inn, because of the advertisement which it would give " to certain propagandists," whilst Mr. Hazleton declared that the Government were merely setting up an act of Parliament " as an Aunt Sally for every Suffragette to come along and have a shot at."

Mr. Keir Hardie stated that in his opinion the Bill was only necessary because of the failure of members of the Government, and Members of the House to redeem their election pledges in regard to Women's Suffrage, and that it was because women felt that they could no longer appeal to the honour of the House of Commons, that they had taken to extreme measures.

In his reply the Attorney General ignored this latter view of the case, but dealt at length with the right of summoning witnesses, pointing to the setting aside of the subpœnas to Mr. Asquith and Mr. Herbert Gladstone, in the case of Mrs. Baines' trial at Leeds, as a proof that this could easily be done again to protect the officers of the House, and especially the "great officers" from being summoned. He promised that stringent provisions with this object should be added in committee, saying "I do not think the House need trouble itself with that objection."

Evidently, therefore, the gradual sweeping away of every safeguard of a free people against coercion, which had been won for us by the suffering and sacrifice and ceaseless effort of generations of our forebears, was as nothing to the Government, in comparison with the staving off of the Women's claim to vote. Now it was one of the fundamental rights of the accused person that they were proposing to tamper with, but the House would not agree. Sir Edward Carson, whilst expressing doubt as to the practicability of the Government's proposals, protested emphatically against the suggestion that there should be a law of subpœna for the House of Commons different to that which prevailed in the rest of the land. Finally the Prime Minister rose to say that though, after the trouble that had been taken in drafting it, he did not like to withdraw the Bill altogether, he yet thought that further time should be given for consideration, and that the debate should be adjourned.

The Brawling Bill was never heard of again. Its final death-blow was dealt on April 27th, exactly a week after it had been discussed, when five Suffragettes effectively showed that no threat of a Brawling Bill could prevent them from demonstrating in the House of Commons by entering St. Stephen's Hall and chaining themselves to the statues of five men —

Walpole, Lord Somers, Selden, and Lord Falkland, whose names are famous in the struggle for British Liberties in Stuart days. Having so chained themselves, the women addressed the visitors and Members of Parliament, explaining that they themselves were engaged in fighting for the liberties of one-half of the British people. With strong pincers the police succeeded in breaking the chains, but there was no prosecution and shortly afterwards the Speaker announced that both the Ladies' and Strangers' Galleries were to be reopened on certain conditions. Before being admitted each visitor must now subscribe his or her name and address to the following printed pledge:

I undertake to abstain from making any interruption or disturbance and to obey the rules for the maintenance of order in the Galleries.

Having signed the pledge, men visitors were to be absolutely trusted, but women were treated as having absolutely no sense of honour, for no woman was to be permitted to get even so far as the signing of the pledge, unless she happened to be related to a Member of Parliament and no Member was to be allowed to introduce any lady to the gallery unless he had previously won a place for her in the ballot.

On May 13th, the Women's Social and Political Union opened in the Prince's Skating Rink, Knightsbridge, a Votes for Women Exhibition in the purple, white and green. Mrs. Lawrence and the Committee of the Union were driven thither by a woman chauffeur in a motor car for which the Suffragettes had subscribed in order that they might present it to the Treasurer on her release from prison. The Rink was covered outside with a mass of waving flags in the colours, and inside these also predominated. The theme of the decorations which lined the walls of the great central hall was " They that sow in tears shall reap in joy and he that goeth forth and weepeth bearing precious seed, shall doubtless come again with rejoicing, bringing his sheaves with him." And indeed in those bright spring days at the Skating Rink, though the victory of the franchise was not yet won, some of the fruits of the struggle were already present in the glad comradeship of the workers. Everyone seemed to be full of high spirits, and all were keenly interested in the success of the enterprise and, in spite of the strenuous militant tactics in which they were engaged and of all the propaganda work which they were accomplishing, every branch of the Union and every organising centre, had its stall laden with goods. Friends from all over the world had sent their contributions, and the Norwegian delegates to the International Suffrage Congress had a stall of their own in aid of the W. S. P. U. funds.

But this was no mere bazaar, for at every turn one was reminded of Votes for Women. Each day as one entered, a ballot paper was always pressed into one's hand and every visitor to the exhibition was invited to record a vote upon some question of the moment; the ballot box and everything connected with the voting being arranged just exactly as it is in Parliamentary Elections. At one end of the hall was a facsimile of a prison cell, in which sat a woman in second division prison dress who herself had actually been to Holloway and could explain exactly how the bed was rolled and the tins were cleaned. Side by side with this was the sort of cell which may be occupied by men political prisoners. Ranged along one wall were glass cases containing clever little cartoon models, prepared by sculptors in the Union and showing numerous representations of Cabinet Ministers in their various encounters with the Suffragettes. Amongst a host of others, there was Mrs. Pankhurst and her deputation at the door of the House of Commons with the Cabinet Ministers hiding fearfully behind a group of stalwart police.

Then there was a picture gallery of Press photographs showing the history of the militant movement, and there were entertainments, all about Votes for Women, by those ardent Suffragists, the members of the Actresses Franchise League.

The exhibition lasted a fortnight, and at the end of the first week, came a great surprise, for a women's drum and fife band, consisting of members of our Union, who had been practising in secret for months past, now dressed in a specially designed uniform of purple, white and green, formed up in the centre of the rink and with Mrs. Leigh as Drum Major, marched out playing the " Marseillaise," and then went round the town to advertise the exhibition.

Hundreds of new members were made during the fortnight, and perhaps the smallest part of the whole achievement was that £5,564 was added to the W. S. P. U. campaign fund. Altogether it was decided that the Exhibition in the Colours was the smartest, brightest and cheeriest exhibition that anyone had ever seen. Strangers visiting it said,

" What happy women you Suffragettes are; we never thought you were like that! " To those who read of this movement in future years it may seem strange that, in spite of the unremitting character of the struggle the Suffragettes, when not actually engaged in the fighting line, should have been so generally merry and light hearted. W. D. Howells, in his *Venetian Life,* and others, tell us that whilst Venice was dominated by Austria the whole town was under a cloud; the Italians gave no balls, dinners or entertainments, and even the great Opera House was closed. But the attitude of the Suffragettes was perhaps more in keeping with the English character. Have we not heard that though the Spanish Armada had long been expected, Drake and the other great sea fighters were playing bowls when the news came that it was in sight? And now, whilst the Exhibition [1] was in progress the fighting campaign was going forward all over the country as briskly as ever.

The protests in connection with Cabinet Ministers' meetings continued almost daily and, whilst the strictest precautions were taken to keep them out, the greatest ingenuity was displayed by them in obtaining an entry. At a meeting of Mr. Birrel's in the Colston Hall, Bristol, two women were found to have hidden themselves amongst the pipes of the organ. When the same Minister spoke with Lord Crew at Liverpool, Mary Phillips, who had lain crouching for twenty-four hours amid the dust and grime in a narrow space under the organ, was there to remind them of Patricia Woodlock, the Liverpool

[1] The Freedom League had also held a successful and interesting Green White and Gold Fair at the Caxton Hall.

The band out for the first time, May, 1909

Suffragette, who was then serving a sentence of three months' imprisonment in Holloway gaol.

Meanwhile during the spring of 1909, eight by-election contests had been fought at Glasgow, Hawick Burghs, Forfar, South Edinburgh, Croydon, East Edinburgh, the Attercliffe Division of Sheffield, and Stratford-on-Avon.

The Scotch constituencies, with the exception of Glasgow, which is not typically Scotch, were the most difficult to fight, for the majority of the Scotch people have long been so rootedly Liberal that a very exceptional degree, not only of sympathy with the cause but of belief in the by-election policy, was needed to induce any of the electors to alter their old allegiance, and to allow a Conservative to be returned. Nevertheless the Liberal majority was in every case reduced. In Glasgow the seat which had been held by a Liberal was wrested from the Government by a Liberal majority of 2113. At Croydon the Liberal Candidate was also defeated by a greatly increased majority, for whilst in the general election it had been 638 it was now 3,948. The elections at Attercliffe and Stratford-on-Avon were perhaps the most striking of the series. In the former contest the Liberals strove to counteract the Suffragette influence in numerous ways, including the issuing of leaflets with such headings as, "WORKING MEN DON'T BE FOOLED BY MRS. PANKHURST," and, " SUFFRAGETTE AND TORY LIES NAILED TO THE COUNTER." In these documents they tried to lead the public to think that the police, and not the Government in power, were responsible for the Suffragist imprisonments. When the result of the polling was made known, it was found that the Liberal nominee had been placed third on the poll, having secured less than half the votes which had been cast for his party in the last election.

At Stratford-on-Avon, another Liberal seat, the Government candidate was again routed, this time by a majority of 2,627 votes.

CHAPTER XX

JUNE AND JULY, 1909

The Ninth Women's Parliament. Attempt to In-
sist on the Constitutional Right of Petition as
Secured by the Bill of Rights. Arrest of Mrs.
Pankhurst and the Hon. Mrs. Haverfield. Miss
Wallace Dunlop and the Hunger Strike. The
Fourteen Hunger Strikers in the Punishment
Cells. Mr. Gladstone Charges Miss Garnett
with Having Bitten a Wardress. Her Acquittal.

When the authorities had first raised the threat
of punishing women under the Statute thirteen,
Charles II, for proceeding to Parliament in a body
of more than twelve persons with the object of presenting a petition to the Prime Minister, the Suffragettes had decided to defy the Statute. We were
indignant at the proposal to enforce against us in the
supposed free and enlightened days of the twentieth
century, a coercive law passed in a bygone time of
great upheaval and of great tyranny. Moreover
the police authorities had stated that if tried under
this Statute of Charles II the Suffragette cases must
be decided by a judge and jury instead of being
hustled through the Police Court. Deputation after
deputation of more than twelve women had therefore gone forth but though these women had again
and again been seized and imprisoned for periods as
long as that prescribed by that Act, the authorities

still did not charge them under the Act of Charles II.

At last, as the seriousness of the whole position grew, our committee decided that it would be wisest to comply with the very letter of the law and to stand on the constitutional right of the subject to petition the Prime Minister as the seat of power. We were advised that the right of petition, which had been to some extent limited by the Act of Charles II, had existed from time immemorial. It had been confirmed by the Bill of Rights which became law in 1869, at the beginning of the joint reigns of William and Mary, as one of the securities for the liberties of the British people, the complete preservation of which had been a condition of the accession of that King and Queen. The Bill of Rights declares that: " It is the right of the subject to petition the King and all commitments, and prosecutions for such petitioning are illegal." As the power of the King had now for all practical purposes passed into the hands of Parliament, the Prime Minister, as the chief Parliamentary official, had become the King's representative and therefore the right to petition the Prime Minister clearly belonged to each and every member of the Community. This right, though it should always be zealously guarded, is of course most essential in the case of persons placed outside of the pale of the franchise.

A ninth Women's Parliament having been called, Mrs. Pankhurst wrote to Mr. Asquith stating that a deputation from the Women's Parliament would wait upon him at the House of Commons at eight o'clock on the evening of June 29th. She informed

Mrs. Lawrence's Release Procession, April 17th, 1909

him further that the deputation could accept no refusal and must insist upon their constitutional right
to be received.

The Prime Minister returned a formal refusal to
receive them but the women proceeded with their
arrangements.

On Tuesday, June 21st, exactly a week before the
day fixed for the Women's Parliament, Miss Wallace Dunlop, visited the House of Commons with
a gentleman who left her and went on into the lobby
to interview a member of Parliament. She passed
into St. Stephen's Hall and sitting down on one of
the seats there, unfolded a large block covered with
printers' ink. She was pressing this block to the
stone wall, when a policeman rushed up, and dragged
her hurriedly away, but there remained displayed
upon the wall the words:

WOMEN'S DEPUTATION,

JUNE 29th.

BILL OF RIGHTS

It is the right of the Subject to
petition the King and all commitments and Prosecutions for such
petitioning are illegal.

Miss Wallace Dunlop was taken to the police Inspector's office opening out of the Palace Yard, but,
after an impression of her notice had been solemnly
made on a sheet of blotting paper, she was allowed
to go. She had been pulled away too speedily to
look at her own handiwork in St. Stephen's Hall,

and the policemen told her that it was " only a smudge." Two days later, therefore, she set out to make a second attempt to stamp on the wall of St. Stephen's her reminder to Parliament that the people's liberties must not be violated. She was able to carefully affix her notice before a policeman appeared, but she was not to be let off this time. On June 22nd she was tried for wilfully and maliciously damaging the stone-work of the House of Commons. She urged in her defence that any damage which she had caused by affixing the notice was entirely outweighed by the great constitutional issue which it had been her intention to impress upon the Members of the House of Commons. " It is claimed by the prosecution," she said, " that it cost ten shillings to erase the impression of the first notice and that it will cost probably a similar sum to wipe out the second. It seems to me that it would have been better if the authorities had spent no money at all but had let the impression stay." She was found guilty and ordered either to pay a fine of £5 and £1. 1. 2 damages or in default to undergo one month's imprisonment in the third division without hard labour.

Meanwhile very great interest had been aroused in the attempt of the Suffragettes to force the Prime Minister to receive them by Constitutional means. There was keen discussion as to what would happen and, when the fateful Tuesday came, vast throngs of people, greater perhaps than at any other demonstration, lined the streets in the neighbourhood of Parliament. In the House of Commons itself there was a strong feeling that the deputation should be received and this was expressed at question time by

Christabel waving to the hunger strikers from a house
overlooking the prison, July, 1909

many Members. Mr. Keir Hardie asked the Speaker whether it was by his instructions that a deputation of eight or nine ladies was to be prohibited from entering the House, but Mr. Speaker replied that this was the first he had heard of it and that he had issued no instructions. When the same question was put to the Home Secretary he also answered, " I gave no instructions," and declared that it was the police who had the responsibility of keeping the approaches of the House open. Mr. Hugh Law asked leave to move the adjournment of the House on a matter of urgent public importance, namely, the refusal of the Prime Minister to receive the deputation and the consequent grave and immediate danger to the public peace, but the Speaker refused, saying that the question had been before the House for at least two years. Mr. Keir Hardie then asked if the Home Secretary would give instructions that so long as the deputation was orderly it should be admitted to St. Stephen's but Mr. Gladstone refused to accept responsibility, saying, " I cannot say what action will be right or wrong for the police to take."

At half past seven the Women's Parliament met and a Petition to the Prime Minister having been adopted Mrs. Pankhurst, Mrs. Saul Solomon of South Africa, Miss Neligan who from 1874 to 1901 had been head mistress of the Croydon Girls' School and was now 76, and five other women were duly appointed to present it straightway. Then Miss Vera Holme was dispatched on horseback with an advance letter announcing that the deputation was about to appear. With all possible speed she rode on, forging her way through the masses of people,

until, close to the House itself, she was met by a
body of mounted police, who demanded her business. She handed the letter for Mr. Asquith to the
Inspector but he merely flung it on the ground where
it was lost to sight amongst the crowd.[1]

Meanwhile the little deputation of eight women
were preparing to leave the Caxton Hall and the
Women's Drum and Fife Band ranged up the steps
was playing out to them the Marseillaise. The
shrill, shrill notes of the fife, were a call to battle,
the heart beat quicker in unison with that drum-
ming and the breath came hard and short. On the
deputation went whilst the cheers of their comrades
mingled with the deeper answering cheer of the
crowd outside. On they went up Victoria Street
and all the way from the masses who watched them
was heard no single cry against them, nothing but
one great cheer. They pressed on, first Mrs. Pankhurst in her light coat, then the two little old ladies
and the other women following behind, but just at
the corner of St. Margaret's Church a long line of
police on horse and foot blocked the road. For a
moment there was a strange pause and the crowd
was hushed. Then the police lines opened and the
deputation passed through to the clear space around
the House. The crowd cheered and they were lost
to sight.

Everyone believed that the women were to be received. But St. Stephen's was closely guarded by
police and, as the deputation reached it, Chief Inspector Scantlebury stepped forward and handed a
letter to Mrs. Pankhurst. She opened it and read

[1] It was afterwards brought back to Clement's Inn by a
stranger who found it still unopened.

aloud: "The Prime Minister, for the reasons which
he has already given in a written reply to their request, regrets that he is unable to receive the proposed deputation." Then she let the missive fall
to the ground and said, "I stand upon my right as
a subject of the King to petition the Prime Minister.
I am firmly resolved to stand here until I am received," but, even whilst she was speaking, Inspector
Scantlebury turned away — he would not wait to
hear her statement. She called to him to stay and
pleaded with the bystanders, Members of Parliament
and others, to bring him back to listen but he disappeared through the door of the Stranger's Entrance.

Then Mrs. Pankhurst turned to Inspector Jarvis,
appealing to him, or to anyone, to take her message
to the Prime Minister, but she was merely told to
go away. "I absolutely refuse," she said, and the
other ladies chimed in, "We absolutely support Miss
Pankhurst." At that, whilst the rows of Members
of Parliament policemen and newspaper reporters
looked on with interest, Inspector Jarvis seized Mrs.
Pankhurst by the arm and began to push her away.

There was no hope now that the deputation would
be received and she well knew that if the women
persisted in their demand to enter the House they
would be arrested in the end. For the sake of their
cause neither she nor they could ever consent voluntarily to retrace their steps. They must refuse to
go and when, as they would be, they were forced
rudely back, they must return again and again until
they could do so no longer because they had been
placed under arrest. This would mean a hard and
a long struggle, for the police would first try every
other means to overcome them. She knew that in

a moment the violence would .begin and that the frail old ladies behind her would he hustled and jostled and thrust ignominiously aside. And so, not for herself, for she had borne this sort of thing before, but to save these older women from ill-usage, she committed a technical assault on Inspector Jarvis, striking him lightly on the cheek with her open hand. As she did so, he said, " I know why you have done that." But one blow was not enough for the police began to seize the other women and the pushing and hustling began. Then she said, " Must I do it again? " and Inspector Jarvis answered, " Yes." At that, she struck him again on the other cheek and he said: " Take them in," and the eight women were placed under arrest and led away.

Meanwhile the people outside the police lines had waited patiently until at last the news filtered through that the deputation had not been received. Then suddenly a woman was seen struggling through the crowd bearing the colours. Cheers were raised at the sight and policemen rushed towards her. This was the signal for a general attempt on the part of the Suffragettes to reach the House of Commons and in ever recurring batches of twelve, that only too soon were to be torn asunder, the women bravely but hopelessly pressed on; whilst more than it had ever done before the crowd showed a disposition to help them and to prevent their arrest.

But Parliament went on as though nothing were happening and when a man in the Central Lobby suddenly shouted, " The women of England are clamouring outside," he was at once seized by numbers of bystanders and police and bundled through the door. Then tranquillity reigned once more. It turned out that the interrupter was Mr. Lawrence Housman, the well-known writer and artist.

At nine o'clock a great force of mounted police cleared the Square, beating the people back into Victoria Street, into Parliament Street, across Westminster Bridge or along Millbank. It was a familiar stratagem and, as on so many other similar occasions, Parliament Square was soon a desert. But now a strange thing happened, for little groups of women, six or seven at a time, kept issuing from no one knew where, and making determined rushes for the House. As a matter of fact the W. S. P. U. had hired thirty different offices in the Square for that night and in these offices women lay concealed and dashed out at preconcerted moments.

Whilst this was happening in the Square other Suffragettes succeeded in carrying out a time-honoured means of showing political contempt by breaking the windows of the official residence of the first Lord of the Admiralty, and of the Home Office, the Privy Council Office and the Treasury Offices in Whitehall. Having gone just after dusk, when the lights are lit in rooms where people are, they chose windows on the ground floor that were still dark. Then to small stones, around which were wrapped petitions, they tied string, and, holding fast to the end of the string, they struck the stones against the windows, and, having thus made holes, dropped them through. So they accomplished their purpose without the risk of injuring anyone. One hundred and eight women were at last taken into custody.

Long accounts of the affair appeared in the Press

next morning and these were on the whole very much more favourable to the women than any that had gone before, as the following gleanings from some of the papers indicate:

The record of these attempted raids has been one of remarkable persistency in the face of every possible discouragement from the authorities.— DAILY TELEGRAPH.

The same paper also published a humorous pen-and-ink drawing of a mounted policeman, four constables and an inspector marching off to prison the tiny figure of Miss Neligan with the inscription, " Seventy-nine years old!   Liberal treatment."

It is the most successful effort that the militant section of the party have made. . . .   However much one may deplore their methods one cannot overlook their earnestness; they are out to win.— THE SCOTSMAN.

Principle and tact alike are wanting in the Asquith administration, otherwise there would have been none of the suffragette scenes in to-day's police court, and none of the tumult and expense of last night. . . .   No one supposes for a moment that such a large and influential body as the Suffragettes would have been denied a hearing by Mr. Asquith and his colleagues had it possessed voting power.— THE MANCHESTER COURIER.

It is not likely that any one of the thousands of men and women who saw the Suffragist deputation to Mr. Asquith to the House of Commons on Tuesday night will ever forget the scene, much as he or she may wish to do so.   There are some things which photograph themselves indelibly on the sensitive plate of the brain and that was one of them. . . .— EAST ANGLICAN DAILY TIMES.

The Prime Minister has shockingly mismanaged the business from the beginning.— YORKSHIRE WEEKLY POST.

There is some concern among liberals at the Prime Minister's persistent refusal to receive a deputation from the Suffragists. They doubt if he is wise in showing so unyielding an attitude to them.— MANCHESTER DAILY DESPATCH.

As the deputation of women had complied with the very letter of the law, the W. S. P. U. determined to prove, if possible, that the Government had broken the law in refusing to allow them to present their petition. Mr. Henle was retained to deal with the legal aspect of the case and he pressed home his contention with so many forceful arguments that when he had finished Mr. Muskett who was conducting the case for the prosecution, asked to be allowed time to prepare an answer.

When the case was continued on Friday, July 9th, a sensation was created by the discovery that Lord Robert Cecil had been retained to defend the case of Mrs. Haverfield upon which all the others hung. Mr. Muskett now began by suggesting that the women had had no intention of presenting a petition and that the claim that they had gone to the House of Commons in the endeavour to do so was an afterthought, got up for the purposes of the defence. He was soon obliged to abandon this line of attack for the speeches and articles of the leaders, the leaflets published by them and the official letters of the W. S. P. U. to Mr. Asquith, together with the fact that each member of the deputation had carried a copy of the petition, clearly demonstrated the absurdity of this contention. The whole case as to the right of petition and of the way in which that right should be exercised was then discussed, first by Mr. Muskett and then by Lord Robert Cecil. Afterwards Mrs. Pankhurst quietly told her own story of the happenings on June 29th. In conclusion she said to Sir Albert de Rutzen, " I want to say to you here, standing in this dock, that if you deal with us as you have dealt with other women on similar occasions, the same experience will be gone through; we shall refuse to agree to be bound over because we cannot in honour consent to such a course and we shall go to prison to suffer whatever awaits us there, but in future, we shall refuse to conform any longer to the regulations of the prison. There are 108 of us here to-day and just as we have thought it our duty to defy the police in the streets, so, when we get into prison, as we are political prisoners, we shall do our very best to bring back into the twentieth century the treatment of political prisoners which was thought right in the case of William Cobbett and other political offenders of his time."

Then looking rather pained and blinking his eyes very nervously, the amiable-looking elderly magistrate proceeded to give his decision. He said that whilst he agreed with Lord Robert Cecil and Mr. Henle that the right of petition clearly belonged to every subject, he yet thought that when the police had refused permission to enter the House, and when the Prime Minister had said that he would not receive the deputation, the women had acted wrongly in refusing to go away. He should therefore fine them £5 and if they refused to pay, should send them to prison for one month in the second division. This punishment should not take immediate effect because he understood that he was desired to " state a case " upon the legal point as to the right of petition, and as he was quite prepared to do this, the matter would be taken to a higher court for further consideration.

Mrs. Pankhurst then claimed that the charges against every one of her fellow prisoners should be held over until her own case had been finally decided as they all turned on the same point. This was agreed to except in regard to the fourteen women charged with stone-throwing and attempted rescue, who on Monday, July 12th, were tried and sent to prison for periods varying from one month to six weeks.

And now the evening paper placards were announcing a strange thing that had been taking place in Holloway gaol. Miss Wallace Dunlop, who had gone alone to prison, had set herself to wrest from the government the political treatment which her comrades demanded, and had seized upon a terrible but most powerful means of attaining her object. On arriving in prison on Friday evening, July 2nd, she had at once claimed to be treated as a political offender, and, when this had been denied, she warned the Governor that she should refuse to eat anything until she had gained her point. On Monday morning she put her breakfast aside untasted, and addressed a petition to Mr. Gladstone explaining that she had adopted this course as a matter of principle and for the sake of those who might come after. Miss Wallace Dunlop has not the vigour and reserve force that belong to youth and she is of fragile constitution, but she never wavered and went cheerfully on with her terrible task. Every effort was made to break down her resolution. The ordinary prison diet was no longer placed before

her, but such dainty food as at other times is not
seen in Holloway, and this was left in her cell both
day and night in the hope that she would be tempted
to eat, but though her table was always covered,
she touched nothing. Tuesday was the day on
which she felt most hungry, and then, as she says,
" I threw a fried fish, four slices of bread, three
bananas and a cup of hot milk out of the window "
Threats and coaxing alike failed to move her. The
doctor, watching her growing weakness with concern, came to feel her pulse many times during the
day, but her calm steadfast spirit and gentle gaiety
never deserted her. She had always a smile for him.
" What are you going to have for dinner to-day? "
he would ask, and she would reply, " My determination." " Indigestible stuff, but tough, no doubt,"
he would answer. So Monday, Tuesday, Wednesday, Thursday passed; by Friday it was clearly
realised that she would not change her mind but
would carry on her hunger strike even to the
gates of death. Hourly she was growing more
feeble and so on Friday evening, July 9th, she was
set free.

The fourteen women who had been sentenced on
the day of her release and heard the news of what
she had done as they were being hurried to gaol decided to follow her example. On reaching Holloway
they at once informed the officials that they would
refuse to deliver up any of their private property,
to undress and to put on the prison clothing, to obey
the rule of silence, to perform prison tasks and to
eat the prison food and that in every way that was
open to them they would protest against the regulations. The Governor agreed for the time being to

allow them to retain their own clothing, but told them that when the visiting magistrates next came round they would be charged before them with mutiny. The women then addressed petitions to the Home Secretary, demanding that, in accordance with international custom, they should receive the treatment due to political prisoners, and decided to wait a day or two for a reply before beginning the hunger strike.

The Suffragettes had always condemned the inadequate ventilation of the cells which they felt to be exceedingly injurious to the health of every prisoner. On those burning summer days the stifling heat became almost unbearable and after several times appealing that more fresh air should be allowed to them, the women at last determined to break some of the panes.

On Wednesday morning Christabel and Mrs. Tuke, anxious for news of their comrades, went up to Holloway and obtained admittance to a house opposite the gaol. There from a back window, they called to the prisoners, who eagerly stretched out their arms to them through the broken panes, and in a few shouted words told them of what had taken place. The same afternoon, a committee of visiting magistrates arrived in the prison and sentenced the Suffragettes to from seven to ten days' close solitary confinement. The women were then all dragged away to the punishment cells. Miss Florence Spong, one of the prisoners, describes her experience thus:

Entering a dim corridor on either side of which were cells, I was conducted to the last one and the double iron doors were clanged and locked behind me; the cell damp, icy cold and dark struck terror in me, but the principle for which I was fighting helped me to overcome my fears. In the dim light I discovered a plank bed fixed in one corner of the cell about four inches from the ground, with a wooden pillow at the head. Opposite was a tree stump, clamped to the wall for a seat, and in another corner was a small shelf with a filthy rubber tumbler full of water. High above the bed was a small window and through the tiny panes of opaque glass a faint light filtered. Realising how quickly the light was waning I hurriedly examined my cell. I discovered two pools of water near the head of the bed which never dried up. There was a small square of glass high above the door and through this the light of a tiny gas jet flickered from the corridor outside. This was lit at five o'clock and just enabled me to see the objects in my cell. At eight o'clock three wardresses brought me a mattress and some rugs, and again the doors clanged to and I was alone. I will not speak of that night; I leave it for your imagination. At six the next morning I was told to get up, my mattress and bed clothes were taken from my cell and a tiny bowl of water was brought me to wash in, and that was the only wash I was allowed every twenty-four hours.

" It is wrong that there should be such places to-day," Miss Florence Cooke told the Governor, " they would drive any ordinary prisoner mad," and she tells us:

I saw all means of protest had been taken from me except one, and that was to do what Miss Wallace Dunlop had done, to refuse to take any food. The hardest time was the first twenty-four hours. Milk was brought to me which I felt I could have taken very willingly, but I put it from me. Then the wardress brought me in some food. I said to her, " Will you please take that out? " She refused.

The hunger strikers waving to Christabel from their prison cells, July, 1909

I therefore took the tin in which the food was and rolled it
out of the cell and what was in it went upon the ground.

This is important, because Mr. Gladstone afterwards charged the Suffragettes with having thrown
food at the wardresses.

Miss Cooke goes on:

I was particularly careful in what I did to be polite and I
believe all the other Suffragettes were the same. On Friday
I took to my bed and the doctor told me that if I persisted I
should get a fever, but I was absolutely determined to do my
part, at whatever sacrifice, and I told the Governor that so
long as I was responsible for my action I should refuse to take
food.

On Sunday night I was removed to the hospital and there
a fresh effort was made to get me to take food. Medicine
was brought to me, which I absolutely refused, knowing that
it was either food in disguise or else intended to aggravate
my hunger. On Monday afternoon my head felt exceedingly bad and I hardly knew what I was doing, but I determined that I would not give in. In the evening the
Governor came to me and said, " Be very calm." I said to
him, " There is a supreme power which gives us strength to
bear whatever comes to us." He said, " I have orders to
release you," and I said to him, " Does Mr. Gladstone prefer this to doing us justice? "

The other prisoners all told similar stories, each
of which unconsciously displayed the most wonderful heroism. One day Miss Mary Allen fell fainting on the stone floor of her punishment cell and
when, weak and numb with cold, she regained consciousness, she sang the Women's Marseillaise to
cheer herself, and to her delight the occupant of the
next cell joined in. So, bravely struggling, each

of the women won her way out to freedom, having fasted bravely, some for six and a half, others for six, five and a half, or five days.

Think of the courage of it! To be confined there in semi-darkness when a word would procure release. To withstand the terrible pangs of hunger with food always before one's eyes, distracted by the fever of that unhealthy and fœtid place. To feel oneself growing gradually weaker and weaker, and to know that but a little more, perhaps suddenly, any moment without warning, and the heart will stop. And yet never, never to falter, always to cling on to the word of their faith and the great impersonal ideal. Think of the wonderful courage of it! And after their release it was only with utmost care and cherishing that these dear women were won back to life and in their feeble weariness they felt, even when lying on the softest bed, as though they were stretched upon iron bars.

There were some generous souls, the Reverend Hugh Chapman of the Royal Chapel of the Savoy and others, who raised their voices in protest, and in appeal to the authorities to withdraw their obstinate opposition to the cause for which the women fought, or at least to extend to them the recognised usages of political warfare. It was shown that even according to the strict letter of the law, the women, their stone-throwing notwithstanding, had an unassailable claim to political treatment. In the case of *In-re-Castioni,* reported in Pitt Cobbett's " Leading Cases on International Law," a Swiss subject named Castioni had been arrested in England at the requisition of the Swiss Government, on a charge of murder. Under the provisions of the Extradition Act of 1870, the prisoner could not be extradited if the offence was of a political character, and the judges unanimously held that even such offences as murder and assassination must be considered political, if committed in the belief that they would promote the political end in view, and as part of, and incidental to, a genuine political agitation, rising, or disturbance.

But the legal and moral justice of their claim, and the heroic courage of the women, were alike disregarded by the Government, and when, on July 21st, private Members of Parliament pressed Mr. Gladstone to relent, and to do justice to the women political prisoners, he retaliated by asserting that they had both kicked and bitten the wardresses. The charge was indignantly repudiated by every prisoner and after careful enquiry the W. S. P. U. issued a statement denying the accusations. Three days later it was announced by the press that Mr. Gladstone had held an enquiry at the prison, as a result of which he had decided that the allegations of assault against the Suffragette prisoners had been clearly proved. The W. S. P. U. then wrote urging that the case ought not to be judged on one-sided evidence and claiming that the Home Secretary should allow the fourteen Suffragettes, against whom the charges had been made to put their side of the matter before him. Mr. Gladstone merely replied that he had already directed proceedings to be taken against Miss Theresa Garnett and Mrs. Dove-Wilcox, two of the Suffragettes concerned, and that these proceedings would afford full opportunity for them to swear to their version of the facts before the Court.

On August 4th these trumped-up charges were heard at the North London Police Court. During the whole course of the agitation the Suffragettes had never sought either to conceal or to deny what they had done, or to escape punishment for their actions, and the police had always readily admitted that they could unhesitatingly accept the word of a Suffragette. It is unnecessary, therefore, to give at any length the evidence put forward at the trial of these two women. Their own statements, calmly and carefully given, even the magistrate, although he punished them, certainly believed.

Miss Theresa Garnett was accused of biting one wardress and striking another. In defending herself against these charges she said:

On Wednesday, July 14th, wardresses entered my cell and ordered me to come down to see the visiting magistrates. I stopped to pick up my bag [1] to bring with me. Immediately the wardresses intervened between me and my bag to prevent me taking it and a scuffle ensued, in the course of which I found myself on my back, and two or three other wardresses came into my cell. In this struggle I did not strike or bite or assault any of the wardresses in any way, but used such force as I was able to put forth in order to regain possession of my property. One of the wardresses tore my dress and it is quite likely that as I took hold of her her dress became torn. I was then conducted to the head of the stairs, and seeing that further attempts to retain my property would be of no avail, I walked quietly down into the magistrates' room. When I was there the

[1] In this bag Miss Garnett had a change of clothing and other necessaries and she realised that if this were taken from her, her determination not to wear the prison garments would be frustrated.

charges of breach of prison discipline were made against me and the matron further charged me with having torn the dress of one of the wardresses whilst I was being brought into the room, but no charge of biting the finger of the wardress was made against me. I was then asked whether I had any apology to make. . . . I was sentenced to eight days' solitary confinement and I made no resistance as I was marched away to a punishment cell. Since I learned that this charge was to be brought against me I have been wondering how it could have arisen. I do not believe that the wardresses would purposely fabricate a charge against me. I am led therefore to suppose that this charge rests upon a mistake. You will have noticed, Sir, that no charge of biting the wardress's finger was preferred against me in the presence of the visiting magistrates, whilst a charge of tearing the wardress's dress, which occurred at the same time that my other act is alleged to have happened, was reported to them then and there. I can only suppose therefore that this charge was an afterthought and that, finding a wound on her finger, the wardress concluded that it had been produced by a bite. Now, Sir, I have dressed myself to-day exactly in the way in which I was dressed that day in Holloway and you will notice that I am wearing this portcullis brooch on my left side.

At this Miss Garnett unbuttoned and took off the coat she was wearing and the magistrate rudely said: " I suppose you could bite as well in one dress as in another."

" I have already told you that my dress was torn," she went on. " You will see that it is torn close to the brooch. I think it is exceedingly probable that the wardress who tore my dress received a wound in her finger from the brooch I was wearing and this wound would exactly resemble the wound caused by a bite."

Miss Garnett now unpinned the portcullis brooch which since April of that year had been presented as a badge of honour to every member of the W. S. P. U. who had suffered imprisonment for the cause, and which, like a genuine portcullis, had five sharp little tooth-like projections at its base.

" Here is the brooch," she said, handing it to the the magistrate, " you can look at it for yourself. I have only this to add that if, in spite of the true facts which I have narrated to you, you send me to prison on account of the charges which have been made against me, I shall go there prepared to carry out afresh my protest against the treatment in prison."

Mr. Fordham said that evidently there had been a great struggle and that at such times it was difficult to say exactly what had taken place. He believed that the wound had been caused accidentally, though he thought it was more likely that the wardress's hand had been struck against Miss Garnett's teeth than that the wound had been caused by the brooch. He therefore dismissed the case, but though Miss Garnett had been acquitted of this charge Mr. Gladstone never retracted the statements which he had made in Parliament as to the Suffragette prisoners having bitten the wardresses.

As soon as this first case against Miss Garnett had been disposed of, a second charge of striking one of the wardresses was preferred against her. She then said:

On the day following that on which the visiting magistrates came to Holloway, the wardress entered my cell and ordered me to get up off the bed. I did not do so and she seized hold of the bedding and rolled me on to the floor, injuring my knee. I then said to her, " Is this what you do?" and she said, " It is." I said to her, " In a civilised country?" and she said, " You are a set of uncivilised women." I then asked her to leave the cell and she refused to do so, whereon I pushed her without using any unnecessary violence out of the cell. Later in the day she was exceedingly insolent to me in her behaviour and she further reported me to the Governor and I was moved into a more severe punishment cell. I informed the Governor of the manner in which she had treated me and from that time onwards her behaviour was marked by ordinary courtesy.

Mr. Fordham then sentenced Miss Garnett to a month's imprisonment in the third division.

After this two charges were also brought against Mrs. Dove-Wilcox of Bristol, who was accused of having kicked several of the wardresses, both whilst she was being taken from the cell to the visiting magistrates' room and on the way to the punishment cell afterwards. To the first charge she returned an absolute denial, saying that when summoned to appear before the magistrates she had gone quietly and willingly, and that when she had been charged before them, no attempt had been made to suggest that she had assaulted any of the wardresses. She was sentenced to eight days' close confinement in a punishment cell, but, as she explained:

I refused to accept this treatment and said that if they insisted I should have to be dragged away by force. Several wardresses accordingly seized me to take me away. I offered such resistance as I was able to, but was overpowered. Outside the room some of the wardresses commenced to pummel me very severely, inflicting serious bruises upon me and at last I deliberately kicked two of them. I had on a pair of thin house-shoes at the time, because, as you

know, we had insisted upon our right to retain our own
clothing, so that I could not have hurt either of them very
much. They then picked me up and carried me to the cell
and on the way treated me very cruelly, twisting my arms,
almost throttling me and tearing at my hair with great violence. I remonstrated with them, saying, "You have no
right to treat me in this way and I shall complain to the
Governor of this cruelty." They carried me into the cell
and threw me roughly onto the wooden bed, taking away
my shoes, which they did not return for some time. At first
I determined to complain to the Governor and to show him
the bruises on my arms, but on consideration I remembered
that my quarrel was with the Government and not with
the wardresses. I did not wish them to get into trouble.
Moreover, I regarded the incident as closed, as I heard nothing of any complaint as to my action. I consider I was
perfectly justified in what I did and that anyone with arms
pinioned, assaulted as I was, would have taken similar action.

The magistrate refused to accept Mrs. Dove-Wilcox's denial of the charge of kicking the wardresses
on her way to the visiting magistrates' room, but
said that it was "not of a very serious kind," and
that he would sentence her to pay a fine of 40 shillings or to go to prison for ten days. He also found
her guilty of the second charge of kicking the wardresses on being removed from the visiting magistrates' room, and sentenced her to pay a further 40
shillings or to go to prison for ten days. If she suffered imprisonment, the two terms were to run concurrently, that is to say, she would serve ten days
in all. As she had already stated that she would
not pay any fine, this was tantamount to punishing
her for one of the charges only.

The two women were still weak from their first

hunger strike, but they determined to again make the same stand.   On their arrival at Holloway, the officials forcibly stripped their clothes from their backs, flung the prison garments upon them, and forced them into the punishment cells, where, in spite of the continual faintness from which they suffered, they steadfastly refused all food until Saturday, August 7th, the third day of their imprisonment, when the order of release was brought.

CHAPTER XXI

JULY TO SEPTEMBER, 1909

Mr. Lloyd George at Lime House; Twelve Women
Sent to Prison; Another Strike. Hunger Strikers in Exeter Gaol. The Scenes at Canford Park
and Rushpool Hall. Mrs. Leigh on the Roof at
Liverpool; Liverpool Hunger Strikers. Manchester Hunger Strikers; Leicester Hunger
Strikers; Dundee Hunger Strikers. The Cleveland By-election.

The vindictive attitude of the Government and
the sufferings and heroism of the women in prison,
spurred on their comrades outside to deeds of renewed bravery and daring. Everywhere vast
throngs of people supported the Suffragettes in their
protests and no precautions, however great, or barricades, however high and strong, could keep the
women's voices out. " Shame on you, Mr. Asquith," they cried, as he was unveiling a statue in
the Embankment Gardens. " Shame on you for putting women in dark cells instead of treating them as
political prisoners. Why don't you give us the
vote and end it? " " Ladies and gentlemen,"
thoughtlessly began Mr. Gladstone at a Reading meeting from which all women had been excluded, and when there were shouts of, " Where are
they? " he answered, " Not far off, anyway." He
was right, for soon their speeches, delivered at a

meeting in the street outside, were to be heard within, competing dangerously with his own.

When, on July 15th, Mr. Lewis Harcourt was speaking at the Co-operative Hall, Leigh, Lancashire, the Suffragettes rushed towards the doors. Thousands of people cheered them on, crying: " We will help you to get inside," and though the police arrested Miss Florence Clarkson of Manchester, Mrs. Baines and three other women, all but the first were rescued by the crowd.

On July 17th, Adela Pankhurst held a great meeting outside Mr. Winston Churchill's meeting in Edinburgh and afterwards, amid the enthusiastic plaudits of the crowd, she and Bessie Brand [1] made a dash for the doors, followed and supported by hundreds of men and women. They were arrested by detectives in plain clothes and taken to the police station, whilst cheering men raised their hats and women waved their scarves and handkerchiefs. A second charge led by Miss Eckford of Edinburgh was beaten back by mounted police, and when Mr. Churchill emerged he was greeted with a storm of groans. Those who had been arrested were released after the meeting.

Numbers of men, most of them members of the Men's Political Union, were now also coming forward to demand justice for women at the meetings from which the women were excluded. If they had gone there to heckle Cabinet Ministers on any other question nothing very much would have happened,

---

[1] Daughter of the late Sir David Brand, Sheriff of Edinburgh and Chairman of the Crofters Commission who had been knighted for his services to the Liberal party.

but now most terrible violence was turned upon them.

At Mr. Herbert Samuel's meeting in the Corn Exchange, Bedford, on the 22nd July, four men undertook to make the protest. At the first sound of the word " Women " two whole rows of seats were overturned, and the interrupter was immediately rushed out, whilst Mr. Samuel remarked with a sneer that he was interested to meet " a Suffragist of the male persuasion," but that he suspected the interrupter of being a " Conservative hireling."   A second man rose up and cried: " I am a Liberal and *I* protest," but the stewards at once set upon him and he was thrown through a door at the back of the platform and fell some six or seven feet to the ground floor, where he lay insensible for nearly half an hour; two other men, one of them a retired naval officer, met with a similar fate. At the same time four of the women who were holding a meeting outside the hall, were arrested and kept at the police station until Mr. Samuel had left the town.

When the same Cabinet Minister spoke at Nottingham the police again arrested, and subsequently released, four women, one of whom was Miss Watts, the daughter of a well-known local clergyman. A like procedure was adopted in numberless cases afterwards.   Inside the hall, an unexpected protest was made by Mr. C. L. Rothera, the City Coroner for Nottingham and a prominent Liberal, but in spite of the fact that he was one of the most familiar and respected figures in the town, he narrowly escaped ejection.

At Northampton, Mr. Samuel again encountered the women, for a plucky little band, led by Miss

Marie Brackenbury, attempted to rush the strong iron gates of the hall. They were flung back by the police, but, nothing daunted, Miss Brackenbury climbed to the top of a forty-foot scaffolding adjoining the Exchange, and, though the rain poured continuously, addressed the crowd from that great height.

But the most extraordinary scenes were perhaps those that took place when Mr. Lloyd George and Mr. Sydney Buxton spoke at Limehouse on July 30th. Some twenty men were there determined to see that the women's cause should not be overlooked, and as soon as the singing of, " For he's a jolly good fellow," which heralded Mr. Lloyd George's appearance on the platform had died away, a man was seen climbing up one of the pillars at the back of the hall. Having mounted some fifteen feet from the ground, he uncoiled a rope from around his waist, contriving a sort of swing seat for himself, and, unfurling a purple-white-and-green flag, hung there above the meeting. Numbers of stewards at once rushed from every direction to haul him down, but more than a dozen of his friends had already gathered around the pillar. Instead of beginning their speeches, the Cabinet Ministers sat whispering together. Then one of them went across to Mrs. Lloyd George and a companion, and immediately these two, the only women present, left the meeting and the struggle began. Gradually the defenders of the pillar were wrenched from their posts. An eye-witness declared that he saw " one man frog-marched out by half a dozen stewards between two rows of infuriated blackguards, who were raining blows with their fists on his defenceless face." A gentleman, quite unconnected with the Suffragists men, who had taken no part in the struggle, protested against this excessive and cowardly violence, but was at once set upon and himself flung outside. One man, home from the Colonies, had his shoulder fractured, another had one wrist broken and the other sprained; another received black eyes and a broken nose; whilst a Cambridge undergraduate had his collarbone broken and a dozen other men needed medical attendance, one fainting through loss of blood some time after he had been ejected. At last the stewards reached the pillar, the rope was cut and the man aloft with the flag was hauled down and set upon by the mob of stewards, who tumbled over each other in the attempt to kick and strike at him; one man deliberately hit him over the face with a glass bottle. When finally he was thrown outside, the police carried him to a doctor.

Now the Cabinet Ministers proceeded with their speeches, but when Mr. Lloyd George began to speak of the "people's will," there came a megaphone chorus from a little workman's dwelling close to the hall where the Suffragettes were lying concealed, "Votes for Women," "Votes for Women," "Votes for Women." The stewards rushed to the windows on that side of the hall and shut them hurriedly, but the sound penetrated still for the people of the neighbourhood joined in and supported the megaphones with cheers and cries of "Stick to it, miss, stick to it." Even this was not all, for a desperate charge was being led against the police cordon that guarded the doors of the Hall and in this struggle thirteen women were placed under arrest.

These women were summoned to appear before

Mr. Dickinson at the Thames Police Court on the following morning, when they were charged with obstruction and as a result, twelve of them were taken on to Holloway for terms varying from ten days to two months. They were all determined to protest as those who had gone before them had done, against the prison treatment, and when ordered to undress and to proceed to the cells, they refused and linking arms stood with their backs to the wall. The Governor then blew his whistle and a great crowd of wardresses appeared. They fell upon the women and after a long struggle dragged them apart, forced them into the cells, and ordered them to change into prison clothes. Worn out as they now were with vain resistance, they still bravely refused to give in and their clothes were literally torn from their backs.

Who would not shrink from such an ordeal! Who would not rather huddle quietly into the prison clothes, however ill-fitting, coarse and objectionable they might be than be subjected to such a thing as this, well knowing that whatever happened one must be overpowered in the end? And these women did shrink from the ordeal, but bore it for all their shrinking. " A long file of wardresses fairly ripped my clothes off, leaving me only half covered," says Lucy Burns; " I counted twelve wardresses in my cell. They tried to taunt and goad me," says Mable Capper, " but I bit my lips."

When the prison clothes had been forced onto them or they had been left half covered with the garments lying beside them, to put them on as best they might, even then they went on bravely with their protest. The ventilation of the cells was inadequate — it was their duty to break the panes, and, though they well knew that as a consequence they would be taken where the want of air was even greater and where they could not break the glass, not one of the twelve shrank back. The windows were scarcely broken when vengeance followed. They were dragged away to the punishment cells and in these unwholesome dungeons they carried out the Hunger Strike, some of them under conditions even worse than those borne by their previously imprisoned comrades.

In some of the punishment cells, including that of Mrs. Leigh, a sanitary convenience, in appearance exactly like an ordinary closet without a lid, was fixed against the wall. There was no water supply for keeping this clear, the inner vessel being withdrawn through the wall from the corridor outside, when it required emptying. When it is realised that the prisoner remained in the cell both night and day without a moment's intermission, and that the ventilation was in any case absolutely inadequate, the objectionable character of this arrangement will be clearly understood. When the matter was made public and commented upon afterwards, Mr. Gladstone stated that this closet was only put there in case of emergency and that in every case the prisoner would be readily allowed to go to the W. C. in the corridor on ringing her bell. Unfortunately none of the Suffragettes who had been placed in the cells in which these closets were, had tested the matter, but those who are familiar with the Holloway régime, will, for various reasons, doubt the truth of this statement, though Mr. Gladstone probably believed it. When a prisoner is told that she will not be allowed to leave her cell at all for several days and instead of being sent each morning to fetch her own washing water, as is usual, she has it brought to her by a wardress; when at the same time she finds a sanitary convenience in her cell and the usual cry of " lavatory," is omitted, she naturally concludes that the receptacle is there for her use, and that she will not be permitted to use any other. Anyone who has asked questions in Holloway, where questions are discouraged, knows that, especially if the prisoner were under punishment, questions upon this point would probably not receive either polite or pleasant replies.

For two nights Mrs. Baker and Mrs. Leigh were denied even a mattress and were obliged to sleep on the hard wooden plank. The long sleepless nights were for all the prisoners the hardest part of the trial and as they grew weaker, their minds, as happens to people during illness, were often filled with strange fancies which could only with difficulty be subdued. They feared that they might walk in their sleep and eat the food which was always left in their cells during the night. Threats to feed them forcibly were constantly being made and the horror of being suddenly overpowered was always upon them. Lucy Burns tells how once in the night she heard a sudden scream. " That cannot be one of our women," she thought, " it is too incoherent," but holding her breath she listened with quickly beating heart. The cry came again and again and at last she heard quite plainly, " No, no, take it away." Then she leapt from her bed and stood at the door hour after hour waiting for what might come, until at last, worn out and stiff with cold she wrapped herself in her blanket and fell asleep with her head against the door. Saturday evening, Sunday, Monday, Tuesday passed.

On Wednesday the visiting magistrates came round. The prisoners whom they had come to punish were now all weak and haggard and some were unable to rise from their beds. Nevertheless further sentences of close confinement in the punishment cells, which they had never yet left, were passed upon them all. But the authorities dared not attempt to carry out these sentences. The chances of life and death had become too evenly balanced now, and Mrs. Baker and Mrs. Leigh were set free that evening and the remainder of the women on Thursday and Friday, August 5th and 6th.

Meanwhile three young Suffragettes, Vera Wentworth, Mary Phillips and Rose Howey had gone through the hunger strike in Exeter having been arrested in that town on Friday, July 30th, whilst leading a crowd of 2,000 people to the doors of Lord Carrington's Budget meeting in the Victoria Hall there. Their arrest had excited great popular indignation and with shouts of " Let them go, you cowards," the people had rushed to their rescue but the soldiery had been called out to beat them back.

Suffering born for a cause begets sympathy with that cause and coercion arouses sympathy with the coerced. Nevertheless tyranny and cruelty beget their like, a crowd, however hostile, will hesitate to throw the first stone but when that has been flung, many missiles will often follow. Thus, when it was shown that rather than do them justice the Government was prepared to thrust women into unwholesome dungeons and to leave them to starve there for

many days, a more brutal and vindictive temper began to manifest itself amongst the more disorderly
sections of its supporters than had ever before been
shown.

On August 2nd, a great Liberal fête was held at
Canford Park, near Poole in Dorsetshire. There
were sports and games and Mr. Churchill was to deliver an address on the Budget. Annie Kenney with
three companions attended the fête and the story of
what took place is best told in her own words. She
says:

As we entered the Park together we saw two very young
girls being dragged about by a crowd of Liberal men,
some of whom were old enough to be their fathers. They
had thrown a pig net over them, and had pulled down their
hair. We heard afterwards that these girls came from a
village near by, but the Liberals suspected them to be Suffragettes and ordered them out of the Park. Before
Miss Brackenbury and I had been in the place many minutes, though we had never opened our lips, we were followed by a howling mob of Liberal men. We thought we
could get away from them if we went and watched the
sports instead of going direct to Mr. Churchill's meeting,
but they crowded round us and the language they used is
not fit for print. After a time a police officer came up and
told us that we must clear out of the place, as we were causing all the trouble, though we had never replied back to anything that had been said. As soon as the crowd saw the police were against us the trouble began. There seemed to
be thousands of them surging round us and they divided
Miss Brackenbury and myself, but she tried to keep me in
view as much as she could. They did not seem to want
to do anything to her, because she looked strong and big,
but they all came and attacked me. They were calling out
to each other to get hold of me and throw me into the

pond which was very near. I shall never forget at this point seeing a carriage in which were two old ladies come driving up. The carriage was almost turned over and the two women were white with fright and breathing very quickly, but though I appealed to the men on behalf of the two ladies they took no notice. Luckily the crowd just swerved round the corner and I consider the lives of the two women were saved not through good management or through any feeling on the part of the Liberals, but it was just a piece of luck. After that they seemed to become more enraged. I then turned and faced the crowd, and, strange to say, when I could turn round and face them they never attempted to do anything to me, but as soon as my back was turned they started dragging me about in a most shameful way. One man who was wearing the Liberal colours pulled a knife out of his pocket, and to the delight of the other staunch Liberals, started cutting my coat. They cut it into shreds right from the neck downwards. Then they lifted up my coat and started to cut my frock and one of them lifted up my frock and cut my petticoat. This caused great excitement. A cry came from those Liberals, who are supposed to have high ideas in public life, to undress me. They took off my hat and pulled down my hair, but I turned round upon them and said that it would be their shame and not mine. They stopped then for a minute, and then two men, also wearing the Liberal colours, got hold of me and lifted me up and afterwards dragged me along, not giving me an opportunity to walk out in a decent way.

So they dragged her out, the little fragile woman with her torn garments and her masses of golden hair falling below her waist, her sensitive face flushed and her blue eyes, wide with pain and horror. They dragged her close past the house of the great Wimbourne family who owned Canford Park, but though the guests and members of the family who were watching from the balcony and from the lawn in front, were appealed to by others, they made no attempt to intervene and saw the great gates opened and the little ragged, exhausted figure with her streaming hair, thrust outside, well knowing that the nearest railway station was more than three miles away.

Truly it needed some courage to face things like this for the sake of any cause, and this was not an isolated happening.

On August 8th, Miss Helen Tolson had a similar experience at Rushpool Hall, Saltburn by the Sea. This is her own description:

The day was beautiful and the private grounds in which Mr. Churchill and Mr. Samuel were to speak were thronged with a great crowd of their supporters, a large number of whom were miners. About ten of us had obtained admission in one way or another and had stationed ourselves at different points. As each woman spoke there was a great roar from the crowd, who nearly all left the speaker to follow and ill-treat her as she was being taken out. When my own turn came I started to ask a question, but was stopped by the hand of a Liberal steward, which was thrust into my mouth. The next thing I remember is two stewards holding my arms and a third coming up and deliberately kicking me in the body. This was a sign to the crowd to do what they liked with me and they thrust me forward with cries of " Throw her in the pond." They dragged me to a steep bank above the pond and here three men, seeing that my hold upon a small tree was giving way, tried to help me. Nothing of what happened during the next ten minutes is at all clear in my memory. I was often full length on the ground and I know I was bruised from head to foot. The crowd abated their efforts to tram-ple me underfoot when the word was passed that the police were at last coming. When I was pulled up the bank again I found that my skirt and underclothing had been nearly torn off.

A Miss De Legh, daughter of Dr. De Legh of Coatham, a guest at Rushpool Hall, quite unconnected with the Suffragettes, was set upon by one man who pushed her into some bushes and blew tobacco smoke into her face. She afterwards brought an action for assault against her assailant and he was fined £3. His defence was that she had cried " cowards " to those who were ejecting the Suffragettes and had thus angered the crowd so that if he had not seized her she would probably have been swept into a pond.

On August 20th, when Lord Crewe spoke at the great St. Andrew's Hall, Glasgow, Miss Alice Paul succeeded in climbing to the roof and in the hope of being able to speak to the Cabinet Minister from this point, she lay there concealed for many hours in spite of a downpour of rain. When she was discovered and forced to descend she was heartily cheered for her pluck by a crowd of workmen, one of whom came forward and apologised for having told a policeman of her presence, saying that he had thought she was in need of help.

Later, when the women attempted to force their way into the building, the people needed no urging to lend their aid, and the police who were guarding the entrance were obliged to use their truncheons to beat them back. When the officers of the law attempted to make arrests, the women were rescued from their clutches again and again. Eventually

Adela Pankhurst, Lucy Burns, Alice Paul and Margaret Smith were taken into custody, but even when the gates of the police station were closed upon them, the authorities feared that they would not be able to hold their prisoners for the crowds shouted vociferously for their release and twisted the strong iron gates. It was only when the women themselves appealed to them that they consented to refrain from further violence.

When Lord Crewe had safely left the town, the friends of the women were allowed to bail them out, on the understanding that they would appear at the police court at nine o'clock the following morning. Nevertheless though they arrived before the appointed time, there was no one to show them the Court room and whilst they wandered about in the passages, trying to find their way, their case was disposed of behind locked doors and with the public excluded. The bail was escheated and a warrant was issued for their arrest before five minutes past nine. At this Mr. Thomas Kerr, one of the bailees, rose to protest and asked two minutes leave to find the defaulting prisoners, saying that he was sure they were already in the building, but he was abruptly told that the court was closed. He went outside and immediately met the ladies and brought them in before Bailie Hunter, who presided, had left the Bench, but though the Bailie saw them he hurried away, whilst the Fiscal [1] tried to put all the blame upon him. The bail was never refunded and the women never answered to the warrants and so the matter dropped.

[1] The Scotch Fiscal is the officer who prosecutes in the case of petty criminal offences.

The same Friday, August 20th, on which Lord Crewe had spoken at Glasgow, Mr. Haldane, the Secretary of State for War, was addressing a meeting at Liverpool and Mrs. Leigh, who was in command of the Suffragette army there had organised her forces in such a way as to give an effective reply to his jeering reference to what he described as the "bodkin tactics." Early in the day she and a number of others had taken up their quarters in an empty house separated from the hall by a narrow passage only. When the meeting began she clambered through the window and swung herself on to the roof with the most extraordinary agility at so great a height and with so slender a foothold, that observers were thrilled with horror.

A loud clear woman's voice, calling attention to the women's demand, through a megaphone, and then crash after crash; that was what the people in the hall knew of the scene, whilst outside great crowds were surging and those who looked up could see what the *Liverpool Courier* called, " the frail figure of a little woman peeping out from behind a chimney stack," who as her comrades at the windows passed ammunition up to her, hurled it onto the roof of the hall "with a dexterity which was nothing short of marvellous." When everything that they had brought with them had been exhausted she tore the slates up from the roof and flung them after the rest.

The police rushed to the scene and pressed a passing window cleaner into the service but his ladder was too short and the fire escape had to be sent for before Mrs. Leigh could be brought down. Then she and her six comrades were driven away in

" Black Maria " to the Central Bridewell and, having been allowed out on bail at a late hour, were brought up the following morning at the Liverpool police court charged with doing wilful damage to the Sun Hall.

They were remanded until the following Tuesday, August 24th, but refused to find bail and were detained in prison where, on being expected to conform to the ordinary rules, they began the hunger strike and were placed in the punishment cells. They had already fasted three and a half days when their trial took place. It was stated in the Court that no one had been hurt by their action on the night of the Sun Hall meeting but that damage had been done to the extent of £3. 19. 0. Sentences of from one to two months' imprisonment in the second division having been passed upon them, they were taken back to the punishment cells, where, owing to the cold and damp many of them were stricken with shivering fits. The order of release came for Miss Healiss on the following day and for the six others on Thursday evening.

During the summer months, Mr. Asquith had been golfing at Clovelly and three of the younger Suffragettes, girls of between twenty and twenty-five, had approached him in the midst of his game and had told him pretty forcibly what they thought of him and his Government. On the first Saturday in September these same girls, Jessie Kenney, Vera Wentworth and Elsie Howey, visited Littlestone on Sea where Mr. Asquith and Mr. Gladstone were playing golf together. They caught sight of Mr. Asquith as he was leaving the club house and Elsie Howey made a dash towards him. He tried to run back into the house but was caught just as he reached the topmost step. As soon as he felt the girl's touch on his arm, he cried out, " I shall have you locked up," but she replied, " I don't care what you do, Mr. Asquith," and as Jessie and Vera also appeared, he called for help and Mr. Herbert Gladstone came to his aid. The two men then tried to push the three girls down the steps but this was not easily accomplished. As Jessie said, " There were blows received from both parties and plenty of jostling. Mr. Gladstone fought like a prize-fighter and struck out left and right. I must say he is a better fighter than he is a politician. The Suffragettes have often been called hooligans, but the two Cabinet Ministers certainly showed that they too could be hooligans when no one was looking."

At last two other men came to reinforce the Cabinet Ministers and the girls were all three knocked down in a heap. The two Ministers then made good their escape and Mr. Gladstone motored to Hythe police station and arranged with the superintendent of the County Police for a body of constables to be sent to guard Lympne Castle, where he was staying. Of course the Suffragettes were severely condemned for having " annoyed " the Cabinet Ministers on their holiday, and the escapade of these three girls was described as an " outrage," but nevertheless many jokes were made on the subject, at Mr. Asquith's expense. Several detailed accounts of his playing golf with an escort of upwards of six policemen (some of which he took the trouble to deny) appeared in the Press.

On Saturday, September 4th, whilst Mr. Asquith was being waylaid at Lympne, scenes in which there

was a curious mingling of grave and gay, were taking place in Manchester where Mr. Birrell was addressing a Budget demonstration at the White City.
The platform from which he was to speak and all
the neighbouring roofs had been carefully searched
for Suffragettes and with 200 stewards and fifty
policemen in the Hall it was thus hoped that they
would be excluded. But the women entered the
American Cake-Walk show which adjoined the concert hall where the meeting was taking place on the
one side, and the American Dragon Slide which
came next it on the other, and from these two points
they threw small missiles through the glass windows
and succeeded in making their voices heard. It was
impossible to arrest the Suffragettes who were on the
cake-walk machine without cake-walking also and
when a policeman mounted the machine in order to
effect their capture, he found, to the great amusement of the onlookers, that he had got on to the
wrong platform and so was forced to play his part
in what the *Liverpool Courier* described as " a spectacle, which from the point of its ludicrousness, must
stand unparalleled in the annals of police adventure "; for, as he was obliged to cake-walk forwards,
so the offending women were compelled to cake-walk
backwards. But if, as is possible, the Suffragettes
in company with the rest of the public, found the
spectacle amusing, their fun was soon at an end, for
on Monday, they were sentenced to from one to two
months' imprisonment in the second division.[1]

[1] An attempt was made to charge some of the women with
unlawful wounding because a man's hand had been cut by the
falling glass, but on the wound being found to be very slight,
the charge was reduced to one of common assault.

At Strangeways Gaol, terrible punishments were meted out to them on the refusal to obey the rules, but these punishments were tempered by kindly acts on the part of many members of the staff. Some of the women were sentenced not only to close solitary confinement but to wear handcuffs for twenty-four hours and one of them tells that, when, after a sleepless night, the matron took pity on her and ordered the handcuffs to be removed, she nearly fainted with pain, whilst the wardress worked her arms to restore the circulation. To another prisoner who refused to wear the prison clothes, was brought a " strange unclean leather and canvas jacket with straps and buckles attached." Into this she was forced and locked but somehow or other she managed to wriggle out, all but one arm, and the matron then appeared and ordered that the remaining strap should be unlocked. These Manchester prisoners were all released on Wednesday, the 8th September, after a four days' fast.

On the same day were released six women who had been arrested in Leicester on the previous Saturday for holding a meeting of protest outside that addressed by Mr. Winston Churchill in the Palace Theatre. They also had carried out the hunger strike.

In Dundee at three o'clock on the morning of Monday, September 13th, Miss Isabel Kelley, clad in gymnastic dress, was climbing a high scaffolding erected on the Bank of Scotland from which in the darkness she let herself down some twenty-five feet onto the roof of the Kinnaird Hall where Mr. Herbert Samuel was to hold a meeting the next night. There she lay concealed for seventeen hours until the meeting began. Then by means of a strong rope about twenty-four feet in length at one end of which was an iron hook, which she attached to the roof, and at the other a running noose, she entered the building by a skylight and found herself on the stairs leading to the gallery of the hall. She was able to rush in, but before a word had passed her lips she was seized by the stewards, handed over to the police and driven off in custody.

Meanwhile other Suffragettes were leading a great charge of people to the door of the hall, but they too were arrested. This was the second time that women had been arrested in Scotland in connection with Cabinet Ministers' meetings. In Glasgow, as we have seen, the officials had escheated the bail and allowed the prosecution to fall to the ground. Here in Dundee Miss Kelley and Miss Fraser Smith who had also succeeded in getting into the hall, were released, whilst the women who had been arrested outside were sent to prison for from ten to seven days in default of paying fines varying from £5 to £3. They all refused to obey the prison rules and carried out the hunger strike, and were released on Friday, the 17th of September, at 10:30 P. M. after having gone without food since the time of their arrest on the Monday.

As soon as it had been announced that Mrs. Pankhurst and those arrested with her were to go free until after their case had been discussed by the High Court, she had made her way to Cleveland in Yorkshire where a by-election was taking place owing to Mr. Herbert Samuel's elevation to the Cabinet as Post Master General. Mr. Samuel had hitherto acted as Under-Secretary at the Home Office, the Governmental Department which was responsible for the treatment of the Suffragettes in prison. Mr. Samuel began by scoffing at the opposition of the Suffragettes, referring to them as " wild women from Westminster "; but the people of Cleveland soon became ardent supporters of the Women's cause and flocked eagerly to their meetings. He then found it necessary to devote large parts of his speeches to combating the Suffragette arguments. He declared that it was a " wicked calumny " to say that the Government had sent women to prison for asking for votes and specially dissociated himself from any part in the responsibility. At one moment he stated that Mr. Asquith had already promised to give women the vote and at another than the present Parliament could not do it, and again and again he accused the women of fighting with " Tory Gold."

All this betrayed his fear that the women were turning votes. Even *The Times,* that anti-Suffragist newspaper which had always condemned the Suffragette tactics and minimised the effect of their work, acknowledged now that their attack was damaging the Government candidates' chances, and, on July 6th, the special correspondent of this paper wrote:

The women suffragists have made a favourable impression upon the electorate and the miners specially appear to have been thoroughly converted by the new propaganda. . . . Some miners with whom I have talked would even vote for the candidate who was in favour of Women's Suffrage without respect to his opinions upon other subjects. To put it more emphatically, a Women's Suffrage candidate, pure and simple, as a third candidate, would probably have endangered Mr. Samuel's re-election quite as much as a candidate of the Labour party.

Finally on the eve of the poll Mr. Herbert Samuel found it necessary to draw up a special leaflet against the women, the only one on any subject which was sent out in a similar way. The result of the contest was, as the Liberals admitted, "disappointing" from their point of view, for, although Mr. Samuel was returned, in spite of his added prestige as a Cabinet Minister, his majority was enormously decreased.

The figures were:

> Mr. H. Samuel, Liberal............... 6,296
> Mr. Windsor Lewis, Conservative........ 5,325
>
> Liberal majority 971

At the General Election of 1906 Mr. Herbert Samuel had been returned unopposed.

> Mr. H. Samuel, Liberal................ 5,834
> Mr. Jeffrey Drage, Conservative......... 3,798
>
> Liberal majority 2,036

Meanwhile another by-election was being fought in Dumfriesburgh where the Liberal majority was again reduced.

CHAPTER XXII

SEPTEMBER TO OCTOBER, 1909

The Arrests at Birmingham; Forcible Feeding in Winson Green Gaol. Mr. Keir Hardie's Protest; Opinions of Medical Experts; Resignation of Mr. Brailsford and Mr. Nevinson.

And now on September 17th the Prime Minister was going up to Birmingham to hold a meeting of 10,000 people at the great Bingley Hall. A "bower bedecked" special train was to carry the Cabinet Ministers and Members of Parliament up north straight from their duties in the House, and back again. Tremendous efforts were being made to work up enthusiasm for at this meeting, Mr. Asquith was to throw down his challenge to the House of Lords, to proclaim that their power of veto should be abolished, and that the will of the people should prevail. But the Suffragettes were determined that, if the freedom to voice their will were to be confined to half the people alone, there should be no peace in Birmingham for the Prime Minister.

Mrs. Leigh and her colleagues, who were organising there, began by copying the police methods so far as to address a warning to the public not to attend Mr. Asquith's meeting, as disturbances were likely to ensue, and immediately the authorities were seized with panic. A great tarpaulin was stretched across the glass roof of the Bingley Hall, a tall fire escape was placed on each side of the building and hundreds of yards of firemen's hose were laid across the roof. Wooden barriers, nine feet high, were erected along the station platform and across all the leading thoroughfares in the neighbourhood, whilst the ends of the streets both in front and at the back of Bingley Hall were sealed up by barricades. Nevertheless, inside those very sealed up streets, numbers of Suffragettes had been lodging for days past and were quietly watching the arrangements. At the same time outside in the town a vigorous propaganda campaign was being carried on by their comrades, and this culminated in an enthusiastic Votes for Women demonstration in the Bull Ring the day before the great Liberal meeting.

When Mr. Asquith left the House of Commons for his special train, detectives and policemen hemmed him in on every side, and when he arrived at the station in Birmingham, he was smuggled to the Queen's Hotel by a back subway a quarter of a mile in length and carried up in the luggage lift. In the hotel he took his meal alone in a private room away from his guests. Though guarded by a strong escort of mounted police he thought it wisest not to enter the hall by the entrance at which he had been expected. Meanwhile tremendous crowds were thronging the streets and the ticket holders were watched as closely as spies in time of war. They had to pass four barriers and were squeezed through them by a tiny gangway and then passed between long lines of police and amid an incessant roar of " show your ticket." The vast throngs of people who had no tickets and had only come out to see the show, surged against the barriers like great human waves and occasionally cries of " Votes for Women " were greeted with deafening cheers.

Inside the hall there were armies of stewards and groups of police at every turn. The meeting began by the singing of a song of freedom led by a band of trumpeters. Then the Prime Minister appeared. " For years past the people have been beguiled with unfulfilled promises," he declared, but during his speech he was again and again reminded, by men of the unfulfilled promises which had been made to women; and, though men who interrupted him on other subjects were never interfered with, these champions of the Suffragettes were, in every case, set upon with a violence which was described by onlookers as " revengeful," and " vicious." Thirteen men were maltreated in this way.

Meanwhile amid the vast crowds outside women were fighting for their freedom. Cabinet Ministers had sneered at them and taunted them with not being able to use physical force. " Working men have flung open the franchise door at which the ladies are scratching," Mr. John Burns had said. So now they were showing that, if they would, they could use violence, though they were determined that, at any rate as yet, they would hurt no one. Again and again they charged the barricades, one woman with a hatchet in her hand, and the friendly people always pressed forward with them. In spite of a thousand police the first barrier was many times thrown down. Whenever a woman was arrested the crowd struggled to secure her release and over and over again they were successful, one woman being snatched from the constables no fewer than seven times.

Inside the hall Mr. Asquith had not only the men to contend with, for the meeting had not long been in progress, when there was a sudden sound of splintering glass and a woman's voice was heard loudly denouncing the Government. A missile had been thrown through one of the ventilators by a number of Suffragettes from an open window in a house opposite. The police rushed to the house door, burst it open and scrambled up the stairs, falling over each other in their haste to reach the women, and then dragged them down and flung them into the street where they were immediately placed under arrest. Even whilst this was happening there burst upon the air the sound of an electric motor horn which issued from another house near by. Evidently there were Suffragettes there too. The front door of this house was barricaded and so also was the door of the room in which the women were, but the infuriated Liberal Stewards forced their way through and wrested the instrument from the woman's hands.

No sooner was this effected however than the rattling of missiles was heard on the other side of the hall, and, on the roof of a house, thirty feet above the street, lit up by a tall electric standard was seen the little agile figure of Mrs. Leigh, with a tall fair girl beside her, both of whom were tearing up the slates with axes, and flinging them on to the roof of the Bingley Hall and down into the road below, always, however, taking care to hit no one and sounding a warning before throwing. The police cried to them to stop and angry stewards came rushing out of the hall to second this demand, but the women calmly went on with their work. A ladder was produced and the men prepared to mount it, but the only reply was a warning to "be careful" and all present felt that discretion was the better part of valour. Then the fire hose was dragged forward, but the firemen refused to turn it on, and so the police themselves played it on the women until they were drenched to the skin. The slates had now become terribly slippery, and the women were in great danger of sliding from the steep roof, but they had already taken off their shoes and so contrived to retain a foothold, and without intermission they continued "firing" slates. Finding that water had no power to subdue them, their opponents retaliated by throwing bricks and stones up at the two women, but, instead of trying, as they had done to avoid hitting, the men took good aim at them and soon blood was running down the face of the tall girl, Charlotte Marsh, and both had been struck several times.

At last Mr. Asquith had said his say and came hurrying out of the building. A slate was hurled at the back of his car as it drove away, and then "firing" ceased from the roof for the Cabinet Minister was gone. Seeing that they had now nothing to fear the police at once placed a ladder against the house and scrambled up to bring the Suffragettes down and then, without allowing them to put on their shoes, they marched them through the streets, in their stockinged feet, the blood streaming from their wounds and their wet garments clinging to their limbs. At the police station bail was refused and the two women were sent to the cells to pass the night in their drenched clothing.

Meanwhile, amid the hooting of the crowd, Mr.

Asquith had driven away through the town and as the special train in which he was to return to London, left the station, a shower of small stones rattled against his carriage window, whilst a great bar of iron was flung into an empty compartment in the rear. The two women who had done these things were at once seized by the police and were also obliged to pass the night in the cells, whilst six who had been arrested in the crowd earlier, met the same fate.

Eventually eight of the women received sentences of imprisonment varying from one month to fourteen days, whilst Charlotte Marsh was sent to prison for three months' hard labour, and Mrs. Leigh for four. We knew that Mrs. Leigh and her comrades in the Birmingham Prison would carry out the hunger strike, and, on the following Friday, September 24th, reports appeared in the Press that the Government had resorted to the horrible expedient of feeding them by force by means of a tube passed into the stomach. Filled with concern the committee of the Women's Social and Political Union at once applied both to the prison and to the Home Office to know if this were true but all information was refused.

The W. S. P. U. now made inquiries as to the probable results of this treatment, and were informed that it was liable to cause laceration of the throat and grave and permanent injury to the digestive functions, and that, especially if the patient should resist, as the tube was being inserted or withdrawn there was serious danger of its going astray and penetrating the lungs or some other vital part. The whole operation, together with all the attendant circumstances, could not fail to put a most excessive strain upon the heart and the entire nervous system, and, if there were any heart weakness, death might ensue at any moment. In the *Lancet* for September 28th, 1872, a case was reported of a man under sentence of death, who had been forcibly fed by means of the stomach pump, that is to say by means of an india-rubber tube passed through the mouth into the stomach, the method used in the case of the Suffragettes. The man had died. In the same issue of the *Lancet,* appeared the opinion upon this question of several prominent medical men. Dr. Anderson Moxey, M.D., M.R.C.P., had said: " If anyone were to ask me to name the worst possible treatment for suicidal starvation I should say unhesitatingly, forcible feeding by means of the stomach pump." Dr. Tennant stated that this method of feeding produced " an incentive to resistance," and that the exhaustion thereby introduced was sometimes so great as to cause death by syncope. Dr. Russell had met with a case in which death had occurred immediately after the placing of the tube " before it could be withdrawn, much less used "; and Dr. Conolly was " appalled by the dangers resulting from the forcible administration of food by the mouth." Amongst the various important medical experts consulted by The Women's Social and Political Union was Dr. Forbes Winslow, whose wide experience in cases of insanity could not be questioned. When asked professionally to give his views on the subject he said:

So far as the stomach pump is concerned it is an instrument I have long ago discontinued using, even in the most

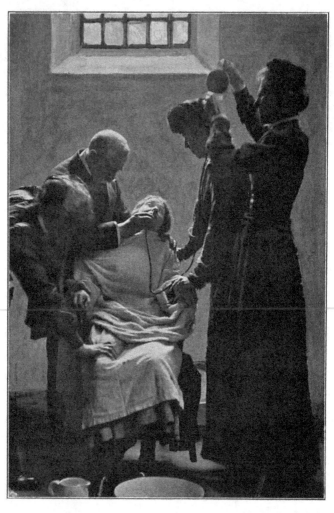

Forcible Feeding with the Nasal Tube

serious cases of melancholia, where the victim, perhaps from some religious delusion, refuses all nourishment. It possibly may be regarded by some as the most simple means of administering food, but this I challenge by saying at once that it is the most complicated and the most dangerous. . . . I have known some of the most serious injuries inflicted by the persistent use of the stomach pump. I have known a case in which the tongue has been partly bitten off where it has been twisted behind the feeding tube.

He added that forcible feeding was especially dangerous in cases of heart or lung weakness or of rupture or hernia, and that the result of persistent use would be to seriously injure the constitution, to lacerate the parts surrounding the mouth, to break and ruin the teeth.

When the House of Commons met on Monday we learnt that our fears were only too well founded for Mr. Keir Hardie drew from Mr. Masterman, who spoke on the Home Secretary's behalf, the admission that the Suffragettes in Winson Green Gaol were being forcibly fed by means of a tube which was passed through the mouth and into the stomach and through which the food was pumped. The unprecedented and outrageous nature of the assault was glossed over by the use of the term, " Hospital treatment," in connection with it. Mr. Masterman admitted, however, that there were no regulations which authorised the proceeding, but he stated that it was resorted to in the case of men and women prisoners who were " weak minded " or " contumacious."

Mr. Hardie's indignant protest and reminder that the last man prisoner to whom such treatment had been meted out had died under it, were met with shouts of laughter by the supporters of the Government. Horrified by their heartless and unseemly levity in the face of so serious a question, he at once addressed a statement to the Press in which he declared that he " could not have believed that a body of gentlemen could have found reason for mirth and applause " in a scene which had " no parallel in the recent history of our country." As far as he could learn, no power to feed by force had been given to prison authorities, save in the case of persons certified to be insane. He concluded by warning the public of the danger that one of the prisoners would succumb to the so-called " hospital treatment," and by appealing to the people of these islands to speak out ere our annals had been stained by such a tragedy.

Others hastened to second this protest. Mr. C. Mansell-Moullin, M.D., F.R.C.S., wrote to *The Times*, as a hospital surgeon of thirty years' standing, to indignantly repudiate Mr. Masterman's use of the term " hospital treatment," declaring that it was a " foul libel " for that " violence and brutality have no place in hospitals as Mr. Masterman ought to know." Dr. Forbes Ross of Harley Street wrote to the Press saying:

As a medical man, without any particular feeling for the cause of the Suffragettes, I consider that forcible feeding by the methods employed is an act of brutality beyond common endurance, and I am astounded that it is possible for Members of Parliament, with mothers, wives and sisters of their own, to allow it.

A memorial signed by 116 doctors, headed by Sir Victor Horsley, F.R.C.S., W. Hugh Fenton, M.D. M.A., C. Mansell-Moullin, M.D., F.R.C.S., Forbes

Winslow, M.D., and Alexander Haig, M.D., F.R.C.P., was organised by Dr. Flora Murray and addressed to Mr. Asquith, protesting against the artificial feeding of the Suffragette prisoners, on the ground that it was attended by the gravest risks and was both unwise and inhuman. To this memorial many of the doctors added descriptive notes of their own. Mr. W. A. Davidson, M.D., F.R.C.S., wrote: "A most cruel and brutal procedure. Were the tubes clean? Were they new? If not they have probably been used for people suffering from some disease. The inside of the tube cannot well be cleaned; very often the trouble is not taken to clean them." [1]

In spite of every form of discouragement and ridicule, Mr. Keir Hardie continued constantly to raise the question of forcible feeding in the House of Commons only to be met by evasive, and sometimes grossly, inaccurate replies from the Home Office. Mr. Gladstone tried to shelter himself behind the officials who were his subordinates, and to place the responsibility on the medical officers. For this he was strongly condemned by the *British Medical Journal* which characterised his conduct as contemptible. [2]

In reply to the protests of medical men and the

[1] Mr. Gladstone afterwards stated in the House that the tubes were carefully cleaned and kept in boracic solution between each operation, but Miss Dorothy Pethick, who was imprisoned in Newcastle, saw the tube lying open and exposed in a basket in the reception room.

[2] The *British Journal of Nursing* stated that even under the most favourable circumstances forcible feeding required "delicate manipulation," and that it was an operation which should only be performed by medical practitioners or trained nurses

memorial from doctors, which had been addressed to him, Mr. Gladstone succeeded in drawing a statement from Sir Richard Douglas Powell, the President of the Royal College of Physicians, who said that he thought the memorial exaggerated, though he admitted that forcible feeding was not " wholly free from possibilities of accident with those who resist." He added that, in dissenting from the view expressed by the memorialists, he was assuming that the feeding of the prison patients was " entirely carried out by skilled nursing attendants under careful medical observation and control." We, of course, know that this was not the case.

A large number of doctors, including Dr. R. G. Layton, physician to the Walsall hospital, replied to Sir Douglas Powell by again recapitulating the dangers of forcible feeding. But indeed the opinions of medical men were unnecessary to those who afterwards came in contact with the women who had been forcibly fed. Their exhausted condition was a form of evidence that no argument could upset. It is important to note also that during the year 1910 two ordinary criminals, a man and a woman, were subjected to forcible feeding. The man died during the first operation; the woman committed suicide after the second.

Meanwhile the bulk of the Liberal Press were defending the action of their Government. The *Daily News* had acclaimed Vera Figner for assaulting one of the Russian prison officials in order to secure better conditions for her fellow captives. It had characterised as the " one healthy symptom and pointed out that the prison wardresses were quite unqualified to take part in it.

in Spain " the revolt of the Spanish people against
their Government in regard to the Riffian War
though this revolt had entailed the burning down of
convents full of women and children who were
in no way responsible for the trouble, and other
dread acts of violence. At the same time in regard to events at home this paper was declaring that,
if the House of Lords were to tamper with the Irish
Land Bill, there would be " no wonder if all the old
methods of cattle-driving and other violence were
revived in Ireland." Yet the *Daily News* had had
nothing but chiding and dispraise for the hunger
strikers, and, in regard to forcible feeding, it now
said, " it is the only alternative to allowing the
women to starve themselves." Thus the two most
obvious ways out of the difficulty, firstly, that of
treating the women as political prisoners, and,
secondly, the more reasonable one of extending the
franchise to women and thus ending the strife, were
entirely ignored.

Revolted by the hypocritical and inconsistent attitude of this paper, two of its foremost leader
writers and of the ablest journalists in this country,
Mr. Henry Nevinson and Mr. H. N. Brailsford,
resigned their posts upon its staff, writing publicly to
explain their reasons for so doing. Many sincere
Liberals resigned their memberships and official posts
under the Liberal Association including the Rev. J.
M. Lloyd Thomas, Minister of the High Pavement
Chapel, Nottingham, resigned from the Liberal Association, and there were many other resignations,
among them the following: Mrs. Catherine C.
Osler, the President, Miss Gertrude E. Sothall, the
Hon. Sec., and Mrs. Alice Yoxall, the Treasurer of

the Birmingham Women's Liberal Association; Mrs. S. Reid, the chairman of the Egbaston Women's Liberal Association; Lady Blake, the President of the Berwick Women's Liberal Association; and Mrs. Branch, one of the most prominent members of the Northampton Women's Liberal Association. At the same time prominent men and women of all shades of opinion, including Mrs. Ayrton, Flora Annie Steel, Lady Betty Balfour, the Rev. J. R. Campbell and the Hon. H. B. T. Strangeways, ex-premier of South Australia appealed to the Government to give votes to women and bring this useless warfare to an end.

Meanwhile, except for the admissions of Mr. Gladstone and Mr. Masterman in the House of Commons, nothing definite was known as to the condition of the outraged prisoners. No direct communication had been held with them and even a petition from their parents and relatives to be allowed to send their own medical attendant into the prison, had been refused. The fearful anxiety and suspense endured by all concerned may well be imagined. Again and again Messrs. Hatchett, Jones, Bisgood and Marschall, the solicitors engaged to act on the prisoners' behalf, applied for permission to interview their clients, but Mr. Gladstone obstinately refused until he was informed that legal proceedings were being taken for assault against him and the Governor and Doctor of the Birmingham Prison, and that writs were being issued, and that Miss Laura Ainsworth would shortly be released so that the full details would be known in any case. Thus at last he grudingly consented to the interview, and sworn statements were made by all the women. Mrs. Leigh explained that on arriving at Winson Green Gaol on Wednesday, September 22nd, she had broken her cell windows as a protest against the prison treatment. As a punishment she was thrust that evening into a cold dimly lit punishment cell. A plank bed was brought in and she was forcibly stripped and handcuffed with the hands behind during the day, except at meal times when the palms were placed together in front. At night the hands were fastened in front with the palms out. Potatoes, bread and gruel were brought into her cell on Thursday but she did not touch them and in the afternoon she was taken, still handcuffed, before the magistrates who sentenced her to a further nine days in the punishment cell. At midnight on Thursday, her wrists being terribly swollen and painful, the handcuffs were removed.

She still refused food and on Saturday she was taken to the doctor's room. Here is her account of the affair:

The doctor said: "You must listen carefully to what I have to say. I have my orders from my superior officers" (he had a blue official paper in his hand to which he referred) "that you are not to be released even on medical grounds. If you still refrain from food I must take other measures to compel you to take it." I then said: "I refuse, and if you force food on me, I want to know how you are going to do it." He said: "That is a matter for me to decide." I said that he must prove that I was insane; that the Lunacy Commissioners would have to be summoned to prove that I was insane. I declared that forcible feeding was an operation, and therefore could not be performed without a sane patient's consent. He merely bowed and said: "Those are my orders."

She was then surrounded and held down, whilst the chair was tilted backwards. She clenched her teeth but the doctor pulled her mouth away to form a pouch and the wardress poured in milk and brandy some of which trickled in through the crevices. Later in the day the doctors and wardresses again appeared. They forced her down on to the bed, and held her there. One of the doctors then produced a tube two yards in length with a glass junction in the centre and a funnel at one end. He forced the other end of the tube up her nostril, hurting her so terribly that the matron and two of the wardresses burst into tears and the second doctor interfered. At last the tube was pushed down into the stomach. She felt the pain of it to the end of the breast bone. Then one of the doctors stood upon a chair holding the funnel end of the tube at arm's length and poured food down whilst the wardresses and the other doctor all gripped her tight. She felt as though she would suffocate. There was a rushing, burning sensation in her head, the drums of her ears seemed to be bursting. The agony of pain in the throat and breast bone continued. The thing seemed to go on for hours. When at last the tube was withdrawn, she felt as though all the back of her nose and throat were being torn out with it.

Then almost fainting she was carried back to the punishment cell and put to bed. For hours the pain in the chest, nose and ears continued and she felt terribly sick and faint. Day after day the struggle continued; she used no violence but each time resisted and was overcome by force of numbers. Often she vomited during the operation. When the

Lady Constance Lytton before she threw the stone at New Castle, October 9th, 1909

food did not go down quickly enough the doctor pinched her nose with the tube in it causing her even greater pain.

On Tuesday afternoon she heard Miss Edwards, one of her fellow prisoners, cry from an open door-way opposite, " Locked in a padded cell since Sunday." Then the door was shut. She applied to see the visiting magistrates, and appealed to them on behalf of her comrade, saying that she knew her to have a weak heart, but was told that no prisoner could interfere on another's behalf. She protested by breaking the windows of the hospital cell to which, owing to her weakness, she had now been taken, and was then thrust into the padded cell as Miss Edwards was taken from it, the bed which she had occupied being still warm. The padded cell was lined with some India rubber-like stuff, and she felt as though she would suffocate for want of air. She was kept there till Wednesday, still being fed by force.

On Saturday she felt that she could endure the agony of it no longer, and determined to barricade her cell. She piled up her bed and chair, but after three hours men warders forced the door open with spades. Then the chief warder threatened and abused her and she was dragged back to the padded cell.

In Miss Ainsworth's case the feeding was done through the mouth. Her jaws were pried open with a steel instrument to allow of the gag being placed between her teeth. She experienced great sickness, especially when the tube was being withdrawn.

Miss Hilda Burkitt's experiences were very

dreadful. She had already fasted four days and
was extremely weak when she was seized by two
doctors, four wardresses and the matron, who tried
for more than half an hour to force her to swallow
from the feeding cup. Then a tube was forced up
her nose, but she succeeded in coughing it back
twice and at last, very near collapse, she was carried to her cell and put to bed by the wardresses.
" This will kill me sooner than starving," she said,
" I cannot stand much more of it, but I am proud
you have not beaten me yet." Still suffering
greatly in head, nose and throat, she was left alone
for half an hour and the matron and wardresses
then returned to persuade her to take food. On
her refusal they said, " Well, you will have to come
again; they are waiting." " Oh, surely not the torture chamber again," she cried; but they lifted her
out of bed and carried her back to the doctors, who
again attempted to force her to drink from the feeding cup. Still she was able to resist and then one
of them said, " The Home Office has given me
every power to use what force I like. I am going
to use the stomach pump." " It is illegal and an
assault; I shall prosecute you," was her reply, but
as she spoke a gag was forced into her mouth and the
tube followed. She had almost fainted and felt
as if she were going to die, and now for some reason
the tube was withdrawn without having been used,
but in her great weakness the officials were now
able to overcome her resistance and to pour liquid
into her mouth with the feeding cup.

    This sort of thing went on day after day. On
Thursday morning she was unconscious when they
came into her cell, and they succeeded in feeding her.

During the night she was in agony. She told the doctor he had given her too much food and cried: " For mercy's sake, let me be, I am too tired," but brandy and Benger's food were forcibly administered. During the whole month she only slept four nights.

But the story of these sufferings had no power to influence the Government. They were determined to persevere with the forcible feeding and were so far from abandoning this hateful form of torture, that, evidently thinking the women who had won their way out of prison by the hunger strike had been let off too easily, they proceeded to rearrest a number of them upon the most flimsy charges. Evelyn Wurrie, who had been arrested with Mrs. Leigh and the others, but afterwards discharged by the magistrate, had been refused bail between the time of her arrest and trial and kept for seventeen hours as an ordinary prisoner in the insanitary police court cells. She might have been thought, therefore, to be entitled to claim damages for wrongful arrest and detention, but was nevertheless rearrested because she had broken the cell window to obtain more air, and was sentenced either to pay a fine of eleven shillings or go to prison for seven days. She chose imprisonment, but her fine was paid by a member of the Birmingham Liberal Club. Miss Rona Robinson, Miss Florence Clarkson, Miss Georgina Heallis and Miss Bertha Brewster, who had all gone through the hunger strike in Liverpool, were also summoned for breaking their cell windows, in spite of the fact that they had already been severely punished in prison for these offences. On their refusal to answer to the summons, warrants were issued for their arrest.   Rona Robinson, who was said to have committed damage to the extent of two shillings, was arrested on October 15th in Manchester, and was taken the same night to Liverpool. Though her doctor had certified her to be suffering from laryngeal catarrh and a weak, irregular action of the heart, she was sent back to prison for fourteen days' imprisonment in the third division.   Owing to the state of her health, the Liverpool authorities refused to take the responsibility of feeding her by force and she was accordingly released after a fast of seventy-two hours.

The other warrants were not executed for some time; that against Miss Florence Clarkson being held over until December, when she happened to notify the Manchester police of a burglary that had taken place in the W. S. P. U. offices in that city.   She was then immediately arrested on the old charge; bail was refused and she was kept in custody from Saturday to Monday, when she was punished by a further fortnight's imprisonment for having committed damage to the value of 6d. three months before.   After three days (on December 15th), she was released in a state of complete collapse.   The warrant against Miss Bertha Brewster was held over until January, when she was sentenced to six weeks' hard labour to pay for her 3/9 damage.

Arrest of Miss Dora Marsden outside the Victoria University of Manchester, October 4th, 1909

CHAPTER XXIII

OCTOBER, 1909, TO JANUARY, 1910

ARREST OF LADY CONSTANCE LYTTON AND OTHERS AT
NEWCASTLE. SUFFRAGETTES ATTACKED AT ABER-
NETHY. HOSE PIPE PLAYED ON MISS DAVISON IN
STRANGEWAYS GAOL, MANCHESTER. MR. ASQUITH AT
THE ALBERT HALL.

WHILST our comrades were thus enduring ago-
nies in prison, protest meetings were being held in all
parts of the country. The *Daily News* said of the
people in our movement: " They are no longer men
and women; they are a whirlwind."

During the first three days of forcible feeding
£1,200 was collected. At a great demonstration in
the Albert Hall on October 7th, a further £2,300
was subscribed, and the £50,000 campaign fund being complete, a fund of £100,000 was started. At
this meeting a procession of women who had already
gone through the hunger strike marched up to the
platform carrying the purple, white and green tri-
coloured flags of the Union, and here Mrs. Pankhurst, who was on the eve of her departure for America, decorated them with medals in recognition of
their services to the cause. The scene was one of
the most tremendous enthusiasm; it was one which
none of those present will ever forget.

On October 9th a great political pageant was held
in Edinburgh, when a procession of women, led by

Scotch pipers and Mrs. Drummond in her general's uniform, astride a prancing charger, marched through the streets, accompanied by a number of tableaux representing the figures of heroic women famous in Scottish history.

On October 4th, Lord Morley, as Chancellor of the Victoria University, visited Manchester to open the University's new chemical laboratory. Deeply moved by the sufferings of Mrs. Leigh and her comrades in Winson Green Gaol, Miss Rona Robinson, M.Sc., and Miss Dora Marsden, B.A., both graduates of the University, and the former a subscriber also to the new laboratory, attended in their academic robes, and, with Miss Mary Gawthorpe, advanced down the central aisle of the Whitworth Hall of the University, just as Lord Morley was about to speak. Each one raising a hand in appeal, they said in concert: "My Lord, our women are in prison."

The rowdiness of the young men students of our British universities is time-honoured; their almost deafening shouts and yells and practical jokes, always in evidence at functions such as this, are invariably received with amused tolerance by the authorities. Mr. Asquith himself, when addressing the students of the University of which he is Chancellor, did not disdain to wait with a smile until their play was done before he could address them. Nevertheless the earnest, quietly-spoken words of these three young women were scarcely uttered when they were pounced upon by a number of strange men, who dragged them out of the Hall, and as soon as they were lost to sight by the audience, fell to striking, pummelling, and pinching them, as they pushed them into the street. The passers-by rushed

up to know what had happened, and at once the police ordered the three women to move on. They replied that they would not leave until their graduates'
caps and other belongings, which had been torn from
them, were restored, and until the names of
the men who had ejected them were given. Thereupon, without further argument, the police seized
them and dragged them to the police station, where
they were accused of disorderly conduct and abusive
language, in Oxford Street. These ridiculous
charges could not be substantiated and were afterwards withdrawn by the Chief Constable of Manchester and the Vice Chancellor of the University.

Such women as Mrs. Baines and Mrs. Leigh, both
capable of the firiest zeal and the most reckless heroism, spurred on by stern first-hand knowledge of the
crushing handicaps with which the woman wage-
earner has to contend, and the terrible disabilities
which are rivetted upon her, had found it not difficult to become rebels. The torture of women in
prison was now making it easy for gentler and happier spirits to cast aside also the mere going on deputations and asking of questions and, whilst doing
hurt to none, yet by symbolic acts to shadow forth
the violence that coercion always breeds.

On October 9th Mr. Lloyd George was to speak
at Newcastle and the town was prepared as though
for a revolution. Police and detectives were to
be seen in hundreds and great barriers were
erected across the streets. The night before the
meeting twelve women met quietly together to
lay their plans for opposing these tremendous forces.
Amongst them was Lady Constance Lytton, who
had already served one imprisonment for the cause

in the previous February, and who, as daughter and sister of an English peer, wished to place herself side by side with Mrs. Leigh, the working woman who was being tortured in Birmingham,— to do what she had done, prepared to suffer the same penalty. Mrs. J. E. M. Brailsford, who had joined the Women's Social & Political Union but a few weeks before, was another who had come forward to bear her share in this fight. (It was Mrs. Brailsford's husband who with Mr. Nevinson had recently thrown up his post as leader writer to the *Daily News,* because of his sympathy with the Suffragettes). Amongst these women were also two hospital nurses, whilst two of the others, Miss Kathleen Brown and Miss Dorothy Shallard, had already won their way out of prison through the hunger strike.

Next night, whilst vast throngs of people lined the streets and the police were massed in their thousands to guard from them the Chancellor of the Exchequer, " the son of the people," as he called himself, the twelve women quietly proceeded to do their deeds. It was rumoured that Mr. Lloyd George was to stay with Sir Walter Runciman, and, seeing the latter gentleman's motor car driving through the streets, Lady Constance Lytton threw a stone at it, carefully aiming at the radiator in order that, without injuring anyone, she might strike the car. Miss Dorothy Pethick and Miss Kitty Marion entered the General Post Office and, having carefully selected a window in the neighbourhood of which there was no one to be hurt, they went out and cast their stones through it with a cry of " Votes for Women." A number of other women were also arrested for similar acts. Mrs. Brailsford walked quietly up to one of the police barriers and stood resting an innocent-looking bouquet of chrysanthemums upon it. Suddenly the flowers fell to the ground disclosing an axe which she raised and let fall with one dull thud on the wooden bar. It was a symbolic act of revolution, and, like her comrades, she was dragged away by the police. By direct order of the Home Office bail was refused and eight of the Suffragettes were kept in the police court cells from Saturday until Monday, without an opportunity of undressing, without a mattress, and with nothing but a rug in which to wrap themselves at night.

Whilst the women who had thus been lodged in prison had been making their protest outside Mr. Lloyd George's meeting, there were men who were speaking for them within. As the Chancellor of the Exchequer was running through the list of taxes in the Budget, a man complained that " there was no tax on stomach pumps." The whole house rose at that and the man was violently ejected. Many others followed his example. Mr. Lloyd George taunted them by saying: *" There are many ways of earning a living, and I think this is the most objectionable of them! "* and by asking: " Are there any more of *these hirelings?* " Evidently he thought that there were no men disinterested enough to support the cause of women unless they received pay for it.[1]

On Monday, whilst the other women received sentences varying from fourteen days to one month's hard labour, Lady Constance Lytton and Mrs.

[1] Mr. Lloyd George's baseless insinuation was of course indignantly and publicly repudiated by the men concerned.

Brailsford were ordered to be bound over to be of good behaviour, and on refusing were sent to prison in the second division for one month. The authorities were evidently very loath to convict these two ladies, one of them because of her rank, and the other because of her own and her husband's association with the Liberal party, but both were determined to stand by their comrades and steadfastly refused to express any regret for what they had done.

Their hope that their courageous action might save Mrs. Leigh and the other Birmingham prisoners from further suffering proved to be vain, and on Wednesday, October 13th, Lady Constance Lytton and Mrs. Brailsford, both of whom had refused food, were released after having been imprisoned for no more than two and a half days. Mr. Gladstone asserted that in deciding to release them, he had not been in any way influenced by regard for their position, but that they had been turned out of prison on purely medical grounds. It was indeed true that Lady Constance was exceedingly fragile and delicate and that she suffered from a slight heart affection, but Mrs. Brailsford protested that she herself was perfectly well and strong.

The eight other women were all forcibly fed and all but two were retained in prison till the end of their sentence. In most cases the nasal tube was used; it always caused headache and sickness. The nostrils soon became terribly inflamed and every one of the women lost weight and suffered from great and growing weakness.

On Saturday, October 16th, Mr. Winston Churchill was to speak at an open-air gathering at Abernethy, some sixteen miles from Dundee. The

W. S. P. U. had no intention of heckling him or creating any disturbance, for after much pressing and a lengthy correspondence he had agreed to fulfil a promise made to the Women's Freedom League in the previous January to receive a Woman's Suffrage deputation on the following Monday. Nevertheless the occasion was thought a suitable one for distributing Suffrage literature and for holding a meeting somewhere in the neighbourhood. Adela Pankhurst, Mrs. Archdale, the daughter of Russell, the founder of the great Liberal newspaper, "The Scotsman," Mrs. Frank Corbett, the sister-in-law of a Member of Parliament, and Miss C. Jolly accordingly decided to motor over there.

They started off on a crisp bright autumn day, the clouds high, the sun shining and the trees all turning gold, and the little frost sparkles gleaming on the good hard road. Everything began auspiciously but before long they were held up by a punctured tire. Owing to this delay they lost the opportunity of giving out leaflets to the people as they arrived, for the audience had already entered the big tent where the speaking was to take place when the Suffragettes drove up. Standing in the road were some thirty or forty men, all wearing the yellow rosettes of official Liberal stewards, and as the car slowed down, they rushed furiously towards it, shouting and tearing up sods from the road and pelting the women with them. One man pulled out a knife and began to cut the tires, whilst the others feverishly pulled the loose pieces off with their fingers. The Suffragettes tried to quiet them with a few words of explanation, but their only reply was to pull the hood of the motor over the women's heads and then to beat it and batter it until it was broken in several places. Then they tore at the women's clothes and tried to pull them out of the car, whilst the son of the gentleman in whose grounds the meeting was being held then drove up in another motor and threw a shower of pepper in the women's eyes. The shouts of the men reached the tent where Mr. Churchill was speaking, and numbers of people flocked out and watched the scene from over the hedge, but only two gentlemen had the courage to come to the aid of the women, and their efforts availed little against the large band of stewards. At last, fearing that his motor would be entirely wrecked, the driver put on full speed and drove away. The only excuse for the stewards who took part in this extraordinary occurrence is that many of them were intoxicated.

On Monday, as he had promised, Mr. Churchill received the deputation from the Women's Freedom League. He then entirely departed from what he had said during the elections both in Manchester and at Dundee itself. In Manchester, when asked what he would do to help to secure the enfranchisement of women he had said: " I will try my best as and when occasion offers." He had added that the women Suffragists had " now got behind them a great popular demand," and that their movement was assuming " the same character as Franchise movements have previously assumed." In Dundee he had said that Women's Suffrage would be " a real practical issue " at the next general election and that he thought that the next Parliament " ought to see " the gratification of the women's claim. Now that no election was in prospect he said: " Looking back over the last four years I am bound to say I think your cause has marched backwards." He further said that the mass of people still remained to be converted and that, so far as he could see, women's enfranchisement would not "figure either in the programme of any great political party" or "in the election address of any prominent man," and that, until militant tactics were discontinued, he himself would render no assistance to the cause. A more flagrant example of political dishonesty than that which these conflicting statements of Mr. Churchill's presented, it would be difficult to find and not merely the Suffragettes but the people of Dundee freely expressed their disapproval.

On Tuesday, Mr. Churchill was to speak in the Kinnaird Hall, and huge crowds then filled the streets and in spite of the tremendous force of police the barricades were stormed. Led by Mrs. Corbett, Miss Joachim, and Mrs. Archdale, they shouted "Votes for Women," and rushed again and again at the doors of the Hall. The three women who led the crowds were arrested but the storm still went on.

Adela Pankhurst and Miss C. Jolly, who had lain concealed there since the previous Sunday, had raised the cry, "Votes for Women," in a little dark room, the windows of which overlooked the large hall. After a tussle with the police and stewards, which lasted three quarters of an hour, they were arrested and with the three who had been taken in the street, were eventually sent to prison for ten days. They immediately commenced the hunger strike, and were set free on Sunday, 24th October, after having gone without food for five and a half days. Whilst they were in prison, huge crowds came to the gates every night to cheer them, and on the next night after their release the men of Dundee organised a meeting of protest, in the Kinnaird Hall.

Meanwhile, four Suffragettes were suffering the torture of forcible feeding in Strangeways Gaol, Manchester. They had been arrested in connection with a meeting held by Mr. Runciman at Radcliffe, and sentenced to one month's imprisonment, with hard labour, on October 21st. They had gone into prison on the Thursday, and had begun the hunger strike at once, and on Friday the doctors and ward-resses came to feed them by force. Miss Emily Wilding Davison urged that the operation was illegal, but she was seized and forced down on her bed. "The scene which followed," she says, "will haunt me with its horror all my life and is almost indescribable." Each time it happened she felt she could not possibly live through it again. On Monday a wardress put her into an empty cell next door to her own, and there she found that instead of one plank bed there were two. She saw in a flash a way to escape the torture. She hastily pulled down the two bed boards, and laid them end to end upon the floor, one touching the door, the other the opposite wall, and, as the door opened inwards, she thus hoped to prevent anyone entering. A space of a foot or more, however, remained, but she jammed in her stool, her shoes, and her hairbrush, and sat down holding this wedge firm. Soon the wardress returned, unlocked the door, and pushed it sharply, but it would not move. Looking through the spy-hole she discovered the reason and called, "Open the door," but the prisoner would not budge. After some threats and coaxing the window of her cell was broken, the nozzle of a hose pipe was poked through, and the water was turned full upon her. She clung to the bedboards with all her strength gasping for breath, until a voice called out quickly, " Stop, no more, no more." She sat there drenched and shivering, still crouching on the bedboards, the water six inches deep around her. After a time they decided to take the heavy iron door off its hinges, and, when this was done, a warder rushed in and seized her, saying, as he did so, " You ought to be horsewhipped for this." Now her clothes were torn off, she was wrapped in blankets, put into an invalid's chair, and rushed off to the hospital, there to be plunged into a hot bath and rubbed down, and then, still gasping and shivering miserably, she was put into bed between blankets with a hot bottle. At 6 P. M. on Thursday she was released.

Meanwhile, the whole country had heard of the incident and an outcry had been raised. A correspondent wrote that he had seen a hose-pipe played on drunken stokers at sea. They were Norwegian stokers, the officer would not have dared to do it had they been English, but the passengers had intervened at what they felt to be revolting and unjustifiable brutality. The thought of turning that fearful force of ice-cold water upon a woman already weak from several days of fasting, was horrible indeed to anyone who realised what it meant.

Mr. Gladstone himself admitted that the Visiting Committee who had ordered it were guilty of a grave error of judgment and ordered the discharge of Miss Davison; but later on he addressed a letter to the officials of Strangeways Gaol through the

Prison Commissioners expressing his appreciation of the way in which the medical officers had carried out their duties and commending "the efficiency of the prison service, the carefulness and good sense shown by the staff," and "the tact, care, humanity and firmness" with which the problem of the Suffragette imprisonments had been "handled by all concerned."

The other Manchester prisoners were obliged to complete their sentences, being forcibly fed during the whole time.

At this point the Government had an opportunity of learning the view of the electorate as to their treatment of the women, for a by-election was now taking place in Bermondsey and the Suffragettes were, as usual, actively opposing the Government candidate. In order that every elector might understand as far as possible what forcible feeding really meant, a pictorial poster showing the operation was displayed throughout the constituency and models representing forcible feeding were shown at the W. S. P. U. committee rooms. A manifesto against the Government was also issued by nine representative men, including Mr. Brailsford, Mr. Nevinson and Dr. Hugh Fenton, which urged the electors "in the name of chivalry and humanity as well as in the interests of true Liberalism to see to it that whatever else may happen at this particular election the Government candidate is left at the bottom of the poll." The Suffragettes worked, if possible, more vigorously than ever, and after the first three days of their campaign, Liberal workers came to them in despair, saying: "Why have you come down to boss our election?" The Suffragettes never go to Liberal meetings at election times, but the Liberal speakers were constantly being heckled by the men and women of Bermondsey as to the forcible feeding of the Suffragettes. The Suffragettes themselves were greeted with cheers and words of encouragement wherever they went. " All the policemen in this constituency are going to vote for you," one of the constables said, and others testified that they preferred to keep order at the women's meetings than at any other because " they talked sense." In the result the Liberal candidate was defeated and the Liberal poll was reduced by more than 1,400 votes. The figures were:

Mr. Dumfries, Unionist	4,278
Mr. Spencer Leigh, Hugh, Liberal	3,291
Dr. Salter, Socialist	1,435
Unionist majority	987

The figures at the last election had been:

George J. Cooper, Liberal	4,775
H. J. Cockayne Cust, Conservative	3,016
Liberal majority	1,759

On polling day an unlooked-for, and to the Women's Social and Political Union, unwelcome incident occurred. The Women's Freedom League endeavoured to render the election void, because they objected to any election being held at which women might not vote. The W. S. P. U. were against this, because their policy was to prove that the electors were prepared to defeat the Government candidate in order to show their belief in

Votes for Women. The attempt of the Freedom League members to render the election void was carried out in the following manner. Two members of the League, Mrs. Chapin and Miss Allison Neilans, each entered a separate polling booth with a glass test tube filled with a solution of ink and photographic chemicals which had been carefully prepared to destroy the ballot papers without any risk of injury to any person who might happen to touch it. In each case the woman concerned broke the test tube by striking it on top of the ballot box so that the black liquid might fall into the slot. When this was done by Mrs. Chapin a Mr. Thorley rushed forward, and some of the black liquid splashed into his eye. In Miss Neilans' case a man stretched out his hand and some of the liquid fell upon it. In both cases the men asked if the stuff would burn, and were told it would do no harm if it were washed off at once. Miss Neilans' own hands and gloves were soaked with the fluid, but she suffered no harm. Only five papers were touched by the fluid and none of these were indecipherable.

A great outcry was raised, however, for it was declared that Mr. Thorley would be blind for life. For some time he went out wearing a black shade over his eye, but when he was called upon unexpectedly by some members of the Women's Freedom League, he was found to be without the shade and his eye appeared perfectly normal. The cases hung over for some time and eventually, on November 24th, Mrs. Chapin was sentenced to three months' imprisonment for interfering with the ballot box and four months for a common assault upon Mr. Thorley, the sentences to run concurrently; whilst Miss Neilans was ordered three months' imprisonment. After a time it leaked out that the slight injury from which Mr. Thorley had suffered, had been caused, not by the liquid which Mrs. Chapin had thrown, but by some ammonia which he had used to counteract any after-effects. Two days after Miss Neilans' release Mrs. Chapin was granted the King's Pardon.

On October 30th Mrs. Leigh was suddenly released from Birmingham Gaol, in a very critical state, though two months out of the four to which she had been sentenced still remained to run. She was at once removed to a nursing home.

November 9th was Lord Mayor's Day, and, as usual, the Lord Mayor had invited the Cabinet Ministers to a banquet in the Guild Hall. Knowing this, Miss Alice Paul, an American citizen, and Miss Amelia Brown disguised themselves as charwomen, and, carrying buckets and brushes, entered the building with the other cleaners at nine o'clock in the morning. There they hid themselves and waited until the evening, when they took their stand in the gallery outside the Banqueting Hall. When Mr. Asquith was about to speak, Miss Brown, having carefully selected a pane of the stained glass window upon which there was no ornament, and which she thought might be easily replaced, stooped down, took off her shoe and smashed the chosen pane in order that her shout of " Votes for Women " might be heard by those below. Miss Alice Paul also took up the cry. Both women were arrested and afterwards sent to prison for one month's hard labour on refusing to pay fines of £5 and damages of £2 ten shillings each. They were both forcibly fed and as a result of this Miss Brown was attacked with severe gastritis.

Three days later, on November 13th, Mr. Winston Churchill visited Bristol to speak at the Colston Hall. Miss Theresa Garnet, the woman who had been twice through the hunger strike, and whom the Home Secretary had wrongfully accused of biting, resolved to humiliate Mr. Churchill, both as a member of the Government which preferred rather to imprison women than to enfranchise them and to torture them rather than to extend towards them the ordinary privileges of political prisoners; and also on his own account for his slippery and disingenuous statements in regard to the Votes for Women question.

She therefore met the train by which he was arriving from London and found him on the platform in the midst of a large force of detectives who formed a semi-circle around him. She rushed straight forward, and they either did not, or would not, see her coming, but the Cabinet Minister saw her, he paled and stood there as though petrified, only raising his arm to guard himself. She reached him and with a light riding switch, struck at him three times, saying, "Take that in the name of the insulted women of England." At that he grappled with her, wrested the switch from her hand, and put it in his pocket. Then she was seized and dragged away to prison.

She was charged with assaulting Mr. Churchill, but eventually this charge was withdrawn (presumably because Mr. Churchill knew that he would be subpœnaed as a witness) and, on being accused of having disturbed the peace, was sentenced to one month's imprisonment on refusing to be bound over.

Meanwhile 30,000 men and women had turned

out to help the Suffragettes in their protest around the Colston Hall where Mr. Churchill was speaking, and during the evening four women were arrested, and afterwards punished with from two months' hard labour to fourteen days in the second division, whilst several men who had spoken up for them inside the Colston Hall were beaten unmercifully by the stewards. Forcible feeding was resorted to in Bristol Prison also, and handcuffs were used in some cases.

Meanwhile the supporters of the Liberal Government were adopting militant tactics on their own account. What was called " A League against the Lords " had been formed with the warmly expressed approval of many of the Liberal leaders, and, though the leaders had kept in the background, the members of the League had twice assembled in Parliament Square to hoot the peers as they drove by in their carriages, and had come into collision with the police.

At the same time the Liberal newspapers were openly commending the efforts of gangs of men who were going from meeting to meeting held by the Conservatives, and with shouts and violence were making it impossible for their political opponents to speak. Columns were devoted to describing the doings of what was called " The Voice " which persistently heckled Tariff Reformers and supporters of the House of Lords.

Mr. Winston Churchill was now arranging to hold a campaign of public meetings in Lancashire, and the W. S. P. U. publicly and openly appealed for funds to insure that protests and demonstrations should be made in connection with all his meetings. Thousands of pounds were, on the other hand, spent by the authorities to defeat the women's intentions. In

Preston, in addition to many other precautions, seventy men were employed and £150 spent on barricading the windows and roof of the Hall where Mr. Churchill was to speak, and at Southport £250 was laid out on mounted police to protect the Empire Music Hall alone.

When the Southport meeting began Mr. Churchill looked ill at ease and turned about sharply from time to time as though expecting an interruption. But at last he seemed to gain confidence and was proceeding briskly with his remarks, when, suddenly, there floated down from the roof a soft voice, faint and reedy, and peering through one of the great porthole-like openings in the slope of the ceiling, was seen a strange little elfin form with wan childish face, broad brow and big grey eyes, looking like nothing real or earthly but a dream waif. But for the weary paleness of her, she might have been one of those dainty little child angels the old Italian painters loved to show peeping down from the tops of high clouds or nestling amongst the details of their stately architecture. It was Dora Marsden who with two other women had lain concealed on the roof since two o'clock in the small hours of the previous morning. So unexpected and pathetic was this little figure that leant further forward to repeat her message that the audience could not forbear to cheer her. They stood up, waving their hats and programmes, " looking delighted," as the loftily placed intruder herself observed. Mrs. Churchill smiled also and waved her hand and even Mr. Churchill, though this was probably because of his wife's presence, and of the general feeling of the audience, himself looked pleasantly up and said, " If some stewards will fetch those ladies after my speech is concluded, I shall be glad to answer any questions they may put to me."

But the stewards, who by this time had found the women, were not disposed to bring them into the hall. A hand was thrust over Dora Marsden's mouth and she and the others were roughly pulled back from their coign of vantage, pushed through a window, and sent rolling down the steep sloping roof. " Stop that, you fools," someone cried out, " you will all fall over the edge," but one of the stewards answered, " I do not care what happens." Fortunately two of the Suffragettes were caught in their perilous descent by the edge of a water trough whilst a policeman seized Dora Marsden by the ankle, telling her, " If I had not caught your foot, you would have gone to glory." Once safely on the ground the women were placed under arrest, but the case against them was eventually dismissed.

At Preston, Suffragettes dressed in shawls and clogs sallied forth at night and pasted forcible feeding posters on the street pillar boxes, the prison and other public buildings and the windows and doors of the Liberal Club, as a welcome to Mr. Churchill, and in connection with turbulent scenes which occurred whilst his meeting was in progress, four women were arrested. At every other town he visited the same kind of thing occurred. At Waterloo, there was one arrest, at Liverpool there were two, and one at Bolton and one at Crewe.

Meanwhile Mr. Harcourt had held a series of meetings in the Rossendale Valley. On December 1st the door and windows of the house in which he was staying were found to have been covered during the night with forcible feeding posters. The next evening three men were set to watch with large hose-pipes attached to the main, but somehow or other the connection was mysteriously cut and the windows were broken without their being aware of it by some person or persons unknown.   Two women were arrested in connection with disturbances on the following Monday, and were sent to prison for one month and fourteen days respectively.   They both adopted the hunger strike, and were both forcibly fed.   Two women were arrested outside Sir Edward Grey's meeting at Leith on December 4th, 1909.

A general election was now announced and on December 10th Mr. Asquith was to speak at a great meeting in the Albert Hall and whilst the authorities were making every attempt to keep them out, the Suffragettes were, of course, making every attempt to get into the building.   Some of them did succeed in concealing themselves inside, but were discovered. Jessie Kenney, who disguised herself as a telegraph boy and tried to get in while the meeting was in progress, was also detected and turned back, but three men sympathisers protested during the meeting.   To these Mr. Asquith replied, " Nearly two years ago I declared on behalf of the present Government that in the event of our bringing in a Reform Bill we should make the question of Suffrage for Women an open one for the House of Commons to decide.   My declaration survives the General Election and this Cause, so far as the Government is concerned, shall be no worse off in the new Parliament than it would have been in the old."   Thus Mr. Asquith was cheerfully preparing for another general election without one word of regret or apology to those women who had been misled by his promise to introduce the Reform Bill before Parliament came to an end. That was almost the last of the old false promise.

Meanwhile Charlotte Marsh, who had gone into Winson Green Gaol with the first batch of prisoners to be forcibly fed, was still being detained there, whilst Mrs. Leigh and all the rest had been released. Those who went to visit her once at the expiration of each month were only allowed to look at her through a small square of perforated zinc. They could neither see her clearly nor hear distinctly what she said. Nevertheless they gathered that she was suffering greatly. Our hearts ached for that noble girl. Often there came before our eyes the picture of the tall, straight figure that had carried the colours of our Union before us in so many gay processions. We saw the fair, fresh face with its delicate regular Saxon features, those masses of bright golden hair, the head so proudly held, and the faint flicker of a shy smile that always came when one spoke to her; we heard the boyish ring in her voice, and realised again her earnestness and enthusiasm, and the unaffected gentleness of her address. There was always something about her that made many a woman think of some dear young brother. Her father called her " Charlie," and thought of her as his only boy amongst a family of girls.

It was expected that she would have been released on December 7th, but the Government who had held her in torment for so long were anxious to extort from her the very last ounce of their pound of flesh. They determined not to grant her the remission of one-sixth of the sentence usually allowed, but to withhold it as a punishment for her refusal to take food, and they did this though they knew that her father was dangerously ill and though her mother had appealed for her release on that ground a week before. There was no fine that could be laid down to buy her out, for she had been sentenced without that option, and so perforce she must wait the pleasure of the Government. On the 8th of December, it was known that Charlotte Marsh's father was dying and her family made another urgent appeal that she might be brought to him. But it was not until the 9th that the Home Secretary at last tardily let her go. She hurried at once to her home in Newcastle, so thin and worn with what she had suffered, that her sisters scarcely knew her as she came into the house, only to find that her father was unconscious and would never wake to know her any more.

CHAPTER XXIII

DECEMBER, 1909, TO JANUARY, 1910

THE APPEAL OF PANKHURST AND HAVERFIELD V. JARVIS.
THE FREEDOM LEAGUE PICKETS. MRS. PANKHURST
RETURNS FROM AMERICA. MRS. LEIGH'S ACTION
AGAINST THE HOME SECRETARY AND THE GOVERNOR
AND DOCTOR OF WINSON GREEN GAOL, BIRMINGHAM.
MISS DAVISON'S ACTION AGAINST THE VISITING JUS-
TICES OF STRANGEWAYS GAOL, MANCHESTER. ILL
TREATMENT OF MISS SELINA MARTIN AND MISS LESLIE
HALL AT WALTON GAOL, LIVERPOOL. LADY CON-
STANCE LYTTON IMPRISONED IN WALTON GAOL AS JANE
WARTON.

WHILST Mrs. Pankhurst was still in America, the
case in which she, Mrs. Haverfield and the ninety-two
other women were concerned, which had been hanging over since the summer, was heard in the Divisional Court on December 1st. It will be remembered that the Suffragettes had sought to put into
practice the constitutional right to petition the Prime
Minister as the representative of the Government
and of the King. They held that this right was especially defined by two Acts, the Bill of Rights which
declares that, " It is the right of the subject to petition the King and all commitments and prosecutions
for such petitioning are illegal," and the Statute 13,
Charles II, which states:

That no person or persons whatsoever shall repair to His Majesty or both or either Houses of Parliament upon pretence of presenting or delivering any petition, complaint, remonstrance, or declaration or other address, accompanied with excessive number of people, nor at any time with above the number of ten persons; upon pain of incurring a penalty not exceeding the sum of £100 in money or three months' imprisonment without bail or mainprise for every offence; which offence to be prosecuted at the Court of King's Bench or at the Assizes or general quarter sessions within six months after the offence committed and proved by two more credible witnesses. Provided always that this act or anything therein contained shall not be considered to extend to debar or hinder any person or persons not exceeding the number of ten aforesaid, to present any public or private grievance or complaint to any Member or Members of Parliament. . . .

Though the women had complied with every provision of the Act, Sir Albert de Rutzen had decided at Bow Street that they had broken the law. In appealing against that decision in the Divisional Court, Lord Robert Cecil contended that in this country there was, and always had been, a right of petition and he urged that this right was a necessary condition of all free and indeed of all civilised Government. He pointed out that the right of petition had three characteristics; in the first place it was the right to petition the actual repositories of power; in the second place it was the right to petition in person, and in the third place it must be exercised reasonably.

In support of his contention that petitions might be presented in person he quoted several historic instances including a petition of women to Humphrey,

Duke of Gloucester in the reign of Henry IV, many petitions to various powerful personages from all sorts of men and women in the time of the Civil Wars and the disputes immediately preceding them; and petitions to the Lord High Steward asking for the conviction of Strafford. In addition to these he cited numbers of petitions presented in 1640, when deputations came to the House of Commons and the Members were instructed to go out and interview the petitioners and hear what they had to say; a great petition of 1680 as well as the petitions from the Gentlemen of Kent in 1701; that of the Silkweavers in 1765; and that of the Trade Unionists in 1834; all of which were presented in person. Throughout our history it was clear, he declared, that petitions had been presented, sometimes to the Houses of Parliament, sometimes to powerful individuals and sometimes to the King. He referred to a case mentioned in Sir Walter Scott's " Fortune of Nigel," in which, on King James II complaining of the way in which a petition was thrust into his hand in the streets, a gentleman named Jingling Geordie, had taken the opportunity of presenting a petition to him then and there in his private closet.

Even without these historic examples the Statute 13, Charles II (already quoted) was enough to establish the right to present petitions in person. The Bill of Rights had specially confirmed the right of petition in so far as the King was concerned because the right to present a petition to the King had recently been called into question by the case of the seven Bishops, which had taken place on June 29th and 30th, 1688, in the reign of James II.

The case had arisen because the King had ordered

that his Declaration of Indulgence should be read in all the Churches in the country and the seven Bishops headed by the Archbishop of Canterbury being of opinion that the Declaration of Indulgence was beyond the power of the King. had therefore presented a petition to him setting forth this view. The King declared the petition to be a seditious libel, and the Bishops had been brought before the Court of King's Bench. In summing up the case for the jury, Mr. Justice Holloway said, " So that if there was no ill-intent and they were not (as it is not nor can be pretended they were) men of evil lives, to deliver a petition cannot be a fault, it being the right of every subject to petition. The jury found the seven Bishops to be guiltless and the right of petition was thus confirmed.

In quoting Mr. Justice Holloway's summing up, Lord Robert Cecil pointed out that the use of the words " to deliver a petition " clearly indicated that the right was to present the petition *in person*. If that were so, the women who had gone to Parliament Square on June 29 had done so in the exercise of a *constitutional right*. So long as they were denied votes, this was their only *constitutional* method of agitation for the redress of their grievances.

If, as was contended, the right not only to petition, but to petition in person, belonged to each and every subject, the only point left to consider was as to whether the right had been exercised reasonably. If one wished to interview the Prime Minister or any Member of Parliament it was surely reasonable to go to the House of Commons by means of the Strangers' Entrance. The evidence clearly showed that Mrs. Haverfield and the others had been on the public highway and had been brought up to the door of the House of Commons by Superintendent Isaacs of the Police, so that up to that point they could not possibly have done anything wrong. Opposite the door of the House of Commons an open space had been kept clear by the presence of a police cordon, the crowd not being allowed to reach this point. Within the cordon there were only members of the police force, persons who had business in the House of Commons and the eight members of the Women's deputation. Therefore it was absurd to say that these eight ladies had caused an obstruction.

It was suggested that the women ought to have gone away because, as he put it, "a casual policeman" had said that the Prime Minister was not in the House of Commons, but that was really not a sufficient answer. The ordinary procedure certainly was not to take an answer from a policeman in the street if one wished to interview a Member of Parliament. The police had no right to stop anyone from going into the House of Commons. It was also said that the women had been given a letter from the Prime Minister saying that he would not or could not see them. "Had he said, 'I cannot see you here and now, but I will see you on such and such an occasion, this is not a convenient time,' that," argued Lord Robert, "would have been a sufficient answer, because the right to petition must be exercised reasonably, but his letter contained an unqualified refusal, and if the right to petition exists, that is no answer at all."

Lord Robert then submitted that if there is a right to petition a Member of Parliament there must be a duty on the part of a Member of Parliament to receive that petition, and that no one is justified in interfering with the exercise of that right. If the women were legally justified in insisting upon the right to present their petition they were also justified in refusing the order of the police to go away for there was no obligation to obey the police if the police were acting beyond the scope of their proper duties or contrary to the law of the land. In the case of Codd v. Cave a warrant had been issued against a man and a policeman had gone to his house to arrest him without taking a warrant with him. The man had declined to go with the policeman and had knocked him down and injured him severely but it had been held by the Court that the man was not guilty because the policeman had no right to arrest him without a warrant.

In delivering judgment the Lord Chief Justice said that he entirely agreed that there was a right to present a petition either to the Prime Minister as Prime Minister or as a Member of Parliament, and that petitions to the King should be presented to the Prime Minister. But he said the claim of the women was not only to present a petition but " to be received in deputation." Had it been only to present the petition he did not think that Mr. Asquith would have refused, and he expressed the opinion that his refusal to receive the women in deputation was not unnatural, " in consequence of what we know did happen on previous occasions."

In making this remark the Lord Chief Justice showed that instead of concentrating his mind upon the actual case before him he was allowing himself to be biassed by inaccurate reports as to what had taken place on previous occasions. As a matter of fact Mr. Asquith never had received a deputation of women since he had been Prime Minister and never at any time had he received a deputation of the Women's Social and Political Union in the House of Commons. Therefore it was absurd to talk about what had taken place on " previous occasions," and, moreover, even if Mr. Asquith had received deputations on previous occasions and trouble had resulted, the Lord Chief Justice would have had no right to take these occurrences into account unless reliable evidence as to what actually had occurred had been laid before him in connexion with the case.

Relying on the Metropolitan Police Act of 1839, which provides that it shall be lawful for the Commissioner of Police to make regulations and to give directions to the constables for keeping order and for preventing any obstruction of the thoroughfares in the immediate neighbourhood of the House of Commons and the Sessional Order which empowers the Police to keep clear the approaches to the House of Commons, the Lord Chief Justice decided that Mrs. Pankhurst, Mrs. Haverfield and the other women had broken the law when they had insisted that they had a right to enter the House of Commons and that for this reason they had been properly convicted and that the appeal must be dismissed with costs.

By this decision the Ancient Constitutional right of petition secured to the people of this country by the Act of 13, Charles II, and the Bill of Rights, was, for all practical purposes, rendered null and void. What is the use of a right that one may not put into practice? Does anyone suppose for one moment that the right of petition would have been cherished as it has been, and that people would have

suffered heavy punishment for putting it into practice, in troublous times, if it had merely consisted
in sending a written document obscurely, through
the post, or by a messenger, to the person in power
whom it was intended to influence? No, for the
right could never have been anything but valueless
had the presentation of the petition not been accompanied by the pomp and circumstance, and the dramatic and spectacular character, of a public deputation, and by the influence that only personal pleading
can lend. Every scrap of evidence tends to show
that the right of petition was to be exercised personally. If it were otherwise why should the Act
of Charles II have insisted that the signatories to the
petition should be represented by a limited deputation? Moreover there is no suggestion that a written document was required and that the petition
might not have been made, as it frequently was, by
word of mouth.

Shortly after this case of Pankhurst and Haverfield v. Jarvis had been decided the Divisional Court
was again occupied with an appeal case bearing upon
the right of petition, this time at the instance of the
Women's Freedom League. In July the League
had followed the example of the W. S. P. U. in
claiming the constitutional right of personal petition
to the Prime Minister. After much preliminary ne-
gotiation a deputation of their number had appeared
at the Strangers' entrance to the House of Commons on July 5th and on being told that Mr. Asquith would not receive them they had announced
their intention of waiting there until he should
change his mind. They were allowed to wait and,
reinforced by relays of others, continued to do so

right on into the New Year and were constantly to be seen standing outside on the pavement both day and night, whenever the House was sitting. Many Members of Parliament appealed to Mr. Asquith to receive them and so bring their weary vigil to an end but he obstinately refused and always evaded " the Suffragette pickets," as they were called. Usually he left the House by one of the underground passages but it was said that one night he hurried unrecognised through their lines. *Punch* then published a cartoon by E. T. Reed, entitled " Mr. Asquith's disguises," showing the Prime Minister as a cab driver, a postman, a policeman, an elderly maiden lady and in other characters.

On July 9th, the pickets were also put on at No. 10 Downing Street, where they succeeded in waylaying the Prime Minister at about 2 o'clock in the afternoon and ran towards him crying, " A petition ! A petition ! Will you give us a hearing, Mr. Asquith ? " As he rushed past he snatched the document from one of them, saying, " Well, I will take the petition," and then fled on up the steps and banged the door. The pickets were still waiting for the interview when the police arrived to arrest them. They were afterwards sentenced to three weeks' imprisonment in default of paying fines of £3.

On July 15th four women again picketted Downing Street, but were arrested and sent to prison without even so much as catching a glimpse of the Premier. On August 16th a line of women was drawn up between the House of Commons and the door of 10 Downing Street, where stood Mrs. Cobden Sanderson and Mrs. Despard. This time they saw Mr. Asquith, but though some of the women spoke to him, he hurried on without making any reply. Three days later, on the 19th, the line of women was again formed, but Mrs. Despard, Mrs. Cobden Sanderson and six others were placed under arrest. Mr. Tim Healy, the well-known Irish member of Parliament, was briefed for their defence, but on August 27th, Mr. Curtis Bennett decided to fine the women forty shillings or to send them to prison for seven days. He stated a case for the High Court and this was heard on January 14th, 1910, when the Lord Chief Justice decided against the women, saying that there were other means of presenting petitions than going in numbers to do so.

Meanwhile it was announced that the cases against the ninety-four women who were concerned with Mrs. Pankhurst and Mrs. Haverfield would be withdrawn, but at the same time application was made by the authorities for the fines recorded against Mrs. Pankhurst and Mrs. Haverfield and it was intimated that unless these were forthcoming, steps would be taken to arrest and imprison them. But immediately after this, on Monday, December 6th, an official receipt for the amount of Mrs. Pankhurst's fine was sent to Clement's Inn and it was stated that the money had been paid by some unknown person.[1] Two days later Mrs. Pankhurst returned from her lecturing tour in the United States and Canada, which had been a most triumphant success.

On December 9th, the action by Mrs. Leigh against Mr. Gladstone as Home Secretary, and the Governor and Doctor of Winson Green Gaol, which

[1] A few days later the same thing happened in the case of Mrs. Haverfield, and later still in regard to the members of the Women's Freedom League.

Jessie Kenney as she tried to gain admittance to Mr.
Asquith's meeting on Dec. 10, 1909 disguised
as a telegraph boy

was to decide the question of the legality of forcible feeding by the prison authorities, was tried before the Lord Chief Justice. It was pointed out on Mrs. Leigh's behalf that there was no rule or regulation to justify forcible feeding. Dr. Ernest Dormer Kirby, who had attended her on her release, testified that her condition was " distinctly grave," and that she had then weighed no more than six stone six pounds. Sir Victor Horsley, Mr. William Hugh Fenton, Senior Surgeon at the Chelsea Hospital for Women, and Mr. Mansell-Moullin all declared forcible feeding by means of the nasal tube to be painful, dangerous, injurious to health, and incapable of providing adequate nourishment. Dr. Maurice Craig, Consulting Physician of Welbach Street, and late Senior Assistant Physician at Bethlehem Hospital, who was called as a witness for the defence of Mr. Gladstone and of the officials, said that the operation of nasal feeding was " a simple one on the average." He considered it more dangerous to leave a patient starving than to overcome resistance.

Sir Richard Douglas Powell, also called for the defence, admitted that he would not willingly resort to artificial feeding unless it was " quite necessary."

The Lord Chief Justice said that he should rule that it was the duty of the medical officer of the prison to take all reasonable steps to preserve Mrs. Leigh's life and to prevent her committing suicide. The only question he should leave to the jury would be whether the governor and doctor had taken the right steps. In his summing-up he assumed throughout that the jury must decide against Mrs. Leigh. They did as he directed, and she thereupon lost her case.

On January 19th, an action was begun by Miss Emily Wilding Davison against the visiting justices of Strangeways Gaol, Manchester, for having ordered that a hose-pipe should be played upon her. Judge Parry said that the use of the hose-pipe was both ineffective and unnecessary; that the duty of the visiting justices was to prevent any abuse of authority by the officials of the gaol; and to report and make suggestions. Therefore he held that they were not justified in ordering the assault, and decided the case in Miss Davison's favour. In assessing the damages, however, he said that he should take into account the fact that the hose-pipe incident had resulted in the prisoner's release before the expiration of her sentence; had provided her with " ' copy ' for a vivacious and entertaining account of the affair in the Press "; and had advertised her cause. Under these circumstances the damages should be no more than forty shillings, a nominal sum. The costs which were charged against the visiting magistrates were however placed on the highest scale because the case was held to be one of great importance.

Meanwhile there was no lack of turbulent scenes all over the country. Cabinet Ministers' meetings were daily being interrupted both by women who had succeeded in concealing themselves and by men who urged the question of Votes for Women on their behalf. When Mr. Lloyd George spoke at Reading two women started up from under the platform, during his speech. In the Queen's Hall, London, a few days afterwards, a forcible feeding tube was suddenly flung at him and he caught it in his hands. As the stewards fell upon the man who had thrown it, Mr. Lloyd George cried, " I do not envy him his paid job."

When speaking in the Louth Town Hall, Mr. Lloyd George was referring to the House of Lords as an " unrepresentative chamber " when a voice from the roof remarked, " So is the House of Commons as far as women are concerned." " I see some rats have got in; let them squeal, it does not matter," said the Chancellor of the Exchequer, and, amidst a terrible uproar, Miss Hudson and Miss Bertha Brewster were dragged down from amongst the rafters where they had lain concealed for many hours. They were taken to the police station, charged with infringing the Public Meeting Act, and detained in custody from Saturday until Monday, both in the same small cell, which contained only one narrow prison mattress and some rugs. On Monday the magistrate discharged them with a caution, complimenting them on their pluck. The Government was averse to allowing them to be let off so lightly, and on Wednesday Miss Brewster was rearrested for having broken her cell windows in Walton Gaol, Liverpool, in the previous August. She was sentenced to six weeks' imprisonment, but gave notice to appeal against the sentence on the ground that she had already been specially punished for this offence whilst in prison. On January 31st she was released in order that she might prosecute the appeal, and evidently thinking that the case hardly did him credit, Mr. Gladstone announced that she would not be asked to complete her term of imprisonment. The appeal was therefore dropped.

On December 20th, Mr. Asquith had arranged to

speak both at Liverpool and Birkenhead, and owing to his desire to avoid the Suffragettes, detectives smuggled him across the river, amongst the luggage. Nevertheless outside the Liberal Club Miss Selina Martin and Miss Leslie Hall, who stood in the gutter, the one disguised as a match girl, and the other as an orange seller, spoke to him as he stepped from his motor car, and urged upon him the necessity for granting the franchise to women. He dashed away without answering, and in protest, and by way of warning, Miss Selina Martin tossed a ginger beer bottle into the empty car which he had left.

Both women were at once arrested, and were afterwards remanded in custody for six days. Bail was refused, though Miss Selina Martin promised that she and her comrade would refrain from militant action until the case should come on.[1] The women were removed to Walton Gaol, and were there treated as though they had been ordinary convicted criminals. They protested by refusing to eat just as so many of their comrades had done before them. Miss Martin also barricaded her cell, but the officials forced their way in, pulled her off the bed and flung her on the floor, shaking and striking her unmercifully. Shortly afterwards her cell was visited by the deputy medical officer, who ordered that she should get up and dress. She explained that she had been wet through by the snow storm on the previous day and that her clothes were still saturated, for no attempt had been made to get them dry, but she was forcibly dressed and, with her hands handcuffed behind her, was dragged to a cold, dark pun-

[1] Miss Martin's promise was reported in the Liverpool *Daily Post* and other papers.

ishment cell and flung on the stone floor. She lay there in an exhausted state for some hours, being unable to rise without the aid of her hands and arms, which were still fastened behind her back, until, at last, a wardress came in and lifted her onto the bed board. The irons were kept on all night. On Friday, the third day of her imprisonment, Miss Martin was brought up before the visiting magistrates. She protested against the way in which she was being treated, pointing out that she was still an unconvicted prisoner, but she was told that the officials were quite justified in all that they might do. The same evening several wardresses entered her cell and ordered her to go to the doctor's room to be forcibly fed.

"I refused," she says, "and was dragged to the foot of the stairs with my hands handcuffed behind. Then I was frog-marched, that is to say, carried face downwards by the arms and legs to the Doctor's room. After a violent struggle I was forced into a chair, the handcuffs removed, my arms being held by the wardresses, whilst the doctor forcibly fed me by that obnoxious instrument, the stomach tube. Most unnecessary force was used by the assistant medical officer when applying the gag. The operation finished, I walked handcuffed to the top of the stairs but refused to return to the punishment cell. Then two wardresses caught me by the shoulders and dragged me down the steps, another kicking me from behind. As I reached the bottom step they relaxed their hold and I fell on my head. I was picked up and carried to the cell."

Next day she was forcibly fed and afterwards again refused to return to the dark cell, but she says, "I was seized by a number of wardresses and carried down the steps, my head being allowed to bump several times."

Meanwhile, Miss Leslie Hall had also broken her windows and had been placed in a punishment cell and kept in handcuffs continuously for three days. After two and a half days' fasting she was fed by the stomach tube. The doctor had taunted her meanwhile, and jokingly told the wardress that she was " mentally sick," and that it was " like stuffing a turkey for Christmas."

On Monday, December 27th, the women were again brought into court, when Miss Leslie Hall was ordered one month's imprisonment with hard labour, and Miss Selina Martin two months. On returning to prison both the women refused to wear prison dress and recommenced the hunger strike. Each one was then clothed in a straight jacket and placed in a punishment cell. Forcible feeding was continued and they both grew rapidly weaker until February 3rd, when they were released.

Meanwhile the facts as to their treatment whilst imprisoned on remand had been widely circulated, for they had dictated statements for their friends' use whilst their trial was being conducted. Mr. Gladstone wrote to the *Times* denying the truth of the statements, declaring that the reason for refusing bail to the women was that they had refused to promise to be of good behaviour until their trial came on, that no unnecessary violence had been used and that the women themselves had made no complaint. But indeed, the inaccuracy of Mr. Gladstone's statements had become proverbial, for he was constantly denying the truth of charges which were clearly substantiated by the most reliable evidence.

Now Lady Constance Lytton, in spite of her fragile constitution and the disease from which she suffered, again determined to place herself beside the
women in the fighting ranks who were enduring the
greatest hardship.   Believing that she had been released from Newcastle prison on account of her rank,
and family influence, she determined that this time
she would go disguised.   She knew that, not only
her family, but the leaders of the militant movement
would try to dissuade her on account of her health.
She, therefore, decided to speak of her intention to
no one except Mrs. Baines and a few local workers
whom she pledged to secrecy.   On January 14th,
she and Mrs. Baines organised a procession to
Walton Gaol.   A halt was called opposite the
prison, and, having told the story of what was happening inside Lady Constance called the people to
follow her to its gates, and demand the release of
the tortured women.   Then she moved forward
and, as she had foreseen, she was immediately placed
under arrest.   At the same time Elsie Howey
dashed into the prison yard and broke one of the
windows of the Governor's house by striking it with
a purple-white-and-green flag.   She, too, was taken
into custody and, bail being refused, the two comrades passed the night in the cells.   Lady Constance
had disguised herself by cutting her hair, wearing
spectacles, and dressing herself in poor and plain
garments, and now she gave Jane Warton, seam-
stress, as her name and occupation.   Next morning
she was sentenced to fourteen days' hard labour without the option of a fine, whilst Elsie Howey was sent
to prison for six weeks' hard labour.   Then they
were dragged ruthlessly away to the torture which

they well knew was to come. On arriving at the prison, on Saturday, January 15th, they made the usual claim to be treated as political prisoners, and, on this being refused, signified their intention of refusing to conform to any of the prison rules. Thereupon they were forcibly stripped by the wardresses and dressed in the prison clothes. At five o'clock, on Tuesday, the doctor entered Lady Constance Lytton's cell with four wardresses and the forcible feeding apparatus. Then, without testing her heart or feeling her pulse, though she had not been medically examined since entering the prison, he ordered that she should be placed in position. She did not resist, but lay down on the bed board voluntarily, well knowing that she would need all her strength for the ordeal that was to come. Her poor heart was palpitating wildly, but she set her teeth and tried to calm herself. The doctor then produced a wooden and a steel gag and told her that he would not use the latter, which would hurt, unless she resisted him; but, as she would not unlock her teeth, he threw the milder wooden instrument aside and pried her mouth open with the steel one. Then the stomach tube was forced down and the whole hateful feeding business was gone through. "The reality surpassed all that I had anticipated," she said. "It was a living nightmare of pain, horror and revolting degradation. The sense is of being strangled, suffocated by the thrust down of the large rubber tube, which arouses great irritation in the throat and nausea in the stomach. The anguish and effort of retching whilst the tube is forcibly pressed back into the stomach and the natural writhing of the body restrained, defy description. I forgot what I was in there for, I forgot women, I forgot everything, except my own sufferings, and I was completely overcome by them." The doctor, annoyed by her one effort to resist, affected to consider her distress assumed, and struck her contemptuously on the cheek as he rose to leave, but the wardresses showed pity for her weakness, and they helped her to wipe her clothes, over which she had been sick. They promised to bring her others in the morning, but she was obliged to pass the night as she was, for, owing both to the low temperature of the cell and her own lack of vitality, she was always so cold that she wore her nightdress and all her clothes both night and day; even then her limbs remained stiff with cold, and though, at last, as a special favour, she was allowed first one, and then another extra blanket and the cape which the prisoners wear at exercise, she remained cold, for she says, " It was like clothing a stone to warm it." When she was fed the second time the vomiting was more excessive and the doctor's clothes suffered. He was angry and left her cell hastily, saying, " You did that on purpose. If you do it again to-morrow I shall feed you twice."

How very much easier would it have been to have given in or never to have started this resistance? How very much more natural to this gentle creature whose whole life had been one of affectionate deference to the wishes of others, who, because of her kindly sweetness had been named by her family " Angel Con," would it have been to save others trouble and quietly to submit to the discomforts of prison life. But where principles were in question, none could be stronger or firmer than Constance

Lytton, and she was determined to go on with the bitter thing until the end. Yet, through it all, her gentle nature was apparent. She could not bear that any of the ordinary prisoners should be brought in to clean up the mess on her cell floor and, except upon one or two occasions she always managed to do it for herself in spite of her weakness and distress. Notwithstanding his brutal rudeness to her, she even tried to wipe the doctor's clothes, if anything was spilt upon them. For the sake of the other prisoners she tried, too, to help him with his hateful task by making suggestions to him as to how it might be rendered more efficacious and some of its horrors mitigated, but her suggestions were contemptuously disregarded. The third time she was fed she vomited continuously, but the doctor kept pouring in more food until she was seized with a violent fit of shivering. Then he became alarmed. He hastily told the wardresses to lay her on the floor and called in his assistant to test her heart, but, after a brief and superficial investigation, it was pronounced " quite sound " and the pulse " steady." Next time he appeared he pleaded with her, saying, " I do beg of you, I appeal to you, not as a prison doctor, but as a man, to give over. You are a delicate woman, you are not fit for this sort of thing." " Is anybody fit for it? " she answered. " I beg of you, I appeal to you, not as a prisoner, but as a woman, to refuse to continue this inhuman treatment."

From Wednesday, January 19th, and onwards, she began to find that not only did she receive greater consideration from the doctor, but that there was a marked change in her treatment generally. This led her to conclude that her identity had been discovered or at least suspected, and she therefore tried to take advantage of whatever privileges might be made to her in order to secure concessions for her comrades and to induce the officials to act with more humanity. But, though she considered that she had been treated with more kindness than was usual, we learn that obvious simple necessities were denied her. The processes of digestion were entirely stagnant and she was losing weight daily, and though she made several suggestions as to remedies and at last an aperient drug was promised to her, it was never supplied. She was right, however, in thinking that her identity had been discovered. On Friday the authorities made up their minds that she was not Jane Warton, and on Sunday morning both the governor and doctor appeared and told her that she was to be released and that her sister had come to fetch her.

Lady Constance Lytton now sent a careful statement to Mr. Gladstone asserting that the forcible feeding was performed with unnecessary cruelty and without proper care. He declared that all her charges were unfounded, and the visiting magistrates, having held a one-sided enquiry into the matter, announced that the regulations had been carried out with the greatest care and consideration.

CHAPTER XXIV

1910

The General Election, The Truce, The Conciliation Committee, a Series of Great Demonstrations.
War is Again Declared. Another General Election. Conclusion.

With the opening of the new year, 1910, whilst
many of the women were still in prison, the General
Election began. The Women's Social and Political
Union fought the Government in forty constituencies. In almost every one of these contests the Liberal vote was reduced, and eighteen of the seats,
which had been held by Government representatives
at the dissolution, were wrested from them. During
the election the Liberal Government's absolute majority over all sections of the House had been swept
away, and they were now dependent for their existence upon the votes of the Labour and Irish parties.

The Suffragettes were now advised in many quarters that the militant tactics had forced the Government to the point of wishing to gain peace by
granting votes to women, but that Cabinet Ministers
were now afraid to do so lest they should seem to have
given way to coercion. The contest for supreme
power in the new Parliament being over, the women
therefore decided to give the re-elected Government and the Parliamentary supporters of Women's
Suffrage a quiet opportunity to settle the matter be-

tween them. On February 14th, the W. S. P. U.
proclaimed a truce, and the Women's Freedom
League followed suit.

During the past year more than twenty thousand
meetings had been held by the W. S. P. U. alone,
in addition to the many thousands organised by
the other suffrage societies. Now that militancy was
to be laid aside a period of even greater effort in
the direction of building up the organisation and
extending the purely educational work was to be entered upon.

Important developments were also to take place
within Parliament itself. For many years a committee of Parliamentary supporters of Women's
Suffrage, had existed. This was originally inaugurated on June 10th, 1887, under the influence of
Miss Lydia Becker. It was strictly non-party,
Members from all sections of the House having belonged to it. During the Parliament elected in 1906,
however, the old committee had been allowed to
lapse. The Liberal supporters of the question
formed a Women's Suffrage Committee of their own,
and, abandoning the attempt to secure votes for
women, and seeking instead to extend the franchise
all around, they had put forward Mr. Geoffrey
Howard's Reform Bill, which had had no chance
of being carried.

Now, largely owing to the efforts of Mr. H. N.
Braitsford, a " Conciliation Committee " was formed
with the object of uniting all sections of opinion
favourable to women's enfranchisement and of coming to a common agreement upon some particular
measure. The Earl of Lytton acted as Chairman
of this Committee and Mr. Braitsford, himself, as

Secretary. Its members consisted of twenty-five Liberals, seventeen Conservatives, six Irish Nationalists, and six members of the Labour Party. In discussing the terms of the Bill to be adopted, the Unionist members urged that it should be moderate, whilst the Liberals insisted that it must give no loophole for increasing the possibilities of plural voting or of adding to the power of the propertied classes. Though the majority of the women who attend the English Universities do so as a preparation for earning their livelihood, the Liberals did not wish to see the Franchise for University graduates, which is exercised by men, extended to women because, as they said, the poorest women do not graduate. For similar reasons they opposed the granting of votes to women under the Joint Household qualification, which applies only to houses rented at twenty pounds a year and upwards; under the Lodger franchise, which applies only to those who pay at least four shillings a week for an unfurnished room; and under the Ownership franchise. To overcome the objections of the self-styled democrats, the old Women's Enfranchisement Bill which would have given bare justice to women by extending the Parliamentary vote to them on equal terms with men was therefore abandoned, and a measure was drafted on the lines of the existing Municipal Franchise of which the basis is occupation and under which there is no qualification for Owners, Lodgers or Graduates.

Local Government was the earliest form of government in this country; it has been the most persistent and staple. Government from the centre was of later growth, and has many times been interrupted. The Municipal Franchise as it exists to-day is chiefly dependent on the Municipal Corporations Acts of 1835 and 1839. Before the passing of the first of these Acts women possessed and exercised equal voting rights with men in regard to matters of local Government, but the act of 1835 deprived them of these rights in all towns incorporated under it. In 1865, however, Women's Suffrage societies, demanding the admission of women to both national and local franchises, sprang into being, and when the Municipal Corporation's Act of 1869 was before Parliament, Mr. Jacob Bright succeeded in carrying an amendment to restore to women the rights of which the Act of 1835 had deprived them. It was a Liberal Government that framed and carried the Municipal Corporation's Act of 1869, and that Government accepted the amendment to extend its provisions to women. There was no suggestion then, nor has any since been made, that that franchise, when exercised either by men or women, is undemocratic when applied to municipal purposes.

Therefore, following the lines of the existing municipal franchise, the Conciliation Committee proposed to extend the Parliamentary vote to women householders and to women occupiers of business premises paying ten pounds a year and upwards. It was estimated that ninety-five per cent. of the women who would be enfranchised under this Conciliation Bill would be householders. To the householder franchise no monetary qualification whatsoever is attached, and every one who inhabits even a single room over which he or she has full control is counted as a householder.

As soon as this bill had been decided upon by the members of Parliament, who formed the Conciliation Committee, it was submitted to the various suffrage and other women's organisations, with a request to adopt it. Many of the societies, including the militants, at first demurred on the ground that though the number of women enfranchised would not differ greatly, the principle of equality between men and women, which the Women's Enfranchisement Bill had laid down, would be sacrificed by the new measure. Mr. Braitsford and others urged, however, that the Conciliation Bill was the only one to which the various sections in the House who supported Women's Suffrage would agree. They also pointed out that, as the women whom it was proposed to enfranchise were already upon the Municipal Register, no difficulty would be experienced in adding the lists of their names to the Parliamentary Register also before the next General Election, even should this take place within the year. Therefore, on condition that it should be passed during the session, all the various women's organisations worked wholeheartedly for the measure.

On June 18 the W. S. P. U. organised in support of the Conciliation Bill a greater procession of women than had ever yet been held, in which joined numbers of organisations, both national and international. Headed by a company of six hundred and seventeen women in white dresses carrying long gleaming silver staves tipped with broad arrows, each representing an imprisonment, the massed ranks with their gay banners took more than an hour and a half to pass a given point. The Great Albert

Hall was able to contain but a section of the processionists.

No place for Women's Suffrage had been obtained in the private Members' ballot. The Conciliation Bill had been drafted in the hope that the Government would provide time for its discussion, and five days after the great procession, the Prime Minister, in reply to an influentially signed petition of Members of Parliament, promised to give facilities for the second reading of the Bill. At the same time he stated that he could not provide an early date for this, but, just as the militant forces were preparing for action, he agreed to fix Monday and Tuesday, July the 11th and 12th, for the discussion of the Bill.

The object of the Conciliation Bill's promoters was, of course, not merely to secure the passage of the second reading by a substantial majority, but also that it should be sent for discussion to one of the standing committees instead of being referred to a Committee of the whole House; because, if the latter course were pursued no further progress could be made unless the Government were prepared to provide more time.

As usual the attitude of the Government was anxiously awaited. It was rumoured that Mr. Lloyd George would speak in opposition to the bill, but those who believed his professions of friendship for the women's cause hoped against hope that he would not do so. Mr. Winston Churchill had been several times in conference with the officials of the Conciliation Committee and had expressed sympathy with their object. They counted confidently upon

his help. It is true that some days before the debate, they had received a letter from him criticising
the terms of the Bill, but they still regarded him
as a friend to the measure. Nevertheless early in
the second days' debate he rose to make a bitter and
uncompromising attack upon it. He began by seeking to prove that the grievance of excluding women
from the franchise was greatly exaggerated, that
they did not suffer any legislative disability there-
from, and that neither the mass of the women
themselves nor of the male electorate desired the
enfranchisement of women. He went on to speak
vaguely of the danger of creating " a vast body of
privileged and dependent voters who might be
manipulated, manœuvred in this division or in
that." Then, having elaborately striven to build
up a case against the granting of votes to women
on any terms, he proceeded with an air of considerable magnanimity to admit that a slight grievance
existed because all women were disfranchised. He
was of the opinion that this grievance could only
be redressed in one or two ways; either by giving
the vote " to some of the best women of all classes "
or by giving the vote to every woman. The former
method he described as " the first way," and he said,
" I always hoped the Conciliation Committee would
travel along that road." In particularising his
favourite method of proceeding by means of his
proposed special franchises he admitted that no
doubt these would be " disrespectfully called ' fancy
franchises,' " and explained that they would give the
vote to " a comparatively small number of women
of all classes on considerations " of " property,"
" earning capacity " or " education." These special

franchises would, he said, " be fairly balanced, one against the other, so as not on the whole to give an undue advantage to the property vote as against the wage earning vote." " That," he said, " would not be a Democratic proposal . . . " It would provide for the representation of the sex through the strongest, most capable and most responsible women in every class and that would meet the main grievance in my humble judgment."

Thus the loudly professing democrat, Mr. Churchill, proposed to enfranchise only those women whom the members of the Conciliation Committee, in the earnest and patient effort to comply with Mr. Asquith's proviso that their Bill must be democratic, had gradually weeded out. They had excluded the property owners as such in favor of their poorer sisters, the graduates, because only the comfortably circumstanced can go to college, and the lodgers, because the majority of women wage earners, to the shame of our country, cannot afford to pay four shilling a week for their rooms. These three classes, the women who own property, those who have graduated at college and those who earn comparatively high wages, were surely those whom Mr. Churchill had intended to indicate. The women had agreed to their exclusion because, as compared with the householders, their numbers were small. This was the very reason for which Mr. Churchill had selected them for inclusion, for he described the Conciliation Bill as " an enormous addition to the Franchise," though it would only enfranchise one million women as against seven million men.

He went on to attack the terms of the Conciliation Bill describing it as " anti-Democrat," and declaring that it gave representation to property as against persons. " The more I study the Bill," he said, " the more astonished I am that such a large number of respected Members of Parliament should have found it possible to put their names to it." He complained that the bulk of married women would not be able to qualify, but that a man who owned a house and stable would be able to qualify his wife for the former and himself for the latter, as though that would not also be the case under his own proposed " fancy franchises." He asserted that the young inexperienced girl of twenty-one would be enfranchised under the Conciliation Bill, whilst " the woman who keeps by her labour an invalid husband and his family " would get no vote. Yet in practice we all know that girls of twenty-one are not usually qualified either as householders or occupiers, and in justice, and let us hope in its practice also, the woman who works to maintain her husband and family, is counted as the responsible householder and would vote instead of the husband she maintains.

He ended with a final appeal to Members to vote against the Bill, saying that a vote on the Second Reading of this Bill was equivalent to that on the Third Reading of any other, and that those who cast their votes for it, should be able to say, " I want this Bill passed into law this session regardless of all other consequences. I want it as it is; and I want it now."

Mr. Asquith spoke against the principle of Women's enfranchisement in general, and against the Conciliation Bill in particular. He began by saying that a franchise measure ought not to be sent

to a standing committee but to one of the Whole
House. He declared also that his conditions that
proof must be shown that the majority of the women
desired any proposed measures for their enfranchisement and that the measure should be democratic in
its character, had not been complied with.

Towards the end of the debate Mr. Lloyd George
also threw the weight of his influence into the scale
against the Bill. He stated that he agreed with
every word both relevant and irrelevant that had
been uttered by Mr. Churchill. Nevertheless he re-
frained from depreciating the abstract principle of
Women's Suffrage as the Home Secretary had done,
and directed his attack wholly against the terms of
the Bill. In defiance of the fact he persistently declared that the Conciliation Committee which had
drafted the Bill was " a committee of women meeting outside the House," and that they had come to
the House saying, " not merely must you vote for
Women's Suffrage, but you must vote for the particular form upon which we agree, and we will not
even allow you to deliberate upon any other form."
He said that this was a position which " no self-
respecting legislature could possibly accept; " yet
the Government had all the Parliamentary year at
their disposal to introduce what measures they chose,
and for years and years the women had been calling upon them to formulate a Women's Suffrage
measure of their own. It had been urged, he said,
that this Bill was better than none at all.

" Why should that be the alternative? " he asked.
But when a member called out, " What is the
Other? " he answered evasively, " Well I cannot
say for the moment; but allow me, I am trying to

concentrate for the sake of others who desire to follow me in this debate."

Later he said: " If the promoters of this Bill say that they regard the Second Reading merely as an affirmation of the principle of Women's Suffrage, and if they promise that when they reintroduce the Bill it will be in a form which will enable the House of Commons to move any Amendment either for restriction or for extension I shall be happy to vote for this Bill."

" Will the Government give time? " asked Mr. Roch, a Liberal member, but the only answer was: " That is a question for the Prime Minister."

Mr. Snowden, winding up the debate for the promoters of the Bill, replied to Mr. Lloyd George's challenge. He said: " We will withdraw this Bill, if the Right Hon. gentleman on behalf of the Government or the Prime Minister himself, will undertake to give to this House the opportunity of discussing and carrying through its various stages another form of franchise Bill. If we cannot get that, then we shall prosecute this Bill." Mr. Lloyd George and the other members of the Government sat silent. They well knew the difficulties under which the Conciliation Committee laboured, and they knew, too, that the women were striving at great cost and sacrifice to obtain for their sex the largest possible measure of representation; but with the power to speedily bring the matter to a satisfactory conclusion, they preferred to hamper the efforts of both with obstructive criticism. As Mr. Snowden aptly put it:

" It would pass the wit of man to put that principle into a Bill which would meet with the approval of the Chancellor of the Exchequer and the Home Secretary."

Mr. Balfour, Mr. Haldane, and Mr. Runciman were amongst those who spoke in support of the Bill, but the two Ministers urged that it should not be allowed to pass to one of the standing Committees.

After thirty-nine speeches had been delivered the division was taken. The Second Reading was then found to have been carried by 299 votes to 190, giving a favourable majority of 109, a majority larger than that cast during the Parliament for any measure and even for the Government's vaunted Budget and House of Lords Resolutions.

A division was next taken on a resolution to refer the Bill to a Committee of the Whole House. The Anti-Suffragists, in the hope of shelving the Bill, those who feared to anger the government and those who genuinely believed that so important a measure should be considered by the Whole House in each of its stages combined to carry this resolution by 320 votes to 175.

The question was now whether the Government would allow the few days necessary for the Committee and other final stages. Practically all other important legislative work was hanging fire because of the deadlock in regard to the House of Lords controversy. The Conference between the leaders of the Conservative and Liberal parties, which, after King Edward's death, had been set up to discuss this matter, was still sitting and until its deliberations were at end no progress towards a settlement would be made. Therefore for the moment Parliament had plenty of time on its hands, and urgent pressure was brought upon the Government to give out of this abundance to the Women's Bill.

On July 17th the Men's Political Union for Women's Suffrage, the Men's League for Women's Suffrage and the Conciliation Committee held a joint meeting in Hyde Park, in support of the Bill. On July 23rd, the Anniversary of the day in 1867 on which the pulling down of the Hyde Park Railings won the vote for the working men in the towns, the Women's Social and Political Union held another great demonstration there for which a space of half a square mile was specially cleared. There were forty platforms, many societies co-operated and two fine processions — one from the East and the other from the West — marched to the meeting. The older Suffragists had also demonstrated in Trafalgar Square, but on the very day of the W. S. P. U.'s big Hyde Park meeting the Prime Minister wrote to Lord Lytton refusing to allow any further time for the Bill that session.

But Parliament was to meet again in the Autumn. It was still hoped that the Government might concede the time then. Resolutions urging them to do so were sent in from numbers of popularly elected bodies including the Corporations of Manchester, Liverpool, Bradford, Nottingham, Glasgow, Dundee, Dublin, Cork, and thirty others.

There were signs that the truce of the militants, which had lasted for nine months, would soon be at an end. This time it was men friends to the cause who gave the first warning. On October 17th young Mr. Victor Duval, now secretary of the Men's Political Union for Women's Suffrage was arrested for seizing Mr. Lloyd George by the lapel of his

coat and rebuking him for his hostility to the
Women's Bill as he passed into the City Temple
where he was to speak. Mr. George Jacobs, an
elderly man saw that the police were treating Duval
roughly and called out to them, " Do not hurt him."
He also was arrested and both men were imprisoned
for a week.

Mr. Lloyd George had been speaking against the
Conciliation Bill in Wales, and numbers of Welsh
women Liberals plainly showed their disapproval
of his action. The women constituents of several
other Cabinet Ministers were pressing to be received
in deputation, and in view of the General Election
they could scarcely be denied. On October 27th,
Mr. Asquith consented to see the women of East
Fife. He told them that facilities could not be
granted before the close of the year and even when
asked what of next year he merely answered, " Wait
and see." Other Ministers seconded him. They
were all agreed in refusing to allow the Bill to pass
into law that year.

Therefore at a great meeting in the Albert Hall
on November 10th the truce broke — war was once
more declared. Mrs. Pankhurst announced that
another deputation would march to the House of
Commons to carry a petition to the Prime Minister.
She herself would lead the deputation, " If I were
to go alone," she said, " still I would go," but at
that hundreds of women's voices cried out from all
parts of the Hall: " Mrs. Pankhurst, I will go
with you," " I will go ! " " I will go ! " Then
Mrs. Pethick Lawrence called for funds for the
campaign, and nine thousand pounds was immediately subscribed.

The Autumn Session lasted but a few days, for on November 18, Mr. Asquith announced that Parliament would be dissolved on November 28th, and that a general election would take place. Even whilst he spoke, the women,— 450 of them, divided into companies of less than twelve to keep within the law,— were marching from the Caxton Hall and Clement's Inn. Mrs. Pankhurst, Dr. Garrett Anderson, founder of Girton College and one of the medical women pioneers now over seventy years of age, Mrs. Hertha Ayrton, the scientist, Mrs. Cobden Sanderson, and Miss Neligan and Mrs. Brackenbury, both of whom had reached the great age of seventy-eight, were amongst the first little band. They soon learnt that the Prime Minister had refused to see them. Some of their number were hurled back into the crowd. The remainder were kept standing on the porch for hours with the shut door before them and a surging crowd behind.

The companies of women who came after were torn apart, felled to the ground, struck again and again, bruised and battered, and tossed hither and thither with a violence that perhaps excelled anything that had gone before. One hundred and fifteen women and four men were eventually arrested. But the full story of that day's happenings belongs to another, and, let us hope, to the last chapter of this long fight.

Meanwhile the Prime Minister forgot to reply to Mr. Keir Hardie's question as to the fate of the Conciliation Bill. Lord Balcarries then moved a resolution which was practically a vote of censure upon the Government for their treatment of the women. Fifty-two Members voted for it, but it was lost. Eventually Mr. Lloyd George said the Prime Minister would make a statement on the following Tuesday.

Tuesday saw the Women's Parliament again in Session and the women waiting eagerly for the news. Mr. Asquith said: " The government will, if they are still in power, give facilities in the next Parliament for effectively proceeding with a Bill which is so framed as to admit of free amendment." He refused, however, to promise that this should be done during the first year of the New Parliament.

Facilities for the Conciliation Bill had been asked for; the reply that facilities would be given to a Bill so framed as to admit of free amendment was too vague to please the women. But the refusal to grant an opportunity for passing a Suffrage Bill into law during the first year of Parliament was more serious. The Parliament now to be dissolved had lasted less than a year. Who could insure a longer life for its successor? Mr. Asquith had given the women scant reason to trust any vague promises of his.

Therefore Mrs. Pankhurst announced to the women, " I am going to Downing Street. Come along, all of you; " and the women went. The police, however, gradually beat them back, and over a hundred arrests were made. On Wednesday, there were eighteen further arrests, and twenty-nine more on Thursday. Many of the women were discharged, but seventy-five received sentences of imprisonment varying from fourteen days to one month.

Then came the general election, and again the Suffragettes strenuously opposed the Government. In almost every constituency fought by them the

Liberal vote was reduced. A notable instance was that of Cardiff, where a Liberal majority of 1555 was converted into a Conservative majority of 299. Here the 800 members of the Women's Liberal Association abstained from working for their party because its candidate, Sir Clarendon Hyde, was opposed to votes for women. The end of the election saw the Liberal government still in power.

During the year the Women's Suffrage societies had all grown largely. The Women's Social and Political Union's salaried staff now stands at 110 persons. Its central offices at Clement's Inn occupy twenty-three rooms, and a shop and thirteen rooms have also been taken for the Woman's Press at 156 Charing Cross Road. There are also 105 local centres of the Union. The income of the central organisation of the W. S. P. U. during 1910 was 34,500 pounds excluding 9,000 pounds made by the Woman's press and many thousands collected by the local Unions. The twenty thousand pound campaign fund is now complete.

The Conciliation Bill has been again introduced. Again its scope and title have been modified to please the " democrats." Its text now is: —

Every woman possessed of a household qualification within the meaning of the representation of the people Act (1884) shall be entitled to be registered as a voter and when registered to vote for the county or borough in which the qualifying premises are situate.

For the purposes of this Act a woman shall not be disqualified by marriage from being registered as a voter provided that a husband and wife shall not both be registered as voters in the same Parliamentary Borough or County Division.

In reply to a deputation of women who waited upon him in October, 1910, Mr. Birrell said: " I am strongly of opinion that in the course of next year facilities must be given for the Bill. You are perfectly right," he added, " in feeling irritated and annoyed at the delay that has taken place and in insisting on a date for Parliamentary action."

Mr. Asquith's promise is that facilities for a Women's Suffrage measure will be granted during this Parliament. Such statements as these must now be held as binding, and the long standing Government veto of this question must be withdrawn.

So the gallant struggle for a great reform draws to its close. Full of stern fighting and bitter hardship as it has been, it has brought much to the women of our time — a courage, a self-reliance, a comradeship, and above all a spiritual growth, a conscious dwelling in company with the ideal, which has tended to strip the littleness from life and to give to it the character of an heroic mission.

May we prize and cherish the great selfless spirit that has been engendered, and, applying it to the purposes of our Government — the nation's housekeeping — the management of our collective affairs, may we, men and women together, not in antagonism, but in comradeship, strive on till we have built up a better civilisation than any that the world has known. For surely just as those children are fortunate who have two parents, a mother and a father, to care for them, so is the nation fortunate that has its mothers and its fathers, its brothers and its sisters, working together for the common good.

THE END

INDEX

507

A CATALOG OF SELECTED
DOVER BOOKS
IN ALL FIELDS OF INTEREST

A CATALOG OF SELECTED DOVER BOOKS IN ALL FIELDS OF INTEREST

100 BEST-LOVED POEMS, Edited by Philip Smith. "The Passionate Shepherd to His Love," "Shall I compare thee to a summer's day?" "Death, be not proud," "The Raven," "The Road Not Taken," plus works by Blake, Wordsworth, Byron, Shelley, Keats, many others. 96pp. 5 3/16 x 8 1/4. 0-486-28553-7

100 SMALL HOUSES OF THE THIRTIES, Brown-Blodgett Company. Exterior photographs and floor plans for 100 charming structures. Illustrations of models accompanied by descriptions of interiors, color schemes, closet space, and other amenities. 200 illustrations. 112pp. 8 3/8 x 11. 0-486-44131-8

1000 TURN-OF-THE-CENTURY HOUSES: With Illustrations and Floor Plans, Herbert C. Chivers. Reproduced from a rare edition, this showcase of homes ranges from cottages and bungalows to sprawling mansions. Each house is meticulously illustrated and accompanied by complete floor plans. 256pp. 9 3/8 x 12 1/4. 0-486-45596-3

101 GREAT AMERICAN POEMS, Edited by The American Poetry & Literacy Project. Rich treasury of verse from the 19th and 20th centuries includes works by Edgar Allan Poe, Robert Frost, Walt Whitman, Langston Hughes, Emily Dickinson, T. S. Eliot, other notables. 96pp. 5 3/16 x 8 1/4. 0-486-40158-8

101 GREAT SAMURAI PRINTS, Utagawa Kuniyoshi. Kuniyoshi was a master of the warrior woodblock print — and these 18th-century illustrations represent the pinnacle of his craft. Full-color portraits of renowned Japanese samurais pulse with movement, passion, and remarkably fine detail. 112pp. 8 3/8 x 11. 0-486-46523-3

ABC OF BALLET, Janet Grosser. Clearly worded, abundantly illustrated little guide defines basic ballet-related terms: arabesque, battement, pas de chat, relevé, sissonne, many others. Pronunciation guide included. Excellent primer. 48pp. 4 3/16 x 5 3/4. 0-486-40871-X

ACCESSORIES OF DRESS: An Illustrated Encyclopedia, Katherine Lester and Bess Viola Oerke. Illustrations of hats, veils, wigs, cravats, shawls, shoes, gloves, and other accessories enhance an engaging commentary that reveals the humor and charm of the many-sided story of accessorized apparel. 644 figures and 59 plates. 608pp. 6 1/8 x 9 1/4. 0-486-43378-1

ADVENTURES OF HUCKLEBERRY FINN, Mark Twain. Join Huck and Jim as their boyhood adventures along the Mississippi River lead them into a world of excitement, danger, and self-discovery. Humorous narrative, lyrical descriptions of the Mississippi valley, and memorable characters. 224pp. 5 3/16 x 8 1/4. 0-486-28061-6

ALICE STARMORE'S BOOK OF FAIR ISLE KNITTING, Alice Starmore. A noted designer from the region of Scotland's Fair Isle explores the history and techniques of this distinctive, stranded-color knitting style and provides copious illustrated instructions for 14 original knitwear designs. 208pp. 8 3/8 x 10 7/8. 0-486-47218-3

Browse over 9,000 books at www.doverpublications.com

ALICE'S ADVENTURES IN WONDERLAND, Lewis Carroll. Beloved classic about a little girl lost in a topsy-turvy land and her encounters with the White Rabbit, March Hare, Mad Hatter, Cheshire Cat, and other delightfully improbable characters. 42 illustrations by Sir John Tenniel. 96pp. 5³⁄₁₆ x 8¼.   0-486-27543-4

AMERICA'S LIGHTHOUSES: An Illustrated History, Francis Ross Holland. Profusely illustrated fact-filled survey of American lighthouses since 1716. Over 200 stations — East, Gulf, and West coasts, Great Lakes, Hawaii, Alaska, Puerto Rico, the Virgin Islands, and the Mississippi and St. Lawrence Rivers. 240pp. 8 x 10¾.
0-486-25576-X

AN ENCYCLOPEDIA OF THE VIOLIN, Alberto Bachmann. Translated by Frederick H. Martens. Introduction by Eugene Ysaye. First published in 1925, this renowned reference remains unsurpassed as a source of essential information, from construction and evolution to repertoire and technique. Includes a glossary and 73 illustrations. 496pp. 6⅛ x 9¼.   0-486-46618-3

ANIMALS: 1,419 Copyright-Free Illustrations of Mammals, Birds, Fish, Insects, etc., Selected by Jim Harter. Selected for its visual impact and ease of use, this outstanding collection of wood engravings presents over 1,000 species of animals in extremely lifelike poses. Includes mammals, birds, reptiles, amphibians, fish, insects, and other invertebrates. 284pp. 9 x 12.   0-486-23766-4

THE ANNALS, Tacitus. Translated by Alfred John Church and William Jackson Brodribb. This vital chronicle of Imperial Rome, written by the era's great historian, spans A.D. 14-68 and paints incisive psychological portraits of major figures, from Tiberius to Nero. 416pp. 5³⁄₁₆ x 8¼.   0-486-45236-0

ANTIGONE, Sophocles. Filled with passionate speeches and sensitive probing of moral and philosophical issues, this powerful and often-performed Greek drama reveals the grim fate that befalls the children of Oedipus. Footnotes. 64pp. 5³⁄₁₆ x 8 ¼.   0-486-27804-2

ART DECO DECORATIVE PATTERNS IN FULL COLOR, Christian Stoll. Reprinted from a rare 1910 portfolio, 160 sensuous and exotic images depict a breathtaking array of florals, geometrics, and abstracts — all elegant in their stark simplicity. 64pp. 8⅜ x 11.   0-486-44862-2

THE ARTHUR RACKHAM TREASURY: 86 Full-Color Illustrations, Arthur Rackham. Selected and Edited by Jeff A. Menges. A stunning treasury of 86 full-page plates span the famed English artist's career, from *Rip Van Winkle* (1905) to masterworks such as *Undine, A Midsummer Night's Dream,* and *Wind in the Willows* (1939). 96pp. 8⅜ x 11.
0-486-44685-9

THE AUTHENTIC GILBERT & SULLIVAN SONGBOOK, W. S. Gilbert and A. S. Sullivan. The most comprehensive collection available, this songbook includes selections from every one of Gilbert and Sullivan's light operas. Ninety-two numbers are presented uncut and unedited, and in their original keys. 410pp. 9 x 12.
0-486-23482-7

THE AWAKENING, Kate Chopin. First published in 1899, this controversial novel of a New Orleans wife's search for love outside a stifling marriage shocked readers. Today, it remains a first-rate narrative with superb characterization. New introductory Note. 128pp. 5³⁄₁₆ x 8¼.   0-486-27786-0

BASIC DRAWING, Louis Priscilla. Beginning with perspective, this commonsense manual progresses to the figure in movement, light and shade, anatomy, drapery, composition, trees and landscape, and outdoor sketching. Black-and-white illustrations throughout. 128pp. 8⅜ x 11.   0-486-45815-6

Browse over 9,000 books at www.doverpublications.com

THE BATTLES THAT CHANGED HISTORY, Fletcher Pratt. Historian profiles 16 crucial conflicts, ancient to modern, that changed the course of Western civilization. Gripping accounts of battles led by Alexander the Great, Joan of Arc, Ulysses S. Grant, other commanders. 27 maps. 352pp. 5⅜ x 8½. 0-486-41129-X

BEETHOVEN'S LETTERS, Ludwig van Beethoven. Edited by Dr. A. C. Kalischer. Features 457 letters to fellow musicians, friends, greats, patrons, and literary men. Reveals musical thoughts, quirks of personality, insights, and daily events. Includes 15 plates. 410pp. 5⅜ x 8½. 0-486-22769-3

BERNICE BOBS HER HAIR AND OTHER STORIES, F. Scott Fitzgerald. This brilliant anthology includes 6 of Fitzgerald's most popular stories: "The Diamond as Big as the Ritz," the title tale, "The Offshore Pirate," "The Ice Palace," "The Jelly Bean," and "May Day." 176pp. 5⅜ x 8½. 0-486-47049-0

BESLER'S BOOK OF FLOWERS AND PLANTS: 73 Full-Color Plates from Hortus Eystettensis, 1613, Basilius Besler. Here is a selection of magnificent plates from the *Hortus Eystettensis,* which vividly illustrated and identified the plants, flowers, and trees that thrived in the legendary German garden at Eichstätt. 80pp. 8⅜ x 11. 0-486-46005-3

THE BOOK OF KELLS, Edited by Blanche Cirker. Painstakingly reproduced from a rare facsimile edition, this volume contains full-page decorations, portraits, illustrations, plus a sampling of textual leaves with exquisite calligraphy and ornamentation. 32 full-color illustrations. 32pp. 9⅜ x 12¼. 0-486-24345-1

THE BOOK OF THE CROSSBOW: With an Additional Section on Catapults and Other Siege Engines, Ralph Payne-Gallwey. Fascinating study traces history and use of crossbow as military and sporting weapon, from Middle Ages to modern times. Also covers related weapons: balistas, catapults, Turkish bows, more. Over 240 illustrations. 400pp. 7¼ x 10⅛. 0-486-28720-3

THE BUNGALOW BOOK: Floor Plans and Photos of 112 Houses, 1910, Henry L. Wilson. Here are 112 of the most popular and economic blueprints of the early 20th century — plus an illustration or photograph of each completed house. A wonderful time capsule that still offers a wealth of valuable insights. 160pp. 8⅜ x 11. 0-486-45104-6

THE CALL OF THE WILD, Jack London. A classic novel of adventure, drawn from London's own experiences as a Klondike adventurer, relating the story of a heroic dog caught in the brutal life of the Alaska Gold Rush. Note. 64pp. 5$\frac{3}{16}$ x 8¼. 0-486-26472-6

CANDIDE, Voltaire. Edited by Francois-Marie Arouet. One of the world's great satires since its first publication in 1759. Witty, caustic skewering of romance, science, philosophy, religion, government — nearly all human ideals and institutions. 112pp. 5$\frac{3}{16}$ x 8¼. 0-486-26689-3

CELEBRATED IN THEIR TIME: Photographic Portraits from the George Grantham Bain Collection, Edited by Amy Pastan. With an Introduction by Michael Carlebach. Remarkable portrait gallery features 112 rare images of Albert Einstein, Charlie Chaplin, the Wright Brothers, Henry Ford, and other luminaries from the worlds of politics, art, entertainment, and industry. 128pp. 8⅜ x 11. 0-486-46754-6

CHARIOTS FOR APOLLO: The NASA History of Manned Lunar Spacecraft to 1969, Courtney G. Brooks, James M. Grimwood, and Loyd S. Swenson, Jr. This illustrated history by a trio of experts is the definitive reference on the Apollo spacecraft and lunar modules. It traces the vehicles' design, development, and operation in space. More than 100 photographs and illustrations. 576pp. 6¾ x 9¼. 0-486-46756-2

Browse over 9,000 books at www.doverpublications.com

A CHRISTMAS CAROL, Charles Dickens. This engrossing tale relates Ebenezer Scrooge's ghostly journeys through Christmases past, present, and future and his ultimate transformation from a harsh and grasping old miser to a charitable and compassionate human being. 80pp. 5³⁄₁₆ x 8¼. 0-486-26865-9

COMMON SENSE, Thomas Paine. First published in January of 1776, this highly influential landmark document clearly and persuasively argued for American separation from Great Britain and paved the way for the Declaration of Independence. 64pp. 5³⁄₁₆ x 8¼. 0-486-29602-4

THE COMPLETE SHORT STORIES OF OSCAR WILDE, Oscar Wilde. Complete texts of "The Happy Prince and Other Tales," "A House of Pomegranates," "Lord Arthur Savile's Crime and Other Stories," "Poems in Prose," and "The Portrait of Mr. W. H." 208pp. 5³⁄₁₆ x 8¼. 0-486-45216-6

COMPLETE SONNETS, William Shakespeare. Over 150 exquisite poems deal with love, friendship, the tyranny of time, beauty's evanescence, death, and other themes in language of remarkable power, precision, and beauty. Glossary of archaic terms. 80pp. 5³⁄₁₆ x 8¼. 0-486-26686-9

THE COUNT OF MONTE CRISTO: Abridged Edition, Alexandre Dumas. Falsely accused of treason, Edmond Dantès is imprisoned in the bleak Chateau d'If. After a hair-raising escape, he launches an elaborate plot to extract a bitter revenge against those who betrayed him. 448pp. 5³⁄₁₆ x 8¼. 0-486-45643-9

CRAFTSMAN BUNGALOWS: Designs from the Pacific Northwest, Yoho & Merritt. This reprint of a rare catalog, showcasing the charming simplicity and cozy style of Craftsman bungalows, is filled with photos of completed homes, plus floor plans and estimated costs. An indispensable resource for architects, historians, and illustrators. 112pp. 10 x 7. 0-486-46875-5

CRAFTSMAN BUNGALOWS: 59 Homes from "The Craftsman," Edited by Gustav Stickley. Best and most attractive designs from Arts and Crafts Movement publication — 1903–1916 — includes sketches, photographs of homes, floor plans, descriptive text. 128pp. 8¼ x 11. 0-486-25829-7

CRIME AND PUNISHMENT, Fyodor Dostoyevsky. Translated by Constance Garnett. Supreme masterpiece tells the story of Raskolnikov, a student tormented by his own thoughts after he murders an old woman. Overwhelmed by guilt and terror, he confesses and goes to prison. 480pp. 5³⁄₁₆ x 8¼. 0-486-41587-2

THE DECLARATION OF INDEPENDENCE AND OTHER GREAT DOCUMENTS OF AMERICAN HISTORY: 1775-1865, Edited by John Grafton. Thirteen compelling and influential documents: Henry's "Give Me Liberty or Give Me Death," Declaration of Independence, The Constitution, Washington's First Inaugural Address, The Monroe Doctrine, The Emancipation Proclamation, Gettysburg Address, more. 64pp. 5³⁄₁₆ x 8¼. 0-486-41124-9

THE DESERT AND THE SOWN: Travels in Palestine and Syria, Gertrude Bell. "The female Lawrence of Arabia," Gertrude Bell wrote captivating, perceptive accounts of her travels in the Middle East. This intriguing narrative, accompanied by 160 photos, traces her 1905 sojourn in Lebanon, Syria, and Palestine. 368pp. 5⅜ x 8½. 0-486-46876-3

A DOLL'S HOUSE, Henrik Ibsen. Ibsen's best-known play displays his genius for realistic prose drama. An expression of women's rights, the play climaxes when the central character, Nora, rejects a smothering marriage and life in "a doll's house." 80pp. 5³⁄₁₆ x 8¼. 0-486-27062-9

DOOMED SHIPS: Great Ocean Liner Disasters, William H. Miller, Jr. Nearly 200 photographs, many from private collections, highlight tales of some of the vessels whose pleasure cruises ended in catastrophe: the *Morro Castle, Normandie, Andrea Doria, Europa,* and many others. 128pp. 8⅞ x 11¼.   0-486-45366-9

THE DORÉ BIBLE ILLUSTRATIONS, Gustave Doré. Detailed plates from the Bible: the Creation scenes, Adam and Eve, horrifying visions of the Flood, the battle sequences with their monumental crowds, depictions of the life of Jesus, 241 plates in all. 241pp. 9 x 12.   0-486-23004-X

DRAWING DRAPERY FROM HEAD TO TOE, Cliff Young. Expert guidance on how to draw shirts, pants, skirts, gloves, hats, and coats on the human figure, including folds in relation to the body, pull and crush, action folds, creases, more. Over 200 drawings. 48pp. 8¼ x 11.   0-486-45591-2

DUBLINERS, James Joyce. A fine and accessible introduction to the work of one of the 20th century's most influential writers, this collection features 15 tales, including a masterpiece of the short-story genre, "The Dead." 160pp. 5³⁄₁₆ x 8¼.
                                                                                 0-486-26870-5

EASY-TO-MAKE POP-UPS, Joan Irvine. Illustrated by Barbara Reid. Dozens of wonderful ideas for three-dimensional paper fun — from holiday greeting cards with moving parts to a pop-up menagerie. Easy-to-follow, illustrated instructions for more than 30 projects. 299 black-and-white illustrations. 96pp. 8⅜ x 11.
                                                                                 0-486-44622-0

EASY-TO-MAKE STORYBOOK DOLLS: A "Novel" Approach to Cloth Dollmaking, Sherralyn St. Clair. Favorite fictional characters come alive in this unique beginner's dollmaking guide. Includes patterns for Pollyanna, Dorothy from *The Wonderful Wizard of Oz,* Mary of *The Secret Garden,* plus easy-to-follow instructions, 263 black-and-white illustrations, and an 8-page color insert. 112pp. 8¼ x 11.   0-486-47360-0

EINSTEIN'S ESSAYS IN SCIENCE, Albert Einstein. Speeches and essays in accessible, everyday language profile influential physicists such as Niels Bohr and Isaac Newton. They also explore areas of physics to which the author made major contributions. 128pp. 5 x 8.   0-486-47011-3

EL DORADO: Further Adventures of the Scarlet Pimpernel, Baroness Orczy. A popular sequel to *The Scarlet Pimpernel,* this suspenseful story recounts the Pimpernel's attempts to rescue the Dauphin from imprisonment during the French Revolution. An irresistible blend of intrigue, period detail, and vibrant characterizations. 352pp. 5³⁄₁₆ x 8¼.   0-486-44026-5

ELEGANT SMALL HOMES OF THE TWENTIES: 99 Designs from a Competition, Chicago Tribune. Nearly 100 designs for five- and six-room houses feature New England and Southern colonials, Normandy cottages, stately Italianate dwellings, and other fascinating snapshots of American domestic architecture of the 1920s. 112pp. 9 x 12.   0-486-46910-7

THE ELEMENTS OF STYLE: The Original Edition, William Strunk, Jr. This is the book that generations of writers have relied upon for timeless advice on grammar, diction, syntax, and other essentials. In concise terms, it identifies the principal requirements of proper style and common errors. 64pp. 5⅜ x 8½.   0-486-44798-7

THE ELUSIVE PIMPERNEL, Baroness Orczy. Robespierre's revolutionaries find their wicked schemes thwarted by the heroic Pimpernel — Sir Percival Blakeney. In this thrilling sequel, Chauvelin devises a plot to eliminate the Pimpernel and his wife. 272pp. 5³⁄₁₆ x 8¼.   0-486-45464-9

AN ENCYCLOPEDIA OF BATTLES: Accounts of Over 1,560 Battles from 1479 B.C. to the Present, David Eggenberger. Essential details of every major battle in recorded history from the first battle of Megiddo in 1479 B.C. to Grenada in 1984. List of battle maps. 99 illustrations. 544pp. 6½ x 9¼. 0-486-24913-1

ENCYCLOPEDIA OF EMBROIDERY STITCHES, INCLUDING CREWEL, Marion Nichols. Precise explanations and instructions, clearly illustrated, on how to work chain, back, cross, knotted, woven stitches, and many more — 178 in all, including Cable Outline, Whipped Satin, and Eyelet Buttonhole. Over 1400 illustrations. 219pp. 8⅜ x 11¼. 0-486-22929-7

ENTER JEEVES: 15 Early Stories, P. G. Wodehouse. Splendid collection contains first 8 stories featuring Bertie Wooster, the deliciously dim aristocrat and Jeeves, his brainy, imperturbable manservant. Also, the complete Reggie Pepper (Bertie's prototype) series. 288pp. 5⅜ x 8½. 0-486-29717-9

ERIC SLOANE'S AMERICA: Paintings in Oil, Michael Wigley. With a Foreword by Mimi Sloane. Eric Sloane's evocative oils of America's landscape and material culture shimmer with immense historical and nostalgic appeal. This original hardcover collection gathers nearly a hundred of his finest paintings, with subjects ranging from New England to the American Southwest. 128pp. 10⅝ x 9. 0-486-46525-X

ETHAN FROME, Edith Wharton. Classic story of wasted lives, set against a bleak New England background. Superbly delineated characters in a hauntingly grim tale of thwarted love. Considered by many to be Wharton's masterpiece. 96pp. 5³⁄₁₆ x 8 ¼. 0-486-26690-7

THE EVERLASTING MAN, G. K. Chesterton. Chesterton's view of Christianity — as a blend of philosophy and mythology, satisfying intellect and spirit — applies to his brilliant book, which appeals to readers' heads as well as their hearts. 288pp. 5⅜ x 8½. 0-486-46036-3

THE FIELD AND FOREST HANDY BOOK, Daniel Beard. Written by a co-founder of the Boy Scouts, this appealing guide offers illustrated instructions for building kites, birdhouses, boats, igloos, and other fun projects, plus numerous helpful tips for campers. 448pp. 5³⁄₁₆ x 8¼. 0-486-46191-2

FINDING YOUR WAY WITHOUT MAP OR COMPASS, Harold Gatty. Useful, instructive manual shows would-be explorers, hikers, bikers, scouts, sailors, and survivalists how to find their way outdoors by observing animals, weather patterns, shifting sands, and other elements of nature. 288pp. 5⅜ x 8½. 0-486-40613-X

FIRST FRENCH READER: A Beginner's Dual-Language Book, Edited and Translated by Stanley Appelbaum. This anthology introduces 50 legendary writers — Voltaire, Balzac, Baudelaire, Proust, more — through passages from *The Red and the Black, Les Misérables, Madame Bovary,* and other classics. Original French text plus English translation on facing pages. 240pp. 5⅜ x 8½. 0-486-46178-5

FIRST GERMAN READER: A Beginner's Dual-Language Book, Edited by Harry Steinhauer. Specially chosen for their power to evoke German life and culture, these short, simple readings include poems, stories, essays, and anecdotes by Goethe, Hesse, Heine, Schiller, and others. 224pp. 5⅜ x 8½. 0-486-46179-3

FIRST SPANISH READER: A Beginner's Dual-Language Book, Angel Flores. Delightful stories, other material based on works of Don Juan Manuel, Luis Taboada, Ricardo Palma, other noted writers. Complete faithful English translations on facing pages. Exercises. 176pp. 5⅜ x 8½. 0-486-25810-6

Browse over 9,000 books at www.doverpublications.com

FIVE ACRES AND INDEPENDENCE, Maurice G. Kains. Great back-to-the-land clas-sic explains basics of self-sufficient farming. The one book to get. 95 illustrations. 397pp. 5⅜ x 8½. 0-486-20974-1

FLAGG'S SMALL HOUSES: Their Economic Design and Construction, 1922, Ernest Flagg. Although most famous for his skyscrapers, Flagg was also a proponent of the well-designed single-family dwelling. His classic treatise features innovations that save space, materials, and cost. 526 illustrations. 160pp. 9⅜ x 12¼.
0-486-45197-6

FLATLAND: A Romance of Many Dimensions, Edwin A. Abbott. Classic of science (and mathematical) fiction — charmingly illustrated by the author — describes the adventures of A. Square, a resident of Flatland, in Spaceland (three dimensions), Lineland (one dimension), and Pointland (no dimensions). 96pp. 5³⁄₁₆ x 8¼.
0-486-27263-X

FRANKENSTEIN, Mary Shelley. The story of Victor Frankenstein's monstrous cre-ation and the havoc it caused has enthralled generations of readers and inspired countless writers of horror and suspense. With the author's own 1831 introduction. 176pp. 5³⁄₁₆ x 8¼. 0-486-28211-2

THE GARGOYLE BOOK: 572 Examples from Gothic Architecture, Lester Burbank Bridaham. Dispelling the conventional wisdom that French Gothic architectural flourishes were born of despair or gloom, Bridaham reveals the whimsical nature of these creations and the ingenious artisans who made them. 572 illustrations. 224pp. 8⅜ x 11. 0-486-44754-5

THE GIFT OF THE MAGI AND OTHER SHORT STORIES, O. Henry. Sixteen cap-tivating stories by one of America's most popular storytellers. Included are such classics as "The Gift of the Magi," "The Last Leaf," and "The Ransom of Red Chief." Publisher's Note. 96pp. 5³⁄₁₆ x 8¼. 0-486-27061-0

THE GOETHE TREASURY: Selected Prose and Poetry, Johann Wolfgang von Goethe. Edited, Selected, and with an Introduction by Thomas Mann. In addition to his lyric poetry, Goethe wrote travel sketches, autobiographical studies, essays, letters, and proverbs in rhyme and prose. This collection presents outstanding examples from each genre. 368pp. 5⅜ x 8½. 0-486-44780-4

GREAT EXPECTATIONS, Charles Dickens. Orphaned Pip is apprenticed to the dirty work of the forge but dreams of becoming a gentleman — and one day finds himself in possession of "great expectations." Dickens' finest novel. 400pp. 5³⁄₁₆ x 8¼.
0-486-41586-4

GREAT WRITERS ON THE ART OF FICTION: From Mark Twain to Joyce Carol Oates, Edited by James Daley. An indispensable source of advice and inspiration, this anthology features essays by Henry James, Kate Chopin, Willa Cather, Sinclair Lewis, Jack London, Raymond Chandler, Raymond Carver, Eudora Welty, and Kurt Vonnegut, Jr. 192pp. 5⅜ x 8½. 0-486-45128-3

HAMLET, William Shakespeare. The quintessential Shakespearean tragedy, whose highly charged confrontations and anguished soliloquies probe depths of human feeling rarely sounded in any art. Reprinted from an authoritative British edition complete with illuminating footnotes. 128pp. 5³⁄₁₆ x 8¼. 0-486-27278-8

THE HAUNTED HOUSE, Charles Dickens. A Yuletide gathering in an eerie coun-try retreat provides the backdrop for Dickens and his friends — including Elizabeth Gaskell and Wilkie Collins — who take turns spinning supernatural yarns. 144pp. 5⅜ x 8½. 0-486-46309-5

HEART OF DARKNESS, Joseph Conrad. Dark allegory of a journey up the Congo River and the narrator's encounter with the mysterious Mr. Kurtz. Masterly blend of adventure, character study, psychological penetration. For many, Conrad's finest, most enigmatic story. 80pp. 5³⁄₁₆ x 8¼. 0-486-26464-5

HENSON AT THE NORTH POLE, Matthew A. Henson. This thrilling memoir by the heroic African-American who was Peary's companion through two decades of Arctic exploration recounts a tale of danger, courage, and determination. "Fascinating and exciting." — *Commonweal.* 128pp. 5⅜ x 8½. 0-486-45472-X

HISTORIC COSTUMES AND HOW TO MAKE THEM, Mary Fernald and E. Shenton. Practical, informative guidebook shows how to create everything from short tunics worn by Saxon men in the fifth century to a lady's bustle dress of the late 1800s. 81 illustrations. 176pp. 5⅜ x 8½. 0-486-44906-8

THE HOUND OF THE BASKERVILLES, Arthur Conan Doyle. A deadly curse in the form of a legendary ferocious beast continues to claim its victims from the Baskerville family until Holmes and Watson intervene. Often called the best detective story ever written. 128pp. 5³⁄₁₆ x 8¼. 0-486-28214-7

THE HOUSE BEHIND THE CEDARS, Charles W. Chesnutt. Originally published in 1900, this groundbreaking novel by a distinguished African-American author recounts the drama of a brother and sister who "pass for white" during the dangerous days of Reconstruction. 208pp. 5⅜ x 8½. 0-486-46144-0

THE HUMAN FIGURE IN MOTION, Eadweard Muybridge. The 4,789 photographs in this definitive selection show the human figure — models almost all undraped — engaged in over 160 different types of action: running, climbing stairs, etc. 390pp. 7⅞ x 10⅝. 0-486-20204-6

THE IMPORTANCE OF BEING EARNEST, Oscar Wilde. Wilde's witty and buoyant comedy of manners, filled with some of literature's most famous epigrams, reprinted from an authoritative British edition. Considered Wilde's most perfect work. 64pp. 5³⁄₁₆ x 8¼. 0-486-26478-5

THE INFERNO, Dante Alighieri. Translated and with notes by Henry Wadsworth Longfellow. The first stop on Dante's famous journey from Hell to Purgatory to Paradise, this 14th-century allegorical poem blends vivid and shocking imagery with graceful lyricism. Translated by the beloved 19th-century poet, Henry Wadsworth Longfellow. 256pp. 5³⁄₁₆ x 8¼. 0-486-44288-8

JANE EYRE, Charlotte Brontë. Written in 1847, *Jane Eyre* tells the tale of an orphan girl's progress from the custody of cruel relatives to an oppressive boarding school and its culmination in a troubled career as a governess. 448pp. 5³⁄₁₆ x 8¼.
0-486-42449-9

JAPANESE WOODBLOCK FLOWER PRINTS, Tanigami Kônan. Extraordinary collection of Japanese woodblock prints by a well-known artist features 120 plates in brilliant color. Realistic images from a rare edition include daffodils, tulips, and other familiar and unusual flowers. 128pp. 11 x 8¼. 0-486-46442-3

JEWELRY MAKING AND DESIGN, Augustus F. Rose and Antonio Cirino. Professional secrets of jewelry making are revealed in a thorough, practical guide. Over 200 illustrations. 306pp. 5⅜ x 8½. 0-486-21750-7

JULIUS CAESAR, William Shakespeare. Great tragedy based on Plutarch's account of the lives of Brutus, Julius Caesar and Mark Antony. Evil plotting, ringing oratory, high tragedy with Shakespeare's incomparable insight, dramatic power. Explanatory footnotes. 96pp. 5³⁄₁₆ x 8¼. 0-486-26876-4

THE JUNGLE, Upton Sinclair. 1906 bestseller shockingly reveals intolerable labor practices and working conditions in the Chicago stockyards as it tells the grim story of a Slavic family that emigrates to America full of optimism but soon faces despair. 320pp. 5³⁄₁₆ x 8¼. 0-486-41923-1

THE KINGDOM OF GOD IS WITHIN YOU, Leo Tolstoy. The soul-searching book that inspired Gandhi to embrace the concept of passive resistance, Tolstoy's 1894 polemic clearly outlines a radical, well-reasoned revision of traditional Christian thinking. 352pp. 5³⁄₁₆ x 8¼. 0-486-45138-0

THE LADY OR THE TIGER?: and Other Logic Puzzles, Raymond M. Smullyan. Created by a renowned puzzle master, these whimsically themed challenges involve paradoxes about probability, time, and change; metapuzzles; and self-referentiality. Nineteen chapters advance in difficulty from relatively simple to highly complex. 1982 edition. 240pp. 5⅜ x 8½. 0-486-47027-X

LEAVES OF GRASS: The Original 1855 Edition, Walt Whitman. Whitman's immortal collection includes some of the greatest poems of modern times, including his masterpiece, "Song of Myself." Shattering standard conventions, it stands as an unabashed celebration of body and nature. 128pp. 5³⁄₁₆ x 8¼. 0-486-45676-5

LES MISÉRABLES, Victor Hugo. Translated by Charles E. Wilbour. Abridged by James K. Robinson. A convict's heroic struggle for justice and redemption plays out against a fiery backdrop of the Napoleonic wars. This edition features the excellent original translation and a sensitive abridgment. 304pp. 6⅛ x 9¼.
0-486-45789-3

LILITH: A Romance, George MacDonald. In this novel by the father of fantasy literature, a man travels through time to meet Adam and Eve and to explore humanity's fall from grace and ultimate redemption. 240pp. 5⅜ x 8½.
0-486-46818-6

THE LOST LANGUAGE OF SYMBOLISM, Harold Bayley. This remarkable book reveals the hidden meaning behind familiar images and words, from the origins of Santa Claus to the fleur-de-lys, drawing from mythology, folklore, religious texts, and fairy tales. 1,418 illustrations. 784pp. 5⅜ x 8½. 0-486-44787-1

MACBETH, William Shakespeare. A Scottish nobleman murders the king in order to succeed to the throne. Tortured by his conscience and fearful of discovery, he becomes tangled in a web of treachery and deceit that ultimately spells his doom. 96pp. 5³⁄₁₆ x 8¼. 0-486-27802-6

MAKING AUTHENTIC CRAFTSMAN FURNITURE: Instructions and Plans for 62 Projects, Gustav Stickley. Make authentic reproductions of handsome, functional, durable furniture: tables, chairs, wall cabinets, desks, a hall tree, and more. Construction plans with drawings, schematics, dimensions, and lumber specs reprinted from 1900s *The Craftsman* magazine. 128pp. 8⅛ x 11. 0-486-25000-8

MATHEMATICS FOR THE NONMATHEMATICIAN, Morris Kline. Erudite and entertaining overview follows development of mathematics from ancient Greeks to present. Topics include logic and mathematics, the fundamental concept, differential calculus, probability theory, much more. Exercises and problems. 641pp. 5⅜ x 8½. 0-486-24823-2

MEMOIRS OF AN ARABIAN PRINCESS FROM ZANZIBAR, Emily Ruete. This 19th-century autobiography offers a rare inside look at the society surrounding a sultan's palace. A real-life princess in exile recalls her vanished world of harems, slave trading, and court intrigues. 288pp. 5⅜ x 8½. 0-486-47121-7

THE METAMORPHOSIS AND OTHER STORIES, Franz Kafka. Excellent new English translations of title story (considered by many critics Kafka's most perfect work), plus "The Judgment," "In the Penal Colony," "A Country Doctor," and "A Report to an Academy." Note. 96pp. 5³⁄₁₆ x 8¼.	0-486-29030-1

MICROSCOPIC ART FORMS FROM THE PLANT WORLD, R. Anheisser. From undulating curves to complex geometrics, a world of fascinating images abound in this classic, illustrated survey of microscopic plants. Features 400 detailed illustrations of nature's minute but magnificent handiwork. The accompanying CD-ROM includes all of the images in the book. 128pp. 9 x 9.	0-486-46013-4

A MIDSUMMER NIGHT'S DREAM, William Shakespeare. Among the most popular of Shakespeare's comedies, this enchanting play humorously celebrates the vagaries of love as it focuses upon the intertwined romances of several pairs of lovers. Explanatory footnotes. 80pp. 5³⁄₁₆ x 8¼.	0-486-27067-X

THE MONEY CHANGERS, Upton Sinclair. Originally published in 1908, this cautionary novel from the author of The Jungle explores corruption within the American system as a group of power brokers joins forces for personal gain, triggering a crash on Wall Street. 192pp. 5⅜ x 8½.	0-486-46917-4

THE MOST POPULAR HOMES OF THE TWENTIES, William A. Radford. With a New Introduction by Daniel D. Reiff. Based on a rare 1925 catalog, this architectural showcase features floor plans, construction details, and photos of 26 homes, plus articles on entrances, porches, garages, and more. 250 illustrations, 21 color plates. 176pp. 8⅜ x 11.	0-486-47028-8

MY 66 YEARS IN THE BIG LEAGUES, Connie Mack. With a New Introduction by Rich Westcott. A Founding Father of modern baseball, Mack holds the record for most wins — and losses — by a major league manager. Enhanced by 70 photographs, his warmhearted autobiography is populated by many legends of the game. 288pp. 5⅜ x 8½.	0-486-47184-5

NARRATIVE OF THE LIFE OF FREDERICK DOUGLASS, Frederick Douglass. Douglass's graphic depictions of slavery, harrowing escape to freedom, and life as a newspaper editor, eloquent orator, and impassioned abolitionist. 96pp. 5³⁄₁₆ x 8¼.
0-486-28499-9

THE NIGHTLESS CITY: Geisha and Courtesan Life in Old Tokyo, J. E. de Becker. This unsurpassed study from 100 years ago ventured into Tokyo's red-light district to survey geisha and courtesan life and offer meticulous descriptions of training, dress, social hierarchy, and erotic practices. 49 black-and-white illustrations; 2 maps. 496pp. 5⅜ x 8½.	0-486-45563-7

THE ODYSSEY, Homer. Excellent prose translation of ancient epic recounts adventures of the homeward-bound Odysseus. Fantastic cast of gods, giants, cannibals, sirens, other supernatural creatures — true classic of Western literature. 256pp. 5³⁄₁₆ x 8¼.
0-486-40654-7

OEDIPUS REX, Sophocles. Landmark of Western drama concerns the catastrophe that ensues when King Oedipus discovers he has inadvertently killed his father and married his mother. Masterly construction, dramatic irony. Explanatory footnotes. 64pp. 5³⁄₁₆ x 8¼.	0-486-26877-2

ONCE UPON A TIME: The Way America Was, Eric Sloane. Nostalgic text and drawings brim with gentle philosophies and descriptions of how we used to live — self-sufficiently — on the land, in homes, and among the things built by hand. 44 line illustrations. 64pp. 8⅜ x 11.	0-486-44411-2